Forms in the Abyss

Forms in the Abyss

A Philosophical Bridge between Sartre and Derrida

STEVE MARTINOT

TEMPLE UNIVERSITY PRESS
Philadelphia

Temple University Press
1601 North Broad Street
Philadelphia PA 19122
www.temple.edu/tempress

Published 2006
Printed in the United States of America

∞ The paper used in this publication meets the requirements of the American National Standard for Information Sciences—Permanence of Paper for Printed Library Materials, ANSI Z39.48–1992

Library of Congress Cataloging-in-Publication Data

Martinot, Steve.
Forms in the abyss : a philosophical bridge between Sartre and Derrida / Steve Martinot.
p. cm.
Includes bibliographical references and index.
ISBN 13: 978-1-59213-440-3 (paper: alk. paper)
ISBN 10: 1-59213-440-8 (paper: alk. paper)
1. Sartre, Jean Paul, 1905–1980. 2. Derrida, Jacques. I. Title

B2430.S34M366 2006
194—dc22 2005054884

2 4 6 8 9 7 5 3 1

Contents

Acknowledgments

THE TRUE INCEPTION of this work was in Akron, Ohio, a long time ago, where some art students first taught me a sense of esthetics, that is, of artistic form. For this I wish to thank in particular Pat Millar (now Boas), Chuck Chipps, and Jim Thompson. It was in Boulder, Colorado, that I began to understand the richness of philosophy as an art form. And for this I particularly thank Forrest Williams, Hazel Barnes, and Betty Cannon. The ability to form these elements into a coherent project was a long journey, involving a few false turns, and some audacious inventions (some of which worked and some of which didn't). I thank in particular Robert Steiner, Liz Locke, Phyllis Keneven, Bill McBride, Gerda Norvig, and Holly Arrow for this; and for just being crazy enough to lead me into yet more invention, Randy DiDomenico, Judy Acquaire, and Laura Marshall. There are many people I met along the way who taught me how to refuse to lose touch with a sense of the world, even in the most abstruse discourses: Bob Stone, Betsy Bowman, Stephen Barker, Cliff DuRand, Charles Mills, and Bill Martin. Finally, for seeing me through this project, for their dialogue, for their interest in ideas, the history of philosophy, and the history of discourse, and for supporting what I was trying to do, I want to thank Richard Terdiman, Tom Vogler, Marshall Leicester, Sandra Luft, Clare Braz Valentine, and Harry Berger.

Abbreviations

BN	Jean-Paul Sartre, *Being and Nothingness*
BT	Martin Heidegger, *Being and Time*
CDR	Jean-Paul Sartre, *Critique of Dialectical Reason*
Con	Jean-Jacques Rousseau, *The Confessions*
DD	David Wood and Robert Bernasconi, *Derrida and Différance*
Dis	Jacques Derrida, *Dissemination*
DTP	Richard Rorty, "Is Derrida a Transcendental Philosopher?"
DTS	John Llewelyn, *Derrida on the Threshold of Sense*
DZ	Roland Barthes, *Writing Degree Zero*
EH	Jean-Paul Sartre, *Existentialism and Human Emotions*
ES	Roland Barthes, *Elements of Semiology*
Glas	Jacques Derrida, *Glas*
Gram	Jacques Derrida, *Of Grammatology*
HD	Herman Rappaport, *Heidegger and Derrida*
HS	Joseph Fell, *Heidegger and Sartre*
ID	Martin Heidegger, *Identity and Difference*
IF	Jean-Paul Sartre, *L'idiot de la Famille*
IMT	Roland Barthes, *Image, Music, Text*
LH	Martin Heidegger, "Letter on Humanism"
LI	Jacques Derrida, "Limited, Inc."
Marg	Jacques Derrida, *Margins of Philosophy*
MN	Richard Rorty, *Philosophy and the Mirror of Nature*
Myth	Roland Barthes, *Mythologies*
Nouvel Obs	Jacques Derrida, interview with Catherine David in *Le Nouvel Observateur*
OS	Fredric Jameson, *Sartre: The Origin of a Style*
OWL	Martin Heidegger, *On the Way to Language*
PI	Jean-Paul Sartre, *The Psychology of Imagination*
Pos	Jacques Derrida, *Positions*
Prose	Denis Hollier, *The Politics of Prose*
PS	Dominick LaCapra, *A Preface to Sartre*
Reveries	Jean-Jacques Rousseau, *The Reveries of the Solitary Walker*
QLH	Robert Bernasconi, *The Question of Language in Heidegger's History of Being*
SHP	William R. Schroeder, *Sartre and His Predecessors*
SP	Jacques Derrida, *Speech and Phenomena*
S/Z	Roland Barthes, *S/Z*

TM	Rodolphe Gasché, *The Tain of the Mirror*
VI	Maurice Merleau-Ponty, *The Visible and the Invisible*
WD	Jacques Derrida, *Writing and Difference*
WL	Jean-Paul Sartre, *What Is Literature?*

1 Introduction

History and Writing

In the half-century since the end of World War II, three philosophical currents have contested social thought in the West and thrown themselves against institutional ideology: Marxism, existentialism, and post-structuralism.[1] While the Marxism of this period attempted to rejuvenate its nineteenth-century progenitor, and succeeded only in re-axiomatizing it in contemporary terms, the other two currents addressed and critiqued the structure of axiomatics and presupposition themselves, emerging as centers of non-ideological thinking.[2] Surprisingly little has been researched, however, on a possible interface or conjunction between existentialism and post-structuralism;[3] and in particular, very little attention has been paid to a possible relation between the two central (and most prolific) figures of these movements: Sartre and Derrida. What astonishes is that the two figures address some common socio-political questions in a significant manner from their different respective directions, in particular, the role of language in the techniques and technologies of social control, domination, and political manipulation.[4] Yet this has not served to bridge the gap of their differences.

Indeed, so great a separation has been discerned between them that most commentary has been content to enhance it, as if the existence of the hiatus itself had some overriding historical importance. Nothing testifies to the intensity of this hiatus more than the paucity and hesitancy of discussion on it. Very few commentators or critical thinkers have ventured to address it as a critical space. Philip Wood, reviewing the state of dialogue between Sartre and the post-structuralists in 1989, finds it singularly sparse. "Extended confrontation with Sartre's work has been noticeably absent in the post-Sartrean philosophy, being restricted, when reference has been direct, to scathing dismissals without recourse or argument, or when reference has been allusory, to superior scorn." And conversely, "Sartre himself never bothered to develop the testy remarks proffered in the interview [in the journal *L'Arc*] into a sustained engagement with his critics."[5] (That Sartre and Foucault at least were on good terms personally seems to have had little effect on this generally tense philosophical stillness.)

Sartre seems not to have addressed Derrida in particular in writing at all. Until 1996, Derrida made only brief polemical mention of Sartre; specifically, in "The Ends of Man," in *Glas*, and in two interviews.[6] Of course, Sartre was a dominant figure in the milieu into which Derrida stepped; he could pretend to the hauteur of the established in the face of young *arrivistes*. But could Derrida afford such a luxury? Nevertheless, Derrida consistently distances himself from Sartre, at times with what sounds like a certain bitterness (which is addressed below).

One could say that the hiatus was in fact a mutual refusal between them. In general, Sartre thought both the structuralists and post-structuralists were somewhat misguided for having emptied their discourses of what he himself considered essential to philosophy and philosophical politics: an account of the subject, an approach to history, and a confrontation with the a prioris and presuppositions of traditional philosophy (cf. *L'Arc* interview on Foucault, no. 30, October 1966, pp. 87–96). The post-structuralist response, however indirect, was that each account of the subject already constitutes its construction; in other words, one constructs the subject by investigating it. And similarly, an investigation of history as such assumed its own history as its foundation, while a confrontation with presuppositions only prioritized a different set of presuppositions as the condition for the confrontation in the first place. In general, the post-structuralist critique argues that the referential subject matter of a text ultimately acquires its meaning and being from the collectivity of social texts that purport to describe or refer to it. Thus, when Sartre claims that nothing human is strange to him because all subjectivities are expressions of freedom,[7] Derrida points out (in "The Ends of Man") that Sartre has merely substituted one presuppositional universal (albeit posed in the negative) for another.

Sartre and Derrida are perhaps most disparate in their approaches to writing. Sartre wants to be definitive about what he says. He desires language that is direct, unequivocal, message-bearing; he wants it to say what he thinks.[8] The Derridean critique of writing suggests this is an idle endeavor, that the polyvalence of language calls into question what *say* and *think* mean, and what the *who* that does it is, as well as "about-ness" itself.[9] At the core of this approach is the notion that textual form—namely, the modes, structures, and genres of writing, including reasoning, stylistic constructions, tropes, and self-referentialities—not only operates as a carrier of meaning or expressed content, but has meaning itself. That is, the structure of textuality is understood to purvey meaning, as well as be the means of expression. And that meaning cannot avoid transforming or undermining the textual content it is used to express. As Gayatri Spivak says, "What one is saying is undermined by the way one says it."[10]

Derrida made this point in 1996 in a contribution to the fiftieth anniversary issue of *Les Temps Modernes* (the journal that Sartre had founded in 1946 with Simone de Beauvoir and Maurice Merleau-Ponty). It was his first friendly approach to Sartre,[11] and he only mildly alluded to his earlier seemingly visceral reaction to Sartre. In this article, called "Il courait mort" ("He runs while dead"), Derrida turned to a short piece Sartre had written in 1948 called "Writing for One's Times" ("Ecrire pour son époque"). Such an essay was, of course, a "natural" one for Derrida to address in an anniversary issue recalling an earlier "time" in the midst of a far different one. And Derrida affirmed that he considered *Les Temps Modernes* to be of his (Derrida's) times, but also that it was not insofar as it did not address what was of primary concern for him. He suggested that Sartre's attempt to secularize writing as engaged in its times was in its form messianic, a soteriology of the writer. Many commentators had previously noticed the programmatic undertone in Sartre's writing, and some had rejected it on that score; but few have seen fit to position Sartre's text, so insistent on its secularity, in the realm of the religious, as does Derrida (Wilfrid Desan comes close to doing so in *The Tragic Finale*). Derrida's point is that the form of the text is messianic, which inserts a subversive meaning into a text that bespeaks a secularity in content. Nevertheless, Derrida embraces Sartre for having lived that contradiction and its ambiguities without pretense.

The post-structuralist critique of textuality thus puts in question the ability of language to be unambiguous, or univocal, to say something with clarity and precision without the means of "saying it" turning it into something else. In particular, it regards the capacity of textuality to multiply meanings for itself, to set itself against and beyond its own literal significations, to be of the essence of language and writing. Against Sartre's desire that his writing say what he thinks, the post-structuralists argue that there is always more than we think in what we say or write. With respect to the Sartrean or phenomenological notion of consciousness, the post-structuralists argue that consciousness only apprehends itself in the language that purveys or articulates that apprehension to itself; that is, in finding itself only in the means it must use to describe what it finds, consciousness remains nothing but the content of cultural and philosophical (textual) practices. Thus, post-structuralism might mirror Sartre's sentiment that consciousness produces writing as its text, by affirming that writing produces consciousness as its text.[12] But the issue remains essentially unengaged; Sartre tends to avoid a critique of language as much as Derrida avoids speaking about consciousness, in a form of mutual refusal.

For Philip Wood, it is precisely the philosophical and cultural critique that a reconsideration of Sartre in the light of post-Sartrean philosophy would make possible that would be of benefit. On the one hand, the post-structuralist critique is itself an "engaged" act, while on the other, there is an openness (an untotalized and untotalizable dimension) in Sartre's notion of totalization that has yet to be fully explored (especially by post-structuralism). He seeks to conjoin the critical concreteness of the Sartrean discourse with the discursive insight into cultural and ideological structures of the Derridean critique. If one can recognize an existentiality in the post-structuralist endeavor, and a deconstructive dimension to Sartre's thinking, Wood concludes, then a foundation should exist for a mutual rereading of each through the other; and that would be, for him, of inestimable historical value, because of what it might make possible for critical thinking, and for social and political understanding. In other words, it is the space between them that Philip Wood seeks to valorize.

Ultimately, the indisposition of Sartre and Derrida toward each other fascinates, in that the aura of innovation that emanates from both contains a misty suggestion of some distant alluring Arcadia in which their thinking flows together. What power would critical thinking gain from some philosophical "unified field theory" conjoining their efforts?

Indeed, the analogy to theoretical physics is not far-fetched. Einstein found little to applaud, from his relativistic point of view, in quantum mechanics in general, and the Heisenberg probabilistic description of matter in particular. Relativity concerned itself with the very large, while quantum theory addressed the very small, with little occasion for overlap. The question of fundamental forces teased at the physicists as a possible link, while evading their every effort, leaving them to circle each other across untraversable conceptual distances. Sartre and the post-structuralists have similarly found few areas of overlap. For the post-structuralists, Sartre seems to remain in the ranks of the rationalists; and they critique rationalism precisely for its assumption of universality as a rationalist pretension, just as the quantum theorists critiqued relativity's assumptions of continuity and an inability to admit discrete transformations or quantum leaps. Sartre looked askance at what appeared to him to be irrationalism, as Einstein did toward quantum theory. Nevertheless, if this analogy were to have any merit, it would not be for some philosophical "unified field theory," but for the adjoining of realms of understanding, the opening of space between disparate theoretical landscapes in which to think.

However, as things stand today, to ask how the texts of Sartre and Derrida relate is to enter a negative space of incommensurability, and to seek to navigate discourses of mutual refusal. To examine this mutual refusal, because it occurs in the form of language, unstated and all the more emphatic for that articulatory absence, a consideration of some commentators who themselves have gingerly approached that space will be required, in order to see what has held them in thrall in doing so. This will be an introduction not only to the question of incommensurability (something that effects itself minimally between any two writers, and in the extreme in this case) but to the metaphysical obstructions to a common language, to narrativity as the possibility of common experience, and to a common historicity that would need to dimension a traversal of the space between.

Critical commentary mostly served to map the separate rims of this canyon and only allusively appreciate the grandeur of the landscape between. Critics of one have tended to exclude the other, thus ratifying the hiatus. In addressing these commentators, as a context for this present investigation, the question one would need to pose is what those who have not entered the space between have gained by not doing so. One might also ask what they had to do to avoid it. This "between" of an existentiality and an ephemerality, or of historicity and an allohistorical multiplicity, is only part of the problem with respect to commentary. The rest of the problem lies in the attempt to historically understand or tell the story of what has not happened. Let us briefly consider some of the commentators who have approached the space between Sartre and Derrida, and look at the ways they have succeeded in not entering it.

THE METAPHYSICS OF A COMMON LANGUAGE

Generally, when Sartre has been addressed from a post-structuralist point of view, it has been not only deconstructively but polemically as well. Sartrean thinkers have been content, for their part, to ignore or marginalize Derrida as being beyond the purview of their own thinking.[13] One author who attempts to touch both sides is Hugh Silverman, and his book, *Inscriptions: Between Phenomenology and Structuralism*, is quite exemplary of the perplexity.[14] Silverman is an excellent reader (and expositor) of both Sartre and the post-structuralists. His book's central focus is Sartre's relation to Merleau-Ponty and various structuralists (among whom he includes Foucault). But in the main body of Silverman's discussion, Derrida is given scant mention; he appears only in the final chapter, one devoted wholly to him. In those final moments, Silverman's brief mention of Sartre seems almost beside the point. As the heading of Silverman's chapter on Derrida, "The Difference Between (and Beyond)," suggests, Derrida and deconstruction become the "beyond" of contemporary thinking. The relationality that Silverman still finds possible between Sartre and the structuralists has all but eroded away.

Christina Howells is another "evenhanded" reader. She makes an intensive attempt to bring the texts of Sartre and Derrida into philosophical relation. In a short and very interesting article titled "Sartre and Derrida: Qui Perd Gagne," she addresses Derrida's seeming animus against Sartre, which she seeks to mitigate (as had Wood) by suggesting that Derrida's notion of *différance* is sufficiently analogous to the Sartrean notion of consciousness to warrant a more positive connection.[15] *Différance* is a neologism Derrida employs to signify the inherently aporetic nature of the sign. Derrida reasons that signs produce meaning only within a system or structure; and they do so through their difference from each other rather than because of any inherent connection between themselves as entities and their meaning. But if so, and if meaning is produced through systems of differences, then it is differing rather than entityhood that is central to a sign's signification, and each sign then must defer to other signs (from which it differs) as the condition for its meaning. Difference and deferral must then be seen as the central operations characteristic of linguistic signs, their spatiality and temporality within a structural system; and it is the conjunction of the two that Derrida seeks to encompass at once in the term *différance*.

For Howells, as the interstice between spatialized and temporalized modes of difference, différance is nothingness. For Derrida, différance is "neither concept nor name" (*SP*, 130) and has "neither existence nor essence" (*SP*, 134). Howells argues that if "différance is not," then it is congruent with Sartre's notion of nothingness, namely, that the for-itself is not. She argues that both resist inclusion in a Hegelian identity, both reside in nothingness rather than being, and both are withheld from presence. She points out that for Sartre, self-presence is "a way of not coinciding with oneself, of escaping identity"; and for Derrida, "the present of self-presence is not simple, . . . it is constituted in an originary irreducible synthesis" ("Sartre and Derrida," 26–7). Thus, she develops certain "basic analogies between Sartre's thinking and Derrida's own," which extend to questions of knowability, the production of meaning, and in particular, to the form of "paradoxical logic" peculiar and common to the for-itself and to différance. Ultimately, she suspects that both thinkers are at pains to prevent their "*logique paradoxale* from slipping into a recuperative mode," in order not to be imprisoned there, but instead to continue overflowing the boundaries of their respective discourses.

Howells's article ultimately became the final chapter in a book on Sartre (like Silverman, she reserves Derrida for the finale).[16] In that book, she maps out the systems of paradox or aporia that appear continually in Sartre's writing, paradoxes that both characterize and represent his philosophical issues. For example, in the Sartrean account, "hate" is always in check, always doomed to failure. It desires a cancellation of the Other's existence, an end to the Other's ontological freedom, while in so doing, it must recognize and grant that existence and that freedom to the Other (*BN*, 412). In effect, it must bring about the opposite of what it intends, as the very condition for intending it. Howells reads Sartre's notions of nothingness, absence, and the inarticulability and inapprehensibility of the Other's subjectivity within the paradoxical logic. And for her, it is the ability to sustain a reasoning in the mode of paradox that opens Sartre to correlation with corresponding aspects of Derridean thought. Overall, she reflects on their common recognition that language's universalizing properties destroy the individual aspects of either experience or writing, and lead to a falsifying and alien codification of the human (*Necessity*, 137).

In singling out the "*logique paradoxale*" in both texts, Howells puts her finger on a formal correspondence that is important in the present essay. Yet she is content to rest at recognition of the formalism. That is, she stays within the literal meaning of a logic, and thus loses a certain perspective on the significance of the difference bestowed upon *this* common logic by the disparity of (textual) languages from which it emerges. Instead, her analogy embeds both discourses in a single language. To assume a common language for this logic means to choose one as the common one, and for her, that is ultimately the language of ontology. Thus she privileges the substance of the logic rather than the parallelism of structures that she has discerned. The structural connection she makes seems to decontextualize her approach, but the philosophical content she insists on recontextualizes it—within the ontological.

This is actually a common phenomenon. From within the Sartrean tradition, a number of commentators have attempted to focus on apparent ideational similarities. Sebastian Gardner, for instance, argues that Derrida implicitly describes a notion of the subject quite close to Sartre's, one that can be resolved through Sartre's critique. And Noreen Keohane-O'Connor reads a phenomenological parallel by arguing that Derrida's text contains within it an implicit theory of intentionality.[17] Where Keohane-O'connor privileges Sartre's critique of self-presence and considers it within the relation of the self to the other, Gardner privileges Sartre's sense of the subject by entering Derridean discourse to discover it there by using a (Sartrean) criteriology from elsewhere.

It is this endeavor that collides with the central problem and thus discloses it, namely, the difference in philosophical languages of the two. Seeking to engage both thinkers within a single discursive framework requires choosing one of those languages for the conjuncture. Whichever one chooses, the other gets absorbed into that chosen language and rewritten in its terms. The effect of adopting a phenomenological language is to transform (translate) Derrida's text and to co-opt Derrida's language into a philosophical realm that is not its own. It is to this disparity that Derrida refers when he mentions that *Les Temps Moderne* is of his times and yet not. To adopt a deconstructive language would be to transform Sartre's terms, against their own internal logic, revealing his inner assumptions, but leaving his text other than it is. To deconstruct Sartre's text would mean to submit it to its own hidden aporias, to reveal how its underlying presuppositions were precisely what it had produced for itself as its foundation, and from which it drew its justification; it would demonstrate that there is always a self-justifying dimension to whatever authority a text pretends to claim for itself. With what, then, would the Derridean text be brought into relation? Ironically, while the choice of a critical language is made pursuant to a critical endeavor, it obstructs its own project by obviating the possibility of a critique of the difference dispelled by the act of choosing.

This suggests a dimension of the problem, the extant incommensurability of language between Sartre and Derrida. To choose a language in which to relate them would be to exclude one and thus obviate the possibility of relation. Either choice would establish one of the languages in question as a metaphysics of that relation. The attempt to enter the space between them seems to erect a barrier to entering that space. The resolution of this problem, if one wished to bridge the hiatus between them, would be to somehow speak of both while respecting and preserving the disparity of language. Howells's work is significant in being as close as anyone has come in daring to venture into that Sartre/Derrida space in that way.

In general, the central value that deconstruction has bequeathed the world is to show that though traditional metaphysics claims to refer to the world, it cannot. It deconstructs through disclosure of the pretensions of metaphysics to coherence, while hiding beneath presuppositional disguises and ploys the inconsistencies to which all language is heir. To show where the language of metaphysics is self-referential is to reveal where its pretensions to referentiality and explanation become infinite, and thus where the text plays god. This is not merely circular reasoning; it reveals the places where critical thought brings itself to a halt—those places where it must realize that a text brings into existence what it refers to in the manner by which it refers to it in the very act of referring. While the world of reference continues to exist, as does the referential text, their inseparability signifies aporetically that all reference remains self-reference. It is the valorization of aporia, the embrace of its inescapability in language, the richness of our relation to the world that the nonrejection of aporia provides, that the post-structuralists, and Derrida in particular, have given us. (This is what has driven some people fairly to distraction; the poets don't mind because they knew it all along, but the logicians get upset.)

This would seem to suggest why a deconstructive language could not be used to bridge the gap between Derrida and Sartre. Under such an operation, Sartre's text would itself become what filled the abyss between itself and deconstructive critique, since it would be transformed into a self-referential language that referred back to itself as Sartre's text (on the other side of the abyss of language). But interestingly, deconstructions of Sartre do not simply render Sartre just another deconstructed text. Something else happens; a different process of philosophization occurs, perhaps because, for Sartre, the aporias are open and practically flaunted (the stylistics that Howells noted as their common paradoxical logic). Dominick LaCapra provides an example in his book *A Preface to Sartre*.

LaCapra's book was the first deconstructive critique of Sartre written in the United States. In it, he addresses the realms of both writing and ontology. His goal is to reveal how Sartre's text undermines itself because it does not escape or critique the language of the philosophical tradition from which it attempts to depart. In particular, LaCapra argues that the distinction Sartre establishes between poetry and prose (in *What Is Literature?*) by which he theorizes how writing is "engaged" (*engagé*) produces a truncated notion of prose that undermines Sartre's ability to conceptualize *engagement* (*PS*, 67ff.). The source of the problem, for LaCapra, is Sartre's unquestioned affirmation that writing is an instrumentality, which in effect reifies writing.

In making this argument, LaCapra is following a lead given by Derrida in "The Ends of Man." There, Derrida takes Sartre to task for not submitting the very central terms of his philosophical discourse such as "Man," "consciousness," or "human reality" to critique, while pretending to go beyond their traditional philosophical meaning. By leaving them unexamined and unquestioned, Sartre ends up appropriating the tradition from which they come and being appropriated by it in turn. That is, in disregarding the assumptions of that philosophical tradition, he tacitly accepts the meanings given to those terms by history, which then reimposes on his text the very tradition he claims to contest. For Derrida, these (non)acts (of leaving unquestioned) have a meaning. To ignore the "history of the concept" (such as "human," "reality," or "man") renders the concept "self-evident," as if it had "no origin, no historical, cultural, or linguistic limit," and transforms it thereby into an a priori. The concept becomes self-referentially presuppositional, rather than something to be investigated. Though Sartre's project is to existentially transcend the assumptions of previous metaphysics, he does not transcend those assumptions in the language by which he does this, which then continue to reside at the interior of his enterprise.[18]

LaCapra argues that this insulates Sartre's project from, and reinforces, what he wishes to contest, namely, certain aprioristic ideological constructions of the world (Sartre focuses specifically on Christianity and Marxism). For Sartre, such ideological structures seek to dragoon writing to their causes. And it is to free writing from such constraints that he proposes the notion of being *engagé*. The deconstructive critique should itself be wholly engaged in the heart of this project. And Sartre's notion of *engagement* almost does this, but not quite.

For Sartre, the writer is engaged in writing in and for his/her time, and not simply in and for the language that the writer inherits or might invent, capriciously or purposefully. To be engaged, the writer must reveal to his/her readers more options and choices for living and dealing with the world than are extant, to free all readers to think beyond the terms and constraints given by their world. The necessary condition for doing so is to guarantee the freedom of the reader as such. Since all writing is a gift given without obligation, all writing does this; that is, it is already engaged. And Sartre's injunction to the writer is be authentic in this, to take responsibility for it.

To demonstrate how the writer is engaged, Sartre makes a distinction between the prose writer and the poet. For the former, language is transparent, instrumental, and capable of representing the world; for the poet, on the contrary, words are objects, capable only of relating to, and gaining sense from, each other.

> For the [prose writer], words are domesticated; for the [poet], they remain in the wild state. For the former, they are useful conventions, tools that wear out little by little and that one throws away when they are no longer serviceable; for the second, they are natural things that grow naturally on the earth like grass and trees (*WL*, 7).

If prose can be engaged, it is because it can represent the world to itself, and do so transparently, without getting in the way. Poetry and other arts cannot do this; they always represent themselves. "The man who talks is beyond words and near the object, whereas the poet is on this side of them" (*WL*, 7).

For LaCapra, this amounts to a return to symbolism, for which poetry has sense but without referential signification (*PS*, 73). He interprets it as creating a binary "categorical opposition between prose and poetry" (*PS*, 68, 70), a "sharp" analytic distinction between pure identity and pure difference. That is, poetry must stand in analytic antithesis to prose, as of a different substance. But LaCapra then argues that, from the point of view of engaged writing, poetry must be in bad faith. It seeks not to represent the world, in order to be poetry. As Sartre puts it, the poet "engages himself to lose," "is certain of the total defeat of the human enterprise and arranges to fail . . . in order to bear witness to human defeat in general" (*PS*, 74). That is, for Sartre, the poet cannot represent if his/her words are to remain of the poetic substance, as things, yet they must represent that nonrepresentation. And LaCapra then concludes that Sartre's notion of prose must be in bad faith as well because, in reducing language to the purely instrumental, to pure identity, Sartre "mystifies that which is literary in the use of prose"; he ignores the artistic, the literary or poetic in prose writing itself (*PS*, 72). Ultimately, Sartre himself must be in bad faith if he does not see either form of bad faith (*PS*, 71).

The polemical issue at stake for LaCapra is clear; it is the politics of what writing is. Yet one could ask, based upon the above quotations, on what basis could words wear out and get thrown away? It could only be metaphorically as objects; that is, prose words have the character of objects as well, at least metaphorically. In that case, what wears away can only be a word's meanings and the meaning of its use. This introduces a sense of impurity, a nonstrictness, into Sartre's distinction between poetry and prose that LaCapra is ignoring in seeing the distinction as analytic. In fact, Sartre's metaphoricity concerning the distinction between prose and poetry would itself render LaCapra's distinction less than (more than?) analytical. Perhaps LaCapra has attributed a strictness of distinction to Sartre that is not Sartre's (*PS*, 72). Indeed, he further quotes Sartre as saying,

> the poet has withdrawn in one stroke from the language-instrument; he has chosen once and for all the poetic attitude that considers words as things and not as signs. For the ambiguity of the sign implies that one can at one's will penetrate it like a pane of glass and pursue the thing signified, or turn one's gaze toward its reality and consider it as an object. (*PS*, 71)

The distinction, then, is not between modes of writing, but between choices, intentionalities toward the double character of the word as sign. And it is the double character of the sign that becomes Derrida's focus in his initial critique of language.

For Derrida, the "natural order of relationships between linguistic and graphic signs" (*Gram*, 35) (between meaning and object) is the foundation for the deconstruction of what he identifies as a philosophical or metaphysical binary between speech and writing (that writing is only a representation of speech, a dependent and secondary form of the sign). He argues that both have the same structure as a confluence of signifier and signified (the Saussurean schema), which is more profoundly discernible in writing than in speech (I return to the import of this later in this book). But if signifier and signified are incommensurable and yet inseparable aspects of the sign itself, then they do not stand in binary opposition to each other; instead, they present the possibility of focusing on either of their two aspects, of conceiving this doubleness without the possibility of sundering it, either as "reality" or as writing. Rather than being analytic, Sartre's distinction accepts the impossibility of any ontological boundaries between prose and poetry. In other words, his distinction is grounded elsewhere, in the writer's project, rather than in the ontology of words where LaCapra locates it. LaCapra is perhaps a little too eager to be deconstructive, forcing a separation between prose and poetry, in order to find it reflected between writing and political engagement.

One might add, since LaCapra uses it to buttress his case, that strict binary divisions are not at all foreign to Sartre. In *The Psychology of Imagination*, imagination and perception are seen as mutually exclusive. For Sartre, they cannot be done at the same time. And for LaCapra, both binaries present us with totalities that expel to a radical otherness all sense of alterity that inhabits them (*PS*, 127). That is, self-identity and difference are radically separated and strictly prioritized. The political implications are clear for LaCapra; Sartrean freedom obscures its own foundations in "a logic of mastery and domination."[19] And indeed, Sartre would agree that mastery and domination are precisely what are at stake in such analytic distinctions.

But again, Sartre is more complex than this allows. As he explains, "Imaginative consciousness may be said to be representative in the sense that it goes out in search of its object in the realm of perception . . . as does perception in relation to the object perceived."[20] But it is creative in its representative aspect, whereas for perception that "representative element corresponds to a passivity of consciousness. . . . The object of an image is never more than the consciousness one has of it." And the context for this distinction is the phenomenological notion (from Husserl) that perception constitutes its object for itself from an infinity of determinations while the imagined image comprises only the finite determinations of which we are already conscious (*PI*, 21).

To read this as a "sharp analytic distinction" (*PS*, 126) is to forget that, for Sartre, different modes of consciousness nevertheless remain inseparable even in their mutual exclusion. Though the poet "withdraws from the language-instrument," that can imply a withdrawal neither from the imaginative use of language nor from the perceptive use of it. The poet perceives words as objects as part of his imaginative use, and the prose writer imagines a world represented in the transparency of his sentences that represent his perceptions. The idea that one cannot do both (perceive and imagine) at the same time means that one is in effect "doing" neither; rather, what one is "doing" is elsewhere, "at" the intentionality constitutive of image, meaning, and recognition. One apprehends the world as meaning, recognizes it imaginatively, and images it perceptively.[21] Again, there is both an incommensurability (of infinite and finite) and an inseparability (of realm) of the two.

Furthermore, Sartre's distinction between perception and imagination could not be analytic, since an analytic totalization of difference would have to rely upon a certain commensurability. It is here that the meaning of his "mutual exclusion" resides. Imagination and perception are incommensurable and inseparable at the same time. Ultimately, there is a kind of skewed relation between perceiving imaginatively and imagining perceptively. And thus too between consciousness and representation. If LaCapra sees an analytic distinction, it is because he has imposed an analyticity upon what remains inseparable precisely because it involves an incommensurability instead.[22] In effect, to submit Sartre's text to its own aporias, one faces an ironic necessity of displacing those aporias first in order to render them recoverable or rediscoverable beneath the metaphysics created by that displacement. In other words, while approaches to the "space between" from the Sartrean side end by imposing a phenomenological language on the nonphenomenological, those from the deconstructive side run the risk of similarly imposing a metaphysics in order to deconstruct it. One constitutes language as a metaphysics of the text in either case.

Though LaCapra's adventure with Sartre suggests that certain serious boundaries exist between Sartre and analytic philosophy, Howells's argument concerning a "*logique paradoxale*" goes further and suggests why analytic philosophers themselves have in general had a problem with both Sartre and Derrida.[23] Richard Rorty, for instance, relegates them to a kind of philosophical background for himself.[24] He divides philosophy into two camps: philosophies of public account, of objectivity and consensus (what we know how to talk about), and world-disclosure philosophy, or "philosophy that leaps in the dark" toward world transformation or transcendence (philosophizing on what we do not know how to talk about; DTP, 210). The first comprises those who deploy problem-solving rigor and reference in their arguments, and the latter those who deploy poetry and transcendence. And he can imagine no synthesis between them.[25] "Poetic world-disclosers like Hegel, Heidegger, and Derrida have to pay a price, and part of that price is the inappropriateness to their work of notions like 'argumentation' and 'rigor'" (DTP, 211). There is thus no place in Rorty for a metadiscursive argument, a discourse about discourse, because it would be about a non-referent. Derrida's textual world has "as little room for transcendental deductions, or for rigor, as for self-authenticating moments of immediate presence" (DTP, 208). Thus, Rorty renders deconstruction unintelligible for himself, ironically by being metadiscursive toward it.[26]

He treats Sartre comparably (in *Philosopy and the Mirror of Nature*), though in slightly different terms. Dividing discourses into the epistemological (natural philosophy or science; again, what we have adequate articulations for) and the hermeneutic (phenomenology; what we have inadequate articulations for), he claims that consciousness can be considered either as essentially unknowable (insofar as it produces incommensurate discourses), or no less knowable than things (articulable through commensurate discourses). Sartre and existential philosophy in general, of course, fall on the hermeneutic side (*MN*, 315ff.). But Rorty likes Sartre as a theoretician of bad faith, which has value for Rorty's approach to systematic philosophy of mind. The problem one confronts in describing the human subject is that one must render it an object and thus not describe it. Though Sartre theorizes bad faith within the unknowability or undecidability of ontological freedom, he shows one can develop a certain epistemological explicitness in speaking about it. Rorty finds the existential suspicion involved in that move difficult because it must critique the definitive without itself being definitive (*MN*, 371); but he sees that Sartre seems to manage. Sartre's existentialism becomes a kind of self-awareness for systematic thought, the conscience of philosophical activity itself.

In sum, for Rorty, both Sartre and Derrida are marginal to what philosophy is about. While he would leave Derrida at the artistic periphery, he would employ Sartre as a witness. If Sartre can tell us something about ourselves, as a mirror of self, Rorty's opinion of Derrida is that he produces what is behind the mirror, beyond telling, behind the self. Where Derrida exemplifies a boundary between spaces, Sartre is their interface, the connecting link. Thus, Rorty reaffirms the sense of incommensurability so far discerned as a hiatus between these thinkers. But he nevertheless does not believe in incommensurability. As he says, "There is no metaphysical reason why humans should be capable of saying incommensurable things" (*MN*, 347). That is, for him, the difference between discourse and metadiscourse is without significance. Though Rorty grants both a certain respect, in his taxonomization of philosophical ideas he places both on a common plane, relating across common boundaries constituted by his notion of philosophical reasoning. Thus, he collapses to a mere interstice the more essential space that opens between them.

The Narrative of Metaphysics

The question of writing that LaCapra raises, and of prose versus poetry, is important and bears further discussion, since for both Sartre and Derrida, it is where one goes beyond "what we know how to talk about." Sartre's sense of *engagement* defines a threshold that Rorty considers nonmarginal insofar as it signifies how the writer opens the present to greater possibility for his/her readers. For Sartre, it is not writing that contextualizes *engagement*, but *engagement* that contextualizes writing. Sartre dissociates poetry in the context of the writer's being engaged in his/her "times" because poetry has a different project; it is a different use of language. Prose seeks to express the world transparently, to which a perception and imagination of meanings are relevant, while poetry self-concernedly uses words as objects for its own constructions, to which a perception and imagination of structures and relations (rather than representations) are relevant.

But Sartre is not attempting to posit a mutual exclusion between them when he says that poetry (or the poetic element of a text) fails. For him, it "fails" because it defeats our attempt to communicate or to have been communicated with. In that case, however, it fails in our project, not its own. It has not set out to succeed where prose does. In its own project, its failure is its success (precisely at defeating communication, in calling the transparency and intention of communication into question). Derrida performs roughly the same operation deconstructively in "Signature Event Context" (*Marg*, 309ff.), in which he asks "whether the word or signifier 'communication' communicates a determined content, an identifiable meaning" or not; and if it does not, if it contains a nonsemiotic as well as a semiotic sense, and if that is contingent upon the "problem of context," then not only is context not "absolutely determinable" for the same reasons, but language itself calls the concept of communication into question. In other words, for Derrida, what Sartre posits for poetry would seem to hold for language in general. Sartre's issue is simply directed the other way, namely, that poetry must fail to be engaged in order to succeed as poetry; this is what constitutes its particular *engagement*. It is on this basis that Sartre found Mallarmé to be in good faith, writing in unparaphrasable poetic forms; for Sartre, Mallarmé had taken poetry's being into fullest account.[27]

This notion of *qui perd gagne* by which Sartre characterizes poetry (in his fashion) becomes critical insofar as it signals the incommensurability of those media. If it does not imply the poet's bad faith, nor represent the nature of the poetic medium or the poetic enterprise, then it points to the aporia of speaking from within prose about a poetic medium that is incommensurable with it. In referring to the problem of the writer, it differentiates the poet from the prose writer precisely in that their situations are different. Poetry and prose do not stand in binary opposition; such a dialectic would require them to be in the same situation. Poetry does not simply "hang on" the ambiguity of language, whether "lived" or "surpassed," as Joseph Fell would have it, for instance. He interprets Sartre's distinction as meaning that "poetry and prose are to be understood relative to a perpetual dialectic."[28] But Sartre has obviated the dialectic in positing the prosaic and the poetic as mutually exclusive while remaining inseparable in their incommensurability. As a form of "*logique paradoxale*," this amalgamation of inseparability and incommensurability takes on the aura of an inner logic in Sartre's writing that transcends the reasoning in his prose.

In addition, should we extend Sartre's sentiment (that the poet "is certain of the total defeat of the human enterprise and arranges to fail") to metaphysics, we would find Sartre describing a defeat that is not dissimilar to Heidegger's notion of *destruktion*. When Heidegger etymologically recuperates a word, while projecting it forward to a meaning he enjoins for it—giving it residence between the already and the not-yet—he is not counterposing it to the already but to its present and its presence, which it defeats in Heidegger's analytic by always being other than that presence.[29] When Sartre's poetic word projects itself into the milieu of other words in its poem, it only makes itself the object that they then make of it, through a contextualization that the word provides for itself only through them. Or, as Fell says in a somewhat Sartrean vein in reference to Heidegger, "In order to build at all I must take over these existing materials and make them my own by subordinating them to my own ends" (Fell, 273). By counterposing prose to poetry, Sartre has not generated a binary opposition, but what Derrida will call a supplementarity.

In this sense, the distinction Sartre makes between prose and poetry reaches forward tentatively toward the post-structuralist critique of language. But it has a further significance. Grasping the word as an object, as Sartre's poet does, raises the question of seeing language as an object. The post-structuralist critique does not do so because it understands language as what one sees with rather than something that will loom into view. Sartre refuses objecthood for language in a different way, through an unabashed nominalism, a drive for the particular. Echoing Heidegger, any objecthood for language disappears between the already and the not-yet of language itself. If the Sartrean objecthood of the word looks forward to the not-yet of the post-structuralist critique, the Sartrean nonobjecthood of language stands in relation to the already of a philosophical history.

All this comes together in Denis Hollier's complex deconstructive homage to Sartre, "The Politics of Prose"—again a critique of Sartrean *engagement*.[30] Hollier addresses Sartre's novel *Nausea*, engaging in a form of guerrilla theater whose purpose is to reveal the general crisis of the sign. He discursively envelopes and harasses a "personage" named Sartre whom he isolates as a character in Sartre's own novel, and simultaneously narrates Sartre as a personage in the historical moment in which he, Hollier, finds himself acting as an (ostensibly) minor character. That is, he places Sartre between two narrativizations, where he toys with him, with his (Sartre's) language, and with the language of his own critique of Sartre's language.[31] But in all this, there is a tribute to Sartre in that Sartre must himself be narrativized in order that his philosophical language be deconstructed.

Hollier focuses on those narrative moments in *Nausea* when Roquentin is writing (the novel is a found diary in which Roquentin is both writer [diarist] and the written [character]). At those moments when he is writing about writing, the novel's tense becomes idiosyncratic (*Prose*, 70ff.). Past and present conflate themselves, as if Roquentin were doing something and writing at the same time. When Roquentin writes in the present tense, he is no longer a narrator of past action; he is enacting himself by writing, while enacting something else, represented in his writing as a narrative in which he is the character—thus, a character twice over. In the present tense, he is self-conscious about writing, about being "there" writing, while he cannot be "there" because he is elsewhere, doing what he is narrating. Roquentin's self-consciousness about the act of writing shifts to a self-consciousness in the act of writing that itself is effaced in writing narratively. There is for him a double failure; the "character" (Roquentin) either fails to be "there" for what happens, or the "writer" (Roquentin) is unable to be writing because he is doing something else.

In effect, the diary, in the present tense, must be doubly elsewhere, prior to the event as a narrative consciousness, and subsequent to it as a diary. When the diary tells of its own past (the past of Roquentin's writing), it (the diary) is elsewhere than the present or the past of the novel. The novel, as a diary, takes its place in a present that is later, written after the event, even in the present tense. In effect, the novel and the diary circle each other, like boxers looking for an opening.

Thus, what Hollier narrates in his critique is not what is absent in the narrative, but narrative absence itself. Writing becomes impossible because there is too much of it; it produces a murkiness of supplementarities, rather than an ontological clarity for itself. What constitutes writing exists only in a temporal space that opens in the time of the novel, in which it becomes impossible. And Hollier concludes that writing cannot be engaged in one's time because writing cannot occur in one's time. It becomes an empty hope, a back-to-back confrontation of a narrator with himself across a difference in tenses.

When Hollier decides that Roquentin represents Sartre's supplement or alter ego (*Prose*, 83), it is to signify that he (Hollier) has wryly narrativized a certain character status for Sartre as his own *engagement* in and with Sartre, a "Sartre" who paraphrases Sartre in the same way Roquentin's diary can only paraphrase Roquentin. This supplementary "character" then represents literary *engagement* in practice. That is, *engagement* becomes a form of character status. Sartre's practice of literature engages itself as a *mise en abîme*; the literary must constitute a character who will write the work of literature that will then be engaged "in its time."

Of course, this "deconstruction" of Sartre's narrator looks suspiciously like the structure of temporality in *Being and Nothingness*, in which the past exists as an object in the present, for an intentionality whose future is imaginary, but that is constructed using that past as its language. It only remains to add that the present does not exist, because one is always ahead of oneself in terms of the objects that lie behind, as the language by which one situates oneself up ahead. The present becomes merely the flutter of the metaphysical imagination as it allows brief unanalyzed quanta of perception, ignited by intentionality's projection into the future, to shine into the darkened chambers of past certainty through the cracks of recognition—like the diary as the future of the event shines only briefly back upon it through the moments of writing it only imagines in the present. But such a critique would suggest that Sartre's account of temporality is also a deconstruction, which Hollier's renarrativized supplementarity only serves to highlight. If Sartre is actually accounting (philosophically) for the facticity of time, then the space between Hollier's critique and the novel's temporality repeats that space as that which Sartre generates between the ontological and the situational. Hollier's double reading (in two characters) constitutes both a deconstructive and an ontological metatext to the novel's text (which is itself double).[32]

In other words, there is not only a confrontation at work between Sartre's nominalism and the post-structuralist critique of language, but an interwovenness. In "The Ends of Man," Derrida suggests that the meaning of a sign (such as "man") has to have its story told, as a history, in order not to become itself philosophically presuppositional. Though, for Derrida, a history is a story only in a philosophical sense, an etymology or archaeology of a concept, for Sartre, it is the operation of philosophy that always has narrative unfolding. To place or to see something in "its" situation is to narrativize it, to give or permit it its own self-generated context, its history, and its project. This is the center of Sartre's nominalism. However unwritten or underarticulated such a narrativization may be, its attachment to a history and a project is a mode of residence in the particular.[33]

For instance, Sartre says that in the world of others, "I meet with meanings which are mine and which I have not given to myself" (*BN*, 510), meanings which are revealed, but which "resist me and remain independent of me" (*BN*, 511). While this is standard phenomenological fare, it is couched in a complex of narratives of coming upon and counterevasion. As a binary of narrated movements, it does not differ from the Saussurean distinction between langue and parole, that is, the specific acts of coming upon each spoken phrase, and the givenness of rules that withhold themselves from the meaning for which they are essential. They embed themselves in each other with no preexistence except with respect to their common moment. The multiplicity of interfaces efflorescing here, between the synchronic and the diachronic of the Saussurean sign, or philosophy and narrative, or the already and the not-yet, come together when Sartre says, "If the phrase is necessary to illuminate the given and to make the word understandable, then the sentence is a moment of the free choice of myself" (*BN*, 516).

Thus, language is not transparent. Neither does it build its meanings through itself, nor does it make transparent the thought of the speaker, as a worldly object. For Sartre, one discovers one's thought in discovering the words that express it. This is not an escapable circle, but an inescapable mutual conditioning of narrative and meaning. The "I" of an utterance must already discover him/herself to be different from the "I" who had spoken. Or, as Sartre says somewhere, "I have a rendez-vous with myself in the future, but I don't know who will show up."[34]

Two things follow from this. First, when Derrida argues that the history of the term must be included in its use, Sartre responds that there is no history, that the term leaves it behind in surpassing it toward the end of the speaker who uses the term, and who makes his/her own history in using it. The fundamental level of language is the contextualization of the phrase or sentence, in which the term loses itself by generating itself there. Second, both escape psychology's linearizing rejection of the hermeneutic circle and its mutual conditioning: Sartre by contesting and transcending it through the notion of the undiscoverable, in that "speech refers to thought and thought to speech"; and Derrida in questioning whether we even discover thought since the language we speak must always multiply its meanings beyond reference to an already that is not there and a not-yet that is not that to which reference is ostensive.

Thus, they tug at each other by ignoring what the other uses to push the one away: Sartre dissolving "the history of the concept" in an affirmation of the speaker's constitution of himself or herself in the act of speaking, and Derrida ignoring the remaking of language through his own affirmation of the word's constitution of the speaker in each act of speaking. That is, where speech (or writing, reference) is for Sartre an instrumentality whose historicity is precisely its escape from historicity, the conditions of possibility for reference (as speech, or writing) are for Derrida precisely the conditions for its impossibility. They evoke each other across an inversion of the possible and the impossible, of narrative and philosophy that constitutes their incommensurability. Rather than a dialectical convergence, there is a much more complex discursive relation involving narrative, circularity, the structure of language, and the space between temporalities and temporalizations.

Yet when, in *Glas*, Derrida makes passing reference to Sartre, mostly through innuendo, as if to say that his point goes without saying, he suggests that what there is to say is what must remain unsaid. To conceive of a confrontation between Sartre and Derrida is perhaps to confront the inconceivable.

The Historical Dimension

Historically, phenomenologist critics have regarded what came after Sartre with a certain dismay, though at times turning to it with serious interest. They saw themselves too often rewriting what Derrida was doing in order to understand him or critique him, threatening to violate his project by ontologizing his escape from ontology. But no strategy for entering into the space between revealed itself. Of course, reaching back toward Sartre from the post-structuralist side tended to incur an analogous misadventure. As suggested above, to critique Sartre deconstructively, one has to give him a metaphysical aspect he may not always have had, which threatens to transform his aporias into a form of metaphysical coherence in order then to reveal them as hidden aporias. At best, each strategy turns the other into a dramatic character whose acts of critique are then narrativized and restaged. At worst, both become forms of violence that render the subject of critique other than it is, thereby delegitimizing itself as a critique and obviating any understanding of a relation. In both cases, rather than understanding the narrative dimension of philosophy, narrative is turned against philosophy.

Perhaps, as Hollier suggests, postwar France was too philosophically dominated by Sartre to permit direct confrontation or leave space for a bridge. Those who came upon the problem found the scene too much in Sartre's shadow. New philosophical thinking could thrive only through a modicum of rejection or rebellion.

In addition, post-structuralism emerged in an era of political upheaval that not only sought to change the world's political configuration but called into question its accepted foundational philosophical notions. In the wake of World War II's horrors, with its Nazi invasions and occupations, and the discovery of assembly-line genocide—whose possibility still remains an unanswered question today—a refusal of complicity with further political criminality became an important issue. And an important dimension of that refusal was a nonacceptance of the philosophical ground of the culture that had produced such criminality. In the flush of newness, the post-structuralist practitioners saw themselves on a one-way street moving to overthrow the dominant Euro-American discourses. They took to heart many of the questions that had emerged from the anticolonialist movements and national liberation revolutions of the time, especially in Africa, which had begun a vast problematizing of the accepted categories of Western Eurocentric philosophy. These categories included the nineteenth-century class analyses of history and the white Western account of the subject and of agency in the world, along with its universalist ethics and conception of culture and civilization.

In this context, for the post-structuralists, Sartre presented a difficult problem. He represented, in his philosophical thinking, both a continuation of the philosophy the new thinkers sought to transcend and a thinker who stood on the front line against colonialism and chauvinism. To openly confront and critique him philosophically would entail a stance against the man in a realm in which he was to be respected; and not to critique him would be to accept the constraints of the philosophical tradition he represented, and indeed dominated. It was not an enviable position to be in. One possible resolution to the dilemma was to address philosophical issues or concepts specific to that tradition, even in Sartre's thinking, without locating them in Sartre. Thus, without confronting the systematic totality of his thought, one could at the same time walk side by side with him in the world's streets. Many chose this route. Roland Barthes perhaps keynoted it as an approach in *Writing Degree Zero* (a veiled response to Sartre's *What Is Literature?*). There, he takes Sartre to task almost allegorically on the question of writing while mentioning him only marginally, as merely another figure on the cultural horizon. Others followed suit.[35] The effect was to intensify the philosophical abyss while leaving untorn the fabric of certain political motivations.

In this context, a 1983 interview with Derrida in *Le Nouvel Observateur* is instructive.[36] Derrida explains that Sartre initially constituted a model for him, toward which he had gravitated. Under the aegis of Sartre, he was introduced to the pantheon of the moment: Husserl, Heidegger, Blanchot, Bataille, and so on. And he found himself reading these texts against Sartre, concluding that Sartre had misread them himself. Ultimately, he came to see Sartre's influence as ill-fated, and even "catastrophic" for himself. It constituted, Derrida intimates, a traumatic process for him (*DD*, 75; *Nouvel Obs*, 86). Yet Derrida's focus, in the interview, is not on Sartre as such but on Sartre's France, and the boundary between Sartre's thinking and his intellectual world. Derrida asks, "What must a society like ours be if a man who, in his own way, rejected or imperfectly understood [*méconnu*] so many theoretical and literary events of his time . . . came to dominate the cultural scene." Derrida admits a certain self-historicization inherently attaches itself to one who disrupts or overturns [*bouleverser*] the literary and philosophical landscape, but he does not think Sartre did that. Rather, he charges that Sartre valorized his particular philosophical (mis)understandings through a popularity bestowed upon him through his academic and publishing connections, in spite of his self-exile from the academy.

One might ask, however, in response to Derrida, how discernible a boundary there is between misunderstanding and innovation. How would one recognize it? From which understanding, reading, or interpretation of a text will "an understanding" be judged to have misunderstood [*méconnu*], misrecognized, or simply be "less than perfect"? Is it not the nature of a "perfect understanding" (and one is implied in Derrida's judgment) to be blind to the innovative, to have already per force obviated the point of view, inventive or not, that produces a different understanding? One would have to ask how Derrida is reading the texts Sartre had supposedly misread in order to read Sartre as having misread or misinterpreted. How is the question of "misunderstanding" more than only "imperfectly" separable from that of "a different reading"?

That the question of "misreading" is always only "imperfectly" separable from "a different reading" is not only at the core of Derrida's every reading, but is something he has theorized. In "Ousia and Gramme," Derrida writes that a text exceeds metaphysics because a "trace must be inscribed within the text of metaphysics, a trace which continues to signal not in the direction of another presence, or another form of presence, but in the direction of an entirely other text." That is, a deconstructive critique of metaphysics relies upon "misreading" it against the terms of its own reading of itself.[37] Robert Bernasconi accuses Derrida of doing this himself, of rendering Levinas's text metaphysical in order to give it "another reading," and he quotes this passage (*DD*, 24).

Ultimately, to be "imperfectly understood," or even misunderstood, is the necessary fate of previous thinkers when viewed through an innovating perspective—the fate of Heidegger at Sartre's hands, and similarly the fate of Sartre at Derrida's. That is precisely the way innovation historicizes itself, the way historicization occurs. Granted, a certain popularity enters the process, as a cultural acceptance of one's particular (mis)understandings. And one's innovations of thinking may emerge as special only from a larger innovative milieu or movement. But these aspects only serve to transform one's "misunderstanding" or misrecognition into one of the understandings or recognitions of one's time. Sartre's popularity, his misunderstandings of previous or contemporary thinkers, his effect on the literary or philosophical landscape, his domination of the cultural scene (however momentary), his self-historicization, and his innovativeness are all simply facets of the same thing.

That it will always be the fate of an innovator to be subsequently misunderstood at the hands of yet another innovator's subsequent self-historicization is the very dynamic that carries Sartre toward Derrida. It is Derrida's own role as innovator that renders Sartre his context, his victim, and the necessary milieu of Derrida's own reading against Sartre's France, against the society that itself produces the force of Derrida's question, the force of his own self-historicization against Sartre. And indeed, in his concern about the intellectual's relation with a cultural milieu, Derrida leaves himself no less free than Sartre to misread, to misinterpret, as a function of his own innovation. As he says in the interview, "What I write resembles . . . a dotted outline of a book to be written in what I call . . . the 'old new language,' the most archaic and the newest, unheard of, and thereby, at present unreadable" (*DD*, 73; *Nouvel Obs*, 86).

But what is the "reading" Derrida has given Sartre? In the few ("counter-hegemonic") moves Derrida has made toward Sartre, including this interview, Derrida decries having discovered Sartre to be metaphysical—in the "catastrophic" sense of being "merely another metaphysician." But it is Derrida's critique of metaphysics that produces the situation he decries; that is, it is his critique that sees Sartre's own critique of metaphysics as still metaphysical, and renders Sartre's thinking catastrophic for him. Derrida's critique has engendered for itself what it then discovers. There is a self-reflexiveness in the historicity of his critique of Sartre that Derrida ignores, though he embraces that historicity in most of his other writing, where it appears as an attention to his own textual form. This omission testifies to a polemical component in Derrida's approach to Sartre, as well as to a blind spot concerning a refusal, an unacknowledged legislation of Sartre's status.

On the other hand, Derrida is also indicting the star system of the "cultural scene" that ostensibly gave Sartre his fame, his meaning as "Sartre"—even for Derrida in his youth. In other words, the catastrophe could not be Derrida's discovery of the necessity to read "against Sartre" vis-à-vis Sartre, or even to give Sartre another (a mis-)reading; it could only be catastrophic for Derrida (and perhaps also apostrophic) to read against Sartre vis-à-vis the "cultural scene." But Derrida's own historicization as innovative also depends upon the star system. It is what provides him with an outside from which to critique Sartre. What then constitutes the misfortune in Derrida's relation to Sartre is actually his confrontation with a star system that embraces (misreads) a metaphysician, and his (Derrida's) enthrallment to that same system while recognizing its misreading of the misreaders as his own destiny, his own future anterior limit. To reproach that boundary, and the intellectual world it guards, is then to pay homage to Sartre's innovativeness precisely as a misreading that came to dominate the cultural scene.

In other words, Derrida is understating the case when he says of Sartre, "I do share the affection, almost the kinship, which many feel for this man . . . who doesn't belong to the period of works which are important to me" (DD 75; *Nouvel Obs*, 86).

But then, too, which "period" does this exclude Sartre from? Is it the metaphysical tradition (from Plato to Husserl) that Derrida has overturned to which Sartre does not belong? Is it from Sartre's own time, that of Husserl, Heidegger, and Blanchot, with whom Derrida is in continual dialogue? Or is it that of Sartre's future, whose "works" Derrida so rarely discusses (Foucault, Lacan, and Sollers are the major exceptions)? Does not this temporal exclusion-in-general of Sartre precisely conjoin Derrida to Sartre in the same (atemporal) historical elsewhere, that of innovation? In his double enthrallment (to Sartre displaced onto the milieu, and to the milieu displaced onto Sartre), Derrida is indeed claiming Sartre as a kindred soul.

A Common Uncommonality

On their disparate planes of endeavor, Derrida and Sartre do emerge as kindred souls, addressing what can surprisingly be seen as common themes. Each proposes a critique of the rationalist view of the subject: Derrida shows it to be a concept, a text, while Sartre discloses it in and as narrative. Each offers a notion of history that is itself a critique of an ideological dimension inherent in all historical discourse. For Derrida, each historical text is a simulacrum, a representation that reconstructs the past and a construction that the past then represents; for Sartre, history and historical discourse can only be understood as contingent upon a project. And each focuses on writing and the role of writing; for Sartre, it is the overriding form, and for Derrida, the underwriting content.

In all this, Derrida's intention appears to be the more radical. His project is to "shake metaphysics" and to exceed it.[38] Derrida's question is not what makes metaphysics possible, but rather what lies behind and within language that makes metaphysics unavoidable, while making the questioning of metaphysics possible.

Sartre's intention is to understand metaphysics (as totalization) within the realm of human praxis; that is, to understand metaphysics itself as one human activity among others (this is, perhaps, the fundamental theme of the entire first volume of the *Critique of Dialectical Reason*). But both agree that to take a step beyond metaphysics—which, for Sartre, is a step anterior to ideology and givenness, and for Derrida is a step beyond presence, security, and the language of Being—one must use the same (metaphysical) language (*DD*, 68). Derrida argues that if one depends on metaphysics for access to the sign in the first place, then the critique of the sign, "submitting the sign to thought" against metaphysics already occurs within metaphysics.[39] One can move beyond presence only through the trace of non-presence in presence. It is the erasure of the trace of difference that is the central operation of metaphysics, whereby it universalizes itself, whether as an account of the subject or the object. Difference persists within the text of metaphysics, however, and one surpasses the language of metaphysics precisely by returning to the trace within its language (*Marg*, 66/77).

For Sartre, the presuppositions of a thought system eventually show up as bad faith, as the attempt to give transcendence (through ideological determination or definition) to what nevertheless remains contingent. Bad faith discloses itself in a narrativization of presupposition, as the way the subject discloses its unacknowledged abandonment of its freedom. Derrida mirrors this in finding the presuppositions of a text within the text's blind spots, those moments of a text's meaning that its discourse cannot "see" because, as a priori, they are what it "sees" with (*Marg*, 125). History, in particular, cannot see its self-construction as that for which the past it examines is created to be its precondition because that self-construction is the eye with which it then sees, as a history, the past it represents.[40] A similar concept of a blind spot appears in Sartre's phenomenology of the racist mind in *Anti-Semite and Jew*. There he points out that the place where one is in bad faith is precisely where one has created such a blind spot: in the case of the racist, the chosenness of a passion toward an a priori idea of an other. (Derrida suggests that this work was one of the first that drew him to Sartre.) For both, it is not a question of tearing down the structure of metaphysics, as if to punish or avenge its dependence on a prioris, but of understanding apriorism as the limit of metaphysics and of the thinking it engenders.

Thus, though Sartre and Derrida are looking in different directions, their concerns are parallel. In a sense that will be of central concern in this essay, Derrida provides a rhetorical structure for more fully grasping the existentialist attack on the metaphysical a prioris that lie beneath its terminologies and rhetorics. Yet Sartre's very negativity concretizes many of Derrida's deconstructive operations.

Indeed, though they inhabit disparate and incommensurable domains, one could, perhaps, find them both seated at a common historical table, in that broader intellectual movement mentioned at the beginning for which their common though incommensurable concerns have been the conceptual core. This movement's philosophical roster would include Nietzsche, Husserl, Heidegger, de Beauvoir, Merleau-Ponty, Barthes, Foucault, and many others.[41] As a whole, it reflects an extended project striving against metaphysical apriorism, each participant doing so in his/her own way. Despite its shortcomings, it is a liberatory project, to which Derrida and Sartre have been among the most committed.

Within their commitment, a number of analogous theoretical strategies can be identified; and which enunciate the central thematic focuses of this essay. In his exposition of subject-subject relations, in *Being and Nothingness*, Sartre seeks (1) to offer an alternative response to the problem of other subjectivities, (2) to reconceptualize the ontology of persons, and (3) to elucidate the nature and dynamics of interpersonal relations. Sartre arrives at an alternate account of subject-subject relations that breaks radically with traditional accounts: specifically the Hegelian and the Husserlian.[42] Similarly, Derrida's project (as outlined in *Of Grammatology*) can be understood as seeking (1) to offer an alternative response to the problem of language and writing, (2) to reconceptualize the problem of metaphysics in terms of an expanded view of textuality, and (3) to elucidate the dynamics of discourse with respect to the textuality of philosophy. Indeed, *Of Grammatology* can be understood as an alternate response to the problem of alterity, theorizing supplementarity as constituting a change of place (an exchange of presence and absence) between the philosophical and the textual.

Ultimately, however, it is because the existentialist and the deconstructive treatment of the a prioris of Western thought are not the same that a relationship becomes a possibility; the difference is important. Derrida argues that because meaning depends on signs and the use of signs, metaphysics is unavoidable. "From the moment that there is meaning there are nothing but signs" (*Gram*, 50). Signs, whether as speech or writing or the division of a landscape by paths worn down by human footsteps moving across the land, are the condition for there to be meaning. Metaphysics simply emerges as one of the instrumentalities of communication, or that which communication constructs as its instrumentality. We formalize thoughts that represent the meanings signs construct and represent those thoughts as meanings formulated through other formalized signs. For instance, when Sartre argues that language is an instrumentality of consciousness, the Derridean critique would point out not only that "consciousness" represents a presupposition but that the instrumentality to which Sartre refers is already a formularization of articulated meanings and reasoning. All the hidden, ideal, ephemeral, experiential, or objective referents to which one addresses oneself systematically have, as their necessary condition, a metaphysical language. Yet conversely, because it is not possible to use language as an instrumentality if what would instrumentalize it relies for its existence on language in the first place, then the instrumentalization of language is itself a condition for the metaphysical operation. Sartre would not disagree with this, since both pertain to human activity: "We search out language to express our thoughts at the same time that we discover our thoughts in the language we find" (BN, 264, translation modified).

Thus, they would go around and around, not negating each other, but inverting the order of each other's terms, as both a critique of the other and a response to the other's critique. Sartre contests metaphysical presupposition and its pretension to universality at the discursive level by arguing that it is contingent; and he rejects the post-structuralist critique because it has raised contingency to an absolute, overgeneralizing it. Derrida does so by arguing that any discursive system must be inconsistent because of the inescapable ambiguities and structural equivocalities of language itself, that is, at a metadiscursive level; and he finds that equivocality operating within Sartre's very claim to contest the metaphysical. Each would think the other was missing the point and undermining his own efficacy.

But beneath the disparity of points of philosophical difference, there lurks an irreducible divergence. While Sartre may deploy polemical language against post-structuralism, Derrida levies a metadiscursive critique of Sartre's language in general. And such a critique remains unanswerable because it is already incommensurable with what it critiques. This is the nature of a critique of the form of language. What Derrida does in his critique of discursive structure is transform the language of the text he addresses. Should the other (Sartre, in this case) answer such a critique from within his own philosophical language, he would in effect be ignoring the critique by assuming his own philosophical language to be still intact as before; in other words, to reassert his discourse would be to not answer the critique. Should he respond from within the language as transformed by the critique, his very use of that language as his own would signify that he had, by so adopting it as his language, acceded to the critique, and would have no need, and nothing from which, to respond. The deconstructive critique is unanswerable, not in what it says, but in where it says it from. Because it comes from a metadiscursive place, it requires that the other (Sartre) do violence either to his own language or to the critique in order to respond. In effect, what has been generally discerned as a hiatus between these two thinkers is actually a concrete structural incommensurability, which would override and undermine any ideational dialogue. The hiatus represents a differential space between discourse and metadiscourse, between text and metatext, rather than a disparity between one thought and another that could be placed in dialogic relation to each other. Dialogue, in a fundamental manner, is relegated to two separate monologues emerging from disparate levels of discourse. (And one question that I shall pose eventually is what this "discursive difference" means for human interaction and dialogue in general, in which it continually appears.)

It is this inability to engage in a "dialogue" on an ideational plane, because their texts operate on different discursive levels, that constitutes the "mutual refusal" of their texts, and explains the paucity of interrelating critique. If their discourses are fundamentally incommensurable, while seeming to reveal certain commonalities of parenthood, project, and strategy, then any conjunction that would hope to traverse the abyss between them must reveal itself at a certain distance from their disparity of language itself. An attempt to relate the two would then seem to have to begin with deprivileging both the literal content of the texts in question and their disparate languages, and reexamine them through their own formal structures. That is, the form of the incommensurability between them must be an aspect of their "commonality" and of the mutuality of their refusal. A sense of a common language would then have to be derived from elsewhere than in their respective philosophical terms. To encompass both, a mode of discursive construction will have to be found that will transcend this critical difference of discursive level. This would require that one proceed without attempting to existentialize Derrida or to transmute Sartre into a post-structuralist discourse. It will demand absolute respect for the incommensurability precisely because it is structural. It is only by dedicating ourselves to respecting the incommensurability that we may proceed.

In sum, there are critical issues at stake here, which concern the opening or obstruction of dialogue and the notion of the social in a political and informational world. If we recognize that analytic thinking is insufficient, it is because we are already addressing the question of a possible conjunction between incommensurable discourses. And we are posing a problematic that could impact similar incommensurabilities elsewhere. Political power, for instance, can be seen as establishing itself through the exercise, the very invention of incommensurability in the real world, in the sense that the levels of hierarchy it establishes are compelled to speak incommensurable languages—or perhaps a spectrum that ranges from the autonomous, the self-valorization of a domination that deprecates the subjugated, to the acquiescent, the self-depreciation of the dominated, those who are silenced in their every claim to autonomous being.[43] If structural incommensurability obviates the possibility of dialogue, then it presents itself as a possible strategy for congealing oppressive situations or hierarchical impositions; indeed, all acts of imposition rely on a dimension of unanswerability. It would suggest that discourses of domination were thereby always able to insulate themselves, against which the dominated have no channels of response. It would imply that hierarchies always contain a structural ability to transform the autonomy claims of the subjected into an expression of the unlawful, the ungrateful, or of transgressive aggression against which the acts of domination themselves would appear to be in self-defense.

Against the operation of such incommensurabilities, which tend to take on the aura of power and oppression even when that is unintended because they enact themselves critically as a form of silencing, an investigation of possible bridge structures would be of great importance.[44] One of the ironies of the post-structuralist movement has been its palpable inability to bring new thinking to bear on everyday social or political activity in the face of its own certainty that its critique of language and discourse would open a new understanding of the political. Consistently, though with notable exceptions, it ran aground precisely because it constituted an approach to language. The politics of real issues depends upon a language in which issues can be articulated in the terms in which ideological confrontation occurs. To that extent, issues are bound to a certain tradition, within which they are issues. A critique that focuses on how issues are imprisoned in a discursive tradition might actually be fundamentally liberatory, but it would be interpreted as posing a liberation that was already separate from or even irrelevant to what was materially at stake.[45] That is, critically stepping outside traditional language appears only to raise new issues at odds with the issue in question in that traditional language. The shoals on which post-structuralism ran aground were an unavoidable collapse of the difference between the language of an issue and the metalinguistic issue of language. Perhaps there will be a possibility of rectifying this problem by breaking the hermetics of metadiscourse through some formal yet significative connection to what continues to address the language of issues. The attempt to read Sartre in a more up-to-date fashion through Derrida, and the complementary attempt to read Derrida in a more down-to-earth manner through Sartre, might relate to such an outcome if it could bring itself to avoid the usual polemics.

To encounter the structure of each through an encounter with the structure of the other will therefore be the project. It will attempt to examine the nature of incommensurability, as it effects itself specifically in the hiatus between Sartre and Derrida, through the construction of a domain of formal interaction, where an interweaving of forms constitutes a level of signification beyond the capabilities of the literal languages in which each discourse is written. What such "formal" connections would look like, as structures that preserve the strength of conceptual disjunction they seek to traverse, will be part of the investigation itself. While the structural parallels and historical affinities between Sartre and Derrida might provide a certain common foundation, no mere juxtaposition or translation, or even transformation of terms would be adequate. And again, neither can this imply a deconstruction of Sartre with a concomitant existentialization of Derrida, which would not respect nor be able to address the space or hiatus between them. The abyss separating them remains untraversable in the discursive terms of either one.

Because the focus of this project is in the realm of formal connections, an encompassing concern with the breadth of thinking of each thinker will be of contingent interest. It is the form of their thinking, its logic, structures of reasoning, style, and poetic or discursive geometry, that will be elicited, rather than their specific accounts of philosophical notions. I will concentrate on the discursive logics and structures, their primary modes and styles of thinking, in whatever works they may be found, and in whatever order.

2 The Form of Uncommon Logic

THE QUESTION IS the incommensurable. If Richard Rorty does not see any reason it should exist, it is because he assumes that there is a common language.[1] But implicit within that assumption, as its condition of possibility, resides a need for a univocality of terms, agreement (social acceptance) on a conventional and formalized logic, and a universal sense of truth and referentiality. These discursive categories (lexicality, logic, and truth) are precisely the ones that have undergone the most severe critique at the hands of post-structuralism, revealing an unfortunately inherent ambiguity, differentiality, and variability.

If language is a system of differences between signs rather than simply of signs themselves, through which meaning is generated, then the multiplicity of differences that surround each sign must generate a multiplicity of meanings. Understood in its most banal form, this means that meaning changes with changes of context. Or rather, this explains why a change of context incurs changes of meaning; it prioritizes different differences for each sign in a system of differences. The lexical loses its assumed univocality; strict lexicality, such as is required by formal logic, becomes an idle endeavor. But context itself is multiple without having to be changed. In any text, there is both the formal context of the text itself that contextualizes each of its component signs, and the ideological context that the text invokes and through which it asks to be read. Not only can these contexts not coincide because they exist at different discursive levels, but the ideological coherence of a reading depends on an ideational system brought to a reading from elsewhere. There is a loss of immanence of context; the context of a "reading" must be "brought to bear" upon it by the reader, as a form of ideological overlay. Discursive context both resides in a text's self-contextualization and is displaced from immanence through the text's discursive self-presentation. A text is polyvalent both internally as a system of signs and externally as a sign among signs. Hence, all readings of a text differ; no reading can ever be *the* reading. There will be a discoverable "truth" of meaning and reference in any text, but it will be contingent upon the reading given it.

A formal logic becomes problematic once the terms of its propositions can no longer be pinned down unequivocally. A focus on logic becomes, against its own desires, an interplay of literal (lexical) meaning and structure, of specificity and polyvocality. And referentiality gets derailed by the self-referentiality of language. If signs make reference to each other in and through their structure, then reference gets replaced by a pretense of referring. Reference becomes a mode of ideational overlay (along with ideology) by which signs "are understood" to make reference to "something else." Textuality is inherently incommensurable with the acts of reference it facilitates.[2]

Sartre would not disagree with this. For Sartre, truth and meaning are brought into being by and for a subject. This is the centrality of the "project" for Sartre. It is the choice of being in the world by which all is contextualized and given its meaning for the individual in his/her situation. Referentiality and truth are transformed by knowledge as part of one's being in the world, contingent upon a project. These are the terms by which Sartre contests metaphysical presupposition in its generality. He would even refuse the generality of mutual refusal. For Sartre, dialogue proceeds without concern for a conjunction of project. If it subverts itself as incommensurable with the world, that too is part of the individual's project. This is what he elucidates in his plays (in particular, *No Exit* and *Les Jeux Sont Faits*).[3] And his refusal of the generality of refusal would hold for writing as well. For Sartre, writing is an existential act that, like all action, reveals a project that engenders its own referentiality in the situation in which it finds itself and attempts to make itself meaningful. In writing's tactical manipulations of socially given forms of logic and lexicality, it subjects that logic to itself; in other words, logic as reasoning cannot be divorced from style.

The disparity of languages in which Sartre and Derrida write philosophically is not one for which referentiality is a concern (and though both wrote in French, that too is immaterial to our conerns here). Indeed, degrees of referentiality will be not only irrelevant, but irreverent. What one looks at, the other sees with—if we may allegorize referentiality in this way, as itself the heart of their incommensurability. Where Sartre speaks about consciousness, Derrida speaks about the inability to escape the textuality of so speaking. Where Sartre attacks the necessity of philosophical a prioris, arguing for their contingency as chosen, Derrida questions the reality of a prioris themselves. But beyond subject matter, it is the structure of their languages that stands between them as style and reasoning and in the way of any intertextual confluence. There are no textual grounds upon which an intertextual conjunction can be demanded or expected. If there are instances where a conjunction exists, they will only mark where mutual refusal had itself been refused. In other words, intertextual commensurability would amount to an absence of the veto that style always holds at the ready.

Yet they both write in the "same world," with similar concerns. And Sartre personally haunts the philosophical ground where the Derridean critique of metaphysics stakes its philosophical claim. How could their respective interactions with the "same world" only serve to reveal a realm between them in which a common language was not strictly possible? What does this imply about the meaning of the "same world"? The same as what?

While each has shaken the world with his thinking, the differentiality of language and the differential of worlds are what offer themselves to inquiry from the space between them. Yet what would be revealed about the world or about language if we could bring them into concert or communication at some level? To establish communication, we will have to understand the nature of incommensurability; and for that, we will have to go to a different level of discourse, other than the categories, concepts, or lexicalities of their texts. A mode of communication will have to be invented, in order not to fall into the trap of using the language of one to speak about the other. That would only lead to an inability to speak about them both at all, since it would cancel the "between." We must begin with a language that begins elsewhere than the languages given.

The invention (or construction) of a new language of communicability must begin by respecting that critical dimension of their relation, their mutual refusal. It must be one that can live in the space in which they veto connection. Perhaps it is the problem of formulating an underlying intertextuality for which conjunction or accord themselves remain irrelevant. Let us begin with invention itself.

INVENTION

Sartre and Derrida are inventors. At the foundation of each of their respective projects is a neologistic endeavor, which functions both as a refusal of the limits of the language given and as an affirmation of their project to go beyond that. Their respective acts of invention are gateways into the realms they seek to address. For Derrida, the invention is *différance*, and for Sartre, it is *néantisation*. To approach what these terms do, or what they accomplish as discursive acts, one must consider the fact (and meaning) of invention itself.

The invention of a term, or a sign, is not like the invention of anything else. One invents something, like a machine or procedure, with a certain instrumentality in mind, a telos or envisioned outcome that the invention facilitates or manifests. In language, the function of instrumentality might be filled by an act of naming or description, in the sense that naming points to something one already has in mind, and whose representation one wishes to manifest. Naming individuates what it points out, by setting it apart. An act of entitling (a poem or narrative, for instance) fulfills this instrumentality, as does taxonomy or prefacing. It is the process of individuation that Sartre refers to as "totalizing" because in separating something from its background, or clarifying its boundaries, one is rendering it a whole, an entity. Naming totalizes because it does this. In effect, the act of naming gives presence, or brings to light what is already there awaiting individuation and discernment through an added articulation. And as added, it is the deployment of something (a name) that already exists.

But the invention of a word is not like that. One invents in language because the language at hand does not give one the power or ability to name or entitle something. That is, something seems to be "there" that escapes one's ability to signify it. The act of invention points to the absence of a signified, precisely by bringing a signifier into existence that does not yet have one. (The most usual way this happens is with a poem. A poem is an invention in language that brings into existence a meaning which only the poem itself names; the poem becomes the signifier for that meaning as a poem. If the poem then names that meaning, it is only after having brought it into existence as an invention.) The invented signifier at first signifies non-presence; it cannot yet name what had not existed at the moment of invention. The invention points to what is not there and proclaims with respect to what is there (all other meanings) that it is not that. In that way, it makes possible a signified of which no notion was possible prior to invention. One invents a signifier in order to bring a "non-thereness" into existence as a signified, that is, to bring a signified into existence. Invention is not the origin of language; it is where language is originary. It marks the limits of language.

In other words, a word is invented not to be an instrumentality but to be the condition for one. Once invented, a term adumbrates a scene in which an instrumentality becomes possible. The term inscribes within itself the absence it discovers and then functions to fill. By pointing out what is not there, invention engenders what it points to.

This, of course, is the role of the word "*I*", which for each first person, whether fictional character or human being, is ever again reinvented in order to bring a "first person" ("I") into existence. The word "*I*" produces itself as a signifier for each new user that has always yet to discover itself as an instrumentality for that person. The same can be said for a narrative text. A narrative text is an invention that is also a discovery (Barthes: and on a second reading is yet a different discovery). Indeed, this can be generalized; every text, as an invented sign, is a name for what is then discovered in the text, and which discovery that text as a name for itself becomes. Though one entitles a narrative or poem, its being as invention is given by itself as a whole. The invented sign (whether word, poem, or narrative) eventually acquires its meaning only through many readings in the context of, and through, other texts. What characterizes an invented word, poem, or narrative is its singularity; singularity is one of the attributes of the invented.

Thus, invention produces itself in two movements: In place of an absence in language, something is engendered by which a new articulation becomes possible; and what is engendered functions instrumentally to point back toward what is still absent, what is still inarticulable, in the act of bringing into existence what it points to. Invention is thus a conjunction of absence and instrumentality (the two terms most central to the respective critiques of language of Sartre and Derrida). The invented term comprehends the prior absence in engendering an entity that is always ahead of itself, a nonobject whose projected form is its own foundation.

DIFFÉRANCE

Derrida's derivation of "différance" exemplifies the scene of invention (*SP*, 129–60). The term "différance" marks the existence of the fact, which cannot be named, that a signifier makes systematic reference to other signifiers, that it is defined through other signifiers, rather than by reference to the world, and thus signifies through the system of its differences from those other signifiers, continually deferring its own meaning to them through that structure. That is, each sign signifies within a double structure of absence. First, meaning is possible because a sign differs from other absent signs; and second, its meaning projects itself elsewhere in its deferral to other signs. "What defers presence is the very basis on which presence is announced or desired in what represents it, its sign, its trace" (*Pos*, 8). That is, the condition for meaning, for language itself, is the differing and deferral of the presence of what is meant.[4] The term "différance" is invented to signify the impossible space of combination (differing and deferring) in which two separate forms of difference overlap without impinging and impinge without overlapping—presence as absence, absence as presence.

Derrida arrives at this invention by arguing that for difference to exist, it must already be the effect of something that distinguishes and postpones. This "something" can be neither substance nor object, since that would simply imply another system of differences from other substances and objects. Neither is it intentionality, he argues, since that also already presupposes distinction (*SP*, 147). Intentionality exists only because an intentional object has already been distinguished; that is, difference has already served to distinguish it. No originary difference can be given or conceived; no cause for difference can be assigned. Yet to speak of effects without causes destroys the notion of effect.

> Our language has no name for such a différance. But we 'already know' that if it is unnamable, this is not simply provisional; it is not because our language has still not found or received this *name*, or because we would have to look for it in another language. . . . It is because there is no *name* for this. (*SP*, 159)

Difference remains the non-effect of what will have differed as non-presence. The term "différance" is invented to point out this non-originary source or condition for the non-effect of what is not there. Différance reconjoins differing and deferring as a nonfull, nonsimple "origin" (*SP*, 141). It is "the structured and differing origin of differences." As an invention, it brings to discernment the inseparability and incommensurability of difference and deferral, of the impossibility of origin in the continual return to a source by what appears as effect. It effectuates the non-effect that was without cause, by creating (in effect) its own effect.

Thus, différance is to be thought of as what is already implicated in, or the exclusive ground of, difference (as Being, for Heidegger, is implicated in, or the exclusive ground of, beings). It engenders what it points to (which in turn points back to it) by proclaiming with respect to what is already there that it is not that. As such, the notion or operation of différance is (points to) the must fundamental moment of Derrida's critique of language. It marks the place where deconstructive thinking starts, because it already understands that any sign, whether word or text or whatever, does not carry its meaning within it. As Gayatri Spivak puts it, "such is the strange 'being' of the sign: half of it always 'not there,' and the other half always 'not that'" (*Gram*, xvii).

The difficulty of Derrida's term, as a rhetorical move, a metatextual operation, lies in its inconceivability. Though it can be spoken about, it cannot be predicated; and thus whatever immediate apprehension one has of it is always also somehow in the distance. This is part of what Howells embraces in her appreciation of the "*logique paradoxale*" of Derrida's text. While she was satisfied to notice its appearance in both Derrida and Sartre, she did so in order to ask what it might imply about further parallels between them, in the sense of "logic" as discursive form. But others, understandably, have found the implicit challenge irresistible to apprehend différance philosophically, to seek to reincorporate its "logic" back into philosophy (the outcome of such attempts being very much at the inception of the present essay).

Rodolphe Gasché, for instance, in *The Tain of the Mirror*, attempts to deploy an alternate trajectory for it.[5] Gasché's quest is for a philosophical ground for deconstruction. Derridean thinking philosophically challenges him because it resists formularization. Though Derrida himself warns against attempting formularization (*LI*, 141), Gasché hypothesizes that a ground should emerge where deconstructive activity formulates itself beyond metaphysics, if it manages to do so without a return to metaphysics as a telos. That is, deconstruction would appear to ground itself as what is called a heterology because it formulates itself beyond metaphysics.

Heterology is an analytic of the heterogeneous, the incommensurable, the structure of aporia. An example would be the relation of conscious reflection and self-reflection: Self-consciousness becomes an aporia in the sense that, in seeking to reflect upon itself, it determines what it discovers while discovering only what it has already determined. Consciousness becomes incommensurable with itself in this operation, seeing itself looking at itself as other, and looking at what is seeing itself as the same. The aporia is that it knows itself as other but not as object, and it objectifies itself but not as other (*TM*, 87). For Gasché, this should hold for différance in its marking the confluence of a sign's differing and deferring, its being "not there" and "not that," its presence as absence and its absence as presence.

Gasché's notion of heterology is taken from the contemporary German philosopher Werner Flach, who loosely bases it on the Hegelian relation of reflection and speculation. For Hegel, reflection is an act of becoming aware of awareness, of being a subject as such by making the self an object for itself (in the subject-object relation, the subject becomes a subject by having an object of awareness for itself; *TM*, 25). And speculation is the act of making reflection itself the object of reflection.[6] When subjectivity becomes subjectivity as such, it discloses a contradiction between objectivity (the empirical proposition) and subjectivity as self-reflection. The moment of absolute reflection becomes the moment of "speculation" (mirroring) because subject and object change places and reflect themselves in each other; it is their discernment of each other that constitutes the moment or dialectical movement of antithesis.[7]

Flach transforms the Hegelian antithesis into absolute exclusion, a space of incommensurability. He reasons that if each Hegelian moment can be considered metadiscursive to a preceding relation, then metadiscursivity becomes potentially endless, and only absolute exclusion and exclusivity will foreclose that endlessness. But this involves rearticulating the mediating conditions of possibility of antithesis, accepting and embracing the aporia of self-reflection by including what speculation is supposed to achieve rather than how it resolves that aporia (*TM*, 88). Thus, for Flach, heterology refers to "the coupled moments of the absolute relation [that] stand in a relation of mutual exclusion, in which the opposite moments, without negating one another, complete each other to form a totality," where the absolute relation is that of one and its Other as an "exclusive other of the same" (*TM*, 91).

Gasché reads Flach as articulating the moment of originary duplication, the irreducible doubling of any logical origin, as the aporetic moment of pure difference that Derrida finds at the heart of all signification. On Derrida's account, for something to operate as a sign, it must be iterable. For something to be read as a sign, or a meaning, it must be recognized, that is, encountered already. There is never a first encounter with the sign; the first time is always already the second. The possibility of iterability, the sense of self-difference, subverts self-identity; a thing (sign) can never just be itself, contrary to the pragmatics of a system that simply assumes the existence of objects. Self-identity or self-plenitude is impossible since repetition is always already at work. This implies that doubling is not preceded by any originary unity; the notion of an original is always only installed as its own iteration (*TM*, 213). There is only originary doubling (i.e., the simulacrum); to be is already to be double (*TM*, 226).

Heterology presents itself as a way of approaching the impossibility of origin, the idea that origin presupposes its effect and thus finds its source (its origin) in it. Reflection on the aporia of self-reflection becomes heterological because self-reflection is aporetic (*TM*, 70). When transferred to the sphere of discourse, this offers an articulation for the originlessness of signs. And Gasché argues that the aporetic textual moments for which Derrida addresses and coins neologistic terms constitute a heterological structure. Thus, for Gasché, heterology becomes an overarching system that gives Derrida's metatextual operations, and in particular différance, a conceptual coherence, a "philosophical ground."

But there is a difference. For Flach, alterity, separation, and equiprimordiality characterize the Other as the exclusive (and exclusionary) other of the same. For Derrida, on the other hand, reflection splits what it doubles, and is both other and the same (*TM*, 101), an opposition without the negation implied by exclusion. There is no moment of pure difference; only the positivities of inseparability and incommensurability, which Derrida calls hybrid and bifacial. Like that of signifier and signified, they constitute a spacing that is indiscernible in the text, but part of its inner logic.[8] Gasché skirts this issue in order to recast Derrida within a philosophical intertextuality.

Ultimately, Gasché seeks an articulation (of Derrida) that will "say what it means" while paying obeisance to the Derridean rejection of this possibility. While this may render his own project heterological, in systematizing while attempting to be self-reflective on that activity, it falls prey to what Sartre would call a counterfinality, an unwanted concomitant collapsing of language and metalanguage into each other through an alternative systematics (Flach's). Gasché's problem lies in assuming that philosophy must be a system, and thus ideationally coherent (*TM*, 239). For him, to seek to philosophize "the deconstructive" already means to systematize it, to impose a condition (from elsewhere) on the Derridean text in order to return it to the philosophical domain. Gasché has proposed a philosophical project, but it cannot be one because of the heterological nature of that project itself. In attempting to formulate "the deconstructive" heterologically, he has shown his project to be heterological rather than the deconstructive. And he has at the same time, aporetically, abandoned the heterology of his project to the coherence he reserves immanently for philosophy. The signifier of his "philosophization" is "not that" and "not there."[9]

This returns us to the difficulty of différance, its inconceivability as a conflation but not a collapse of text and metatext into each other. Opening the space of this conflation, différance makes room for an erasure at its own hands of what it is ostensibly about, of its "aboutness" as such. Though constituted by a play of meaning, of aboutness itself, différance remains "about" a double system of absence, the double absence of differing from and deferring what it is itself "about." Conceiving it cancels "aboutness" itself (*SP*, 143). Thus, it must travel an entirely different trajectory as a formal structure from what either Howells or Gasché map out for it.

That is, rather than différance having a systematicity that requires philosophical coherence, it presents itself as a structure that operates logically within a text, a structure that could be considered heterological, as a relation of inseparability and incommensurability, that is not systematizable as such. Différance "makes possible the very thing that it makes impossible" (*Gram*, 143). Neither a concept nor a name, neither intelligible nor sensible, its form is precisely its inconceivability, the unnameable grounding of what remains without ground. As the unconceivable form of all language, différance then is about the logic of language; it is the form of that logic, a shift from language to the form of language, and from the logic of language to the language of that logic. "Différance is therefore the formation of form" (*Gram*, 63).

In other words, if différance were to have a content, a "meaning," it would be precisely its nonconceptuality, its inconceivability; that is, its content or meaning is its form as an absence of concept, a noncontent. In sum, its content signifies its form: its form is its content as what is not signified (a concept), and its content is its form as what is not a signifier (a name). Thus, it differs from an ordinary sign, whose existence its operations make possible. For an ordinary sign, the sign is a signifier that signifies its content, its signified. For différance as an invention, the content, its inconceivability, signifies its form, a nonword and nonconcept. Différance is a form that is the signified of its content as a signifier.

NÉANTISATION

Sartre's neologist term *néantisation* (nihilation) evinces a similar structure.[10] Where différance is to be thought of as the exclusive ground of difference, nihilation is to be thought of as the exclusive ground of consciousness. That is, it makes nonreference to that essential and primordial "moment" of the upsurge of consciousness into the world, of which an awareness remains impossible. Sartre broaches the question of nihilation to address in analogue the Heideggerian necessity of questioning a being that questions its own Being. Heidegger begins with the assertion that the question of Being had been forgotten by metaphysics; and Sartre argues analogously that we cannot forget the priority of negation, of what he calls *négatité*, even to the question of Being.[11] To ask a question, to enter into inquiry as such, must leave open the possibility of a negative response, or the possibility that what is questioned is itself nothing. The possibility of the negative, that the answer is "no," is always immanent in the nature of questioning (*BN*, 23).

In addition, an essential condition for a response to one's inquiry is that one not be what is questioned (for Heidegger, to question Being, one must question the Being of a being that questions, which is different from the Being questioned). In short, for Sartre, negativity and non-being are fundamental to one's being in addressing anything.

Sartre pushes this another step. If the questioner must be dissociated from the being questioned, then the possibility of nothingness or of non-being must arise within the questioner's own being. The questioner "wrench[es] himself from being in order to be able to bring out of himself the possibility of a non-being" (*BN*, 23). In other words, to understand Being is to understand that by which nothingness comes into the world, the being that must be its own nothingness. "Nothingness lies coiled at the heart of being—like a worm" (*BN*, 21).

Thus, consciousness apprehends its object in the mode of non-being and in the awareness of not being that object. An object is both individuated against its background (context), as not that background, and made a presence to consciousness without distance as other, as not consciousness. Or, as Sartre puts it in his famous doubly negative expression, consciousness (being-for-itself) "is what it is not and is not what it is" (*BN*, 63). Néantisation is the term Sartre uses for this double negativity, for the mode whereby consciousness is already the "nothinging" of its object and itself.

> By a double movement of nihilation (néantisation) [one] nihilates (néantise) the thing in relation to [one]self... by placing it in a neutral state, between being and non-being—and [one] nihilates [one]self from being in order to be able to bring out of [one]self the possibility of a non-being. (*BN*, 23)

Nihilation interrupts (nothings) the world's space, and it displaces the world's content (the object) as the nihilation of the object's presence. Presence is nothing but this double non-being, the incommensurability of these dual nihilations of continuity and fullness.

It would seem that Gasché's notion of a heterology should pertain to Sartre, as the other "*logique paradoxale*" that Howells described. But like différance, nihilation escapes any causal chain since, as nothing-ing, it must already be separate from the positivity of a caused or causal object or being (*BN*, 23). Nihilation is a detachment from Being, the (non)source of presence to consciousness, in the mode of being inseparable from it. Thus, it likewise reveals both an incommensurability and an inseparability, an aboutness that is "about" a double system of negative absencing, of nothing-ing and non-being.

But the individuation of an object from its background, its nothing-ing, marks its difference from other objects ("between being and non-being"), and the nihilation of consciousness defers the object to the possibility of non-being that is the possibility of consciousness of the object. Again, as per Spivak's aphorism, the object is "not there" in its deferral as non-being, and "not that" in its difference as a nihilated content of consciousness. A congruence appears between nihilation and différance that, like all congrence, can be inverted. Différance can be couched in the terms that constitute the structure of nihilation—that is, expressed in Sartre's formulation of being-for-itself. In its difference from the absent, the sign is what it is not; and as constituting the deferral of the signified, by which the sign empties itself, loses itself in an "elsewhere," it is not what it is.[12]

Finally, because nihilation refers to nothing, to consciousness nothing-ing its object, it names an inarticulable, a form whose content is the absence it was invented to present, a meaning whose form is nothing but reference to that inarticulability, to that nothing-ing. Its act of referring to that inarticulability constitutes its content. Thus, its content, its signified, makes reference to that act of referring; its content refers precisely to its form. Like différance, the form of nihilation is the signified of its content as signifier.

In sum, the terms "différance" and "nihilation" reveal congruent involutions of form and content; they are structured in a congruent fashion as textual operations (inventions). As inventions, neither différance nor nihilation refer; instead, they bring into existence that to which they will have referred. Différance is invented through certain critical operations, and it remains undefinable in the language producing its necessity; nihilation is invented through certain ontological operations, and is irreducible to them. As textual operations, they produce, through being the groundless ground for signs and consciousness respectively, congruent descriptive configurations. That is, they operate analogously with respect to the disparate domains of meanings and objects. Indeed, they seem to be the same kinds of textual machinery—or rather, the same kind of textual animal: in terms of opening an inarticulable to discovery, they exhibit a certain autonomy; and, though they belong to different textual ecologies, with respect to those ecologies, they seem to evince parallel roles and similar metabolism.

The two terms are what one could call homologous. But the notion of homology must be understood. It originated in mathematics and signfied specific types of algebraic operations or topological mappings between structures that were the same, or "congruent," but not geometric. During the last century, it was adopted as an idea of critical discourse in the social sciences and humanities. The anthropologist Franz Boas first employed the concept to describe the function and specificity of totem animals among Native American clans; homology provided him a way of classifying social meanings through their structural relation to natural meanings, thereby specifying more than the nominal relation between totem names and social groups.[13] Levi-Strauss transfers Boas's concept to the realm of sign structure. In *Totemism*, Levi-Strauss argues, against Boas, that a totemic homology must name a relation of relations, rather than an interrelation of referents (10). And he defines homology in general as a system of "differential features," marked by an orderly correspondence between events, texts, or sets of objects, rather than a system of denotations (13).

Lucien Goldmann applies this notion of homology to literature and literary criticism, and in particular to novels in relation to their contemporary world, in order to speak about class structure in novels. For him, there are always sets of "intelligible relations" between the literary form of the novel and everyday life in the individualistic society of market production.[14] And he argues that fictional characters formally reflect the ideological structure of class groupings to the extent that those characters act without being presented as consciously aware of what their actions signify. In effect, Goldmann's homology relations focus on "what goes without saying" within class relations (*Toward a Sociology of the Novel*, 160).

Roland Barthes takes the notion of homology to a higher level of abstraction in literary criticism. For Barthes, there is an overall homological relation between the forms of organization of all semiotic systems, such as discourses or language itself.[15] In proposing a homological "identity between language and literature," Barthes is, in effect, globalizing the Levi-Straussian sense of homology to all sign systems, and localizing the Goldmannian relation of literature to the world to that same level. Barthes's notion differs from Levi-Strauss's in the sense that he extends homology to textual forms, rather than simply to structures of differences. And he differs from Goldmann in that Goldmann writes within class discourses, while Barthes writes within semiotic discourses.

In applying the notion of homology to the structure of inseparable incommensurables found in nihilation and différance, we are using it in its primary function to reveal instances of iteration and recognition. Homology is critical to the problem of recognition of form in textual discourse, since the recognition of structural configurations cannot depend upon critical methodologies that already regard the text primarily at its literal or narrative levels, or use prior methodologies as modes of recognition.[16] For textual form to be discernible, a mode of recognition that also generates an individuation of the structure to be recognized must be available. It must rely on formal congruences within what presents itself to critical discernment. Furthermore, recognition requires a sense of repetition; a sense of sameness of structures hidden in textuality must be articulable to apprehend them as repetitions. And if the signification of textual forms is an issue, along with their discernment, then the question of recognition becomes one of double recognition. It is to articulate the repetition of form between texts that the notion of homology is essential.[17]

What will concern us with respect to the structuralist use of homology is the concept of discursive mapping between congruent structures of language. Since a homological mapping is independent of the textual content composing the mapped structures, it brackets content and abstracts form. It thus presents itself as a way of reading and articulating configurations of a non-textual character within the realm of textuality. What will be of concern in the literary use of homology is its ability to demonstrate the existence of forms in various textual fields, though in hidden or disguised form, when pointed to by an articulated structure in a present discourse, through their congruence, thus rendering the other structures discernible. The ability to constitute a homology between forms will not only point them out but give them definition and a mode of concreteness. The homological operation will provide a certain "entityhood" to textual form, as befits a possibility of recognition.[18] The structures involved can be texts, parts of texts, or different discursive moments in the same text. Ultimately, to discern textual forms as repetitions or iterations of each other, even in their non-textuality (that is, as the object of a critical operation), will be to grasp textual form as a potential sign.

Just as congruence is a stronger term of relatedness than analogy, so homology is a stronger term of relatedness than congruence. If congruence refers to a geometric sameness, homology absorbs that into a structural and functional identity. That is, the aspects of functional structure can be mapped from one onto the other in a more complete and exhaustive manner. Ultimately, the notion of homology and homological mapping will be critical for recognizing form because it serves to individuate structures across textual differences.

But form remains invisible in a text insofar as that text relies on form as its terrain of expression. It is inseparable from the particular "contours" of its discourse. A text cannot reflect on its own form, just as the eye cannot see itself seeing, though it constitutes itself as sight. It requires a metatextual act, a means of stepping outside of the discursive contours to look back at them and individuate them. Sometimes a text provides the ability to do that from within itself, and sometimes an exterior mode of approach, such as homology, is necessary. Because the discernment of textual form requires its individuation against the background of the discourse it contours, it also depends on a deindividuation as peculiar to its particular context. That is, it must be separated from its textual particularity in order to be recognized as repeatable. Deindividuation is the basis not only for recognition but for discernment of the individuated. And this deindividuation is always a critical or metatextual operation. In effect, a double metadiscursive approach to the text is required, in order to critically separate the act of language as textual form from the content of the text's literal expression, with which it is always conflated.

In the case of nihilation and différance, this double critical metatextuality is provided both by the act of neologistic invention in their respective texts, which provides an interior metatextual moment to the act of invention, and an exterior citation or situating of the process of invention in order to deindividuate the terms in their respective discourses, and render them structures.

This last notion of textuality and metatextuality elucidates a terminological problem, however. The homology of différance and nihilation, of the sign that differs and defers, and the for-itself which is what it is not and is not what it is, points to their being parallel structures. However, both are discursive. Sartre, in his characterization of the for-itself, does not put his language in question, in particular, the copula (which appears twice in his phrase), as does Derrida in his derivation of différance (as well as elsewhere; cf. *Marg*, 195ff.). For Sartre, the third-person singular of "to be" is assumed, as is its relation to being. A critical hiatus opens here that disturbs the homology. Sartre has admitted into his formulation a traditional structure of predication that is not present in Derrida's critique of the sign, while at the same time rendering its use ambiguous in referring to "being" and "non-being" as well. Derrida couches his account of the sign, derived from Saussurean semiotics, in terms of presence and absence, rather than being. In Sartre's ambiguous use of "being," it is also dependent upon presence and absence, as are the two predicating relations of Sartre's formulation.

Sartre would respond that such predications, including the ambiguities of the verb "to be," remain primarily "guides to transcendence" (*L'Idiot*, III, 50) in a reader-text relation; that is, in a relation that is both ontological as a reader's freedom, and situational within a historicization of reading. Derrida's questioning of the copula, and his critique of language as a whole, stand in a different relation to Sartre's conception of the "for-itself" than Sartre's critique of consciousness does in relation to Derrida's language. This disparate relation between them conditions their homology. The incommensurability between their texts continues in effect. But it also suggests that their two inventions have a more complex relation than simply two configurations of "groundless ground."

ON HEIDEGGER

To fully savor the difference in direction this incommensurability sends Sartre and Derrida with respect to each other, we need only examine their different approaches to a common precursor: Heidegger. Heidegger stands in direct anteriority to both. The mode of questioning by which Derrida pursues the dismantling of metaphysics derives in great part from that developed by Heidegger in *Being and Time*; and the structure of Sartre's approach to ontology, as an organization of his existentialist argument, follows Heidegger's own sense of organization in the same work, as both Fell and Schroeder have suggested.

The irony of Heidegger's anteriority is that both Sartre and Derrida established their particular directions of investigation through a critique of how Heidegger undermined his own thinking, his own inadequate attempts to do what each then set forth to accomplish or complete. For Sartre, Heidegger failed to resolve the question of the Other as subject. He contented himself with positing an apprehension of other subjectivities on the basis of one's own self-apprehension, of Dasein already aware of itself and thus already knowing what is to be encountered in the Other. For Heidegger, the Other is always already grasped because being-in-the-world can only be founded on Being-with Others (an "ontological coexistence" in which one *is* through others; *BT*, 154ff.). Sartre points out that if, as Heidegger says, one's being as Dasein is that by which there is (*es gibt*) a world, and hence an Other as such, then one is caught in a solipsism (*BN*, 244ff.). To resolve this question of the Other as subject, Sartre develops his ontology of the look, which remains perhaps the most distinctive argument in *Being and Nothingness*.

For Derrida, Heidegger failed to complete his investigation of Being (for Heidegger, "Being" signifies the ontological [existence itself], while "being" signifies the existent, entities, things) because he presumed a language that could be used to escape the metaphysical use of language. Heidegger recognized the need to escape the constraints of metaphysical language in order to address the Being of language, and through it the meaning of Being. But he sought to accomplish this by allowing language's innate poetic possibilities to carry the discourse. Heidegger reasoned that if language were allowed to speak itself (if it were allowed to simply be), it would return thinking to Being. For Derrida, this amounts to the assumption that a natural poetic efflorescence of language would be sufficient to overcome the constraints of referentiality, the defining of beings, and ontic presence—in short, all the presumptions of metaphysics—while at the same time relating to language from within that poetic. Derrida argues that, on the one hand, Heidegger underestimates the disparity between language as such and the referentiality it continually reengenders, even in the "letting be" of poetic language (*Gram*, 22). And on the other hand, he ignores the disparity between language's structural equivocality and its creation of a new definitude for itself through its textual deployment. In seeking to escape metaphysical language in the poetic, Heidegger did not foresee the reincorporation of the poetic into metaphysics. Language is constantly reappropriated by the metaphysical in each text to the extent that it takes upon itself an act of engendering a reference or univocality for itself, even if that is a self-engendered act by the text in question.[19] In deploying a new poetic "clarity," Heidegger essentially succeeds in substituting his own poetic language for that of metaphysics, without arriving at a critique of language as such. Derrida, in turn, would address the way in which metaphysical language deconstructs, through the very Being of language as a structure of differences that resists at every point the univocity that metaphysics depends upon.

The issue of the other as subject leads Sartre to the look; the issue of the Being of language leads Derrida to the deconstructive. Ultimately, Derrida makes Heidegger's text (though not this difference in philosophical trajectory) an issue of substance between himself and Sartre (in "The Ends of Man"), to which we shall return later. But Heidegger's text itself contains an inner fracture of great profundity, an inner incommensurability that this disparity of critiques reveals and expresses. To apprehend the power of this fracture, a few words need be said about Heidegger's project.

Heidegger's original purposes in raising the question of Being in his early work (*Being and Time*) were, first, to investigate how one returns to the meaning of Being, and, second, to interpret the ontological difference revealed in doing so. Where metaphysics thought of Being as entities, reducing the former to the latter, Heidegger argued that Being cannot be understood either through entities or as an entity because it is the condition upon which there are entities in the first place; beings are present, and Being is that presencing of beings. Heidegger's ontological problem emerges because Being nevertheless hides itself by appearing as entities, in which guise it resists understanding. For Heidegger, metaphysics had forgotten all this behind its desire to be definitive and thus to begin with the definitive entity. But Being persists as a trace even in the metaphysics of beings, Heidegger affirms, which means one can return to it by re-posing, or unforgetting (*a-letheia*), the question of the meaning of Being.

The question for Heidegger becomes how to approach the meaning of Being without giving it entityhood, without articulating it with the definitude of an entity, how to (re)pose the meaning of Being without reconstituting a metaphysics. To do so, to understand Being, it is not beings that can be approached. And neither is it a question of approaching Being. The idea is rather "one of laying bare the grounds for [beings] and exhibiting them" (*BT*, 28). The difference is between logical consequence and ontological precedence. If one moves forward toward derived results, as critique, one at the same time moves backward toward foundations, in an identity of subject matter and mode of inquiry. The fact of questioning Being implies that the questioning of Being is an act of Being whose attention to itself as interrogation looks back at where it came from. The act of revealing the presuppositions of ontology takes itself as its presupposition, and presupposition is what is revealed. Thus, Heidegger posits his methodology as a "relatedness backward and forward" by which he relates the logical and the ontological. And to accomplish it, he argues, one must turn to that being for which Being is a question, the being that can question Being, and thus posit itself as the place of inseparability between Being and beings. That being is Dasein, and the inseparability in difference between the ontological and the ontic (beings) constitutes what Heidegger calls the "ontological difference." Dasein is the being for which there is an ontological difference in the sense that it can question the meaning of Being within beings, and for which its own ontological Being and its being as an entity are inseparable in their difference.

Heidegger originally understood this project to involve what he called a destruction (*Destruktion*, *Abbauen*: unbuilding, deconstruction) of metaphysical ontology, by which he meant that an archeology of Being would also entail undermining and dismantling ontology's fundamental assumptions.[20] He subsequently discovered that one could not just return to the question of Being as it had been originally posed before metaphysics, because the very language of metaphysics or ontology, in which ontology couched itself, stood in the way. Metaphysical language had not only transmuted the anterior language of Being given by tradition, it had transformed the meaning of that tradition; one could return to the original question only through a critique of the very language of that return itself, which was no longer the language to which one sought to return.[21]

Like an ouroboros that eats its own tail, metaphysics feeds upon itself; it generates a circle in which it depends upon a language that depends in turn for its meanings upon metaphysics, with its assumptions and ideological determinations. A double approach to language was required, both to critique the language of metaphysics and to apprehend how the language of metaphysics, in its self-assumption, self-production, and self-consumption, could serve as the language in which one critiqued metaphysics as well. Heidegger therefore shifted his focus to language in his later writings, in particular to the language he himself had used in his earlier critique of Being, as a shift from an assumption of that language's content to a critique of its form.[22]

To ask how metaphysics generates its language of Being through this circularity is to investigate the question of the Being of language—which, for Heidegger, is the question of what is hidden in language, or concealed behind the language of metaphysics (in the same way that the question of Being had been hidden behind the metaphysics of beings). That is, the Being of language is disguised by the language of being (LH, 198ff.). The irony of ontology is that metaphysics conceals the Being of language precisely by using language to direct our attention to what language speaks about; that is, it conceals ontology behind discursive content. Heidegger thus shifted his investigation to a critique of metaphysical language and a disclosure of how metaphysics generates itself through its language, that is, from the question of the meaning of Being to that of the Being of language. And he sought to disclose the Being of language as the trace within (as the condition for) the language of Being.

Bernasconi sums up Heidegger's turn to language by giving it a Derridean aura (*QLH*, 67). On the one hand, "Heidegger introduces us to 'non-essence' as essential to the essence" (of language). And "language remains metaphysical precisely because an attempt is made to leave metaphysics behind through taking charge of language; this tight grasp maintains a metaphysical attitude to language." And Derrida in turn adapts this double turn to his own critique of language, giving it a Heideggerian aura. He sets it at the core of what becomes the deconstructive (*SP*, 156).

For Derrida, a sign is always double in that it signifies something and signifies itself as a signifier; it engenders meaning and it means itself (this is the core of what "form" refers to; *HD*, 19; *Gram*, 40ff.). Metaphysics had covered up this double nature of language in order to posit thought as autonomous and self-presencing. For metaphysics, language must be only representational and not self-representational, or self-referential, so that one may judge the extent to which it truthfully and veridically represents the thought it expresses. If language were admitted to be self-referential, capable of generating autonomous meaning, it would attain an independence that would interrupt the immediacy of language to thought and in turn call the very autonomy of thought in question. For this reason, speech, for metaphysics, must constitute the essence of language, because speech has an immediacy to thought that is impossible for the exteriority of writing. As Derrida argues throughout the first part of *Of Grammatology*, speech must be considered by metaphysics as the exemplary representational medium. This explains why writing is understood within metaphysics as merely a representation of speech (as part of reducing speech to pure representation). Conversely, to reaffirm the double nature of language and to overcome the priority of speech over writing, as Derrida does, is to proceed with the dismantling of metaphysics.

Thus, Derrida turns to a critique of writing, as if to the "Being of language." A critique of speech would not reveal the structure of language because speech's momentarity and linearity tend to reduce the investigation to the question of speech sounds and phonetics. In writing, one is able to discern the way language constitutes itself as a system of signs (*Marg*, 317). Behind the difference between speech and writing, one can grasp what conditions both speech and writing as sign systems, that is, what is hidden behind both (as Being hides behind beings). For Derrida, three qualities underlie all inscription and structure the means by which inscription signifies (either as speech or writing): the spacing of signs (their particulate nature; *Gram*, 39); the iterability of what is spaced in an inscription, so that their appearance (or use) always implies their former appearance (or use) in inscription; and the operation of difference between them.

Because these notions condition the existence of signs as signs in whatever form they appear, they constitute a structure that Derrida calls "writing in general," or arche-writing (*Gram*, 9, 44). Arche-writing is what "presences itself" as writing or speech. It names the structure of the fundamental relations of signs.

It generates a form of "ontological difference" for writing insofar as writing in general is the condition for writing and speech in the same sense that Being is the condition for beings.[23] Writing and arche-writing are each other's foundation in the sense that, by moving forward in a critique of writing, one moves backward to what is anterior to language (the fundamental Being of language; *BT*, 27). To the extent that this parallels Heidegger's disclosure of the Being of language behind the language of Being, Derrida has adopted Heidegger's project. But insofar as Derrida incorporates this structure within the operation of language as he has critiqued it, he has transformed the form of Heidegger's analytic into the content of his own discourse on the structure of writing. And the double character of the sign, which makes possible Derrida's completion of Heidegger's analytic of language, is what he encapsulates as différance, as a way of bespeaking the inarticulability of that project, the inarticulable at the core of his project, without articulating it.

Sartre affirms a divergent affinity to Heidegger's project through an alternate apprehension of the form of Heidegger's double turn. For Sartre, consciousness is double insofar as consciousness, in being conscious of its object in a thetic or positional mode, must also be non-thetically conscious of itself as conscious. (One can see a structural analogy to Derrida's notion that the sign signifies and signifies itself as a sign.) By *thetic*, Sartre means consciousness positing its object reflectively, as opposed to living it intuitively, pre-reflectively, in a non-thetic mode (*BN*, 14). In its non-thetic mode, consciousness is not conscious of self (*conscience de soi*), taking itself as an object, but is simply aware of being aware, for which Sartre writes *conscience (de) soi* (*BN*, 14). That is, as the condition for being conscious of its object, consciousness is conscious that it is not that object, and in a mode not identical with itself. For Sartre, this implies that the being of consciousness, which is not the object and not itself, is non-being, nothingness. Consciousness is not, as the condition of its being, and its being is non-being aware of itself. Non-being, as nothingness, is the being of consciousness. The double (aporetic) expression by which Sartre characterizes consciousness (being-for-itself), as mentioned above, is that it "is what it is not and is not what it is" (*BN*, 63). Not only is this analogous, in the negative, to Heidegger's double turn (that is, that the Being of language is the language of Being insofar as it is not the language of being, and it is not what language presents [its content] insofar as it is language), but it is also analogous to Heidegger's original analytic of Being (that Being is not beings, but Being only manifests itself in beings). And it is this doubled character of the ontological, couched in the negative, that Sartre encapsulates as néantisation.

Thus, Sartre incorporates Heidegger's double turn for the comparable formal purpose of preserving an inarticulable (nothingness) at the core of what he is investigating. When Sartre says that being-for-itself apprehends itself as not being its own foundation (*BN*, 79), he is constituting an inarticulable within his account of consciousness that is comparable to what Heidegger leaves unarticulated, as absence, in his approach to the question of Being. Where Heidegger grasps the inarticulable as a positivity, as Being, to which thinking must ever and again return, Sartre posits it as negativity, or as freedom, which escapes articulability, as does Heidegger's sense of Being itself. Both are what one cannot not be, and what one cannot delimit from beyond itself.

Granted, what Sartre is literally addressing arises as conceptuality from a philosophical tradition dependent upon the metaphysical assumption of Being as beings (subject and object) and consciousness as self-presencing, namely, the Cartesian. Sartre is considered a Cartesian thinker because he posits the cogito as foundation, upon which he develops his subject-object system. But Sartre has displaced the categories of subject and object, which depend on positivity to be entities, by couching them in the negative. To charge him with Cartesianism or metaphysical thinking would be implicitly to read his account of subject and object as positive, and thus erase his insistence on the negative. It would be to rewrite him in the sense of undoing the negative operation he has performed. For the subject-object duality to be open to analytic division, as in Descartes, the freedom of the for-itself would have to be reified, rendering it referential within a philosophical description. The cogito would be fixed and defined analytically. Sartre refuses it this role. Ironically, it is LaCapra who points out that Sartre has indeed established an undecidability at the core of the cogito (*PS*, 51–52). He argues that, in transforming Descartes's "ego cogito" into "the cogito," Sartre has rendered it different than the Cartesian notion (more on this later).

But what role is Sartre giving the cogito, if he claims that the for-itself has no foundation? How would that relate to the negativity he gives the subject and object? Sartre himself is fairly explicit. For him, the cogito is a source of certainty, though not a foundation for subjectivity. It could not be such a foundation, since consciousness has none. Consciousness exists in the mode of self-certainty in its awareness of itself as conscious. The question of certainty surpasses that of evidence or objectivity and goes to the very core of being. Where, for Heidegger, Being is the trace that enables one to see Being in beings, by which to return to the meaning of Being, for Sartre, certainty is the trace of the being of self-consciousness, *conscience* (*de*) *soi*, that accompanies all consciousness of its "object." Indeed, it is through Heidegger that Sartre questions the cogito and strips it of all but its character of being certain.[24]

> In truth, the cogito must be our point of departure, but we can say of it, parodying a famous saying, that it leads us only on condition that we get out of it. [Our goal has been] to place us in a position to question the cogito about its being and to furnish us with the dialectical instrument which would enable us to find in the cogito itself the means of escaping from instantaneity toward the totality of being which constitutes human reality.[25]

In its undecidability, in its certainty only that it is, the cogito obviates the possibility of a Cartesian analytic division. (Parenthetically, by casting his terms in the negative, Sartre also escapes the Hegelian dialectic that he so often seems to invoke; his negativity is not that of dialectical negation [or affirmation] but of inversion. His expression for the for-itself, that it is what it is not and is not what it is, is not a dialectical relation but an incommensurability of two inseparable aspects of being.)

Heidegger nevertheless considered Sartre's formulation of the inarticulable in terms of action or freedom to be a regression back to metaphysics, because they pertain to consciousness. Heidegger does not want to speak about consciousness, and he is careful not to. For him, to speak of consciousness is already to separate it from what consciousness is conscious of, and thus to reaffirm the Cartesian duality of subject and object.[26] And Heidegger reiterates that phenomenology leaves unexamined the tradition of its language of ontology when it assumes a transcendence and universality for its concepts and framework. Heidegger's quest is rather the apprehension of the precondition for the duality, and for the cogito—that is, the possibility of thinking in general for which metaphysics and the Cartesian duality are specific (and misguided) forms (LH, 208ff.). It is for this reason that Heidegger sought (in "Letter on Humanism") to differentiate himself from Sartre and existentialism so strongly. Not only does existentialism render a philosophical attitude conceptual and give it entityhood, but for him, the question of Being underlies and is the condition for that transcendence and universality that existentialism gives to existence itself.

Sartre would respond that this would be so if he was deploying the term *existence* in the same sense as Heidegger, but he is not. If consciousness encounters existence beneath meaning, it does so on the condition of its freedom. As Sartre points out in his critique of Heidegger, Dasein is not a metaphor for consciousness (*BN*, 73). And freedom is not a metaphor for Being. Freedom rather is the condition for consciousness, in a structural analogy to Being as the condition for Dasein. It is in this sense that Heidegger's existential analytic provides Sartre with a structural model, though *Being and Nothingness* presents itself also as a response and an alternative to *Being and Time* (*HS*, 66). For instance, he maps the for-itself's ekstasis of being-in-the-world through a structure of existential moments similar to Heidegger's (authenticity, temporality, angst, the Other, etc.; *HS*, 67). But where, for Heidegger, the world is given through Dasein's Being, for Sartre, the for-itself loses itself in order that a world may exist (*HS*, 88). Thus, Sartre posits the world in inverse terms from Heidegger's.

Indeed, a sense of inversion in relation to Heidegger systematically perfuses Sartre's text. Where for Heidegger Dasein is the upsurge, the ekstasis of Being in the world, as an existential structure, for Sartre, consciousness is likewise an upsurge of being in the world, but as nothingness (*BN*, 88). Where Heidegger posits a circularity in language's self-generation and self-grounding, as the Being of language, Sartre understands the for-itself as similarly self-generating and self-grounding in its negativity as non-being. There is both congruence and inversion. When Heidegger refers to language as the "house of Being" (LH, 239) or the "advent of the truth of Being" (LH, 206), he is attempting to invoke a being of language that is anterior to its instrumentality and to a metaphysics of subjectivity. He enjoins humans to let language speak, in order to open their return to the meaning of Being. For Sartre, speech is an action; in centering action, he is attempting to invoke a being of consciousness, a freedom, that is anterior to the instrumentality of activity, as well as to the bad faith of reducing activity to pure instrumentality (as does pragmatism, for instance). And he enjoins humans to be authentic in the freedom of subjectivity itself, and in the autonomy and responsibility of activity in the world. Here, the inversion moves the other way; Sartre casts in the positive as human reality what Heidegger posits in the negative as "letting be."[27] Yet the congruence and the inversion remain.

In short, action and freedom for Sartre play a role other than those Heidegger gives them, which can be apprehended not through a translation of their lexical meanings from Sartre and Heidegger, but through a homological structure that positions them in Sartre's discourse in the same but inverted sense that Heidegger positions the Being of language and the inarticulable. Thus, Sartre's notion of néantisation serves to preserve the centrality of a fundamental inarticulability at the core of being human that Heidegger seeks to preserve through his treatment of Being.

Derrida also inverts Heidegger's discourse, but in a very different manner. He renders the form of Heidegger's argument the content of his own discussion. Derrida turns to Heidegger, first and foremost, for a mode of critique or investigation that escapes the need for foundations. The question of philosophical foundationality cannot be grasped from within a system of thought that is itself dependent on a certain foundation. For Derrida, Heidegger's return to the meaning of Being from within ontology provides an access to understanding nonfoundation, to the trace of thinking or language prior to its being enfolded in metaphysical being. He thus adopts Heidegger's mode of questioning as the undoing of the definitive, the metaphysical, while turning the ensuing critique on the content of Heidegger's text as well.

For Heidegger, Being, as the condition for beings, can be revealed only through beings, which are thus the condition for revealing Being. While Being as such must remain inarticulable in order not to become a being for which it is the condition, the sense of nonfoundation implicit in inarticulability subverts the sense of foundations. For Heidegger, nonfoundation is disclosed within foundations by disclosing the process of disclosure itself. Disclosure differs from itself, within a certain circularity, in that it moves in two directions at once: forward toward what discloses itself, and back toward what disclosure is. In a similar manner, for Derrida, arche-writing (the operations of three forms of difference, which Derrida calls iteration, spacing, and the trace) is a foundation not for writing and speech, but for their condition. If it is a condition to be approached through writing as a specific accessible mode of sign inscription, because the system and operation of difference are more evident in writing than in speech, for instance, it nevertheless discloses what is general to all use of signs.

But difference has no materiality, nor does it have existence as an entity or even as a meaning. It can be neither located nor articulated, because it is the condition for location and articulation themselves. To speak in general of difference, or the condition for difference, is to approach a different form of the inarticulable. If difference is the way signs operate, then différance marks the inarticulable condition for difference, its nonfoundation, a way of positing a trace for difference without defining a foundation for language. Thus, it looks forward toward difference as what it conditions, and backward toward the eliciting of a structure of différance from writing itself as a system of signs. Différance is the condition for revealing difference (*SP*, 136).

While différance is presented as itself a sign, Derrida is justified in claiming it is "neither a word nor a concept" (*SP*, 130), because it refers to an inarticulable; it traverses the hiatus of its interior incommensurability between spatial difference and temporal deferral. In being the condition for both at once (signifying is not if there is "nothing" "there" to signify), différance reflects the structure Heidegger has given to nothingness. "Nothingness" for Heidegger names the inarticulability, the absence or inapplicability of words to the meaning of Being, to what cannot be spoken in the logos. As Bernasconi points out, when Heidegger speaks of "the nothing," he is pointing to Being (*QLH*, 56). "'Nothing' is a title for Being"(*QLH*, 56). Différance marks this same "nothingness," what is inarticulable at the core of what makes articulation possible. It is a title for the operations of difference. Where nothingness is "Being experienced from the point of view of beings," so too the nonconceptuality of différance is what is experienced from the point of view of articulability. But where Heidegger marks this "nothingness" in the form of his argument, Derrida makes the nonconceptuality of différance explicit in his process of invention. Derrida has transformed the form of Heidegger's argument into the substance of his discussion, and the effect of Heidegger's formal approach into a critique of language itself. Thus, he has inverted the form and content of Heidegger's argument.

But in doing so, he has also completed Heidegger's project. With specific reference to writing, Derrida begins by adapting the structure of Heidegger's archaeology of a-letheia (nonforgetting, truth). For Heidegger, a-letheia is the trace of Being as it was thought before metaphysics concealed or forgot it. Against the truth metaphysics defines for beings, Heidegger counterposes the truth of beings, through which "one must let them be seen as something unhidden (aletheia)" (*BT*, 56). Being persists in the fact of metaphysics, rather than in the act, and a-letheia constitutes the disclosure of the meaning of Being unforgotten in it, hidden behind entities. It is by letting what is hidden (Being) appear "as hidden" that a-letheia recalls the question of Being (*BT*, 59; *QLH*, 67). In effect, for Heidegger, where nothingness is the trace that marks the possibility of returning to the question of Being, a-letheia is the trace of disclosure, of the necessity of returning to the meaning of Being.

For Derrida, because the difference between signs is the site of the production of meaning within a system of signs, the production of meaning can be understood only through thinking the trace of difference (concealed in the materiality of the signifier; *HD*, 65). That is, what linguistics concealed and forgot is that meaning emerges from difference, instead of attaching to the concreteness of the sign as an entity. Even Saussure, who understood that language was a system of differences between signs, nevertheless focused his analytic on the signs themselves, rather than on difference (*Gram*, 45). But each sign or text holds concealed, while at the same time revealing in its very existence as a sign or text, the structure of differences that are its essential condition. For Derrida, what is concealed within each sign is the multiplicity of differences that constitute it as a sign in a structure. The trace is the presence to each sign of that multiplicity of absent signs that differ, and through which the sign obtains its meanings; the trace is the absent presence of what differs.

This has dire implications for metaphysical language. The effect of the operation of the trace is to produce an undecidability for each sign, since the trace discloses a multiplicity of differences between the sign and other signs (*Gram*, 65). The space opened by the trace between language's literality (its articulation) and the inarticulability of the necessary conditions for its existence is what is hidden in language (*HD*, 168). This is a space of undecidability because it brings the hidden into play against the literal. Beyond simple connotation, it is a multiplicity of meanings that expresses a polyvalence or indeterminacy inherent in each sign. The immediate implication is that the claim to refer or to be univocal, as in an expression of truth value, is a presupposition that is adjoined to the text, brought from elsewhere as an ideological overlay; a univocality of meaning can emerge only from an artificial operation engendered against the sign's inherent polyvocality. Though texts pretend to establish a univocality or a singularity of meaning for themselves as a prerequisite for their ability to say what they mean, or to state their truth, the very structure of the means by which this is done imparts an ambivalence and a deferral of meaning that transcends textual boundaries.

It is in these terms that Derrida criticizes Heidegger's attempt to use language to escape metaphysics. Heidegger addresses the logos of metaphysics, the centrality and universality of precise reasoning, and seeks to "deconstruct" that by letting "language speak," to say "what is unsaid in what is said."[28] To accomplish this, Heidegger embraces poetic language, which he claims approaches Being by letting language speak from its own Being. "Poetic composition is truer than the exploration of beings" (LH, 240) because it opens thinking to form, not as prioritized over content but as part of the Being of language that does not follow the path of articulation or technical reflection on "doing and making" (LH, 194). Derrida argues that Heidegger could not escape the logos in such a way. However innovative (poetic) language may become to avoid definitude or a presumption of truth, it still requires some terminological specificity in the fact of its presentation for what it represents. And that specificity in turn reasserts a metaphysics (*Pos*, 11). Inevitably, the exigencies of content in discourse return to overcome the freedom of form in discursivity.

Ultimately, for Derrida, a critique of the language of metaphysics does not amount to a critique of language as such. Heidegger's substitution of a poetic for a metaphysical language does not change its role in conceptualization. Being becomes, even in Heidegger's attempt to preserve it as inarticulable, a transcendental signifier that functions like a metaphysical assumption on which a discourse can ground itself as the center of its "truth." In that sense, deconstruction, which always and everywhere puts language itself in question, could be said to be what completes Heidegger's project (*HD*, 60; *SP*, 159). That is, in completing the critique of language, Derrida shows what Heidegger omitted that left his project incomplete.

But now, this is parallel to that "other" inversion, namely, Sartre's, with respect to the notion of nothingness (*HS*, 158). For Heidegger, nothingness is the trace of

Being's oblivion, of its being forgotten in the logos (*QLH*, 54–57), the absence of words to the meaning of Being. If it surrounds all beings with the question of Being, it constitutes the immersion of beings in the meaning of Being. For Sartre, nothingness is what lurks in the heart of Being itself, what is itself surrounded by Being. For Heidegger, nothingness is the nothingness of Being, the inarticulability of Being at the end of an archaeology. His confrontation with nothingness is in apprehending the absence and impossibility of foundations, the place where metaphysics cannot reach in each critique of foundations. For Sartre, nothingness is the nothingness in Being, the nothingness that is freedom, an indeterminacy at the heart of the for-itself; for him, the confrontation with nothingness is a confrontation by freedom with what it cannot not be, and with its own inarticulability as possibility and indeterminacy. It is from freedom that any metaphysics reaches out as one of freedom's projects. In effect, the condition for consciousness formally parallels the nothing that is the condition of the question of Being in Heidegger, but in an inverted sense with respect to the world. For Sartre, nothingness is that "negation" from which the possibility of questioning Being arises, while for Heidegger, nothingness adheres "positively" to the Being in question (*BN*, 21; *HS*, 71). With respect to its ontological operations, Sartre has transformed (inverted) the form of its nothingness.

A concomitant inverse parallel occurs with respect to the "materiality" each gives the term "nothing." Sartre says, about a man negotiating a narrow ledge over a high cliff, that *nothing* prevents him from leaping into the abyss (*BN*, 32). Though Sartre uses the term *rien*, rather than *néant*, its meaning is clearly one of nothingness. Each of the man's choices, whether to push on or to leap, are contextualized by all his other possible choices, and any one of them is as real as the condition for the reality of all, namely nothingness. If he chooses to traverse the ledge, he remains separated from the self that awaits him, who has already traversed the ledge, by a nothingness, by which he is also separated from the self who jumps. The *nothing* that restrains him from jumping is both an absence of restraint and the nothingness of the "who" he is and becomes, for whom all conduct is a possibility, and who decides not to jump.[29] Conversely, when Heidegger says that "nothing is the veil of Being," he is presenting the same ambiguity; namely that there is no veil, and at the same time that there is and it is that nothing (*HS*, 168). While the veil hides the Being of the world behind it in the world, freedom hides its inescapability as nothingness within itself.

In a sense, these modes of presenting nothingness relate as a photograph does to its negative. In the photograph, objects are seen as positivities, for which the space surrounding them is absence. In the negative, this is reversed; what is space in the positive becomes an object in the negative, and what is an object in the positive becomes absence. One could metaphorize the inversive relation between Sartre and Heidegger as a photonegativity.

A comparable inversion occurs with respect to temporality. Sartre understands the present as an absence that exists in the difference between a future toward which one is always involved (what one must be in the mode of not being it), and a past that is both facticity and a being that one is not: the past is what "[one has] *to be . . . in order not to be it* and [what one] *has not to be . . . in order to be it*" (*BN*, 117). "The Present *is not*" (*BN*, 123); it is a conception whose being is that "to which the present [instant] is presence." For Heidegger, the present is what is absent to Dasein through a double displacement to an already (Dasein *is* its past), and a not-yet (the future that Dasein is always "coming toward," as Dasein's "ownmost potentialities"; *BT*, 41, 372). One could recast the already, that Dasein is its past, as that it *is* what it is not (first displacement), and the not-yet as that it *is not* (as possibilities) what it is (ownmost). That is, the structure of Heideggerian temporality invokes the Sartrean expression for the for-itself. The form is the same, but Heidegger's positive terms are cast negatively in Sartre. For Sartre, the double structure of consciousness (that it is what it is not and is not what it is) is precisely its nothingness, not the absence of the present, but the presence of the nothing. The Sartrean structure transforms the double form of Heideggerian temporality from an *existentiell*, an aspect of thinking, to the very center of ontology, the being of the for-itself, and inverts it in the negative. What was an object of investigation for Heidegger becomes a critical space for Sartre, and the positive is rendered negative. This is not a translation of Heideggerian temporality, but a parallel photonegative structure between them.[30]

The most substantial of Sartre's differences with Heidegger is the question of others. For Heidegger, one is not at first separate from others, as an "I," but rather in the world with others as those among whom one already is. Being-with implies that Dasein is like others in a sameness of Being (*BT*, 154). Relatedness, as the condition of all specific relationship, is a priori. One lives in a world made by others, among objects that always already involve others. Sartre argues that the assumption of a sameness of Being, because it implies thinking that one is because one is with others, is aporetic. One cannot be granted one's subjectivity among others by those others without them already being subjectivities that can grant it; and one cannot grant others their subjectivity without having already granted it to oneself. Furthermore, on the ontic level, one's being a "me," a participant in the "they" (das Man), according to Heidegger, must accede to the priority of the *mit-sein* (being-with). If the social logic of the *mit-sein* is that one is always not yet oneself, however, one is also not yet a "me" that must nevertheless exist to participate in that "they" (*BN*, 246).

Heidegger would argue that the "me," as behavior, is precisely what is not fundamental. Others are always already more than their behavior, and the perception of that behavior requires an act of abstraction from the Being of the Other, an act whose condition must be the Other embraced as Being-with. Sartre argues that the Other must already be set at a distance by one's being the source of the Other's existence in order for the Other to be the source of oneself, even as one's Being-with. Either the "me" is fundamental to the *mit-sein*, or it is always deformed, always elsewhere than the subject across a distance to Others among whom the "me" is a *mit-sein*. Sartre counterposes the example of a rowing crew; each rower lives his/her immediate life to the rhythm of the coxswain and the oars of the boat, as a common member of a group, but not with a membership that precedes me-ness. For Heidegger, the "me" among others, and the subject as already *mitsein*, condition each other. For Sartre, there must be a distinction between the way one apprehends others and the way one becomes who one is through others, and this notion cannot assume a unity that necessitates finding oneself in and through the "they" (*SHP*, 140). In other words, the (ontic) Heideggerian notion that "everyone is the other, and no one is himself," is transformed by Sartre to the ontological in order to interrogate the aporia that one always already is and is not yet who one is (*SHP*, 165). Sartre again adapts the form and transforms the content of Heidegger's concept of relationality by shifting it from the space between the ontological and the ontic to the ontological itself.

Finally, a similar shift is discernible in their accounts of instrumentality. For Heidegger, instrumentality already reflects others' purposiveness; it is others, who are known through "what they are about," and who provide the instrumentality of things as part of the texture of the world (*SHP*, 130). For Sartre, the instrumentality of things is produced by one's project to whatever extent it involves one's being toward others. For Heidegger, one's use of a thing is a space delimited by others' purposiveness as positivities, while for Sartre, one's project is an object for oneself in the space of others toward which one is always moving; again, it is a mode of photonegativity.[31]

In sum, to the extent that Heidegger's text functions as a precursor for part of Sartre's philosophical approach, it is in a mode that is already textually disparate from the way it is a precursor to part of Derrida's. For Sartre, difference is something that is to be apprehended ontologically by a consciousness, a freedom, through a project for which difference is always discernible and meaningful. For Derrida, on the other hand, it is the ontological (as a metaphysical discourse) that is to be understood through a system of differences, and whose textuality is a structure that is nowhere ignorable or indifferent. In their common consideration of the Heideggerian ontological difference, Sartre emphasizes the ontological rather than difference, and Derrida emphasizes difference rather than the ontological.

Within this disparity, a common structure glistens. For Heidegger, there is the doubled structure of presence: beings, as presence, disclose Being, and Being is the presencing of beings. For Derrida, the sign, and writing, is always double: the sign signifies, and signifies itself as a sign. For Sartre, there is a double structure of consciousness: consciousness is always conscious of something, and is conscious of itself as conscious.

But one cannot propose a sense of connection through Heidegger. Through nonparallel approaches that look back on inseparable elements in Heidegger, Sartre and Derrida, in a topological sense, remain incommensurable, and disperse incommensurably from their readings of Heidegger. The texts of Heidegger will not serve as a common language between them. It is from the concrete homology of the structure of incommensurability and inseparability within their separate texts that we must start.

3 The Parameters of Homology

THE QUESTION IS the inarticulable. If Heidegger raised this question in two ways before and after the war, first with respect to Being and later in terms of the Being of language, it has been (re)raised, or rephrased, in two ways, by Sartre and Derrida. Not only is the inarticulable the form of their nonencounter, since it was a nondebate, but it was also the content, the absence of a conceptual intersection between their "articulations" of inarticulability. Indeed, when Derrida makes passing reference to Sartre, in *Glas*, he suggests by innuendo that what there is to say is what must remain unsaid.

As we have seen, Heidegger deployed a form of questioning that Derrida then made his own, and developed a scenario for exposition that Sartre in turn appropriated. Where Derrida inverted the form and content of Heidegger's mode of questioning, Sartre turned the scenario inside out, transforming its values photonegatively. While Sartre asks what makes metaphysics possible, Derrida questions what lies behind and within language that makes metaphysics unavoidable.

Derrida is not insensible to the irony that his own neologistic vocabulary, by which he addresses the inarticulable foundation of writing in writing, has ultimately become "socialized" out of its metadiscursive formalist impetuousness; différance, "neither a word nor a concept," is now to be found in the dictionaries of France, as if existentially it had been a word all along. Sartre haunts the scene of contemporary critique because he too formulates an approach to the inarticulable that, perhaps too innocently in its paradoxical logic, is strongly articulated. What remains, in their commonality of origin and disparity of trajectory, is a homology of method or style of "combat." In plumbing the depths of this homological structure, a space for their textual incommensurability must be reserved. But rather than return to questioning that fact (of "refusal"), the hint of structural accord, although in violation of the assumptions of discursive incompatibility, opens a different arena for différance and *néantisation*.

In the operation of différance, a sign defers meaning to other signifiers, which defer meaning in turn. Meaning does not get specified except through a metadiscursive operation (whether socially, lexically, or ideologically), without which, and beyond which, deferral "happens" polyvalently. Meaning is always multiple and the sign polyvalent by default (*Pos*, 45–46). Polyvalence is the subliminality of definitude. No escape from a signifier's systematic referral to a plurality of other signifiers can be offered or promised. The ability to define univocal meaning and reference occurs as a compromise with discursivity in general, and incurs its own ambiguity in turn because it remains discursive.[1]

If the very structure of reference produces a deferral of meaning, then reference is already the absence, the deferral of the referent. Reference happens because no referent occurs, leaving reference itself an infra-discursive non-happening by default. The act of referral is an act which is not one, a non-act produced by a structure of differences. The referential statement that "commits" this non-act of deferral, as a deferral to signifiers different from the referent, at the same time constitutes the factuality, the state of affairs, of this referential "act," the structure of differences that "happens." Where the sign's deferral of meaning is a non-occurrence, a non-act, the sign's diffusion through a system of differences constitutes the state of possibility of its meaning, the state of its referentiality.

Deferral and difference are different kinds of difference; deferral is "done," in the sense that it undoes, or does not do (by default), while difference *is*, as alterity. And each operates as a different kind of absence. In the latter, absence is its state of affairs, while for the former, absence is enacted. Derrida has testified to their incommensurability through his need to invent. And to name this as "state" and "act" is a way of highlighting the incommensurability (it is the "act" of ignoring the incommensurability of state and act, of conflating them, that produces Zeno's paradox). Yet the "act" of deferral appears as a "non-act." As a non-act, deferral empties the sign; as a state, differing establishes its elsewhereness. Hence, the inseparability of difference and deferral in the sign appears as a conflation of state and non-act. "State" and "non-act" become a structural denomination of the state of what is stated, and of what happens in the sense of not happening, in the double absence of différance. The terms *state* and *non-act* do not describe the sign but provide coordinate terms, or parameters, for the form of what is not a sign because it is "neither a word nor a concept": différance.

This parametric form, as a restated conflation of inseparability and incommensurability, has as its characteristic feature non-intersection. Difference and deferral remain distinct, separate, irreducible to any commonality or interaction; they run skew to each other, operating disparately and independently within the dimensions of the same semiotic moment. They refuse to devolve to the planar, the geometric, the mapable. They cannot be negations of each other, since they are incommensurable; and they cannot be out of relation to each other, since they belong to the same operation of différance. As separate and inseparable, they can be apprehended only in the structural relation they constitute as such, which can be described topologically as a *skew relation* or skew configuration. In three-dimensional geometry, two lines can be said to be skew when they have all the attributes of parallels, namely separateness, non-intersection, and mutual identification with each other, but are not parallel because they run in disparate directions. "Mutual identification" (inseparability) means they have some essential relation to each other, while "independence of direction" (incommensurability) means they do not touch or overlap at any point. Escaping the commensurability assumption of the dialectic, a skew relation exemplifies what Howells referred to as a *logique paradoxale*.

The fact that the skew relation does not constitute a dialectic, not only because dialectic depends on a relation of negation or opposition that assumes commensurability but because the dialectical relation also depends on an operant mediation to establish the moments of dialectical opposition,[2] marks the inapplicability of the dialectic to différance. Where the dialectic produces a surplus of meaning through an inner process of overdetermining its terms through the mediation, différance marks the surplus of meaning in the sign, not as a process, but as a prior condition. The skew structure is rather one of heterogeneity in which nothing can be synthesized or amalgamated.[3] Yet it is not a heterology, since it is a structure and not a logic. Heterology is a systematic philosophical pursuit of the logic of aporia, in order to intelligibly interpret its effects. The "skew" is a description of a discursive structure, which happens to pertain to and inhabit Derrida's invention. Rather than point interpretively or philosophically toward explication, it remains a descriptive discovery within what Derrida's discourse has produced.

Such a description is not obviated by Derrida's own thinking. In *Positions* (*Pos*, 39), he asserts that différance is not "astructural." It "produces systematic and ruled transformations" that ground a space of structure itself, a "general structure of economy" (*Pos*, 17). On the other hand, to cast différance in parametric terms moves the discussion from "semiotics" to the metadiscursive space of structure.

As a structure, the skew is further distinguished from the dialectic in being a non-negation, without entelechy. That is, non-act is not the negation of an act, but the trace of an operation in which an effect is produced (in reading, for instance), but which operation is empty, an absence. It means a "textual" enactment in a manner suggestive of the relation between a textual state and its statement. As a non-negation, the skew is without goal or end. It constitutes an irreducible diagram of différance drawn by means of the notions of "non-act" and "state."[4]

There is a certain recursivity in the structure of différance. Both differing and deferring are themselves skew relations. Difference is a state that exists as form because its content is the non-act of differing with other already absent signs. Deferring is a postponing of what is already necessarily elsewhere, that is, an act in form whose content is a situation of prior absence, a non-state. If difference can be characterized, using the same parametric approach, as a state and non-act, deferral can be characterized as an act and non-state. Différance is a skew relation of two skew relations, a non-negation of two non-negations. This composite parametric structure will be referred to as a "double non-negation."

Sartrean "nihilation" can be cast in similar parametric terms. As the Being by which negation comes into the world, the for-itself must, first, dissociate itself from its object, and second, grasp the object as a veil behind which the object's possibilities reside, among which is that of its being nothing (*BN*, 23). Thus, the for-itself's relation to its object can be parametrized as an act (of dissociation) and a non-state (a veil of non-being). But Sartre recasts each of these aspects in the form of skew relations, as non-negations, as well. In the act of dissociation, one "wrench[es] [one]self from being in order to be able to bring out of [one]self the possibility of a non-being"; that is, an act and non-state. And the veil of the object's non-state is produced when one "nihilates the thing questioned in relation to [one]self by placing it in a neutral state, between being and non-being"; that is, a non-act (nihilation) and state (betweenness) (*BN*, 23).

Thus nihilation, like différance, is a skew relation of two skew relations, a double non-negation. But the two non-negations are incommensurable and inseparable in a different way than encountered in différance. Nihilation discloses incommensurabilities between possibility and (subjective) enactment, between actuality and the possibility of acting. Possibility and actuality are at all times inseparable; but in being not yet specified, they reveal a negative valence that differs from the distance and absence of difference and deferral. (That is, though absence reveals negativity in Sartrean phenomenology, it is a non-negative condition for Derrida.) Though both the nihilation of an object and a deferral of meaning are emptying acts whose concomitant is a non-state, the notion of "empty" is different for both (as negativization and promise), and the temporal directions of the act of emptying are opposite, toward a projected neutral state for Sartre, and toward retrieving an anterior absence for Derrida.[5] Nothing-ing and nothingness mark a condition, for Sartre, that is other than default or the prior presence of absence. These differences, whether incommensurable or not, metonymically represent the gap between these two texts.

Perhaps this suggests why the texts of these two thinkers fascinate. The skew relation, which structures the inner form of their thinking, forever escapes the ability to think linearly, to reason either syllogistically or dialectically. It both entices and displeases at once because we do not know how to think with it; that is, "know how" does not accompany the ability to do so. We are at a level at which thetic self-awareness or self-reflexivity are idle epistemic endeavors. For many, this is an untenable place to be. Some have sought to escape by commandeering the skew structure and assimilating it to a dialectical process—which violates the non-negativity of the relation.[6]

The skew contains a double gap, "coiled in the heart" of inseparability and brought out of the core of incommensurability. It constitutes a mode of articulation of what resists articulation or naming by any means other than an abstract parametrics—in this case, through three parameters: act, state, and non-. And as a parametric structure, it is suggestive of a form that is the signified of its operational content (e.g., difference and deferral) as signifier; its parametric articulation signifies its mode of signification as its meaning (inarticulable in ordinary ways). Thus, this parametrics accords with the general form discovered in both inventions, that is, a form that is the signified of its content (in this case, its inner incommensurability) as a signifier.

Finally, the skew relation is not a totalizing principle. There is no necessity for it. It reveals itself only metatextually as a structure of/for difference and deferral, or double nihilation. Yet, if it permits disparate textual forms to be related to each other, then it will have taken on the aura of a formalism (the addition of the "-ism" signifying that the metatextual description of this textual form has been taken to another level of signification). Just as geometric forms provide a "vocabulary" for representing composition in painting or sculpture (which also resists articulation), this form, already a link between these texts, will permit us (as a formalism) to speak about what is sculptural between them.

Parenthetically, the notions of "state" and "act" might seem to be a particularly Sartrean way of putting things. They derive, admittedly, from the phenomenological tradition: the intentional act and the state from which escape through the ek-static and ecstasis is a possibility.[7] For Sartre, the object rather than the sign is in question. Differing and deferring belong to a different way of thinking, a different textuality. This particular parameter set might seem, therefore, to be an imposition on Derrida. But they can be derived in "Derridean" terms from his own semiotics. Derrida speaks of the "operation" of difference, giving it a certain force. It is not the subject that produces this operation within the sign system or text in question, but the sign system that produces these effects in reading, in what constitutes the reading of those signs.

Ironically, because they can be respectively contextualized, these parameters produce a reciprocity of language that both interiorizes the disparity to be preserved and reaffirms it. For Derrida, the Sartrean use of state and act would mark metaphysical notions belonging to phenomenological discourse, rather than to discursive critique. For the Sartrean ontology, the Derridean deployment of state and act would only invoke the emptiness or absence on a semiotic level that nihilation already produces and constitutes as nothingness. But the latter would not be an apprehension of writing in general as an intentional attitude toward difference and deferral as "things," and the former would not mark moments in a phenomenological metaphysics at which it would deconstruct. For each, the parameters would only be a translation and transformation of what would be brought to bear upon it from the other. The contours of the formal structure of the "skew" to which a parametric description has been given would thus preside over such transformation in both cases, leaving it intact in form. And that would be its meaning; its form the signified for its content as signifier.

It remains simply to reiterate that ontology is not semiotics, and semiotics is not ontology. For ontology, the fundamental notions of semiotics are objects; for semiotics, the fundamental notions of ontology are signs. Sartre paints the sign with the immediacy of the object, while Derrida sculpts the way the object and subject are entextualized. Derrida suggests, in his critique of ontology, that it is the ontology of the subject that gives the subject existence. For him, there is both an inadequacy of the language of the subject to its subject (matter) and an inadequacy of "the subject" to what that language sets out for it (cf. *SP*). When Sartre posits the opposite, that the subject gives the ontology of the subject existence phenomenologically, similar inadequacies appear, in invoking a future as a project that is endless, that is always more and less than one sets up for oneself. The conceptualizations of these respective "inadequacies" remain incommensurable. While each can be expressed in the formal terms of the other (the for-itself as difference and deferral, and difference-deferral as intentional), it does not imply a mutual absorption of différance and nihilation into each other as mirror images; it simply testifies to the power of each discourse to address other discourses. But to bracket differences of terrain and textual content by moving to the planes of morphology and ecological structure is to place a different kind of window between them, and a different kind of reciprocity at the level of double non-negation: différance as a state and non-act; nihilation as an act and non-state.

Of course, this reciprocity would satisfy neither one. Derrida's intention is not to engender a formalism, though one may be found metatextually. Sartre's attitude toward language is to deploy it to be direct and unequivocal, though immanent in his discourse may be found the operation of incommensurability and hence of indeterminacy. Yet if each would be dissatisfied for themselves, they would find satisfaction in what this reciprocity engendered for the other. For Derrida, language is continually rendered undecidable by the dissemination of its signs, its structural polyvocality, by the impossibility of an ultimate appeal to context (*Marg*, 316ff.), in short, by its own form. So it would be no surprise that Sartre's was as well. And for Sartre, the intelligibility of Derrida's critique of language must be apprehended as intentional, but thus must reveal certain reasoning structures reflecting Derrida's engagement, indeed, his freedom, above all at the level of form.

EXTENSIONS OF THE DOUBLE NON-NEGATION

Before pursuing the meaning of the skew relation for the discourses of Sartre and Derrida, which will imply approaching it as a form of sign (a kind of sculpted sign in a metadiscursive space), it will perhaps be informative to look at how it perfuses their texts and threads its way through their thinking.

Part of Sartre's discussion of concrete relations with others concerns the body, which Sartre posits as one of the modes of the for-itself's facticity. As a concrete fact of relation to others, the body presents a dual aspect of being for-itself-for-others (the object that it is for others, while being consciousness at the same time), and of being-in-itself (an object for the for-itself). In the sense of being in the presence of others, one apprehends one's physical self as both oneself and a thing.

But consciousness is always ahead of itself. In one's being in the world, one continually turns from the "thing" or state of being in which one finds oneself, as a body and a past, toward a future in which one would be again in the mode of being an in-itself, a different "thing" as the concretization of a project. "The for-itself as the nihilation of the in-itself temporalizes itself as a *flight toward*" (*BN*, 361–62). In pursuing the future, it is in flight toward something that does not yet exist. In going toward itself in the future in abandonment of its present givenness or facticity, it flees from nihilation to possibility, pursued by the present. In effect, it flees and pursues, a pursued-pursuing. In this pursuit, the for-itself empties itself in the sense that what it seeks it is not. The present is a state it nihilates in its flight from it, and the future is an act that always already empties it.

In terms of the body, consciousness pursues itself as a for-itself that is fixed in an in-itself in the future. If this is a possibility for the for-itself, it is because its body is its facticity, providing limits in its spatial relation to others who are the condition of such possibilities. It seeks to escape what is already toward something that is not yet. In temporalizing itself, and thus fleeing its facticity, the for-itself renders itself an enactment, a movement toward an elsewhere. In enacting its flight, it returns to being the pursued, to its flight from the in-itself. As a past, a state, its flight or abandonment becomes a non-act. But in fleeing this facticity, it renders itself again an enactment toward a future that is not yet, a non-state. Thus, it can be apprehended as a double non-negation. And in this, pursued-pursuing reveals its similarity to the operation of différance, in the sense that the sign undermines presence through differing from the absent sign, and promises presence through its own deferral. Pursued-pursuing reflects an operation of the for-itself that is homologous to the operation of différance.

Sartre's texts are in fact replete with comparable examples of the double non-negation; his notions of the reflected-reflecting (*BN*, 298) or transcendence-transcended, for instance. For Sartre, transcendence-transcended is the body of the other, the other as subjectivity apprehended as object. That is, transcendence-transcended is a consciousness (unseen in the other) apprehended in the form of a human as nihilated object, the nihilated body as the object of (one's own) consciousness (*BN*, 291). In the body of the other, consciousness is hidden, absent, yet part of the object that the other is (a state and non-act). The other's consciousness is lived by one through that body, but as the absence that is the other in that body (an act and non-state). It is a reciprocal structure to the pursued-pursuing, again a double non-negation. It is the reliance of these descriptions on nihilation that gives them their parametric character as such.

A similar thread appears in Derrida's work. In *Positions*, he speaks about his own counterposition of textual form to content. On the semiotic level, a text's language means both more and less than it says, (im)precisely because the operation of the trace renders the text's signs polyvalent, and because no context by which the text can be definitively coded is ever wholly immanent in it. That is, there is always a surplus and a lack of meaning. At their intersection, the text reveals an awareness of itself as a text.

> I have attempted not to formalize this motivic regime of the surplus (and the) lack in the neutrality of a critical discourse. . . . it is a question of remarking a nerve, a fold, an angle that interrupts totalization: in a place of well-determined form, no series of semantic valences can any longer be closed or reassembled. By means of this angle, this fold, . . . a mark marks both the marked and the mark, the re-marked site of the mark. The writing which . . . remarks itself . . . can no longer be counted on the list of themes. (*Pos*, 46)

What Derrida configures as a "fold" is the double operation that both signifies (marks the marked, the signified) and signifies itself as a signifier (re-marks the mark). In this, it reveals a structural affinity to the Sartrean doubling of consciousness: namely that it is conscious of its object, and conscious of itself as conscious, *conscience (de) soi*. In the first case, the signified is absent, as the condition for it having been marked, for there to be signification that the mark as signifier enacts: an act and non-state. In the second, the signifier that points to an elsewhere (its signified) also points to itself as something that points. In this non-pointing by which it enacts itself as a mark, it effaces itself as a sign (pointing elsewhere) precisely in calling attention to itself as already a sign: a state and non-act.

For Derrida, this double operation can be extended to the entire range of signification. For instance, in asking how the term *philosophy* can be extended to the deconstruction of philosophy:

> This structure of the double mark [philosophy] (. . . borrowed and still bound . . .) works the entire field within which these texts move . . . every concept necessarily receives two similar marks—a repetition without identity—one mark inside and the other outside the deconstructed system, [which] should give rise to a double reading and a double writing. (*Dis*, 4)

The double reading it should give rise to is that of content and form, of signification and the situation of signifying (in) itself. If there is a reciprocal structural affinity, it is that the sign abandons all its previous significations (while nevertheless carrying them along) toward a meaning that is always up ahead, as a deferral toward the possibility of signification—a repetition without identity.

> [A] reading must always aim at a relationship unperceived by the writer between what the writer commands and does not command of the patterns of the language that he uses. (*Gram*, 158)

That is, it is a relationship between what the writer engenders as a writing, the state of constituting the writer's statement, and what the language enacts (formally, metatextually), that is, what the language does beyond that statement as a non-act. The reading, then, must also aim, as an act, at what is not there, a non-state consisting of what is not stated. In sum, the reader's act conjoins to itself a non-state, and his state as reader conjoins itself to a non-act.

A similar structure is reproduced in Derrida's discussion of metaphor in "White Mythology" (*Marg*). There he discusses the impossibility of theorizing metaphor, because one cannot do so without using metaphors in the process. For instance, relating images of the sun and the sunflower, he argues that the sun can only be experienced indirectly, through Galilean, scientific, or poetic descriptions, for which direct experience, such as the motion of the sunflower, is itself already a metaphor (e.g., of the sun "going by"). In effect, the theorization of metaphor must shift to a level of form that stands self-referentially behind signification; in particular, the dependence on metaphor to explain direct experience of metaphor. A theorization of metaphor thus already assumes its theorization and escapes it. In Derrida's text, metaphor is the form of an exposition whose content is the theorization of metaphor; and metaphor is the content of an exposition whose form is the theorization of metaphor. The form enacts the content that cannot theorize itself (act and non-state), and the statement of that theorization constitutes itself as the content of what does not present itself as form (state and non-act).

All these examples (for instance, the pursued-pursuing of the Sartrean for-itself, and its counterpart, the Derridean mark–re-mark) reveal the same textual form, and at that purely formal level are congruent. But they are also elements of discursive ecologies, across which they are homologous to each other and to other structures in those same ecologies. In the sense of similar ecological situatedness, pursued-pursuing, in its temporalizing, reveals an affinity to difference-deferring, engendered by their homology; and the form of mark–re-mark would stand in similar relation to that between consciousness and *conscience (de) soi*. Beyond the fact that Sartre may be speaking about consciousness, while Derrida rejects the possibility of speaking about consciousness in any but a metaphoric manner, the interior textual forms we have articulated parametrically seem to provide a means of interconnection, independent of thematic enterprise or discursive ecology. Of the multiplicity of instances of the double non-negation encountered here, they all appear as different individuations of the same general form, as repetitions of a single sculpted configuration. In this sense, these forms can be said to constitute a formalism, a structure of textual movement, in the works of both thinkers.

Sartre's Use of the Skew Relation as a Formalism

By "formalism," I mean that the structure serves to organize the process of movement from sentence to sentence, idea to idea, and level to level of discourse. That is, it constitutes the framework of a logic, a stylistics as a reasoning procedure.

Let us consider a passage from Sartre's account of the look. For Sartre, the look is the prototypical event through whose structure he resolves the problem of other subjectivities without falling into solipsism. In the passage below, we are interrupting him *in medias res* as it were, in the middle of his exposition, in order to apprehend the way he does what he does, rather than to examine his argument (which is considered in detail in a later chapter).

> [The other] is the being toward whom I do not turn my attention. He is the one who looks at me and at whom I am not yet looking, the one who delivers me to myself as unrevealed but without revealing himself, the one who is present to me as directing at me [*il me vise*] but never as the object of my direction [*il est visé*]. . . . The other's look as the necessary condition of my objectivity is the destruction of all objectivity for me. . . . I am looked at in a world that is looked at. . . . The other's look . . . denies my distances from objects and unfolds its own distances. This look of the Other is given immediately as that by which distance comes to the world at the heart of presence without distance. (*BN*, 269)

In this passage, there is an interplay of active and passive voices, but the passive mode used throughout, with one exception, is compound rather than reflexive.[8] This accords with the narrative structure of the passage. Let us look at its separate phrases carefully.

> [The other] is the being toward whom I do not turn my attention.

The other is there, as the state of the world, and I (that is to say, the "I") do not act toward that being, neither in actuality nor intentionality, though that is the possibility at the center of the sentence; it conflates a state and non-act.

> He is the one who looks at me and at whom I am not yet looking,

The other's act is not in question, while I am not yet performing a comparable act. For me, the act I would perform is still only potential, among all other potentialities; in the context of the present of the other's unquestionable act, the present is a state that is nihilated in the upsurge of my possibilities, that is, a state that is not. It is an act and non-state. "I am not yet looking" is a non-state and not a non-act because, though an act has been potentiated, it reflects and reflects on the other's act of looking, a state of reflection, while no act has yet been either arrived at, emptied, or negated. My actual state to be emptied is perhaps not even specifiable, except as objectivization. But in the synchronicity of the moment, it has been supplanted, sacrificed to the potentiality, the non-state of the not-yet. And we might notice that these two sentences, the first complete and the second to be followed by two appositives, themselves name a non-act and a state, respectively.

> the one who delivers me to myself as unrevealed but without revealing himself,

An act and non-state: the other's act is a delivering that continues the act of looking, in its unknowability; the other's hiddenness is the non-state that the other is.

> the one who is present to me as an attention to me but not as the object of my directed attention, [translation modified]

A state and non-act: this passage focuses on the fact that I am an object, the content of the other's attention/intention as a state, while finding my own attempts at intending the other to be null, a non-act.

In these two appositives, the central focus has shifted from an overall "exterior" narration of the situation to perspectives interior to it that situate the self and the other in relation—the first centers "myself" (*moi-même comme non-révélé*), and the second centers the other (*qu'il me vise et non pas . . . qu'il est vis*). It is a shift that parallels that of the first two sentences, suggesting that this kind of juxtaposition constitutes a structuring in itself. Insofar as the focus of each phrase is the object of a perspective, and not simply a grammatical subject or object, they constitute semiotic forms that produce their perspectival objects as signifiers rather than ontological entities: "other" and "self" as non-signs. And in direct contrast to the first two sentences, these phrase appositives name an act and a non-state respectively.

By piling these descriptions on each other, each of which constitutes a skewed repositioning of ontological elements, Sartre builds a richly stratified and always nonlinear account or description. And in apprehending Sartre's narrative in a parametric rather than literary manner (engaging metatextual form rather than critical interpretation), we are actually renarrativizing its structure in terms that reveal an already present inner self-narrativization. Based neither on the grammatical nor on the ontological, these parametric renditions make synecdochic reference back to the original phrases by abstracting from their given narrative elements. Thus, these renditions, as renarrativizations, enter the space between the text's discursive content as prose and its discursive form as a reasoning, on a plane other than that of syntactical or phenomenological construction.

Before continuing with the rest of the passage, let us digress momentarily on the subject of grammatical form, in order to grasp the difference between that and the sense of discursive form being developed here. The use of grammatical form to analyze a text has a long tradition in literary criticism. It is a favorite tactic of Northrop Frye, and one of his Seven Forms of Ambiguity. It is the play of grammatical form that Denis Hollier addresses in his demonstration of the way

Sartre's tenses confound and deconstruct themselves, in which one loses the sense of what it means to write for "one's time." And Fredric Jameson deploys it extensively in his book *Sartre: The Origin of a Style*,[9] which provides adequate counterpoint to what is being addressed here.

In addressing Sartre's fiction, Jameson points out a central problem (and paradox) for the represention of Sartrean consciousness. Prereflective consciousness, so fundamental to Sartre's account, remains non-thetic, non-positional as consciousness of something. If a novel is to present a consciousness, however, its fictional presentation must somehow articulate the prereflective, in order to present the full existentiality of the character. But that would render it thetic through representation, and thus not represent it as non-thetic. The problem Sartre's fiction poses, then, is how Sartre could fictionalize a consciousness with all the complexity of his own theorization of it, and leave what must remain unarticulated in that articulation. That is, how could Sartre's fiction escape representing the unrepresentable? Does Sartre's philosophy render Sartre's fiction impossible, or at least un-Sartrean?

Jameson argues that Sartre accomplishes his fictionalizing of consciousness through stylistic modes of grammatical construction. Thetic consciousness can occur as quoted or fully formed thought events (*OS*, 21). Past non-thetic or prereflective consciousness can be looked back upon thetically; or it can be anticipated, perhaps, through a thetic awareness. But in either case, as a future that looks back on the novelistic present as its past, or a past that has taken that novelistic present as its future, non-thetic or prereflective awareness is represented thetically only in a temporal elsewhere in the novel's textuality. And Jameson asserts that the location of such an "elsewhere" is style, insofar as style also resists articulation in the present. This means that Sartre's fiction must play between the presentation of consciousness as fiction (writing the writable) and the presentation of fiction as consciousness (representing the written and the unwritable).

To concretize his assertion, Jameson looks at moments of abruptness, shifts in perspective, or changes of velocity in the narrative that are produced by syntactical turns and breaks (*OS*, 53ff.). Punctuation, for instance, produces discontinuities of diction, direction, flow, or breath. These mark a mode of temporality in the sense that, for Sartre, time is the way one lives the world (*OS*, 46). And the discontinuities present a fracturing between non-thetic and thetic awareness (*OS*, 32). In reflecting on thought, or discovering it "after the fact," one interrupts the subjectivity of an event. And syntactical discontinuities then articulate the difference in modes of conscious as elements of grammatical structure. "It is not content [one] seeks, but a special way of treating content, . . . as if things were being constantly forced to take the shape of subjectivity" (*OS*, 63).

But Jameson's hermeneutic of Sartrean consciousness relies upon a second level of discourse. To contextualize and illuminate the play of grammatical form in Sartre's novel, Jameson calls upon Sartre's philosophical account of consciousness itself. It is in Sartre's philosophical articulations that a certain structure of meanings for his grammatical discontinuities must be found, if his "special way of treating content" is to refer elementally to Sartrean consciousness. That is,

Jameson must enlist Sartre's philosophy as the source of his literary critical categories, in order to decode the moments of Sartre's grammatical style. Thus, he bridges the gap between grammatical form and impossible content in Sartre's fiction by abridging the space between Sartre's fiction and his philosophy. Sartre's use of grammar becomes a production of meaning beyond Sartre's grammar through the construction of a grammatical mapping beyond Sartre's fiction. And this structure is then returned to Sartre's fiction through his use of grammar. This is reminiscent of Hollier, who deploys elements of Sartre's biography to notice and identify certain thematics in Sartre's fiction, and whimsically "re-narrativizes" Sartre as having presaged his own life in a novel written before the event, though it is Hollier who associates the two in reverse (*Prose*, 83, 175). Both critical projects become Sartrean in requiring his past philosophy to provide a philosophical future through which to analyze that future's past as its meaning.

In short, grammatical form structures the lexias of a text by positioning itself prior to the codes that generate the connotative and denotative meanings of that text, and at the same time sets those codes in the future in order to locate itself in a present that will then discover them. The coherence it discovers is rendered prior to the coherence of reading the fiction; and thus it sets the philosophy prior to it as a priori to it. Indeed, to address the form of Sartre's stylistic use of grammatical form, one would have to address how form produced itself through (consequent to) the coherence of a reading, including the coherence given it by grammar.

The skew structure, on the other hand, describes itself on the basis of the full meaning of the text, and not simply its literal content. In the first passage above, the pairing of pure predication (the copula) with a non-enacted activity is part of the grammatical form that the metatextual construction of the skew works with. In the second, the predicate clause combines looking in both the active and passive voice, and so on. This is part of the material of the skew structure, from which it emerges as structuring, but it is not what structures. While there is meaning to be elicited from syntax and grammar, it is not open to homology, only similarity, for which it has to be discerned and analyzed first, rather than discerned through the mapping process itself.

It is now time to say a word about the all-too-neglected third parameter: the "non-." In the second pair of phrases, the emphasis is on the absence of content for an object that can have none. Nothing is missing; but what is already there remains unfilled, form without content, without quiddity. This contentlessness is not a negation; it is an emptiness that is not an absence, and whose elsewhereness is there. That is, the "non-," the third parameter, implies emptiness understood as positivity; it marks a formal operation, rather than a condition of opposition or negation, a positive sense of emptying rather than a dialectic. It represents no clash of opposing entities or actions, that is, of things that would have had to be commensurable or intersecting in order to clash. In the non-negational structure, there is no intersection and no opposition, only inseparability and incommensurability. In Sartre's reasoning, the "non-" refers to the contentlessness of form, to an erasure, a reduction to *potentia*, rather than an inversion of value.

To see this more clearly, the operation of an emptiness-fullness relation can be traced in the rest of the passage.

> The other's look, as the condition of my objectivity, is the destruction of all objectivity for me.

A state and non-act: the state is a filled state, a condition for something concerning myself who fills it, and that prevents my being from escaping into nothingness; at the same time, my ability to fill it, other than as a conditioned object, is emptied, erased. Objectivity becomes for me, in general, a non-act as an obviated possibility toward the world.

> I am looked at in a world that is looked at.

An act and a non-state: this time my objectivity fills an act with an "I," that at the same time renders the look at the world empty, a non-state, because it is elsewhere. The world for the other has lost its worldness for me except as looked at by the other.

> The other's look . . . denies my distances from objects and unfolds its own distances.

An act and non-state: Even my distance from objects, as a *négatité*, is emptied, and rendered a non-state. If distance unfolds, its content is elsewhere for the other's look as the object of an act that fills itself therewith.

> The look . . . is given immediately as that by which distance comes to the world at the heart of presence without distance.

A state and non-act: Actual "distance comes to the world" as a state with a certain content (no one enacts that distance, but it is non-empty); yet its appearance at the heart of presence, at the heart of a distance for the Other (*d'une distance à autrui*), of subjectivity, where it can have no content, no being, is an upsurge of nothingness.

In sum, Sartre's reasoning (style) throughout the passage manifests itself as a particular permutation of the constituent act (what produces or enacts), the constituted as a state (status, passivity), and an emptying, an erasure of content. It is the process of permutation that constitutes, in Sartre's text, a mode of descriptive reasoning. In fact, in the passage examined, it reveals a pattern reminescent of a ballad form: ABBA ABBA (where A is state and non-act; B is act and non-state); or, in pairs, there is an alternation of two forms: AB and BA. This patterning may actually represent an unconscious poetic form in which Sartre thinks; it also suggests one possible reason why some readers find his writing esthetically pleasing and others do not.

Derrida's Use of the Skew Relation in His Thematics

In Derrida's work, one encounters a stylistics that also evinces the formal structure of the skew, but in a more presentational mode, rather than one of reasoning. That is, it plays a more rhetorical part in Derrida's text. I shall look at two forms this takes.

The Middle Voice

In Derrida's play with language, he often engenders juxtapositions that invoke a form of middle voice. In contemporary discourse, because it is a lost grammatical form, the middle voice would present itself as an allo-logical rather than a grammatical category. And Derrida mentions that différance functions in this manner:

> Différance is not simply active (any more than it is a subjective accomplishment); it rather indicates the middle voice, it precedes and sets up the opposition between passivity and activity (*SP*, 130).

Though Derrida gives the idea of the middle voice only passing mention, a number of commentators have remarked upon it, particularly Llewelyn and Gasché.[10] Its connection to an interplay of passive and active, which we have just seen in Sartre's play of the passive and active voice, should not be ignored.

According to Llewelyn, the middle voice (as an extinct verb form) ostensibly resided somewhere between active and passive voices.[11] Certain verbs, in Sanskrit and Greek, took the middle voice: for example, to be born, to lie down, to die, to grow, to speak, and to imagine (*DTS*, 91). What characterizes these verbs, which in modern language can take either an active or passive voice, is that

> the subject is the centre as well as the actor of the process; i.e. he accomplishes something which accomplishes itself in him. . . . He is well and truly inside the process of which he is the agent (Benveniste; referred to in *DTS*, 91).

The agent is both actor and acted upon, act and enacted, subject and object of an action at once. A power or dynamic other than the subject's own autonomy or intention is at work on the subject while at the same time "performed" through that subject. An approximation in English might be: one gets married,[12] or a fish gets hooked. The active voice says the subject effects something; the passive voice says the subject is affected by something. The middle form might say the subject effects something and in so doing is affected, or that a subject acted (was not passive) upon itself but was itself not a wholly autonomous agent in the action.

In a more Sartrean vein, one might understand a middle-voiced act or agent as the space of an act that the agent performs, for which the action performed constitutes the way the agent lives that moment or space. In these terms, the middle voice would be the way space becomes timed and time spaced.[13] To transcribe this parametrically, the agent becomes the space, or state, of an act, and the action becomes the enacted within the situation of an agent (state). The agent acts and the act agents (as a verb; in the same sense that the world worlds, in Heidegger); that is, the agent is both the state of a non-act (since what the agent enacts is not the agent's enactment), and the act of a non-state (the enacted). The middle voice, in Llewelyn's terms, would refer verbally on the one hand to an activity in which the act is space become temporal (viz., a state and non-act), and on the other, in which an imposed state is the temporal become space (viz., an act and non-state). The middle voice, in its classical mode, is a double non-negation.

For Derrida, the middle voice is important as a way to break from the metaphysics of presence and the metaphysics of the subject as autonomous, as self-presence

(*SP*, 147ff.). And he often seeks to express ways of being beyond the two dimensions of state and act (presence and subject) by enacting a warp of language, or a distortion of a text's logic.[14] French lends itself to this endeavor in conflating the passive voice and the self-reflexive mode in the same verb form. The sentence "Henri se trouve en route" can be translated, for instance, as "Henry is (found) on the go," and "Henry finds himself on the road." Though one normally distinguishes the alternatives contextually, Derrida often obstructs this by complicating his syntax in order to problematize context, and thus derail determinateness, or decidability.

For instance, at the beginning of "La Facteur de la Verité," in *La Carte Postale*, Derrida writes: "La psychanalyse, à supposer, se trouve."[15] This is no longer a simple conflation of an active-voiced "discovers itself" and a passive-voiced "is discovered." There is a complicating factor (a truth factor) in this passage. It is the juxtaposition, or apposition, of "à supposer." "À supposer" must be read contextually, while it is, at the same time, the context. In French, it too alternates between an active and passive infinitive, which cannot be translated as an infinitive in English. To give it a literal translation would cancel literal meaning, rendering it half-literal by leaving it half unintelligible: "Psychoanalysis, (to suppose), finds itself, or is found."

"To suppose" (or "to assume") is a miscreant verb in the absence of an agent, one who supposes. In English, the active and passive voice divide the verb between the indicative mode and an act of imposition. Passive-voiced use of "to suppose" becomes an imposition because it assumes something while hiding and protecting the one who assumes from responsibility. That is, an agent is supposed to do something ("you're supposed to wash the dishes"), and the omission of who or what supposes transforms the supposition into a veiled demand. It imposes by shifting the focus of the phrase to the actor and the act already supposed by someone else, and away from the one supposing, determining the act while speaking of the supposition.

Since the active and passive infinitive are already conflated in French, the appearance of the verb is even more problematic. But if it cannot be translated as an infinitive, it can nevertheless preserve an indefinite status in English; "one assumes," "on its own supposition," "it is to be supposed," are cases one might consider. But in these terms, it will be discovered, its ambiguity alternates out of phase with that of the main clause. For instance, suppose "à supposer" is understood as active ("one supposes"). Either it becomes derivative in the face of psychoanalysis's own self-discovery and hence passive, or the passive discovery of psychoanalysis by (absent) others renders supposition active. In either case, the sentence will invoke two subjects, two agents in non-interrelation, one of which is passive in the face of the other. It is the subject of supposition, absent from the infinitive verb "to suppose," that ostensibly would have been specifiable in the middle voice. In the absence of a middle-voiced subject, the sentence's possibilities substitute themselves as a structure; either "to suppose" is a (passive) state, for which "discovers itself" is a non-act; or "to suppose" is an act, for which "is discovered," in the passive voice, is a non-state.

Two other possibilities exist for the verb "to suppose": The first is the reflexive supposition ("on its own supposition"), justified by the reflexive possibility of the main verb; and the second is a literally passive-voiced supposition ("it is to be supposed"). In the first case, the sentence becomes "Psychoanalysis, on its own supposition, discovers itself"; and "Psychoanalysis, on its own supposition, is discovered." Self-reflexivity breaks down here. The agent, psychoanalysis, is passive in the face of an action it supposes toward itself, for itself. And the agent, psychoanalysis, only supposes that it discovers itself, that is, discovers itself only on its own supposition. (And these two instances would accord with Derrida's critique of Lacan and psychoanalytic self-referentiality in the rest of "La Facteur de la Verité.") Discovery is middle voiced, since psychoanalysis becomes an active agent that acts through supposition, pretending to be passive in discovery.

For the second case—"Psychoanalysis, it is supposed, discovers itself" and "Psychoanalysis, it is supposed, is discovered"—only passivity, agentlessness, in the face of supposition, renders the sentence intelligible. If there is to be supposition, and there always is, then it must be passive. That is, supposition is given from elsewhere, and the activity it supposes to be occurring is rendered beyond self-reflexive activity because it is anterior to any such self-reflexiveness. The active agent of discovery (psychoanalysis) acts in an unstated elsewhere, though it remains here. Psychoanalysis becomes isolated, out of place, under this passive assumption, like a hammer left lying on a parlor coffee table. And this interpretation finds a certain echo in Derrida's critique of how Lacan wields the transcendental signifiers of psychoanalysis in the rest of his chapter.

What is at stake here is the effect of two ambiguous phrases, whose interacting significations mutually deconstruct and reconstruct themselves at the limits of their own ambiguities, like an interference pattern of light. At each moment of ambiguity, a confluence or conflation of an enactment and a statement, of an act and a state, occurs. The source of the act or state is always elsewhere, absent or empty, an act and non-state and a state and non-act, where the negative parameter added to each double ambiguity reflects an otherness, a distance that produces non-intersection. In other words, the double non-negation is not simply a reasoning style by which one moves from one idea to the next, but in Derrida's hands a form of presentation that both stops such movement and produces it in a different dimension of meaning, opening a space for multiplicity.

One might hypothesize, since the middle voice became extinct, that it characterized a period prior to the development of the individual self: that is, of the self as an object of self-contemplation, the self as an ideological and ideational entity. In that case, self-reflexivity (as in the ambiguity of the French verb form) would point back to a third-person recognition that the actor was acting on him/herself; and its passive-voiced mode would absorb the recognition, from a first-person standpoint, that one was the third-person recipient of the action, a third-person enactment inside a first-person statement.

Always Already

Another example of Derrida's deployment of the double non-negation is his use of the expression "always already," which at times becomes a mantra in his text, to the point where it takes on a certain rhetorical significance, a meaning beyond itself as descriptive. The expression "always already" has a certain charm and a certain fascination. Its concision in halting thought while setting it in motion, forward and back, is almost blasé, like an expert diver doing a double back-flip off a low diving board. It takes us where it does not go, to a non-origin in the past, and goes where it cannot take us, to a recurrent future in the present.

The notion of "an" Always Already emerges first in Heidegger, for whom it expresses a logic that leads back to Being.[16] In Heidegger's analytic of Dasein, every thought, every being, implies the question of its own foundation or ground (its necessary condition of possibility). Being is always already there, as what is implied by and implicit in each entity. The ontological difference generated by Being always already being there is that "Being and beings are always found to be already there by virtue of and within the difference."[17] In the logic of this difference, one arrives back at what is already there through what is always implied—in effect, up ahead in a "relatedness backward and forward" (*BT*, 28). As he states explicitly in *Identity and Difference*: "The beginning is the result; . . . the result is the beginning" (*ID*, 53). It is reminiscent of Nietzsche's deconstruction of causality. For Nietzsche, an event must have occurred and been named an effect before a cause for the event could become a question, implying that the effect essentially precedes the cause. The Always Already seems to imply prior conditions, but prior conditions that are to be brought into existence by their outcome or implication. Heidegger becomes quite explicit about that. In speaking about speech and its attempts at communication, he says:

> What takes place in our completing the performance of a statement is not that we first transport ourselves, as it were, into the soul of the individual who makes the statement and then put ourselves somehow in relation to the external object spoken of. We are rather always already comporting outselves toward the beings around us. . . . Propositional truth is primordially rooted, rooted in already-being-by-things. The latter occurs "already," before making statements—since when? Always Already! Always, that is insofar as and as long as Dasein exists. Already being with things belongs to the existence of Dasein, to its kind and mode of being.[18]

And this effectively restates the ontological difference. If the ontic (the "things" of Dasein's Being-with) is to be, it must be thought, while thinking the ontic is ontologically other than what it thinks. It is already implied in what is thought but always withholds itself from being contained in what is thought. Indeed, for Heidegger, the logic of the Always Already is what is inconceivable about thinking, what constitutes one of the names of the inarticulability of its primordial existentiality. That is, the inarticulable is what is always already the ground for things, to the extent things are articulable. The proximity of Dasein to the relation of articulability and inarticulability for Heidegger is what induced him to focus on the problem of language. The Being of language constitutes that relation of articulability and inarticulability as separation and as the limit of articulation itself.

But it is with the question of the Being of language that this logic, named by the Always Already, defeats itself in Heidegger. As Bernasconi points out, "Language for the most part conceals itself by directing us away from itself toward what is spoken about. . . . When we speak about language, it is, as something spoken about, reduced to the status of a thing" (*QLH*, 65). That is, the Being of language is the inarticulable that is the inaccessible ground for language itself. Though language is the condition of possibility for stating the truth of the Being of language, for it to do so renders those conditions of possibility essentially metaphysical. And Bernasconi adds that "Heidegger concedes that his thinking seems to remain on the path of metaphysics" on this question (*QLH*, 67). It was a problem that Heidegger did not resolve, but that Derrida opens up by treating language as Heidegger had treated Being.

For Derrida, the Always Already formalizes (renders textual form) the overthrow of origins, the irreducibility of the impossibility of origins—especially the origin implicit in the notion of ontological precedence. If Being precedes beings, is their necessary condition, is always anterior as already ground, then something else prior to Being is there for which the notion that "Being precedes beings," the notion of "anteriority" itself, is an iteration, a repetition; that "something" is the condition for anteriority or precedence, and for representation as such as well, to function as meanings in the first place. In effect, precedence can have no beginning; its meaning recedes back to a "before" that also precedes precedence, always precedes the pure textuality of the statement of origins, and hence of origins themselves. If something else is always already there, it can be grasped only as a trace of a non-origin immanent in all return to origins.[19]

From the programmatic beginning of *Of Grammatology*, when Derrida offers his first unraveling of writing and the signifier, the Always Already is in place, sometimes as a sign rather than a syntactical device, and sometimes as a buoy marking the hidden irregularities under textual waters whose ripples Derrida is carefully recording: "a slow movement whose necessity is hardly perceptible" (*Gram*, 6). Those waves, which already surround metaphysics (as a trace), mark the restlessness always encountered in textuality and, in particular, in the relegation of writing to secondary status, subordinate to speech, which is where metaphysics puts it.

For Derrida, under the metaphysical reduction of writing to the status of "the signifier of the signifier," there lurks the recognition that signifieds (meanings) themselves signify other signifiers. To reincorporate that into one's reading of a text, which constitutes one of the aspects of a deconstruction, is to restore the nature of the sign to its proper place at the heart of language. There the signified always already functions as a signifier. The secondary status commonly reserved for writing turns out to affect every signified in general, always already impresses itself on them the moment they *come into play.*[20] And we can add that if, as Derrida proclaims, this "destroy[s] the concept of the sign, and its entire logic," "overwhelms" it in the moment of "effacing" the limits of language (*Gram*, 7), the very notions of "overwhelm" and "efface" name textual forms that are always already at work in every text. That is, in the rescue of writing from its exile as the "signifier of the signifier," there emerges textual form. If form can be grasped as a signifier as well, it confirms that "either writing was never a simple 'supplement,' or it is urgently necessary to construct a new logic of the 'supplement'" (*Gram*, 7).

That is, textual form as a sign system itself produces meaning that adds itself to the text and obstructs the text in so doing, so that the text always means more than and less than it presents itself literally as meaning. If the unavoidable dynamic of writing is to go beyond and to fall short of itself, then it cannot be the supplement of speech that had been proposed for it.

What Derrida's reasoning implies is that the Always Already participates in the generation of textual form. In particular, the Always Already moves toward the trace of what is always there as absence (act and non-state) and toward a residence in the erasure of what is already there (state and non-act). One encounters this in reading the Always Already, in attempting to follow its double movement; and one encounters the Always Already in reading. In reading, the Always Already jars the forward flow of thought back to a preceding space of the already read. To read is to Always Already have read, and to have repeated the foundations of the possibility of reading. At the same time, what is already read has yet to be read, and can be read only in what follows. Like reading a murder mystery, one feels suspense in a certainty of unfamiliarity, and one feels a non-suspense (having finished reading) in an uncertainty of familiarity. Just as the questioning of beings invokes the question of Being, reading the Always Already calls in question reading itself. One reads at the level of the Always Already at the same time that one reads the Always Already. It maps out a realm of metatextuality that is not literal, but exists only through the literal. Thus, it constitutes the domain of textual form as itself the domain of textual self-referentiality, of self-presentation as neither text nor the metatextuality that the Always Already names. The Derridean Always Already is neither methodological (as it is for Heidegger), nor metatextual; it can neither be separated from textual content nor abandoned to it as a form. Thus, it fascinates because in reading it we encounter it reading itself, self-referentially. It becomes the textual incarnation of the double non-negation, which it individuates as an avatar.

It has a different function for Sartre. Rather than constituting a methodology for thinking intentionality, as it does for Heidegger, the Always Already analogizes the structure of intentionality. For Sartre, consciousness (of something) is concomitant with awareness of not being that of which one is conscious. Non-being is always what is in relation to the object, in that it implies the *négatité* that must already distance the object from the for-itself in order for consciousness to be conscious of it. Sartre's constant use of "in order that" (or "in order to," "in order for," almost to the point of its substituting itself as a rhetorical formula for subjectivity and project[21]) embeds an ephemeral or subliminal narrative of purpose within a discourse of structure; it allegorizes a performative relation in order to reveal the overlap of separation and inseparability, like that found in "the difference between the dancer and the dance." Consciousness cannot be independent of the distance (a distance which is not a distance) that is the condition for consciousness not being its own foundation. And it is across that distance (a nothingness) that the "in order to" operates.

Thus, the "in order to" presents itself as a different avatar for, or form of, the Always Already. The Always Already becomes the logic of a dependence within ontological autonomy (an independence of foundation that depends upon the nothingness of a distance)—a tie to the past that renders the present forever a disconnected future. Or, as Heidegger says, "'Being' ever and always speaks as destiny, and thus permeated by tradition" (*ID*, 51). If, for Heidegger, the Always Already is the backward and forward dynamic of his analytic, for Sartre, it amounts to the hidden purposiveness implicit in a distanceless distance to the object. Once again, what appears in the form of Heidegger's argument is transferred to the content of Sartre's account of consciousness; Sartre's writing enacts what Heidegger's writing states. What is positive in Heidegger becomes negative or absence; it is a reappearance of photonegativity between them. In sum, what Heidegger constructs as method in *Being and Time*, Sartre tells as ontological process in *Being and Nothingness*, and Derrida deploys as a critical operation in *Of Grammatology*—or, as Derrida would list them, formalism, thematicism, and rhetoric, respectively (*Dis*, 35).

Ultimately, not only has a common source been traced in Heidegger, as a source of incommensurability, but Heidegger's formalism presents itself as a possible mediation, a common or parallel logical structure between them. This logical structure goes beyond Howells's sense of paradoxical logic because it discriminates the modes and levels of textuality that it serves in turn to shape. And it does not fall into Gasché's trap of seeking coherence; Gasché's heterology relies upon a leveling of language and metalanguage, which could only linearize intertextual relations.

In sum, the Always Already produces three perspectives from its vantage point as a textual form with respect to the significations constructed by it. As form (for Heidegger), it is a formalism, a thematized logical procedure that makes thinking possible; as a thematized procedure (for Sartre), it is a trope for the structure of intentionality; and as a trope or rhetorical structure (for Derrida), it names a deconstructive access to form in a text, the possibility of signification (metatextual content) accruing to it as textual form.

Where Sartre speaks of awareness, of difference from the object and attention to the object as distant without distance, Heidegger addresses Dasein through a discursivity that structures itself by means of an ontological difference, of identity in difference. The content of Sartre's use of the Always Already (in the thematic mode of the "in order to") appears homologous to the form of Heidegger's own thematizing of the questioning Being. Where Heidegger speaks of Being as always already implied in the question of beings, Derrida points to what is always already implied in the existence of a text, of writing, in order to speak of Being. Through rhetorical invocation of the Always Already, the form of Derrida's argument appears homologous to the content of Heidegger's analytic. And where Derrida speaks/writes of the undecidability of textuality, of writing, because it always already escapes the contexts and modes of signification imposed in order to read it (as for instance the middle voice escapes both the active or the passive), Sartre reasons using strata of incommensurability overlaid upon each other, through which his account of consciousness continually escapes definitude. Finally, the content of Derrida's discourse appears homologous to the form of Sartre's argument through the mapped mediation of the Always Already as a formalism.

There is thus a circularity of the three through the mediation of the Always Already as a textual form. It presents itself as content in Sartre with respect to being form in Heidegger, as content in Heidegger with respect to being form in Derrida, as content in Derrida with respect to being form in Sartre. In effect, the generation of this circular interweaving of form and content constitutes the Always Already as a discursive "object." Without that, it would reduce to contingency, a stylistic element in Derrida, a trope for intentionality in Sartre, and a logical procedure in Heidegger.

Because these pairs of form and content interweave, the circle presents itself like an ecology. More than simply a reprieve from isolation, it conjoins these elements in what appears to contain a nostalgia for that form, as if it were archaic, a space in which logic, project, and rhetoric felt at home with each other. Each element, in isolation a double non-negation, loses that structure to the circle the way ions lose their electrical charge in a greater compound. Perhaps the anxiety involved in the strangeness of the skew relation results from the intuition that it marks a whole that had been broken. What the unbroken circle might suggest is that the Always Already is its own foundation in the mode of being circular. This would be discoverable only after being reconstructed through the interrelations of the works of these three thinkers. The meaning of the Always Already is that it is the effect of an absent origin, an absence of origin, a structure that constitutes itself through its intertextual transformations of textual form and content. To have no foundation other than its own structure is a Heideggerian notion of Being; to have no foundation other than itself, and not to be its own foundation, is a Sartrean notion of being-for-itself; to constitute itself through intertextual movements and transformations, an originless sense of repetition as foundation, is a Derridean notion of language.

4 Form and Structure

THE QUESTION NOW is textual form. The skew relation as a textual form has been shown to function as a logic, a way of organizing a reasoning, a way of structuring a presentation. We can discern it in its hiddenness by means of parametrics and mappings. These have been derived from literary critical and philosophical methods. And thus they have an abstractness that should be applicable elsewhere, beyond this single form, or the peculiarity of these texts. But our preceding discussion has suggested that perhaps a distinction needs to be made between textual form and structure. Not that textual form does not have structure; but does it constitute a structure for the more general domains of language or philosophy? Can it be extracted from its specific textual ecologies, and considered a formalism? The skew relation has a certain entityhood bestowed upon it by its iteration and iterability in the texts discussed. But what does it mean that a textual form, discerned through homology, can function as a formalism?

To address textual form means to shift one's gaze from the content of philosophical discourse, from its ideational presentation, from what its language speaks about, to the constructions and geometries of its presentation, to what provides the contour and topology of its aboutness. To do this, a somewhat different view of the philosophical must be adopted, one that goes beyond reading propositionally, one that deprivileges content and uses it as an opening to textuality itself. That is, form would constitute a sense of objectivity within textuality, a domain of textual objects that could be given entityhood, and between which there would be (textual) space and the appearance of differences and repetitions. To discern form, one must read for form. And the problem of form is how to read for it, recognize it, and relate forms across difference. It will be important to broaden our understanding of this.

ON FORM

The question of form has been given a contemporary significance by post-structuralist thinkers, because an attention to form plays a central role in their critique of language at all levels: that of the sign (Derrida), of style (Barthes),[1] of ideology (Lyotard), discursive formations (Foucault), or historiography (Deleuze and Guattari). It is treating the meaning of form, and analyzing what that means, that has set the post-structuralist discourses apart as a special philosophical project.

Roland Barthes opens the question when he says that form is constituted by "significations apart from their content" (*Myth*, 111). In his literary criticism, he looks at the formal aspects of literary codes, and asks how codes that produce meaning at the same time produce metadiscursive signs that reach beyond that meaning, and beyond signification altogether. This defines a somewhat different project from Derrida's use of form in his deconstructive operations. For Derrida, textual form counterposes itself as alternate meanings to a text's significations, in a manner that recontextualizes discursive content. Such counterpositions allow one to free the text's statement from its ideological assumptions, the assumptions the text makes about what it attempts to say in order to make its statement true and referential. The differential between meaning systems discloses the difference between what the text literally says and what it is made to say through the adjoining of those assumptions. For Barthes, there are codes that are historically given that play beneath a text and provide its sentences with the specific roles they play—as literary, narrative, expository, and so on. For him, the codes reflect a cultural or class tradition, embedded in the history of language, at variance with Derrida, for whom the metaphysical presuppositions of a text are both more general and specific to each text.

Barthes's critical methods often reveal operations that can only be called deconstructive. But one of his constant themes, to which he returns again and again, is an investigation into "significationless signs," or what one might call "contentless form"—that is, textual form that reveals a glimpse of "signness" or the essence of signification, without itself signifying something immediately apprehensible.[2] In this regard, Barthes complements Heidegger's concern with the inarticulable, the moment that remains "nameless" in order to silhouette "formless content."

Textual or discursive form is different from narrative form, which in turn concerns categories of character, action, and intentionality. Discursive form is constituted by formal patterns of meaning: circularities, surface topologies, geometries, knots and interweavings, and so on, as well as reasoning strategies. An attention to form can be considered "constructivist" insofar as what it discloses in a text it constructs discursively from elements of textuality and discursive flow.[3] The discernment of textual form is an activity toward the text, rather than a mere apprehension of its signification.

At the center of Barthes's activity of reading textual form is his use of the Saussurean semiotic system (the understanding of the sign to be composed of signifier and signified) as a tool for describing different orders of discourse. A second-order sign system, such as connotation, myth, or metalanguage, is one that takes a first-order sign system (language or image) as either its signifier or its signified. If it takes the first-order system as its signifier, it becomes what Barthes calls myth or connotation; and if as its signified, a metalanguage. In the latter case, the first-order language is what the second-order language is "about," the domain of its meanings. A metalanguage is a discourse about language (e.g., linguistics, grammar theory, etc.). The first-order language is its "object," the object of its attention.

On the other hand, a second-order language that takes a language or discourse as its signifier is a discourse that transforms the first-order language at the level of its meanings. A turn of phrase that suggests the phrase's connotation is more important than its literal statement is thus a seizure of the phrase by that turn, one which then transforms it. When literary criticism attempts to reveal a literary work's hidden motifs and meanings, its connotations and the import of its metaphor structures, it is functioning as the first kind of second-order discourse, a metalanguage. But when it uses the text it addresses to make certain political points about the world, it is functioning as the second kind, as a form of mythification. Most literary criticism does both.

Let us pursue this second kind of second-order discourse briefly in Barthes's work. In his essay "Myth Today," Barthes presents his now famous discussion of the French colonial mythos contained in a picture on the cover of *Paris-Match* (the French analogue of *Life* magazine). (*Myth*, 116). The photo depicts a black soldier in one of France's African colonies, shown in French army uniform saluting (ostensibly the French flag). For Barthes, the photo is designed to evoke, as its immediate, unavoidable meaning, the greatness of the French empire and the equalitarian cohesion and unity through which it embraces many diverse peoples, races, and territories. The photo assumes that this ideological content will be understood from the photo's image, composition, and the fact that it appears in *Paris-Match* (rather than *L'Humanité*, the Communist Party newspaper, for instance).

Beneath the ideology of its image, it contains a vast array of submeanings, involving the history of Africa, of French colonialism, of militarism, of race and racialization. But the image is of a single African person, saluting. Thus, at the level of the literal photo, there is an invocation of that person's stories, his geography, his biography, an entire African culture and literature, behind what is signified by the fact that he is at the moment a French soldier. The actual picture of the person is thus full, a plenitude in itself. All this gets pushed into the background by the overarching concept, however, which seizes and then "redeploys" it as raw material for something else "unspoken" in the photo. Historicity, person, locale, all that constitutes the specificity of the image, are reduced to what Barthes calls "form," the "material" of a signifier whose signification is ideological. Its ideology, which emerges from a source wholly exterior to the image (from France rather than Africa), attaches to it and speaks connotatively from it. For Barthes, this appropriation of a sign or sign system (the photo as sign, and the data and narratives of the soldier's life as an implicit system of signs) by a concept from elsewhere for its own purposes constitutes the structure of myth. Myth recodes the given (sign or system) to produce a second-order signification. It commandeers the first-order sign system for its own purposes and submerges all the first-order meanings back into the sign to serve as carriers of its own meaning. "It makes us understand something and it imposes it on us" (*Myth*, 117) by imposing it on the sign (the photo).

By commandeering the first-order system, the myth places the African's particularity, and the stories that fill the image, at a distance, in an unseen background for colonial appropriation in the second-order system. In being transformed from meaning to form, the image loses the knowledge it had contained; it is emptied of its own reality in order to contain the different reality of the myth (*Myth*, 119). Myth produces the form it appropriates as part of the act of its appropriation. It "is a pure ideographic system, where the forms are . . . motivated by the concept which they represent" (*Myth*, 127).

In dehistoricizing and emptying the sign (the photo image), the second-order code traps it in a conscripting space between its own (defaced and effaced) meaning and the ideological signification that concretizes itself through that conscription. Between those two, an inarticulable gap opens, the barest separation between discursive fabrics, between first- and second-order systems, through which the inner structure of signification itself is revealed. Between its two readings as image and myth, between meaning and the form that is emptied, the signifier briefly becomes significationless, and the exteriority of its many levels of meaning, their arrival from a distance to it, is invoked. This moment marks the interior limit of its being as a sign, its interior fracture between signifier and signified, between being and signifying. It is a moment of textual singularity produced by a lamination of meaning, a place where meaning implodes, suspends itself as a form without content.

This sense of transformation of meaning into discursive form, which emerges from an ideological imposition of prior meaning, differs from the more traditional sense of myth. Eric Gould, for instance, addresses "mythicity" as that which names the characteristics of a narrative discourse that would render its story element mythic in the sense of narrative presence or power.[4] Unlike Barthes's notion, narrative power preexists the particular narratives or stories from which it emerges. Narrative as story is constituted as mythic by an intentional process, the operation of mythicity. It operates in the gap between event and meaning (in a sense between signifier and signified), rather than between levels of discourse, as it does for Barthes. An event reveals an absence of origin and closure. And meaning is given in a determined way. It is between these two, as their conjunction, that Gould finds the operation of myth. This differs from Barthes's concern with the semiotic transformation of the sign, its becoming mythic (ideological) as the result of a signifying operation. That is, myth attaches to the form of a narrative sign, rather than to the content of a narrative by which an event is told. For Gould, myth is a mode of interpretation that is not ideological but contained within the narrative that precedes the ideological operation in referring to an event. For Barthes, myth is itself an event.

Barthes extends his inquiry into textual form in *S/Z*. His project in that book is to demonstrate the unfolding (sentence by sentence, phrase by phrase) of the discursive codes for narrative. He uses Balzac's short story "Sarrasine" for this purpose. The elements of narrative are produced by codes that overlay certain connotations on the statements of the text, through which they then represent action, plot, character intentionality, and so on. It is through recognition of those coded connotations that one reads the text as narrated acts, characters, class situation, or temporality, and so forth. Discursive representations, under the operations of these codes, produce a sense of literariness, of narrative, that flatten literal sentential and grammatical meaning and connotation into the background of the story itself. Thus, the propositional content of the sentences is transformed into references to character and action, timing, plot, and story development; they are emptied of their literal meaning and disappear as materiality into the greater signifier whose signified the story is. That is, they are transformed by the codes into form, on which the story effloresces as character and action.

To read a story in a way that reveals the underlying narrative codes is to demystify the literariness of the story in the same way that foregrounding the mythifying ideology demythifies the image commandeered—as Barthes does for the colonialist ideology at work on the *Paris-Match* cover. The various textual strategies designed to produce particular effects become discernible as specific interactions of narrative codes. And these strategies produce particular formal configurations in the text which constitute what can be called "discursive form."

Barthes provides a number of examples in *S/Z*. In one instance, he argues that an old man, encountered in the story's first scene, remains enigmatic as long as two identities (Sarrasine or Zambinella) are possible for him. The reader's guess as to who he is hinges on how a particular sentence spoken by the narrator in the story is read.

> The alternative's two elements (error/truth) are attached to a kind of swivel which neutralizes its revelatory power. This swivel is the sentence. Everything about it, the simplicity of its structure, its brevity, its speed (which seems borrowed, by metonymy, from the narrator's impatience) keeps the truth (dangerous to the story's interest) away from the reader. (*S/Z*, 127)

That is, on an ordinary reading, the sentence in question takes the form of a hinge that can swing the meanings of the narrative one way or the other. This image of the swivel, a dissimulating lure that dances enticingly out of reach before the reader—a "meaning that denies the meaning" of the scene—is an interrelation of codes, to which Barthes gives the function of defending the story from being found out too quickly. The sentence in question in Balzac's text, revealing itself as the axis of this "meaning" for Balzac's story, can be seen in the text as a moment of discursive form. The swivel is that form—a structure of narrative logic that, for Barthes, buries a reader's insight behind reading itself.

A second example Barthes gives is an intertwining of codes that he calls a braid. At one point in the narrative, three actions are underway at the same time: an excursion outside Rome, during which Sarrasine reveals the passion of his feelings for Zambinella, and in response to which Zambinella evinces a perplexing terror. The narrative's focus shifts from one to the second, to the third, and so on, in rapid succession; the story loses its linearity to this cyclic weaving of narrative moments.

> The terms of the sequence [of actions are] positions held and then left behind in the course of a gradual invasion of meaning. . . . The grouping of the codes, as they enter into the work, into the movement of the reading, constitute a braid. (*S/Z*, 160)

In Barthes's metaphor, it is as if a "hand" intervenes to weave the strands of narrative voice in order to produce an effect impossible for each voice singly, in a homogeneity of tone. Elsewhere, he considers a "braid" of metanarrative voices, an intertwining of passionate, novelistic, and ironic codes that circle around each other in the scene. In the moment in question, a character is caught in a passionate state; the text, however, assumes a self-consciously literary ("authorial") voice that makes reference to the novelistic, and which the ironic ("narrative") tone parodies in turn, as if from a distance.[5] The braid's effect is to prevent a resolution of the question "who (metanarratively) is speaking?"

But there are two dimensions to this discursive structure that must be distinguished. As an operation affecting itself within and upon the text, the "braid" exemplifies what Barthes calls a singularity, that is, a significationless sign, a contentless form; it metatextually conditions the very existence of signification and takes as its own signification the generation of that condition—an Escher-like hand emerging from within the picture it is in the process of drawing. But Barthes is the one who points it out upon the narrative plane. It is his act of critically discerning the "braid," of articulating its stylistic effect, that elevates it as a form (in his metadiscourse) above the narrative plane, and gives notice of it as a structure against the narrative background. Barthes the critic (or reader) himself becomes a metatextual operation, appropriating that structure as a signifier for the effect he describes and thus playing a role similar to that assigned to ideologizing myth, but with the difference that he is discerning the significance (as a singularity) of the structure at work within the text, rather than ideologically imposing it.[6]

Barthes thus moves us through three ever more complex stages toward a presentation of what "discursive form" means: the operation of myth on a sign, the operation of narrative codes on a text, and the operation of a critical metadiscourse on the formal structures of a text's codes. With the image from Escher, we are getting even closer to it. Let us follow Barthes one more step. In general, to read textual form is to engage in a reading that discovers and produces structures in the text, in terms of the text's own generation of meaning (*S/Z*, 20).

> The text, in its mass, is comparable to a sky, at once flat and smooth, without edges and without landmarks; like the soothsayer drawing on it with the tip of his staff an imaginary rectangle wherein to consult, according to certain principles, the flight of birds, the commentator traces through the text certain zones of reading, in order to observe the migration of meanings, the outcropping of codes, the passage of citations. The lexia is only the wrapping of a semantic volume, the crest line of a plural text. (*S/Z*, 14)

> There is no entrance language or exit language for the textual dictionary, since it is not the dictionary's (closed) definitional power that the text possesses, but its infinite structure. (*S/Z*, 120)

Each text replaces the historically given lexical structure with itself as a language, rendering the given language supplementary, a space or "wrapping" in which to present itself as patterns, motions, or objects. Meanings are given not only being, or particularity, but relational motion within a structure continually remapped and extended by reading into a textual space that has its own language. And Barthes's imagery of a "flight of birds" or "outcroppings of codes" suggests an objecthood, or a "thereness" of paths of interaction that reside in textual space like a kind of hologram that one has only to illuminate with a polarized light source to see.

> When two codes function simultaneously but according to unequal wavelengths, they produce an image of movement, an image of life . . . it is a scene made up by blocks of meaning, at once varied, repeated, and discontinuous (outlined); out of the arrangement of these blocks comes a diagram of the body, . . . the figure is not the sum, the frame, or the support of the meanings; it is an additional meaning, a kind of diacritical paradigm. (*S/Z*, 61)

These "diagrams" are metatextual compositions of textual meaning; it is to such structural compositions that the term *discursive form* refers. These structures cannot simply be "read" but must be constructed through a multilevel and laminated reading. One discerns form in an interpretive operation in the text at the same time that one constitutes it through a metatextual operation upon the text. It is a "chiasmus" of constitution and discovery, a construction of what is encountered as already having been there.[7] Or, as Derrida puts it, "Formality, as convention, is what presents itself of the thing, lets itself be seen, gives itself to thought. That metaphysical thought—and consequently phenomenology—thinks of being as form, that in metaphysics, thought is thought as the thought of form, and the formality of form, is only therefore the sheerest necessity."[8]

In sum, perhaps one way of comprehending this process is through the notion of the sculptural. In metatextually producing forms that are then discovered in the text, one could be said to be sculpting them out of the text's meanings, while discovering the sculptured form within those meanings. In doing so, one is not being metaphoric toward the text; textual or discursive form is not an alternative articulation of it. To be metaphoric, form would in some way have to be about what the literal is about; instead, it is about the way the literal does what it does. While textual form is not "about" the text's subject matter, neither is it metatextual to it. Rather, it is immanent in the text, providing the subject matter for a metatext that discerns and describes it. Thus, textual form is not synecdochic or metonymic either, because it builds a significational mode that is not a part of the whole, and thus neither represents it, as would the metonymic, nor recontextualizes it qualitatively, as would synecdoche.

Form is the invention, the bringing into existence and visibility of a textual "thing." In constituting a structured interrelation of parts, using the literal as its sculptural medium, it decenters the whole without reducing or essentializing. In apprehending textual form, the metatextual discernment of a configuration must pass through a moment when the form discerned is apprehended without signification, a contentless moment on the border between reading literal meanings and discovering possible meaning within the structure and contextual environment of the text in the process of reading it. This moment of contentless form supplements the inarticulable, stands alongside it as the inarticulability of the text's singularities, a meaning the text cannot approach in itself as a meaning. This is especially the case in texts addressing the inarticulable, for which constructivist methods are indispensible. It is in light of inarticulability that form requires homology as a means of discernment.

"Form" occurs to the textuality of a text through what the text does; it belongs to what Derrida suggests is always there in a text that exceeds meaning. A reading of form gives space to the non-text of textuality that exceeds its own meanings.

Indeed, it is that "non-text" that says (in not saying) what is not said (in saying) that makes the text and its logos, its "saying," both possible and polyvocal. In reading for form, discursive textual patterns or structures become discernible, recognizable, and specifiable. The operation of homology then discloses the iterations of those patterns and structures. Homology deprivileges the literal text in order to discern the structuring of textuality behind what its language says. If form signifies, it can only be through its differences from other forms, its iteration of itself within textuality, and with a sense incommensurable with the text's language.

On Structure

But now, let us return to the formal relations, non-negational, homological, and inverted, between Sartre, Derrida, and Heidegger. What we find operating among the three will transform, in its generality, our considerations of form into considerations of structure.

Where discursive form emerges from the interaction of levels of textuality generated by reading, structure as formalism has a more concrete and autonomous existence. Rather than be discerned metatextually in the text, it is constructed by it. Both occur as the content of a metatext, a reading, and both exist in the text in question. But structure contours the reading of the text while form contours its meanings, what one reads. It is the difference between discursive form as read and the metadiscursive forms through which one then reads. We recall that the neologisms Sartre and Derrida invented are discursive forms because they are unreadable as signs—forms that are the signifieds of their content, what they do, as signifiers. But we do not read a text through différance; it is the way the text read provides meaning. We do not live the world and its objects through nihilation; it is the way we provide the world's meanings for ourselves as subjects. But the ecologies of the text, or of the world, are structures. And some of them are discernible and articulable metadiscursively.

Heidegger introduces us to structure at the beginning of *Being and Time*, where he describes his methodological "backward and forward relatedness" (*BT*, 28). The problem he is addressing is that in questioning the meaning of something, there is already implied a prior understanding of what is questioned. "Inquiry, as a kind of seeking, must be guided beforehand by what is sought" (*BT*, 25). That is, implicit prior knowledge conditions the inquiry's terms, which are realized in the explicit articulation of the matter addressed. One returns to the implicit by pressing forward toward explicit conceptualizing.

But when such an inquiry comes into existence, it produces an aporia. "Man's" essence is to stand forth in ek-static emergence from Being, to which inquiry will ostensibly return "him."[9] "The essence of man" is not to preserve the essence of his being in Being, but to return to it. Man is not as he is, simply because he stands forth from Being, enabling (and necessitating) a return. This aporia perfuses Heidegger's inquiry. If the meaning (or the truth) of Being is unknowable because inarticulable, inquiry's prior understanding of Being not only belongs to Being's unknowability, but preserves its inarticulability in inquiry by also questioning the questioner, namely Dasein ("the Being for whom Being is a question"). Dasein's aporia is the incommensurability of inquiring into the meaning of Being and residing in the unknowability of Being.

The terms of this aporia produce a circle: Being reveals itself in the meaning of Being; the meaning of Being reveals itself in the unknowability of Being; and the unknowability of Being reveals itself in Being.[10] The inquiry into Being becomes other than it is because, while the ensemble leaves Being itself undefinable (*BT*, 23), each term on the circle "articulates" another, the one that precedes it, as what it "reveals." Each aporia thus escapes the aporetic by coming back upon itself through a third term, that is, through circularity. And Heidegger had intuited this without "articulating" this circle as such (*BT*, 193–95).

There is a similar circle in Sartre, also produced by a discussion of a fundamental aporia. For Sartre, "man" is not as he is because "man" makes "himself." That is, through activity in the world, one becomes who one is in pursuit of one's project as the making of oneself. If, in making himself, "man" is other than he is, it is because as a product, he is other than a producer; that is, as a project, man is other than simply a for-itself. This generates a circle similar to Heidegger's: The activity by which a person makes him/herself, or realizes his/her project, must be intentional; but intentionality requires a subject; and the subject is engendered by activity.

The similarity of this circle in Sartre's text to that in Heidegger's suggests that the circle provides more than a formal link between the two, because it represents a common textual logic. The circle is an iterable construct at the level of discursive development, rather than simply that of presentation, as with textual forms (the hinge, the braid, the skew relation, even as a double non-negation). It represents an isomorphic logic between the two texts, for which it is the sign, a common configuration encountered in reading them. This adjoins itself to the inversion already discovered between them. Let us look at this double relation a minute, as a way they differ from and defer to each other.

Though Heidegger and Sartre never really engaged each other in dialogue, they mutually critiqued each other. Heidegger addresses himself to Sartre in 1946, in response to the public lecture Sartre had given called "Existentialism Is a Humanism" (*EH*; see note 7, chap. 1). And he wishes to distance and differentiate himself from Sartre, precisely because Sartre had claimed Heidegger as part of his own existentialist tradition.[11] Heidegger focuses on Sartre's "profession" of the Cartesian cogito, which for Heidegger would necessarily lead Sartre and existentialism back to metaphysics. Heidegger's chosen course had led elsewhere. Because metaphysics is presuppositional, it constitutes a "technical interpretation of thinking." That is, it "does not measure up to [thinking]" (LH, 195). For Heidegger, metaphysics sells thinking short. If Sartre begins with the Cartesian cogito, Heidegger argues, he is beginning with the subject, the "I" in "I think." This renders the subject prior to thinking, which is the same as existence being prior to Being. For Heidegger, thinking is what grounds subjectivity. It is itself suspended in something more primordial, in Being as its realm of "accomplishment." "Thinking accomplishes the relation of Being to the essence of man"

(LH, 193). For Heidegger, the essence of man is his existence as a thinking being. It is the ek-static emergence of "man" from Being. The essence of Being is that "thinking is." That "thinking is" says that Being has "embraced its essence" (LH, 196). The "I think," on the other hand, inverts this by being the foundation for existence (the ek-static emergence from Being) as "I am." Thus, the cogito alienates "man" from Being by deferring Being to the subject. To center the essence of man in the subject is to make "man" an ideological construct, an a priori concept. As a reduction of thinking that leaves unrealized the "proper dignity of man" (LH, 210), it sells "man" short.

But Heidegger only partially follows his own injunction. While he reasons that the cogito must be dismissed, he himself has introduced a sense of its transformation instead. In place of the Cartesian "I think, therefore I am," Heidegger has substituted, "There is existence, therefore thinking is." In other words, he has inverted it and cast it in the third-person singular.

This returns us to the sense of inversion that reverberates between Heidegger and Sartre, and continues it. (The relation between them is, of course, extremely rich; richer, in fact, than either Heidegger or Sartre chose to publically acknowledge, as both Fell and Schroeder point out.) Heidegger understands affirmation and nihilation to be aspects of Being and not of subjectivity (LH, 238). Nihilation is what manifests itself as the negative (LH, 237); it is the essence of "thinking the nothing" (LH, 239). If the essence of Being is existence, then with existence, there is already nihilation. For Sartre, nihilation pertains to the upsurge of consciousness; it is not the source of the negative but the space of difference between existence and the world in which the negative, and absence, can exist. It opens the space of existence as a space of activity, which is primordial in the sense that activity is that through which one becomes who one is. In effect, the concept of nihilation functions in an inverted manner between them.

Heidegger, in his critique of Sartre, goes further and argues that thinking must precede experiential activity since the latter necessitates a subject, which is already a conceptualization. Rather than become who one is through (Sartrean) activity, "man" as preconceived subject would cease to know who he is; and activity will not find him for himself. The primacy of the subject only results in man's homelessness. Sartre rejoins in ironic (and inverted) agreement; man is always a project, an engagement in the world; to find himself at home, man must first make himself there in the world. Where, for Sartre, man discovers his being through what he sets for himself beyond himself, Heidegger thinks that man will discover what he has set for himself as man only by returning to Being. Man will find himself only through entry into the meaning of Being, which involves detachment (*gelassenheit*), that is, letting Being be (LH, 237).[12]

This inversive (dis)agreement continues even in Heidegger's effort to rescue the term *existence* from what he sees as a rationalist opposition of *existentia* and *essentia* (LH, 208). Sartre's "formula," that "existence precedes essence," he argues, returns these terms to their metaphysical meaning. Though Sartre reverses their order from the Platonic, he preserves the dichotomy, having left the meaning of "precedence" unquestioned. For Heidegger, "ontological precedence" both predetermines through differentiation (LH, 208) and is an artifact of textuality. For him, "existence precedes essence" must be read: "There is a thing called existence, and it is theoretically precedent, in a theoretical thing called ontology, to something about things that we call essence." And Heidegger seeks to speak of thought without rendering it a "thing." If the essence of "man" lies in his existence, there is no differentiation; precedence (and the differentiation it makes explicit) is a presumption. Because the nondistinction must remain inarticulable, its articulation renders it other than it is, dissociated from the meaning of Being.

It is to preserve the inarticulability of "existence" that Heidegger coins the term *ek-sistence*. Its prefix signifies a "coming out," a non-oppositional "standing forth" of thinking from Being. To say that "Man ek-sists" answers the question of the essence of man, not of whether man is or not (LH, 207). "Ek-sistence can only be said of the essence of man, of the human way to be" (LH, 204). The implication Heidegger draws is that man can escape metaphysics only by not differentiating, by seeking to "exist in the nameless," in the meaning of the inarticulable (LH, 199). And his charge against Sartre is that the cogito articulates what must remain unspoken. In excising the inarticulable, Sartre has not let Being be.

But in the face of the complex system of inversions that exist between their texts, and which suggest a disparity of form rather than substance or concept, this difference of language needs to be pursued.

It is true that Sartre speaks of the cogito and claims to begin with it; but as suggested earlier, it plays a different role for him than for Descartes. Descartes meditatively posits the cogito at the end of skepticism, and "before the fact," to serve as a first certainty that something is "there" (namely, that "I" am). Sartre, on the other hand, argues from the existence of negativity that nothing is "there" in order to arrive at the cogito.[13] And for Sartre, the for-itself (consciousness) is the absoluteness of that nothing; it is the absoluteness of contingency or indeterminacy whose certainty is a freedom unable to escape its own freedom (even in self-denial). Descartes's certainty is that "I exist"; and for this notion, the "ego" of "ego cogito" must be central in order to avoid reduction of human existence to an object. But if Sartre begins with the autonomy of nihilation, as the autonomy of freedom, the indeterminacy of awareness aware of itself (*EH*, 36), then he is centering the "think" of "I think," a "thinking" whose foundation is the inarticulability of freedom. That is, he phenomenologically decenters the Cartesian "hisness," the priority of the "he" (Descartes) that thinks it sees, or thinks it thinks, in the skeptical attitude. For Sartre, certainty begins with the meaninglessness of such a topos or of any predefined substance to activity. There is only the certainty of freedom, the certainty of an indeterminacy in which subjectivity is "always already" free. Sartre names this the "cogito," but insists that the name is permissible only because the (Cartesian) cogito itself can be escaped (*BN*, 85).

In converting Descartes's "ego cogito" into "the cogito," Sartre wrests the "cogito" from Descartes's grasp. This is his critical move beyond the "I" toward the autonomous subject.[14] And the distinction he makes between the subject and the self is important. For the Sartrean subject, there is only autonomy, an autonomy of absence, prior to a self-awareness constituting itself as a self. For the autonomous self, autonomy is an attribute; for the autonomous subject, however, the subject is only an attribute of autonomy. Any critique of the Sartrean cogito, the term he uses to name that autonomy in its indeterminacy, must take this distinction into account—which Heidegger has not. Sartre does not begin with the "I," as Heidegger claims, simply because he deploys the cogito. The "I" emerges later as an object; the ego is but another nihilation.

In other words, freedom is not the product of the cogito; the cogito instead constitutes an act of naming the indeterminacy (the inescapability, the certainty) of freedom. As the impossible (indeterminate) foundation of the subject, it signifies a subjectivity that is far from Cartesian. For Sartre, the "cogito" answers the question of the essence of man ("the human way to be") and not whether man is or not. The Sartrean cogito is the name for the truth of what cannot be said, because there is nothing to be said about it except that it "is." And that unspokenness is congruent to the inarticulability of Heidegger's "truth of Being." As such, the "cogito" plays the same role in Sartre's text as ek-sistence plays in Heidegger's. Though Sartre bespeaks existence, he is not saying that there is man, but rather, like Heidegger, that man begins with an indeterminacy, an inarticulable. Though Heidegger objects to having his unspoken meanings spoken by Sartre, he misses Sartre's own preservation of the unspoken.

This sheds a different light on Heidegger's attempt to open a space between himself and Sartre by charging that Sartre has chosen the language of metaphysics, of existentia rather than ek-sistence. It implies that, between these two texts, there are parallel structures, which emerge from congruent aporias, a similar circularity, and a common centering of an inarticulable for which the circle is a sign. In other words, a coherent structural homology exists between them. Hence, Sartre's use of the term "existence" relates homologically to Heidegger's inverted use of "ek-sistence," and his use of "precedence" to Heidegger's formal enactment of his "forward and backward relating" (and we will excuse Heidegger's own use of "priority" in the section headings of the introduction to *Being and Time*, since we have found him out in his other congruence to Sartre's use of precedence).

This further implies that Heidegger's rejection of Sartre's use of "existence" resides on a different level of discourse. In *Existentialism Is a Humanism*, Sartre chooses Heidegger (and not Aquinas or Berkeley) to be his immediate tradition, and this cannot be taken lightly. The idea that a tradition can be "chosen" is not trivial; it is, as Bakhtin says, one's very choice of language. For Heidegger to read Sartre's term "existence" as existentia and not as ek-sistence is to disregard Sartre's choice, and to impose a different choice upon him. Rather than read or misread Sartre, Heidegger transforms and rewrites him.[15]

Ultimately, Sartre's inarticulable is more convincing than Heidegger's, perhaps because it is more tangible. Against Heidegger's silhouetted absent positivity, Sartre posits (in a further inversion) a manifest present nothingness. It is a nothingness one can apprehend in all one's own everyday refusals and nostalgias. On the other hand, it is difficult to imagine Dasein in the first-person singular without that being already a betrayal. It is in order to escape thingness that Heidegger constructs a discursive space in which some-thing can exist that signifies "this is not a thing" without saying so, without rendering that signifying act a thing. In saying "the essence of man lies in his ek-sistence," Heidegger is attempting to rip the terms away from thingness, and make them signs for non-thingness. Non-expression must be a sign without a signifier, an unexpressed coincident meaning implicit in something else. But even coincident meaning, Derrida argues, only attaches to the system of signs that produces it, be it a language or a text or a set of gestures. The inexpressible would attach to the thingness of its coincident signs. Heidegger wanted the non-thingness of Being to have the full positivity of its Being in (non)expression; but that requires something more subtle than even "the nameless" (or *sinnlosigkeit*, or *gelassenheit*, which reify themselves), something that engenders naming without being a name.

Sartre ironically escapes this necessity while fulfilling its purpose by expressing himself in worldly terms, by attempting to say what he means. Speech expresses the freedom that manifests it while leaving that freedom inarticulable even in its act of "saying what one means." Heidegger asserts that inquiry itself is what means, and that the notion of "what one means" in speech (or writing) is a pretension; that is, to think meaning resides in the language one speaks is only a displacement of meaning from thinking. Furthermore, meaning (thinking) must reside at the level of the expression as well as the expressed. But as we have seen, it is at the level of expression, of textual form, in the form of Heidegger's desire to preserve the inarticulable, that a structural connection appears between Heidegger and Sartre's text.

What effect would this homology of circularities have on the relation between their different categories of ontology?

Sartre gave his public lecture ("Existentialism Is a Humanism") in 1946 as a response to charges by Christian and Marxist critics that existentialism did not sufficiently elevate "man" nor affirm a divine or class ideal. Sartre took pains to refute that existentialism is not humanist, which was a dire charge in the wake of World War II. Delivered in the politically charged atmosphere of newly liberated France, the real purpose of Sartre's lecture was to popularize existentialism in order to engage it in the political landscape of that historical moment. Thus, he tended to be somewhat sloganistic—"Every action implies a human setting and a human subjectivity"; "Existence precedes essence"; "Subjectivity must be the starting point"; and so on (*EH*, 13). In effect, Sartre chose a style that sought to be "in context" with the political situation in which he acted, to speak to "his epoch."

Sartre's philosophical thought is, of course, more elaborate than can be represented by slogans (though Heidegger, in focusing on this "lecture," seems not to be concerned by this). For Sartre, the possibility of understanding the world can only arise through the freedom of the mind that conceives it, a freedom that makes its own meanings and apprehends the world through them. In its freedom, it preempts and precludes all givenness and a prioris, while at the same time choosing them for itself, choosing those presuppositions and a priori notions it will live by in its world. In particular, the very notion of human nature, and of "humanism" itself, is chosen. If "man" him/herself must exist before a conception of him/her is possible, then "man's" existence is the prior (necessary) condition for the conceptualization and discernibility of "man," of the human. Definitions (such as of "human nature") can occur only at his/her own hands.

This is what Sartre means by "existence precedes essence"; conceptualization and self-conceptualization proceed from the activity of consciousness aware of its existence. It is not the existence of consciousness (existentia) that precedes its own essence (essentia) as a thing, for Sartre, but consciousness aware of its existence (what it does rather than what it is) that precedes (and produces) all essence (*EH*, 36). No essence is preordained, neither by class nor divine influence. "We are on a plane where there are only men" (*EH*, 22).[16] "Man's" destiny is only to be, to live the experiential component of the subjective, namely, activity (Man "is nothing else than a series of undertakings"; *EH*, 33).

However, Sartre is not saying that one is simply a subjectivity that acts; one becomes what is manifest by one's actions, pursuant to a project that is both lived and envisioned. The past that conditions the lived, and one's flight to a preenvisioned future (the already and the not-yet), are the foundations for each other. Like Heidegger's inquiry, which moves backward toward the meaning of Being by moving forward to what manifests that meaning, the for-itself as a project engenders its future in terms of a past it only realizes as a past by discovering (inventing) that future. These are congruent (and again, inverted) constructions. (And this suggests the tantalizing notion that Heidegger's sense of inquiry already contains, in a formal congruence, a sense of temporality that nevertheless remained uncompleted in *Being and Time*.)

The homology between them (of the circularity, and the form of "backward and forward" movement that inhabits Heidegger's reasoning and Sartre's conceptualization of their respective inarticulables) now brings Sartre's discourse into a different relation to Heidegger's. First, the homology suggests that the for-itself's (freedom's) relation to its projects parallels Being's relation to Dasein: freedom underlies those projects, is not them, is manifest through them, and is the context in which they are, as Being does Dasein. The difference lies in the narratability of choice, responsibility, flight, and so forth, through which freedom manifests itself, and which Heidegger subsumes in the notion of inquiry. This also suggests that nothing in Heidegger corresponds to what Sartre calls Being-in-itself.[17] For Heidegger, there are beings (*Seiendes*), the ontic, the ready-to-hand, but they do not stand opposite Being; they manifest Being, in the way that the meanings of objects and situations given by one's project manifest one's freedom, for Sartre. But they are not given Being as "in-itself" as in Sartre (*BN*, lxvi).

Second, the homology serves to disclose an unspoken "ontological difference" in Sartre's text. For many commentators, Sartre's notion of freedom is contradictory, in its conflation of the for-itself's absolute ontological freedom and one's relative freedom in a world of determinations and of others.[18] Sartre himself is ambiguous on the question. But if we turn to Heidegger, we encounter a structure that is both comparable and relevant. For Heidegger, if beings are, and as such manifest Being, then Being must persist in beings as a trace; and indeed, Heidegger addresses the question of Being by tracing back the inarticulable presence of Being in beings, and its erasure of itself in the specificity of beings. Beings (entities) point back to Being, and Being presences itself in its absence as the necessary condition for there to be beings. Sartre's notion of ontological freedom can similarly be understood as a trace within each person's situational choices. In order to be unfree or constrained in any way, one's freedom must be there as a trace that constitutes its absence. And that trace must be absolute; in order for one's freedom to be situationally abridged, it must already have been to that extent ontologically unquestionable. Indeed, it is only through the trace of absolute (ontological) freedom that a determined and determining world can be lived as determining. Or, to pose it the other way, situational freedom (which is limited by social conditions and constraints) points back to ontological freedom, and ontological freedom is the necessary condition for there to be situational freedom. In that sense, Sartrean freedom is an "ontological difference" between one's absolute freedom in its indeterminacy and the dependent strategies and tactics through which one lives the world situationally with respect to its conditions and constraints, as rendered meaningful for oneself by one's project.

Third, a certain congruent notion of humanism emerges in both. For Heidegger, the human implies being-in-the-world and care. But "world" means neither the objective nor the spiritualized world, nor what pertains to a subject-object relation, but rather "man's" standing forth in ek-sistence (in "his" essence). Being-in-the-world means "experiencing the essence of man more primordially" (LH, 225) than the level of conceptualized values, logic, or spirit that metaphysical humanism renders "objects" for thought (LH, 229). (And the homological counterpart to this in Sartre is that ontological freedom can never be delimited as "being free from" or "being free for.") The nonmetaphysical humanism that Heidegger attempts to silhouette through "being-in-the-world" is the essence of ek-sistence (LH, 231). Being-in-the-world is not a state or condition, but thinking that is not conceptual, that is "more rigorous than the conceptual" (LH, 235).

Heideggerian humanism is thinking that is not subsumed by a subject-object relation nor by an intentionality structure. Being-in-the-world is an openness of Being in which "man" stands, in which one's primordial attention is to the "not-yet" from the point of view of being with the "already." As activity in the "light of the truth of Being" (LH, 193), it contains subject-object relations as one of its forms. As attention to the "not-yet" in light of the "already," Being-in-the-world is what Heidegger calls "care"; it is "the human way to be." Similarly, the Sartrean notions of responsibility, choice, flight, and so on manifest one's being-in-the-world in the sense that they are the way one lives one's ontological freedom. Thus, they also reside in the "not-yet" from the point of view of the "already." In Sartrean language, it is through their situationality and narrativity that such manifestations of ontological freedom constitute the "human way to be." When Sartre says, "There is no human nature since there is no god to conceive it," (*EH*, 15) he is contesting the same objectivizing (third-person) point of view that for Heidegger characterizes metaphysics.

Thus, through the homology, we arrive at a different and more structured mapping of Heidegger's notions onto those of Sartre's ontology than has been developed up to now (Joseph Fell, for instance, spends a significant amount of time making categorical comparisons). And this would amount to a difference in the way Sartre is read. When read through the homology, Sartrean subjectivity (the for-itself) would be neither an analogue nor a translation of Heideggerian Dasein. Rather, it corresponds to Heidegger's notion of inquiry itself, since "human reality" names more than just Dasein, embracing not only Dasein but its disclosure and the discourse of its advent as well. This implies that human reality is not a human universal for Sartre, and neither is freedom; they are both the very absence of such, an absence that is the only universal: "There is a universality of man; but it is not given, it is perpetually being made" (*EH*, 39). To understand the subject as freedom is not to place "man" (or the "I") at the center of a space called "human reality"; it is instead the emptiness of that space which constitutes the existence of the human.

In sum, being-for-itself maps onto Heidegger's notion of inquiry, being-in-itself has no comparable element in Heidegger's text, and freedom maps onto the ontological difference, the relation between the ontological and the ontic. The Sartrean cogito and the Heideggerian ek-sistence correspond to each other, as do the Sartrean analytic of temporality and the Heideggerian methodology of "backward and forward" movement in inquiry. Human reality is not Dasein, and néantisation is nothing but the space between Being as the condition of beings and the beings in which Being resides.

But now, how are we to read Heidegger's charge that Sartre has fallen back into metaphysical humanism? The difference between them must be reevaluated across the homology. Heidegger calls for a return to "man's" essence, a rescinding of the "technical interpretation of thinking" (i.e., metaphysics), and he calls for "man" to find his way back to the nearness of Being by learning "to exist in the nameless" (LH, 199). This involves replacing metaphysical "humanism" with a different notion of the human. The "nameless," as existence without differentiations, constitutes escape from the false consciousness of objective noninvolvement (the distance from others as objectified); the "nameless" is where "care" can predominate, as precisely living the nearness of Being as the nameless. But the nameless must be named without being addressed, because determination cancels thinking and care. A suspension of all determinations, points of view, ideologies, and so on is required, as in an *epoche*. The call to "think there" (Da-Sein) in "the nameless," prior to determination, means to live the *epoche* (LH, 203) and not simply reflect on thought through it. And Heidegger's leap of faith is that upon realizing the "lived *epoche*," man will be man.

Heidegger's "lived *epoche*" is what Sartre refuses. Though for Sartre, freedom is autonomous of the doctrines and projects that structure the world, it cannot escape them. It must return to them, because it already lives in them in the world (as Being resides in beings). Because ontological freedom resides in situational freedom, there is no ontological freedom without situational freedom as such, in the sense that there can be no situational unfreedom without the absoluteness of ontological freedom. Because one is free, living the *epoche* is an illusion.

And this inversion within their homological attitudes toward "humanism" is again reflected in the question of the universal. Sartre claims that all people are understandable to him, and that no subjectivity need be alien if understood in its situation (*EH*, 39). It recalls the Eurocentric pretension to being the universal human, as the ethnocentrism that has founded European white supremacy. Sartre says, "There is no difference between being free, . . . like an existence that chooses its essence, and being absolute" (*EH*, 40). This would appears to be the foundation of a humanism in which Derrida would discern the "essential operation of metaphysics." But because it must be understood in the negative, as a dimension of néantisation, it is a "universal" that is neither truth nor Being. It is the nothingness from which there emerges the freedom to choose, to adapt, to go beyond, to acquiesce or rebel. No abstract moral principles are possible (*EH*, 47) because any two moralities amount to the same thing insofar as what both "set up as a goal is freedom." What remains "absolute" (nonalien) is the indeterminacy that grounds them, the contingency of social context to which the individual responds (as responsibility) in making that world his/her own. Whether that social context is a system of narratives or a structure of "scientific" reasoning, a mythologized social structure of yearly voting rituals, or communal decision procedures, what is common to all is that each appears as given, foundational, a contingent social reality that each person lives as contextualizing necessity (*EH*, 39).

In short, when Sartre says that all people are understandable to him, he does not mean that they can be measured according to European standards, but that all people must be granted their tradition and the necessity of their world. Indeed, not to do so would be to ignore or even refuse a person's ability to rebel against his/her situation from within it. It is this final possibility that Heidegger does not see in his charge of metaphysical humanism against Sartre, because he must view all Sartre's ontological categories as positive, and thus objectifiable, standardizable, or normative, while for Sartre they are precisely the absence of that.

THE DERRIDEAN CIRCLE

In "The Ends of Man," Derrida addresses both notions of "humanism," not in their generality as ideological, but in their pretensions to speak for others. He too addresses Sartre's language, but not to paint it with the same brush as Heidegger. He recognizes that there is a value in Sartre's deployment of terms like "human reality" that will rise above the presuppositions of tradition. But for Derrida, Sartre's attempt is inadequate because he neglects to historicize either his newly enacted language or the language he seeks to transcend—the "meaning and origin of the *concept* of (human) reality" along with that of "man," for instance (*Marg*, 116). Derrida is emphatic about the unignorability of language's historicity, to which its many dimensions of etymology, association, anagrammatics, and so on point. To ignore the "history of the concept" (e.g., of "man" or "reality") renders it "self-evident," without origin, without "historical, cultural, or linguistic limit." That is, it renders it, as an assumed term whose meaning is "understood," a conceptual a priori, something that "goes without saying." The concept becomes self-referential and closes off investigation, suppressing the play of language. For Derrida, a term's historicity is what it always points back toward, as its necessary condition, and that historicity resides in the term as a trace. Echoing Heidegger's judgment that metaphysics renders thought self-referential, he relates language to its historicity as a form of "ontological difference."

For Derrida, the historicity of language occurs in three forms, which he concretely narrativizes in terms of the difference betwen Sartre and Heidegger, in the context of Sartre's essay on humanism and Heidegger's disavowal of Sartre. First, there is a language of that history itself, which Derrida narrates for the other two in the third person. Second, there is a historicity that both Sartre and Heidegger lived in 1946 in the first person, for which the other provided a discursive counterpoint. And third, there is a language of oblique address, by which each of the three renders another historical for himself, as if in the second person. History, historicity, and historicality couch themselves in a syntax of persons, in the midst of which the "first-person plural," the "we" of philosophy, appears.

For Derrida, the philosophical "we" constitutes the self-referential moment of humanism. The self-referential moment of a text is that singular point where the meaning of a sign or a text reveals itself as self-generating, and speculative—the point of self-contextualization where "nothing cannot be made to make sense."[19] It is that signifier in a text that is assumed to be true or legitimate, and from which all else, even that which seems to ground the sign as singularity, follows. In the case of the "we," Derrida points out that it ineluctably speaks for someone else, includes them in something that may not be theirs or that may not be "proper" to them. What Derrida seeks to address is the supplement to such a "we," the possibility of saying "we" without speaking for someone else. That is, he seeks to open the terms of the question in which to differentiate two senses of "we."

To approach the singularity of the philosophical "we," Derrida historicizes the limits of philosophy's notion of "man," its sense of the "ends" of "man," in particular, in phenomenology. For phenomenology, "man" has always appeared in two modes: first, as an objectification of the human, and second, as what transcends objectification by rendering the apprehension of objectification, or of presence, a form of self-presence. Thus, it includes self-presence in its apprehension of presence (*Marg*, 123). For Hegel, he argues, "man" supersedes himself, and the "we" becomes a reunifying synthesis as self-presence (which leads Hegel back into a metaphysical ideality). For Husserl, "man," as transcendent, transcends himself in order to be himself; but if this occurs as ego, self-presence becomes a self-objectification, which reconstitutes the anthropologism it had sought to escape. In both phenomenologies, Derrida concludes, "the name of man" is simply reinscribed in metaphysics, as both an infinite and finite end (*Marg*, 121)—a confluence of the unlimitedness of "man" to "himself" (a transcendental self-referentiality) with his own limitedness as "man" (an anthropological finitude). "Man" is always between these two ends, as an implicit internal fracture in humanism. Each "end" is the condition for the other; "The transcendental end can appear to itself and be unfolded only on the condition of mortality, of a relation to finitude as the origin of ideality" (*Marg*, 123).

If "man's end" is equivocal—an internal difference in humanism itself—then a difference in the "we" of humanism is implicit. To articulate this difference, Derrida turns to Heidegger's "Letter on Humanism." For Heidegger, metaphysics forgot the question of Being by assuming that Being could be understood as beings, as the named. Though metaphysics purports to be about consciousness, or thinking, it sets at its foundation a naming of thinking, as subject or consciousness, which it then understands self-referentially through that name. Thinking names itself, and then understands itself as the thing named. The suppression of the difference between the naming of thinking and thinking itself is what characterizes metaphysics. (It is under this aegis that Heidegger claims Sartre's "cogito" names something while his own use of "ek-sistence" does not.) This conflation suppresses involvement in thinking, and prioritizes a third point of view on what can only be first person. The "we" (as "we" and as "the we") thus marks the boundary between those two.

For Derrida, this is the problem Heidegger sought to avoid through the notion of Dasein. Dasein is the being in closest proximity to Being because it is the being for which Being is a question; but as an entity questioning, it is farthest from Being because it sets itself in ontic self-presence from which the ontological (Being) retreats into the distance. In questioning the meaning of Being, Dasein is both the nearest to Being (in form, as inquiry) and the most distant (as the subject matter of inquiry). The near and the far, in reflecting the ontological difference, avoid the first/third-person problem posed by metaphysics. Dasein is not expressed in the first person; it is named as the site of inquiry into itself, while being "there." But its aporia (questioning the meaning of Being while residing in the unknowability of Being) provides (reproduces) the inarticulability of Being in Dasein that saves it from being a third-person "thing."

Derrida deconstructs Heidegger's inquiry by noticing that the "near" and the "far" map a structure of metaphor which carries Heidegger's argument into the discursive. "It remains that Being, which is nothing, is not a being, cannot be said, cannot say itself, except in the ontic metaphor" (*Marg*, 131). That is, it is within a "metaphoric insistence that the interpretation of the meaning of Being is produced" (*Marg*, 131). Thus, the metaphorics of the near and the far is anterior to the question of the meaning of Being. In effect, Heidegger deploys the language of ontology as a metaphorics in order to critique the ontology that produces that language.

Heidegger's "explicit" use of the "we" then deconstructs along the same lines. Exemplifying the "historical complicity of metaphysics and humanism," Heidegger says, "We *always already* conduct our activities in an understanding of Being" (*Marg*, 124). That is, Heidegger's "we," as well as the "always already" that accompanies it, are determined in correspondence with an understanding of Being that is already accessible to that "we." Having moved back from the "we" of metaphysics ("we men"), one encounters the "we" within the question of the meaning of Being—reinscribing it, Derrida argues, "within the horizon of metaphysics" (*Marg*, 125). But along with the metaphysical "we" that includes (speaks for) others as soon as it pretends to refer, there is also an anterior "we" that is "always already" beyond the objectivity of "inclusiveness." That "we always already comport ourselves" invokes an anterior condition as the condition for there to be a "we" in the first place. Finally, when Heidegger says, "We do not know what Being means," he includes others in this "we" who do not necessarily have the same priorities. The self-referentiality implicit in the non-impositional "we" remains a trace that constitutes the ability of the inclusive (impositional) "we" to mean. The "we" is both in proximity as anterior (presupposed) and distant as imposed. In the first sense, the "we" is not "that," and in the other, it is not "there."

For Derrida, the interior division and incommensurability in the "we" reflects an ambiguity in the metaphysics of humanism that opens the possibility of a "revalorization of the essence and dignity of man" beyond "the name of man" (*Marg*, 128). If this means, for Heidegger, that "man" "must first learn to exist in the nameless" (*Marg*, 129), it recalls for Derrida the need for a sense of the "dignity" of the human, of "man" as his own "proper end." But the structure of this dignity, of both the "we" and the "ends" of "man" as silhouetted in both humanism and in inquiry, is a structure of incommensurability, of a fracture that is inarticulable in the self-referentiality of language. Between the inarticulability of "we" who "concern ourselves" and the definitude of "the we" of the philosophical "we men," there is, without region of overlap, a persistent inseparability or mutual conditioning. It is again a skew structure, which not only does not reduce analytically to two definitudes (rendering both metaphysical), but remains interior to all definitude.[20] And in the positing of "we" and the "ends" of "man," Derrida is adding a silent non- to man, as if to structure this both as act ("we") and non-state ("ends of man"), and state (humanism) and non-act ("man").

And this thus inhabits Heidegger's metaphorics, the near and the far. The near and far of Being in Dasein's inquiry is a double non-negation, the "near" as an act and non-state, and the "far" as a state (being an entity) and non-act (self-referentiality). The presence of this structure here imparts a different definitude, not in the sense of a concept, but that of a relatedness within the project of preserving inarticulability. For Derrida, not only are "man" and Being inseparable in their incommensurability, but their difference is internal to that inseparability. What the anteriority of metaphor to the meaning of Being implies is that, within this space of the "ontological difference," "man" and Being evince a mutual properness, a "co-propriety." "Man is the proper of Being," and "Being is the proper of man" (*Marg*, 133). These two relations, though they be one notion, resist interpretation in that they articulate a conflation of inarticulables. However, they cohabit in the same house, as it were, whispering, as Derrida says, in each other's ear (*Marg*, 133).

By eavesdropping on this secret "whispering" within "co-propriety," Derrida draws a triad of relationships that all reflect the notion of the co-propriety of "man" and Being. First, "the end of man is the thinking of Being"; second, "man is already the end of the thinking of Being"; and third, "the end of man is the end of the thinking of Being" (M, 134). As sibling paraphrases of "co-propriety," they are softly synonymous. But in their formal differences, they diverge metaphorically toward other meanings. The third suggests that man's mortality is the end of questioning, the self-referential anthropological death that ends one's thinking and the question of Being. The first suggests that every telos that "man" sets for him/herself has the thinking of Being within it as its end—or at least as a trace, as mirrored in Heidegger's metaphorics, for instance. The second, finally, is that "man" cannot escape the (inarticulable) self-referentiality that constitutes the space of these endeavors. One is oneself the thinking of Being. The thinking of Being is not elsewhere, nor does questioning carry "man" beyond him/herself.

Thus, these "metaphorize" the three pivotal notions of Derrida's critique—mortality, infinite telos, and co-propriety itself. As such, they constitute a triadic circle. First of all, the presence of mortality, as the condition of self-presence that leads phenomenology back into anthropology, positions mortality as the form that "man" takes as a thinking being. That is, in the context of a critique of "humanism," mortality and its finiteness is the form that the infinite telos of thinking takes. Second, Derrida's notion of co-propriety, that "man is the proper of Being," expresses the anteriority of language to Being (of metaphor to inquiry), an anteriority that is the inescapable content of the infinite telos of "man." The infinite telos of thinking is the form taken by anteriority as co-propriety; in other words, the infinite is the form co-propriety takes.

Finally, co-propriety, the mutual properness of "man" and Being, shows itself to be the form that mortality takes; to see this, we must simply look at the anteriority of language to Being from the perspective of the inescapability of death implicit in that anteriority. One of the meanings attaching to the anteriority of language (to the question of Being) has been signaled by placing quotes insistently around the word "man." These quotes transcribe Derrida's expression "we men," which is in turn a less covert reference to the exclusion of other people who are not male and/or not of this philosophical "we" (nor of its cultural manifestation: the West). The difference between "man" and "people" (some of whom are elsewhere and others of whom are "here" but effaced by the term "man") is generated by these signals (quote marks) from within their use as "language" (in a manner not strictly separable from the enactment of "grammatical" persons—first, second, etc.—of these texts). Exclusion and effacement are things people do—through the term "man" in this case—but which "man" does not do in "his" own terms. People historicize, while "man" gets historicized; "man" is an effect of reading people through those signals that are neither names nor concepts and thus remain indiscernible in their historicization. The anteriority of language puts people in the place of reading "man," and reads "man" in the place of people.

But how, Derrida then asks, does one encounter the mortality contained implicitly in the historicity (where the story of each death is told) that fills the space between "man" and "people"? It is not simply that death (in its properness, as one's own) is knowable only in metaphor, as an extrapolation to oneself of another's death; the other's death is always elsewhere, a sign for what it is not (one's own). Neither can one ignore that one's thinking always already signifies immortality (infinite telos), precisely in the unknowability of one's own death (if one's own death implies that time stops for oneself, and one can never know that time ever stops because death ends all knowing, then for each person time never comes to an end; one lives immortal in the first person, and only dies in the third). Death is a metaphor that can never be literalized; it remains a sign that is not what it is. In other words, the anteriority of language, in which death is both an endless metaphoricity and a name for what is always elsewhere, is the necessary condition for mortality. That is, co-propriety, as the anteriority of language to Being, including the necessity of metaphor and name to mortality, is the form that mortality (not death) takes. (And we must not lose sight of the fact that the chauvinism in the term "man" and the ethnocentrism of the philosophical "we" are both ineffacable from this argument, thereby locating this notion of mortality only within the Western philosophical deployment of this "man" and this "we.")

The familiar circle thus enacts itself (with a circularity that is Heideggerian, an enactment that is Sartrean, and a self-referentiality that is Derridean). Mortality is the form infinite telos takes; infinite telos is the form co-propriety takes; and co-propriety is the form mortality takes. Indeed, the first moment of this circle represents Derrida's critique of Sartre's acceptance of a unitary humanism, and the deconstructive division to which Sartre had already subjected it between presence and self-presence. The second moment of this circle represents Derrida's critique of Heidegger's acceptance of a unitary Being, as the philosophical "we," and the deconstructive division to which Heidegger had already subjected it in his ontological difference between Being and "Man." The third moment represents Derrida's own discussion of the "ends of man" with respect to his critique of language as anteriority itself, and the deconstructive division of those ends between a metaphorics and a naming, an "always already" as co-propriety.

This Derridean circle raises the question of what it means that the philosophical "we," the "humanism" of Western metaphysics, and the "ends" of "man" are all equivocal in the same way, in pointing to how the double non-negation operates as a sign in each text, and how one is to read it. In Derrida's discourse, it is a structure of incommensurability and a textual form that names the space delimited by the anteriority of language to Being (for Derrida), the anteriority of Being to Dasein (for Heidegger), and the anteriority of the for-itself to language (for Sartre). These three pairs of forms of being (to which they as terms refer) are incommensurable when developed into discourses that investigate their relationships as pairs. But among these three, the circle forms, in which each element becomes no longer an "element" but a mediation of its own form and content, in a braid of themselves around the circle. That is, in the circle, these incommensurable discourses acheive a different kind of coherence.

Mediation

From Heidegger's "backward and forward" analytic method, which Sartre appropriates and incorporates into his account of temporality, and which Derrida structures as the trace in his discourse on systems of differences and absences, circularities emerge. There is Heidegger's circle of the meaning of Being, by which he avoids articulating Being as an entity. There is Sartre's circularity of the subject, by which he wrests an account of consciousness from the grip of the Cartesian cogito. And there is Derrida's circle of humanism between the finitude and infinite horizon of human ends (death, telos, and the historicity of looking back), which he reconstructs as a sense of human co-propriety. What is it that takes us from the "backward and forward" to the circle? What is implicit in the form of the "backward and forward" that needs the circle for its own purposes? Let us look at this, since the circle will occupy a central place in this discussion.[21] The phenomenon of the circle poses the question of what drives its circling.

For Heidegger, the "backward and forward" movement (*BT*, 28) arises from the fact that Being is both the questioning and the questioned; the questioning of Being is an act of Being whose attention to itself as interrogation looks back at where it came from. For instance, consciousness, ahead of itself, looks back at itself as already revealed to be up ahead.[22] Or, in Heidegger's investigation of understanding, understanding is always ahead of itself, while pointing back to what has become it. In addressing the role of presupposition, the act of revealing it takes itself as its presupposition, and presupposition is what is revealed. These are all forms of movement found in Heidegger's text (*Being and Time*), an endless movement that gets transformed into an inner reasoning. It is a form of circularity insofar as, in moving forward toward what is to be investigated, one encounters there, already in place, the foundation from which one's investigation comes; each concept points to the foundation that has already pointed to that concept. It is a formalism that differentiates what Heidegger is doing from that of analytic logic. What rationalist logic sees as a circle, Heidegger sees the circle as—namely, a formalism.[23]

In Heidegger's "backward and forward" analytic, the fact of questioning (the activity contained in inquiry) already implies a knowledge of what is questioned. One is always ahead of oneself, but only in an implicit sense. If the purpose of inquiry is to make this knowledge explicit, to articulate it, then that implicit knowledge is its necessary condition, that which it always points back to. There is an act of questioning ("Inquiry itself is the behaviour of a questioner"; *BT*, 24) that, in explicating the implicit, opens inquiry to a response, to an articulate meaning (what one encounters in the inquiry). But if the response must conform in some sense to the question's explicit terms, then it is those explicit terms that implicitly guide the meaning of the response. Thus, the response as such is always already an implicit understanding in form whose content is opened to explicitness by the fact of inquiry itself. Thus, for Heidegger, the meaning of the response is not what the question lacks in being a question; the question always had implicit knowledge of it. The relation of response to question is not one of signified to signifier, but one of bearing witness, a relation of artifact to the process producing it.

And herein, the circle is produced. The act of response (making the implicit explicit) conforms to the fact of inquiry (what is articulated in questioning); the fact of response (what is articulated explicitly by the investigation) conforms to the act of response (what had been implicit in it as response); and the existence (fact) of inquiry conforms to the fact of response (what the investigation encounters in its forward motion). Thus, an inquiry becomes a circle containing the fact of inquiry, the act of response, and the fact of response, all conditioning each other, each being the mediation between the other two in a whole, an interaction of form and content around the circle that constitutes inquiry itself. And it reveals an interwoven structure. The act of responding, as a recognition of what is implicit, gives form to the fact of questioning, the terms of the question whose implicit projected knowledge becomes its content—that is, the signified for which the act of questioning is the signifier. The actual response gives form to the act of response, the existence of which becomes its content as the knowledge discovered (made explicit) in the investigation. And the existence of the inquiry, the fact of questioning, gives form to that explicit response, that which renders it knowledge discovered in an inquiry, for which the response provides the actual content. Form and content are aporetically divided in each of the circle's three moments, and braided by the act of circling.[24]

This same structure appears again in Heidegger's discussion of "understanding" (*BT*, 194). For Heidegger, "understanding" names the way Dasein existentially confronts its possibilities in the world; it exists in reciprocity with "interpretation," where "interpretation" names the act of rendering possibility explicit. As an act of Being (which is already revelatory), understanding confronts the fact of Being (which is always presupposed). As an act of understanding (which is not yet explicit), interpretation explicates possibility (which leads to the fact of understanding). Understanding grounds itself on interpretation, and interpretation grounds itself on understanding. "Any interpretation which is to contribute understanding, must already have understood what is to be interpreted" (*BT*, 194).

Heidegger is explicit that this is not a vicious (logical) circle. "If we see this circle as a vicious one and look for ways of avoiding it, . . . then the act of understanding has been misunderstood. . . . In the circle is hidden a positive possibility of the most primordial kind of knowing" (*BT*, 195). And it differs from the Gadamerian hermeneutic circle, in which two things mutually condition each other's existence (such as the whole and its parts, which can be seen as "metadiscursive" to each other), in that Heidegger posits a forward dynamic in which each establishes the other in order to reestablish itself. There is an "in-order-that" or "for-the-sake-of-which" (*BT*, 120) whose effect is that each expresses the other ontologically as the other's mode of existence. "The 'circle' in understanding belongs to the structure of meaning" (*BT*, 195). Finally, insofar as this is not a dialectical relationship, while appearing bipolar, it raises the question of what, conceptually, brings it back around in itself.

If the act of interpretation explicates the fact of understanding and gives it form as explicitness, and the act of understanding makes possible the fact of interpretation by giving it aboutness, a more complex interlink is extant. Concerning understanding, Heidegger says, "In every understanding of the world, existence is understood with it" (*BT*, 194); that is, understanding understands both what exists and existence itself. The meaning of understanding is the understanding of existence, implying that all understanding is to be a grasp of Being. Its form as circularity signifies that it understands at a primordial level of inquiry; the meaning of understanding is precisely to inquire into the meaning of Being. Thus, the meaning of understanding is the inquiry into the meaning of Being, which interpretation makes explicit, while the form of understanding to which interpretation applies itself is the understanding of existence (the Being questioned), which is understanding as the meaning of Being. The meaning of Being mediates understanding and interpretation.

Where the act of understanding (its form) makes possible the fact of interpretation (its content), it is in the form of being the Being questioned; and where the fact of understanding (its meaning or content) is made explicit by interpretation (its form), what is made explicit is the inquiry into the meaning of Being. The inquiry into the meaning of Being finds its form in interpretation and its content in understanding. Understanding finds its form in the meaning of Being and its content in interpretation. Interpretation finds its form in understanding and its content in the inquiry into the meaning of Being. That is, the mediation by the meaning of Being runs both ways. The inquiry into the meaning of Being realizes itself (generates its content) in understanding, which realizes itself (generates its content as explicit) in interpretation, which in turn realizes itself (generates its content, what it is essentially about) in the inquiry into the meaning of Being. The form the inquiry into the meaning of Being takes is interpretation, which produces its content as understanding; the form interpretation takes is understanding, which produces its essential content as the meaning of Being; and the form understanding takes is the inquiry into the meaning of Being, which produces its content in the explicitness of interpretation (and I am being a little repetitive here, so that the nature of braiding of form and content becomes clear).

Returning to Heidegger's ontological circle, we see that it takes this same form. Being is the basis for the meaning of Being; the meaning of Being is the basis for the unknowability of Being; the unknowability of Being is the basis for Being. This gets transformed into: The nature of Being is to inquire into the meaning of Being; the meaning of Being is to be the Being questioned; to be the Being questioned is the nature of Being. That is, between each two elements of the circle, the third is the mediation back. Each two elements are in double relation through the third. In other words, in Heidegger, this triadic circle would be the general form of mediation as such. Where he investigates the various dimensions of Being and the meaning of Being through his "backward and forward" method, he must generate a circle to provide a form of mediation for each moment; and those forms of mediation generalize themselves into this triadic circle of elements.[25]

We have previously found similar circles in both Sartre and Derrida. For Sartre, the activity by which one makes oneself who one becomes is intentional; intentionality is the attribute of a subject; and the subject is engendered by activity. Derrida's deconstruction of humanism constitutes a circle: Mortality is the form infinite telos takes; infinite telos is the form co-propriety takes; and co-propriety is the form mortality takes. Indeed, all three circles within the discourses of these thinkers are the structures for their respective versions of "the human way to be."

But we want to be careful here. The triad is not a triplet; we are not dealing with trinities. The elements of the circles are not separable in that sense into independent monadic moments. Rather, the circle provides the structure whereby any element comes back to a prior element from which it had arisen, and between which there is a relation of form and content. Form implies content, but content does not imply a particular form except as mediated by something that is comparably related to both, that can take that content as its form. Hence the necessity for a third element to mediate a return. Mediation is the third. It is not the mediation of pairing, as in the hermeneutic circle, nor the dialectical mediation bringing its relata into existence through their relatedness. The third mediates between the other elements it renders the third for its own relations to them, endlessly, around the circle. The circle constitutes a structure that signifies (and represents) mediation as such.

Thus, the triadic circle presents a generalized and self-referential structure of mediation. It is the most minimal structure for representing mediation abstractly, as a generalized notion. It also signifies that each pair of elements on the circle inherently contains a dimension of aporia, which is surpassed by mediation. In the Sartrean circle, the relation of originarity of activity to the subject, and the priority of intentionality to that activity, represent aporetic relations that appear, in Sartre's discourse, as a paradoxical logic. In the triadic circle, the paradox dissolves into mediation, as a reestablished intelligible connection. Mediation generates the circle by integrating itself and the elements mediated in a form of intelligibility, and the circle generalizes mediation by providing each moment as a third term for an aporetic pair. The circle substitutes itself for axiomatic foundations by means of its self-referentiality, producing itself (as foundational) through the circularity of its endless braiding. As mediation in general, it becomes the "materiality" of inarticulability. For each triad that the circle renders self-referential, it constitutes a ground through its equiprimordiality of component elements, without the necessity of an axiomatics. It is a foundation that preserves inarticulability while dispensing with the necessity of foundations or metaphysical ground.

The Triadic Circle in Its Historical Moment

And this now suggests a way of articulating a structure between Sartre, Derrida, and Heidegger, beyond Heidegger's role as common precursor. There are political questions that arise in this confluence. Philosophy is not devoid of its political bearing. Circling discloses itself in the interior of their texts, engendering a special relationship; it requires contextualization in their common (and singular) history.

"The Ends of Man" is a paper Derrida presented at a conference in 1968, in which he critically addressed both Sartre and Heidegger. His topic was how an ethnocentrism seems to secrete itself paradoxically at the very heart of Western "humanism." Though metaphysical humanism extols universal "Man" and the infinitude of human freedom, it ultimately objectifies the human and anthropologizes "man" in "Western" terms. In other words, it speaks for others in European (Euro-American) terms. The very conference at which he speaks, Derrida suggests, in calling itself an "international philosophical colloquium," is a case in point. In assuming a predefined set of "national" philosophical identities, and a "universality of philosophical discourse" among them, the conference succeeds in absorbing those who may understand philosophy on a different cultural basis, while at the same time excluding others who locate themselves in a different internationality (for example, those peoples involved in resistance against the "forces of order" in Paris, the United States, and Vietnam at the very moment of the colloquium). Though the "democratic" ideal would seem to be served by openly including other traditions, such an invitation would simultaneously undermine that ideal by dint of having extended invitations to those others as "other" (the "other" outside the "universal" that does the inviting).

In short, in thinking the universal figure of "man," the rationalism of metaphysics succeeds in limiting the horizon of thought to "its" figure of "man." "Man" is thus rendered a metaphysical entity rather than the thinker of metaphysics. And at the same time, a chauvinism of Western thinking imposes itself upon a diverse humanity that Western humanism seeks to make universal. The "oneness" of the "family of man" pretends to be all while getting caught in the act of looking at itself. And Derrida asks, is it possible to say "we" without speaking for someone else, without including others in a "we" that is not theirs, nor proper to them? This is the historical context in which he addressed Western humanism and the philosophical "we," as "we" have seen above.

Though Derrida discusses Sartre only briefly and Heidegger at greater length, he nevertheless engages them in a heretofore unengaged (unconfronted) "confrontation," the one that occurred in 1946 between Sartre's invocation of Heidegger and Heidegger's rejection of Sartre. Derrida thus produces an historical encounter that never occurred. Though Heidegger and Sartre speak of each other, their respective critiques pass silently like ships in the night. Like Heidegger, Derrida raises the "issue" of Sartre to distance Sartre from himself, because he reproaches Sartre for having obstructed a certain philosophical movement that was important to him. But if Derrida succeeds in staging a confrontation between Sartre and Heidegger, it is insofar as he sets them on stage in a melodrama in which Sartre plays the (ethnocentric) Cartesian universalizer, while Heidegger is the elusive detective who catches him red-handed in the act of metaphysics. Of course, as both impresario and performer, Derrida places himself on the same stage. When the curtain rises and the drama proceeds, "we" find Heidegger disputing Sartre's terminology (see above), with Derrida off to the side suggesting in stage whispers that perhaps Heidegger is a little too self-righteous in doing so.

> Is not the opposition of the primordia to the derivative [Being to beings, ek-sistence to existentia] still metaphysical? Is not the quest for an archia in general, no matter with what precautions one surrounds the concept, still the "essential" operation of metaphysics? (*Marg*, 63)

While Heidegger looks askance at Sartre's positioning himself in a Heideggerian tradition, Heidegger produces a doubleness in his own discourse that he does not see. In counterposing his use of "ek-sistence" to the metaphysical (Sartrean) "existentia," he is making a language demand on Sartre that Sartre cannot fulfill. That is, he tacitly says to Sartre: Write like me, though to do so will be to codify my language, render it metaphysical, and hence be not to write like me." It is a secretly programmatic aspect of Heidegger's critique, which reflects a political moment in his essay, laminated onto his own inquiry. What neither Heidegger nor

Derrida see is the chauvinism in it; the stock-in-trade of chauvinism is its statement to those it denigrates: "Be like me, though of course you can't, and I will hold that against you." And Heidegger holds just such an inability against Sartre.[26]

Sartre, of course, is Eurocentric in a different way. Though his "universalization" of "man" is one of absence, there is a doubleness in it as well. To relativize through the contingency of social context, and to understand living that context as necessity, even in the absence of a stated universal, is to couch each situation in the Western philosophical binary of contingency and necessity. This binary bestows an objectivity upon a "situation" that obviates some modes of social participation that may be alien to Western thought. It is alienness that Sartre had sought to deny in categorizing a person's project in terms of acceptance and rejection, acquiescence and rebellion. But he cannot prevent the ossification of these terms.

> A man may be born a slave in a pagan society or a feudal lord or a proletarian. What does not vary is the necessity for him to exist in the world, to be at work there, to be there in the midst of other people, and to be mortal there. (*EH*, 38)

Sartre presents these as "invariants," with a certain "thereness" that does not decategorize them, though he claims they are "neither subjective nor objective."[27]

Sartre had the reputation of being a relativist because he respected other cultural traditions, despite the intrusion of such invariants in his thinking. Indeed, the political question of "relativism" has been levied as a "charge" against him, a form of rationalist (and hierarchical) judgment against cultural autonomy and difference. The charge against relativism asserts the existence of absolutes of moral judgment or ethical discourse, which becomes self-contradictory. To judge from an ethical absolute is to reserve for oneself the power to hold an ethical absolute as part of who one is. But an ethical absolute would then have to admit itself elsewhere, granting the same power to all others to be themselves, from within their own ethical absolutes of judgment. The very existence of an absolute, because it inhabits self-identification, necessitates a relativism, if it is not to deny the other's judgment as such through imposition rather than judgment. But relativism is not a question of agreeing with the other; it is a matter of hearing him/her, of listening and responding in coordinate terms, as the basis for dialogue. The act of granting the other his/her own judgment is the absolute necessity upon which dialogue can proceed. Situational (dialogic) relativity implies an absolute; and the absoluteness of one's being implies relativism.

This only restates the Sartrean ontological difference. Situational freedom or unfreedom is possible only on the basis of absolute ontological freedom. Ontological freedom is the trace by which moments of situational freedom or unfreedom can exist. But these too are Western philosophical terms.

Ultimately, the difference between Sartrean Eurocentrism and Heideggerian chauvinism implies a programmatic conflict. For Sartre, we are immersed in the ideologies, doctrines, and projects of the world, from which there is no escape, yet in which freedom remains absolute. And his program is that one be authentic in that (absolute) freedom. Heidegger's program is to live in the "nameless." But if the "real" difference between Sartre and Heidegger in their "humanism" is programmatic, then their dispute on humanism becomes a political one, immersed in a real historicity. The historical context for both is World War II. Postwar France lurks in everything Sartre says in *Existentialism Is a Humanism*: in his choice to popularize, his stories and terms, and the role he gives phenomenology. If the form of his presentation amounts to a promotion of existentialism, then the act he performs in that historical context is what is programmatic. It is a call for liberation from given a prioris (be they Marxist, Christian, etc.), a call to live the world.

For Heidegger too, the war lurks in what he says. He has just been through investigation by Allied de-Nazification procedures and knows he has left much unspoken concerning his membership and activity in the Nazi Party up to 1945.[28] Perhaps he addresses himself to Sartre's lesser text, in a high-powered discussion of a small popularization (rather than to *Being and Nothingness*) because, for a man in his position, it is better to let the unspoken be and not call undue attention to himself, while still attempting to reestablish himself. His text is thus programmatic, while the historical act he performs with it is a promotion—of himself.

In effect, the differentiation in the philosophical "we" that Derrida was looking for has split in more than one way. In Heidegger, it has divided against itself between a "humanist" "we" and a chauvinist "we," while in Sartre, it has divided between an "existential" "we" and a metaphysical "we." And in part, it is to retreat from the chauvinist or metaphysical dimension of their respective steps toward alternate "humanisms" that each becomes programmatic.

However, the same thing happens to Derrida. He criticizes the preconceptuality of Sartre's "human reality" and argues that phenomenological ontology, in the guise of anthropologism, imprisons the human behind its conception of itself. Though Sartre opposes his ontology to a metaphysical unity of Being, Derrida charges that this opposition pretends to be more than it is.

> *It goes without saying* that the metaphysical unity of Being, as the totality of the in-itself and the for-itself, is precisely the unity of human-reality in its project. . . . What was named in this way . . . was nothing other than the metaphysical unity of man and God. (*Marg*, 116)

But Sartre's notion of human reality, his "response" to the question of "the unity of Being," is precisely that no unity is possible between the for-itself and the in-itself, that human reality is the impossibility of the unity of Being. The for-itself, in its being, is "made to be" in relation to its object (being-in-itself), which is in turn nihilated by the for-itself; that is, the for-itself is what it is not, and not what it is. Sartre does not deny that "human reality" is conceptual, but it is so only in silhouetting the inarticulable at its core, from which it emerges.

> Each human reality is . . . a direct project to metamorphose its own for-itself in an in-itself-for-itself and a project of the appropriation of the world as a totality. . . . Man loses himself as man in order that God may be born. But the idea of God is contradictory and *we* lose ourselves in vain. (*BN*, 615)

If this "we" represents "human reality," it shifts Sartre's discourse from a generality of human reality as man (the conceptual dimension for which freedom is the inarticulable), to a "we" who are narrativized, and thus ensconced in the futility of this "end." "We" are both included in Sartre's generalization and excluded in being told "we" cannot do what it is this inclusion requires to be done. Insofar as being-for-itself is what it is not and is not what it is, Sartre's "we" becomes a narrativized case of this structure; that is, "we" become a narratived case of that structure. And what "goes without saying" for Derrida, that the "unity of human reality" can be realized for Sartre, is precisely what is not said.

In other words, Derrida is speaking for Sartre by refusing to recognize his use of narrative. And this is important because Sartre often embeds his discourse of subjectivity in narrativities precisely to preserve specificity, the subject's individuatedness, and the inarticulability of its (non)foundations.[29] Though Derrida insists on the internal difference in the "we" and the "human," he does not extend this to the operation of all signifiers, such as "human reality" in Sartre's text. Finally, if each subjectivity approaches itself anew and as different, then the for-itself is not generalizable as such.

Ultimately, the "we" of philosophy is that through which Derrida historicizes himself, and which provides a rubric for a critique of ethnocentrism. From the initial necessity to historicize the concepts of metaphysics, Derrida has reread and rewritten the language of those concepts, that of "we" and "man," which divide against themselves. The divisions revealed therein point to Derrida's programmatic. For him, the call is to "speak several languages . . . at once" (*Marg*, 135), a deployment of language designed to break the arrow of history that is "played out in the violent relationship of the whole of the West to its other" (*Marg*, 134). And this implies the West's launching an arrow against itself from that "elsewhere" (its own violence) as its own other target. This involves the violence that already attends the power of definitude, the violation of what is "proper" to "man" through an axiomatics of "man," the violence produced by the definitionality of metaphysics, which through its definitude is used to justify colonialism and chauvinism.

It is to launch such an arrow that Sartre constructed his circle of activity, intentionality, and the subject; and Derrida the circle of mortality, infinite telos, and co-propriety; and Heidegger the circle of the meaning of Being, and inquiry into Being, and the unknowability of Being. And within each circle, there is the space of the inarticulable that each posits as an "ontological difference." These also interweave, as a circle of anteriorities—of language to Being, Being to Dasein, and the for-itself to language. However, the fact that a circle of anteriorities exists means that Heidegger does not just mediate between Sartre and Derrida. He becomes a member of their common triadic circle.

Conclusion: The Structures of Ethnocentrism

Out of the inarticulables of each of these discourses, and the incommensurabilities they have generated among these texts, a system of homologous circularities has emerged. The content of each inarticulable is a mode of ontological difference, whose guises are Being and beings, writing in general and sign systems, ontological and situational freedom. But that common role of an "ontological difference" is not sufficient to overcome the incommensurabilities that the disparity of inarticulables generates. Indeed, the formal terms each generates in his respective discursive articulations around it are even more disparate: the near and the far, the "always already," and the for-itself that is what it is not and is not what it is. Yet it is across that disparity that a homology is possible. And it results in a strange circularity that evades philosophical confrontation because it provides a structure in which they seem to reach out to each other. For Sartre, meaning produces writing as its being; for Derrida, writing produces being as its meaning; for Heidegger, being produces meaning as its advent or expression in the world (its writing).

Homological commonality bestows upon the circle a certain iconicity. It signifies the inarticulable and the interrelatedness of inarticulables, without representing a dialogue or mutual involvement between them. By engendering a coherence to their interrelatedness, the circle actually provides an articulation of conjunction. In transcending incommensurability toward such a coherence, it points back to the nature of inarticulability of which it is composed, and from which it differs. Thus, this circle diagrams the scene of an ethics of the inarticulable.

The inarticulable is a signified without a signifier that can only be discerned in the guise of intimations or in the disguise of implications. It exudes a certain inviolability, which in turn implies a desire that its inarticulability remain inviolate. Sartre does not want to violate the absoluteness of freedom; he would have to do so to recognize the discursive distinction between the ontological and ontic "we," since that recognition would ground the subject in a plural context. For him, each subject, through its project, points to a particular context that precedes discourse, and by which it makes itself the project or subject that it is. Heidegger does not want to violate the absoluteness of Being; he would have to do so to recognize Sartre's ontological distinction between freedom and the project, since that would imply recognizing a plurality of inarticulables. For him, ontic beings point only to a oneness of inarticulable Being that precedes ontology, the trace of which then presents itself as beings and indeed as projects. Derrida does not wish to violate the absoluteness of a sign structure's self-referential singularities, of writing in general; he would have to do so to recognize a non-Heideggerian, nontranscendent inarticulable in Sartre's text, since that would affirm a plurality of anteriorities, beyond language as anteriority itself. For him, the extended notion of "text" still points to itself as writing, as a system of signs, that precedes all philosophical systems, and in which a particular structure of differences, sometimes discernible as textual form, constitutes it as the writing that it is.

In effect, each thinker produces the context required to preserve the particular inarticulable that renders it the text (and context) that it is. In so doing, each grants that inarticulable a mode of "philosophical sacredness," the reading of which entails a "taboo" toward any articulation within the space it empowers.

The circle of readings, such as Derrida staged, reveals that each reading participates in what empowers a different space of "sacred" inarticulability. At this level, however, the homological relation across differential forms of "sacredness" provides them with a formal commensurability, which the circle iconizes. Outside the circle, the common desire to preserve inviolability produces a blindness to that commensurability. Blindness excludes, and exclusion represents exclusiveness. It is only the completed circle of interwoven "inarticulables" that becomes what "sees" and articulates plurality and becomes inclusive. To sunder the circle again would leave each of its component discourses in its "sacred" isolation.

As a weave of inviolabilities that thereby transcends inviolability (even as philosophical "sacredness"), the circle generates a space of non-imposition, because the modes of imposition implicit in inviolability, of "we" and "we men" (ontological and ontic, we and the others) divided against themselves, lose their coherence as form and content in being interwoven through the mediation of form and content in the operation of triadic circularity. The circle iconizes a non-impositional "we" that "speaks" more than one language at a time.

And herein a certain access to the question of ethnocentrism and chauvinism resides. When Derrida counterposes Heidegger to Sartre to elicit a difference in the philosophical "we," he reveals a difference in ethnocentrism itself. When Heidegger refuses Sartre's "we," his form of the inarticulable, he exiles Sartre to a "they" of metaphysicians, of those excluded by their refusal of the inarticulability of Being. These are political operations. The first marks the ethnocentrism of inclusion in a "we" that is not one's own, and the second reflects the structure of a chauvinist act. Ethnocentrism is a blindness to the violation of identity produced by inclusion, and chauvinism is a violation via identity avowing itself through exclusion. Though incommensurable, both relations would be mediated by a circle that wove each in with the other. Instead, they rely on a sundered circle. In Sartre's text, the "we" is shown to impose in the name of a universal (albeit a universality of indeterminacy); and Sartre's "I," in filling the space between the indeterminate and the narrative, points to the inarticulable as freedom. In Heidegger's text, the "we" is shown to include the space between the inarticulable and the discursive; and Heidegger's "I" imposes a discourse in the name of a language that points to the Heideggerian unspoken. Each pretends to a humanism of inclusion that would obviate the dehumanization of exclusion, yet excludes through the universalism implicit in their humanism.

Derrida had forewarned of all this in "The Ends of Man." He offers two deconstructions of Western metaphysics and two possible mediations back to the circle. The first deconstruction is the project of using the language of the metaphysical edifice against itself from within, risking a deepening reconfirmation of the very language in which its own definitudes and rationalisms are couched, without undoing the violence (neither as definitude, nor as colonialism, nor as "law and order," for instance). The second attempts to escape that edifice, to engender a differentiation that would oppose it from elsewhere. It, in turn, risks reconstructing a similar edifice on similar though displaced ground through that very process of opposition. Heidegger enacts the trap implicit in the first deconstruction, falling prey to the chauvinist impulse of renewed exclusions, the impossible condition that the other "speak like me" while remaining irremediably other. Sartre enacts the trap implicit in the second deconstruction, falling prey to a reabsorption of difference, even while stepping outside the positive axiomatics of metaphysics, blind to the imposition still contained in the universalization of indeterminacy. Derrida himself sees no structural alternative to these risks, nor to the traps of chauvinist and ethnocentric imposition they entail.

The circle is a sign that seems to point to an alternative, not least of which because both ethnocentrism and chauvinism require its sundering. Chauvinism sunders the circle to generate or preserve the identity for which others are objects, while ethnocentrism breaks the circle to render identity an object. The sundering of this circle throws each text back upon its interior circularity, which now can be seen to insulate its particular inarticulable and preserve its inviolability.

In opposition to this, the "external" homological circle provides certain conceptual possibilities. It preserves the inarticulables without remaining in inarticulability. Thus, it transforms the inviolabilities on which chauvinism depends. Its circularity conjoins identity and non-identity in a manner that is participatory and non-impositional. In mediating incommensurabilities, it defuses the two ethnocentric operations by reimmersing them in the "other" they impose upon. The circle does not present a cultural or a political alternative to chauvinism, because it is only a form. It suggests the possibility of an arena of alternative in which difference and the incommensurability of inarticulables can be respected and thus included in social articulation, without programmatic projects that would reduce to social oppositions reconfirming the structures of chauvinism or ethnocentrism in that very opposition. While the circle is not programmatic, however, it is not a silencing either. Silence is not what resides within the inarticulable; it only clothes an efflorescence of language that can transcend axiomatic thinking. It is axiomatics that silences, by rendering the univocal and the universal a violence and an imposition.

5 The Look and Its Inner Narrativizations

WE HAVE RECONTEXTUALIZED the incommensurability between Sartre and Derrida through Heidegger and arrived at a structure of mediation in general. The triadic circle does not render its components any less incommensurable individually, but it interweaves the threads of discursive form and content in a way that then spans the space between them. And in doing so, it suggests a foundation for discussion among discourses such as these that have called into question the very possibility of philosophical foundations as such, but does so incommensurably. Separately, each of them insists on an indeterminacy at the foundation of their own thinking; and each reveals a structure of mediation in general that concretely obviates foundations. Thus, the forms by which they move from that indeterminacy, as a trajectory of thought, have homologous centers, though they do not take analogous paths.

The structure of the circle provides Sartre and Derrida with a common dwelling place, a philosophical neighborhood where the various structures of their thinking might form a vocabulary of conversation. As members of a "circle," they inhabit an ecological domain of discourse. It is not a commonly recognized domain. Their respective inner reasoning, expressing a double non-negational logic, however, seems to characterize an ideational relationship in the history of contemporary philosophy. Around the double non-negation and the circle that mediates it, a space opens up in which they might talk. This is not a suggestion of a common language between them; the problems of that have been addressed. What their conversation might do is make the discernibility of the world larger.

Finding them in this circle, which composes them as it is composed by them, seems to suggest some kind of triadic primordial Aristophanic relation, is if the circle were the trace of an arcane analysand from which each had been evicted through ineluctable analytic processes, and left to wander diasporically through twentieth-century thought. But their meetings are not accidental. Perhaps it is to allow each to tell the other his story that this circular link becomes compelling. Perhaps the link suggests itself because each has already let it be known that he has a story, and that the other is already engaged in it, beyond the aura of being kindred souls.

That, of course, is not how they saw each other—though Derrida has said that he has never abandoned his understanding of what has always linked him in some fashion to Sartre. But what conjoins them more emphatically is the way they look away from each other. Each knew, during the moment of their contemporaneity in France, that they were seen by the others, critically and in silence. Each was discovered by the other in his respective philosophical location, peering over at what the other was doing.

But having found a common neighborhood for them, and perhaps even a common café table, though still in the absence of that (as yet) common language, let us have them look at each other, in lieu of speaking in all its continuing incommensurability.

THE LOOK

In Sartre's account of the look (*le regard*),[1] for which he tells the story of someone discovered peering through a keyhole, the object of the story is not the voyeur's gaze, nor what the one discovered is seen to be doing. It is about the ontological character given the one who discovers him/her, and the ontological transformations that occur to the one seen upon being discovered. It is a narrative that is perfused with Sartre's paradoxical logic, his deployment (as we have seen) of double non-negations. If we enter this realm of narrative, we unavoidably enter an interface with the social, with the world of people and how people look and notice each other both in recognition and in distance.

As both a topic and an image, the look resides at the center of Sartre's ontology. Sartre's account of one's visibility to another is Sartre's response to the question of the other as subject.[2] For Sartre, the problem is how to give an ontological account of another subjectivity without falling into the solipsism of attributing one's own subjectivity to it; that is, the apprehension of other subjectivities without projection of oneself. Traditionally, philosophy had stumbled on this question as a "solipsist trap" (*BN*, 244ff.). Even Heidegger, Sartre argues, falls prey to it. Heidegger describes Dasein's apprehension of another Dasein on the basis of Dasein already being aware of itself and thus already knowing what is to be encountered in the Other. For Heidegger, the Other is always already grasped because being-in-the-world can only be founded on Being-with others (*BT*, 154ff.). But Sartre detects a solipsism within "Being-with others" insofar as Dasein is already that by which there is (*es gibt*) a world, and hence an Other as such.

Against this, Sartre gives an account in which one apprehends the Other as a subject not through oneself but rather as a disruption of oneself and one's world. For Sartre, the look is a site of discovery, of discovering oneself in the sight of the Other. Already in the world, one confronts an Other in a space that is both one's own and not of one's choosing; in that space, one grasps the Other's subjectivity by becoming an object for that other (*BN*, 259). It is one's sense of being an object for that other which generates one's sense of the other as the subject for whom one is that object. That is, Sartre's sense of being-in-the-world permits the world in turn to beset as a world without one getting lost in the ontic, in the "they" of the world.[3]

The Other-as-Object

Sartre introduces his account of "the look" through its inverse, seeing another in the distance as an object (which he narrates in the first person). The Other, seen in the distance, is an object for me. Yet the Other already appears as a different kind of object because the things of my world are also objects for that Other. The Other "sees what I see"; the world (as "my world") is present to the Other's eyes without distance (*BN*, 256). Seen as seeing, the Other presents a kind of animal center, one that is complete, like an object, yet hidden in its autonomy. And this other center decenters my world and my relation to it. The world "flees" toward the Other; its immediacy to myself is replaced by an immediacy to the Other, precisely because the Other appropriates it by seeing it (*BN*, 254). The Other becomes a hole in the universe through which the world appears to drain away (*BN*, 255).

> The Other is defined not as the absence of a consciousness in relation to the body which I see but by the absence of the world which I perceived, an absence discovered at the very heart of my perception of this world. (*BN*, 256)

"An element of disintegration" is added to the world. Though nothing has changed and the objects of one's world are still there, they now have other meanings. Their differences have become different. As objects they disperse, not to a future (because they are already of the past) but to a temporal elsewhere. One's comprehension can no longer "put itself at the center" of the world (*BN*, 255). Indeed, Sartre's account becomes an allegory for the erasure of all centers precisely in the sense of being a first-person narrative that decenters the first person.

At the same time, the flight of one's world toward the Other provides a foundation for objectivity. To see the Other seeing defers one's world as different and renders each object equivocal in its appearance of simple "thereness." There is no longer a simple "thereness" with respect to which the object can be *this* object for oneself. Its "thereness" for the Other abstracts the object itself from the question of point of view. It provides a different distance whose detachment characterizes the objective view. In short, when I see the Other seeing, I am caught between my world becoming polyvalent and ambiguous, and the world becoming definable by being "there" for the Other as well as myself. The Other-as-object transforms a world written by and for oneself into one that must now be read; that is, one is transformed from a writer of one's own world into a reader of a world. Because the world is rendered equivocal with respect to its "mine-ness," it acquires a sense of "objectivity" through the abstraction of being seen by others, which empties it.

This transformation has a structure. Through the now emptied objects of my (convulsed) world, I look at the Other-as-object, and I see what is not there; I interact with the Other as object, and I interact with what is not that.[4] The first is a deferral of the Other; the Other is a non-act (a hidden consciousness) and a state (the disruption of my world). The second is the appearance of difference; the Other is an act of seeing my world that at the same time empties it by centering it in the other's hidden autonomy (a non-state). The Other-as-object becomes a sign, and the encounter an allegory, for Derridean différance; différance surfaces in the world through immersion in the other's disruptive operation. To read the world through this allegory is to read a world of objectivities whose meanings are deferred to an elsewhere as well, while being different from objects-for-me. In apprehending the other-as-object (in alterity), I apprehend another who stands in a formal relation of allegory, that is, of narrative, to my relation to the world, and to the meanings I apprehend as a system of signs.

The Look

Sartre's account of the look addresses the other as subject, narrated again in the first person. In the look, the visual relation is reversed. One enters the real or imagined perceptual field of another and becomes oneself "present to the [Other's] eyes without distance" (*BN*, 258), like an object. In Sartre's famous example, he is peeping through a keyhole, wholly engrossed in what he sees (that is, prereflectively; not reflectively aware of himself in what he is doing). Suddenly, he hears footsteps and realizes he has been seen. In that moment, the object of his own attention shifts to the Other's look, for which he has become the scene. His preoccupation dissolves, and he resurfaces in self-reflection, awash in shame at being caught. He now finds himself the object of the Other's attention; that is, he is objectivized.[5] And it is by becoming an object for the Other that he apprehends the Other as a subject, a freedom (*BN*, 262). This apprehension does not entail knowing the Other's subjectivity as such (which remains hidden and unknowable). It is not the other that one sees, but rather the look of the other that one apprehends.[6] The other besets as a freedom that remains unknowable as such; one knows oneself to be still a subjectivity but structured as an object with respect to the other—separate yet inseparable, distant yet immediate to the other. What it constitutes is a certainty immanent in becoming an object for the Other that the Other is indeed a subject, a freedom.

The other's subjectivity is thus not a metaphor for oneself, as Hegel or Heidegger would have it. Indeed, the structure of Heidegger's account is inverted. Rather than attribute subjectivity to the Other, one encounters and knows the Other-as-subject as an attribution to oneself, not through the content the other gives to what one is doing, but through the very act for which one is already the content. The other remains unknowable, but apprehended as subject because one becomes the other's knowledge, the object of their subjectivity.

> The appearance of the look is apprehended by me as the upsurge of an ekstatic relation of being, of which one term is the "me" as for-itself which is what it is not, and which is not what it is, and of which the other term is still the "me" but outside my reach, outside my action, outside my knowledge. . . . Through the Other's look I *live* myself as fixed in the midst of the world, as in danger, as irremediable. But I know neither what I am nor what is my place in the world, nor what face this world in which I am turns toward the other. (*BN*, 268)

Three transformations occur to the self-as-object.[7] First, one discovers one has a nature, an "outside" turned toward the world; the self (the "I") finds its foundation beyond itself, in the Other-as-subject (*BN*, 262). Second, there is a loss of project and of instrumentality in the world; one becomes an instrumentality in the Other's project, and one understands oneself as that Other's project. And third, there is a loss of autonomy, or authority, in the world; the once autonomous subject finds itself no longer self-determining. Its foundation abandons it, absorbed and appropriated by the Other's hidden apprehension. Through loss of self, one gains a certain knowledge of the unknowable Other (*BN*, 261) because one becomes the Other's knowledge. One is transformed from being for oneself to an aspect of a situation that is by and for the Other.

> The Other's look makes me be beyond my being in this world and puts me in the midst of the world which is at once this world and beyond this world (*BN*, 261).

In these transformations, one ceases to be pure consciousness, pure project; there is, as it were, a "loss of innocence." No longer an "I" for oneself, one becomes a "me." In undergoing a loss of instrumental contact with the world, and a loss of project, one finds oneself no longer self-determining; instead, one's selfhood, the foundation of one's "self," is discovered outside oneself, lost in and to the Other's hidden apprehension.

In the case of the Other-as-object, the other becomes a hole through which one's world drains away; in the look, one is beset by the other, and one is drained from one's world. In reading the Other's look as an effect on oneself, one is transformed from being a writer of one's world to being part of the world written by the Other; and one becomes the Other's knowledge in being read (as written) by the Other. Thus, the look partially inverts the metaphoric writer-reader transformation of the Other-as-object.

These transformations constitute concomitant facets of a single ontological moment. I shall investigate their inner logic and narrativity in Chapter 6, at which time a series of homological connections will be drawn between them and Derrida's thinking. But preparatory to that, we need to delve further into how reciprocity and existentiality unfold in the look.

In Sartre's account, reciprocating the look returns one to subjecthood by rendering the other an object for oneself—which the other may again reciprocate in turn.[8] The effect would be a potentially endless oscillation of objectivizations. In its extreme, a mode of conflict would ensue, or else some form of contingent mutuality or uneasy balance would evolve. This balance is not of subjectivities, or a mode of intersubjectivity. It is a way in which the Other is apprehended in oneself as an object, equalizing one's being for the Other as an object, in the Other's look. The other is not seen as an Other, but apprehended as an Other looking, an Other-as-a-look. The overarching mode of being that encompasses all the possibilities to arrive out of these encounters Sartre calls one's being-for-others. It contrasts with the Heideggerian *mit-sein*; being-for-others is not being with-others; it is the way others are apprehended as Other and as with one.

Being-for-others is not an ontological structure of the for-itself. That is, it cannot be derived from the for-itself, but must be understood as part of one's being in the world, a facticity of encounter with others, contingent to rather than implicit in being-for-itself (*BN*, 282). Being-for-others is an exterior being to the self, "the condition of my selfness confronting the Other and of the Other's selfness confronting me" (*BN*, 285). In this relation to the existence of the Other in general, the two primary aspects are (1) that the Other is who one has to not-be, who one makes oneself not be, and (2) that one makes the other be in apprehending the other as a subject (*BN*, 285). If one's being-for-others is "irreducibly contingent," it nevertheless emerges through a certain ontological necessity. "The Other whom I recognize in order to refuse to be him is . . . *the one for whom my For-itself is*" (*BN*, 284).

It is by shifting the domain of one's being "for-others" from the for-itself to the "world" that Sartre responds to the Heideggerian *mit-sein*. For Heidegger,

Being-with Others is an existential aspect of Dasein, where being-in-the-world is always Being-with; "the world is always the one I share with Others" (*BT*, 155). Sartre argues that the *mit-sein* is always not yet a self, while relying on that self to participate in the sociality of the "they" (das Man) as the correlate of one's Being-with. For Heidegger, the *mit-sein* only restates the ontological difference that characterizes Dasein. But, Sartre asserts, in the context of the sense of sociality implicit in the *mit-sein*, one cannot be granted one's subjectivity by others without having already granted them their subjectivity, and one cannot grant them their subjectivity without having already granted it to oneself. This is not a circle, in contrast to the hermeneutic circle Heidegger affirms in the ontological difference between the *mit-sein* and the "they." Rather, it constitutes a mode of existential interaction between oneself and Others. The *mit-sein* implies that the self in sociality becomes both impossible and originary. Herein lies the central disparity between the sameness of Being in Heidegger's *mit-sein* and the contingency of the Sartrean Being-for-others. Both start from the recognition that one is always among others, and that one starts with a Dasein that is "one's own" or with Being-for-itself. But from that point, the two diverge—inward toward the ontological difference for Heidegger and outward toward situationality for Sartre.

Sartre does not posit being-for-others as an intersubjectivity, or a project toward intersubjectivity; for him, a desire to reveal oneself as a subject to the other as subject must be self-defeating. To reveal oneself as a subject implies reducing the other to an object in order to do so. For the other to be a subject to whom to reveal oneself, one must submit oneself to becoming an object in turn. Out of reach as a project, one is left only with the desire to reveal oneself as a subject in intersubjectivity; but the situation that desire generates remains unstable and always on the verge of breaking down. Each individual lives under a threat of the other's re-objectivizing look. Both stand ready with a preemptive look in order to preserve their own autonomy, their subjectivity and freedom—in a kind of ontological Cold War. As Sartre himself says, being-for-others "represents the negation of any synthetic totality," (*BN*, 300) a seemingly irresolvable arena of disunion between individuals; "conflict is [its] original meaning" (*BN*, 364). And we might note here that in endlessly obviating synthesis, it suggests that incommensurability is more appropriate to Sartre's account than dialectical reasoning.[9] But these mutual "Cold War stances" should not be interpreted as inherent alienation. The deterence strategies are rather metaphoric for complex conflations of being and individuality, and of living one's world always with and through Others. In part, it is this complexity that Heidegger sought to articulate through the ontological difference; Sartre does it through inclusion of negativity and potential conflict within each moment of active interpersonal conjunction.

It is in this spirit that Sartre claims that the look is always accompanied by shame—the shame of having been rendered an object, the shame of self. But this sense of shame should not be misunderstood. It is an existential shame, rather than a moralistic shame—a distinction akin to that between existential angst and psychological anxiety. It names a mode by which one lives one's freedom; specifically, the mode by which one lives the look as a situation. What Sartre means by "shame" is an allegorical self-confession to being the being that one is (*BN*, 261), of having been "caught in the act" of being who one is. Though "this being that I am preserves a certain indetermination, . . . shame reveals to me that I *am* this being, not in the mode of . . . 'having to be' but in itself" (*BN*, 262). For instance, even for the simple act of sitting down: when alone, one sits without thinking about it; but in the presence of another who is watching, one becomes someone who is "being seating" in a particular way, and the sense of being that someone is what constitutes existential shame. One is given a being and simultaneously beset by it; the other's look irreducibly freezes who one is in the being of one's act, at the same time that the act participates in what one is becoming through it.

There is a danger to which Sartre's concept of existential shame in the look sometimes falls prey. If restricted to morally shameful or negatively valued situations, the sense of shame would restrict the domain of operation of the look by elevating it to the level of essence, conflating existential and moral shame. Many commentators tend to read it that way. Sartre's examples seem to do this, though it is perhaps for purposes of starkness.[10] But other examples are possible. One might be speaking to another person intensely and suddenly encounter the other's look as one of longing, or intimacy. One discovers oneself an object in that intimacy or longing, an object of an unknown, mysterious, perhaps appropriating desire, directed at oneself, in which one apprehends oneself as the Other's hidden knowledge, the other's awareness of desire.[11] Though not a shameful situation, the loss of subjectivity would be experienced as existential shame (perhaps there is blushing). Indeed, one's blushing under the other's look might signify to the other that one has been discovered in the throes of an unwonted behavior and constitute, as a facial expression, a returned look. The reciprocity of the returned look would thus occur wholly within the purview of existentiality. As a footnote to this, it is worth pointing out that while *regarder* in French signifies "to look," it also connotes "to concern" (in the sense that "*il me regarde*" can be read "it concerns me" as well as "he looks at me"). Sartre's narrative of the "look" thus plays across the boundaries between concern, shame, social behavior, and intersubjectivity.

And this brings us to the question of narrativity. A returned look of intimacy, reciprocating its objectivation, would incur the tenuous balance of one's being-for-others, within a reciprocity on the issue of desire or closeness (which is not the same as a reciprocity of desire as such). But how would a person's outward appearance, within a situation of mutual objectivation, and as that situation itself, have become recognizable as representing hidden (let alone reciprocal) desire, in order to constitute that situation? Certain facial expressions, for instance, would already have to be recognizable signifiers, that is, meanings that were to some extent common knowledge. A reciprocity of intimacy would entail mutual readings of facial signifiers in each other's expressions, even within a "tenuous balance" of exchanged looks. Its very tenuousness suggests why love relations require formulation (and continual reformulation) in systems of narratives, of gossip, the love stories of romance magazines, the discourses of marriage ideals and structures, and the methodologies of divorce. Though a "longing look" may seem to come "naturally" to the human face, only narrativization, the *récit* (story) of what a person "has in mind" behind an expression, will enable it to serve as a sign for that secret feeling. It is prior narrativization that enables a facial expression to be recognized and experienced as what is hidden, or to be a signal for détente against alternating objectivations—and ultimately to be a mirror for one's own unseen expressions. In the unfolding of the complex particularities of such encounters, only narrative can fill in for what remains concretely and existentially invisible.

As we have seen, Sartre reserves a special place for narrative in his ontological expositions. Beyond exemplifying or locating consciousness in "its" situation, narrative preserves the subject's particularity. Narrative is, in its broadest, most general form, the account of a particular agent performing a particular action. But we should add that the term *narrative* here does not necessarily mean fiction. It signifies any discourse that recounts an event performed by an individual (or by an "anthropomorphized" object, for that matter). What it does represent, in some fashion, about the "agent" it narrates is some form of intentionality, whether literally or by implication. The narrative of the situationality of a gesture, reaction, or response conceptualizes the gesture or action at the same time that it constitutes that action by narrativizing it; thus, it becomes the account of a conduct. When "the wind caresses the trees," a conduct is described and an intentionality is implied in both the caress and the caressed.

Sartre has explained that he turned to drama and fiction to resolve or investigate questions that could not be explored through philosophical generalization.[12] In his philosophical work as well, his vignettes and examples likewise present the subject as much as represent it. For Sartre, it is the narratable that leads to, rather than follows from, the investigation of persons and world, the intelligibility of the relation between them, and a narrative of the world's actions as well. Narrativity becomes one means of transcending the metaphysics of definability; it opens the way for subjectivity to tell itself rather than to be told. The question of narrativity is thus integral to Sartre's account of the other as subject insofar as both constitute ways of avoiding the generalization of people. Later, the question of the generalization of people will become important.

THE METANARRATIVITY OF THE LOOK

Sartre's account of the look not only contains a narrative, it can be read as a highly complex structure of narratives. In Sartre's well-known example (the story of the peeping tom), there are two entities. The first is the narrator, who is the "I" telling the story of his discovery (at the keyhole) and his objectivation by the (real or imagined) Other;[13] the second is the character narrated, the one who sees, the Other who discovers and objectivizes. What the "I" apprehends, upon becoming an object for the Other (existential shame) through the Other as subject, is a content given his own action—in this case, its moral shamefulness. And that content is inseparable from the first-person narrative (by the "I") of a transformation from prereflectively looking through a keyhole to a self-consciousness of what he is doing morally by doing so, and what he has become.

However, this transformation is not what is discovered by the Other. The Other discovers a person involved in an act. Whether the Other actually considers it a reprehensible act or not is not the question. The Other's judgment is not part of the narrator's knowledge of having become the Other's knowledge. It is the "I," in his transformation to self-consciousness, who recognizes that what the Other has come upon, and is seeing and narrativizing, is reprehensible. It is the "I"'s morality that renders it reprehensible in the eyes of the Other. Though the "I" may know his own reprehensibility (be he peeping from jealousy, vice, or curiosity; cf. *BN*, 259), his act becomes a knowledge for the Other as subject only as an experience of discovery, of seeing. It is that experience of seeing by the Other that the narrator must renarrativize if it is to contain a judgment of reprehensibility.

In other words, there is a complex nesting of narratives. Within the narrator's account of getting caught at the keyhole by an Other, there is first of all a different story, a recognition of himself in a narrative of the other's experience of discovering someone at a keyhole. The narrator of that story (of catching a person in the act) would be the Other who makes the discovery; that is, the other would be the narrator of a narrative of the act of discovering this scene, not the "I"; it is the "eye" of the Other who comes upon it and sees it. What is given to the other to tell in that narrative is also the moral narrative of the discovered act's reprehensibility. Though the "I" tells the story of being discovered, the story of what is discovered experientially and morally is given (by the "I") to the Other to tell—presumably in silence. The other does not act in that narrative; rather, the other undergoes an experience of discovery and a recognition. But the meaning of that recognition (discovering a reprehensible act, for instance) is narrativized by the "I" who is discovered, as part of the transformation of the "I" to becoming self-conscious of having been discovered.

In effect, the story of discovery about the Other (the person making the discovery) is narrated for the Other by the "I" (the one discovered), through which the "I"'s act is given its reprehensibility. That narrative tells of both the experience of discovery and the judgment of what is discovered. The Other "is" only the one who sees the "I" at the keyhole; the Other is subsequently "told" (by the "I") as experiencing a certain meaning or knowledge in that act of discovery. And this all happens in a story the "I" tells himself about the Other. By feeling moral shame in the eyes of this Other, the "I" as narrator (existentially) enacts the Other's knowledge, along with its assumed reprobation. While the Other as a subject remains unknowable to the "I," that "I" as a narrator nevertheless narrates what the Other (who becomes a character in this, the "I"'s narrative) knows, and thus turns the other as character into a narrator of what s/he knows or recognizes in the act of discovery. In a similar fashion, a longing look that renders one an intimate object for the Other is a story whose substance, as the Other's longing, one tells oneself through the Other and for the Other at the moment of discovering oneself the Other's (intimate) object.

In short, the narrative of being discovered is a narrative told through the Other, given to the Other to be told, and by which the Other is narrativized as a subject. That is, for the "I" to apprehend himself as shameful in the Other's look, the Other must be narrated as renarrating for him/herself the act discovered as shameful.

This means that the "I" as narrator becomes a character in a narrative of what is discovered, and which is told by the Other at the same time that the "I" narrates the Other as a character who discovers him at the keyhole in all his ignobleness. The "I" narrates the Other as a character in the act of discovering the narrator, and narrates himself as a character for the Other's narrative, in the Other's narrative of discovery, and through the Other as narrator.

Thus, the look is a double narrative. The narrator as "I" narrates his/her being discovered by another, and in turn becomes a character in a narrative of the other's actual discovery for which the Other is the narrator, but which is told for the Other in the enveloping narrative in which the Other is a character told by the "I" as narrator. The character (Other) in the first narrative becomes the narrator (Other) of a second narrative in which the first narrator ("I") becomes a character ("I"). It is a chiasmic crossing of narrative elements. There are two narrators and two characters that are both distinct and conflated. Specifically, the "I" becomes two, a narrator in the first (outer) narrative and a character in the second (inner) one. As narrator of the first, the "I" then actually becomes a metanarrator of the second narrative, narrating in the guise of the Other the second narrator's (the Other's) narrative of discovery, which experience would be articulated in an act of narration and is thus given to that other metanarratively as an act of narrating ("He sees me in a reprehensible state, and must call what he sees reprehensible"). The difference between "I" as narrator and metanarrator becomes what distinguishes the two. In the narrative in which the "I" is narrator, the Other is a character; in the narrative in which the "I" is metanarrator, the Other is narrator and the "I" is a character.

I will give a name to this structure of doubled narrative, and call it a narrative-metanarrative (NMN) structure. Though this act of naming generalizes it as a structure, the individual subject who narrates, metanarrates, and is narrated nevertheless remains the specifically designated "myself" of the structure. The Other, however, who is apprehended as a subject, is given a different kind of specificity. The Other is grasped in the guise of a character whose role is that of storyteller, telling a specific story (experience) that pertains to the specificity of the "myself" as discovered. This suggests that the Other, as character, is apprehended as a subject, a freedom, precisely by becoming a narrator in his/her own right. That is, the power to narrate is an attribute of the individual subject. Or conversely, what reveals the Other's subjectivity is not his/her being, but the fact of being a narrator of a story, of being able to be such a narrator. The "I" (metanarrator) arrives at knowing the Other as a subject by rendering the Other a narrator of that "I." In effect, the "I" is written by the Other's apprehension, while writing that Other's apprehension itself; in the look, one loses self-authority to objectivation by the Other only through one's own authorship.[14]

In an intuitive way, Sartre saw this narrative duplicity, though he did not articulate its separate elements:

> In so far as I make there be an Other, I apprehend myself as the free source of the knowledge which the Other has of me, and the Other appears to me as affected in his

being by that knowledge which he has of my being inasmuch as I have affected him with the character of Other. (*BN*, 289)

In this ontological description, Sartre articulates the immediacy of the encounter as pure form, rather than through the complex narrativities that would preserve the particularity of the encounter's content. Yet, though the content (knowledge, affect, etc.) remains unspecified and abstract, he still embeds it in the unabandoned essential moment of narrativity, its being told in the first person. And thus, he leaves undisturbed the implicit reference to the Other's narrativizing, as "the knowledge the Other has of me." And indeed, Sartre's entire account depends upon this duplicity of double narrative insofar as he seeks to describe one's becoming an object for another while retaining one's existence as a consciousness that can still describe it. It gains its force and refuses the pitfall into metaphysics by preserving its essential narrativity, even as an abstract ontological description.

A Critique and Extension of the Narrative-Metanarrative Structure

Three points can be made about the NMN-structure, which extend it back into the interface between the ontological and the social. First, it contains a hidden moment of attribution in its structure (though Sartre's account of the look was designed to avoid attribution to the other). Second, it conflates modes of narrative generality and cultural specificity that allow it to be extended to the field of experience. Third, it finds an echo in Derrida, precisely as a structuring of narrative and ontology.

The hidden moment of attribution in Sartre's account of the look is already revealed in the moment of metanarrativity. The character or nature that one receives in the look at the moment of objectivation occurs through the narrative within which one sees oneself seen, in attribution. In the instance given, one's own moral shame (as content) appears to oneself in the form of another's narrative, but it is a narrative attributed to that Other. One feels the shame bestowed upon oneself by the Other because one metanarratively attributes to oneself a characterhood in that Other's narrative. Yet, in fact, this attribution does not stray from the fundamental contingency on which Sartre grounds consciousness. One need not attribute to the other the particular narrative of moral shame; it is possible to be discovered at a keyhole and welcome the chance to involve or include another in the voyeurism, meaning that one metanarrated the other as one who is open to such an invitation.[15] Furthermore, the Other may not actually think one's action shameful, even though one does oneself, and would jump at a chance to take a look if offered. In either case, there is an attribution to one's act through one's attribution to the Other of a narrative of what the character of one's act is. The meaning of one's discovered action is at once an attribution to oneself through the Other and an attribution to the Other through oneself. Neither is an attribution of subjectivity to the Other; they are both attributions of meaning to an Other-as-subject. The look formulates the narrated Other as an unattributed ontological subjectivity by means of non-ontological (narrative) attribution. And this non-ontological attribution is apprehended as ontologized (that is, given being) by the Other in oneself, which one apprehends as a "nature," a "knowledge" the Other has in apprehending oneself as that object. Thus, the interweaving of the ontic and the ontological that Sartre saw as a problem in Heidegger is given narrative articulation in Sartre's response to it.

But now Sartre's account deconstructs; its meaning is not where he locates it. Though it is an account that seeks to be non-attributive, its content is structured through the metanarrative attribution of a narrative of attribution. If the specific content of the narrative (of discovery), and of the subject's objectivation, is immaterial to this structure, the fact of narrative in this structure is not immaterial to Sartre's account of subjectivity. Though Sartre avoids the generality of ontological attribution of subjectivity to the Other, it is only through the specificity of narrative attribution to the Other. The ontology of the Other-as-subject depends upon the narrativity of ontology. The relation between ontology and narrative is thus also chiasmic: narrative depends on ontology, and ontology depends on narrative. As with the Other-as-object, this narrativity becomes the erasure of any ontological center through the multiplication of narrative centers. Narrative is the hidden discursive core of ontology, and ontology is the hidden discursive core of narrative.

But the fact of narrative attribution raises a question: What is the source of the narrative content (reprehensibility and shame, or perhaps approbation, in the discovery) of the double narrative? Because the "I" recognizes (in telling) what the Other recognizes (in discovering), both recognitions mark a familiarity and therefore a prior knowledge. Indeed, an assumed common and prior knowledge is the foundation for both moments of attribution. If the meaning given to the "I" by the Other-as-subject is a story the Other tells in a story the "I" tells, the story the "I" tells the Other telling must already have existed; it must come from beyond the ontological relation, from beyond the look, and from beyond one's self-discovery in the Other's look. To know or to assume a common narrative of shame, approbation, or intimacy (in the case of two people speaking closely and looking at each other), in order to recognize it, is to have already been given that narrative from elsewhere. Though Sartre may blithely locate the content of his story (discovery at the keyhole) in its enactment, the form of his account takes it beyond that. The discursivity of this "scene" overflows.

The narrative's existence as common and prior signifies that its origin is social, if by "social" we understand an environment of interpersonal relations that is "elsewhere" with respect to *this* interpersonal relation, but to which this one is inseparably related within that environmental framework (whose ecological character articulates one aspect of what is meant by the *cultural*). In other words, the narratives of the NMN-structure are of social origin insofar as they are socially given and understood within a particular cultural framework. The story belongs to a social givenness that has to have already arrived to the "I" in order to again arrive to the "I" in the form of the Other's metanarrated story, the attributed story that the "I" gives to the Other by telling it through the Other. It is a social givenness that is never the object of an intention, but only the immediacy of meaning that is experienced as familiar, that can be located in an enactment.[16]

It comes from elsewhere and is given to an elsewhere (an Other) in order for one to submit oneself to it, to recognize it and to recognize oneself in it.[17]

Corollary to this, a question arises with respect to feelings and emotions: Can we continue to understand such things as fear, intimacy, shame, or desire as aspects of human existence that one simply undergoes as if inherent to one's being? To the extent that one is beset by a feeling toward another, can it be understood as something an Other has "done" (e.g., caught one at the keyhole) or enacted (e.g., a sense of intimacy)? To undergo a feeling (of moral shame or personal desirability) is already to recognize it as recognizable (and thus recognized) by another.[18] Despite the feeling that one's feelings are inherent to one's being, or indeed constitute one's very self, the fact of recognition of that feeling by others, one's recognition of it in others, and the ability to name it within a language given to one from elsewhere (a *mother* tongue) and to attribute it to another wholly on the basis of his/her situational presence suggest that the feeling is already in some sense a common experience and can also be named in oneself by others because of that. The question becomes, do people have an awareness of their feelings inherently, or is that awareness given them because, in certain social situations, they have been named by others as evincing certain feelings? If it is from others that one receives the language with which to name one's feelings (as feelings) in the first place, it is also from others that one receives the indication of what it is that is to be thus named—as common to others, and thus common to oneself with respect to them.

Because another's consciousness and feelings are in principle unknowable, a direct experiential apprehension of them, or a meaning given to them experientially, are not possible. And this holds as well for one's own; one enters a society as a child without an apprehension of what one's feelings are, nor what they mean socially, and these are given (and explained) to one from elsewhere, by others. Furthermore, they can only be named, and given a meaning, through narrative, since it is only narrative that can present consciousness, which is unknowable by others, to both oneself and others as a common experience. Only narrative can present subjectivity in its hidden individuality as something different people can apprehend in common, as a common experience. A cultural framework involving language and narratives is the necessary condition for feelings to become common experiences and thus to acquire the meanings they do as the feelings they are, within a particular socius.

This is not to argue that emotions are fundamentally discursive. They are not to the extent that we undergo them; and we undergo them at the somatic level, as well as through the significance of the psychic transformations they constitute. But it suggests that we know feelings such as shame, fear, love, and so on, and individuate them from each other under those names, because we experience them through stories that tell us what those feelings are, and how to know them.[19] And we have to know them in this way in order to be able to attribute to others the experience of having discovered them in us. Part of growing up is being told, in social terms, who one is in terms of the social meaning of the things one does and feels; and being told who one is in social terms is already a process of being constructed as who one is through the narratives that purvey its meanings. One chooses, within that narrative knowledge, one's comportments (as desires, individualities, or socialities, for instance) and what one can express in and through them. But their social meanings are given from elsewhere. Again, an emotion or feeling does not manifest itself contemplatively, without a real somatic substrate; one undergoes emotion in one's entire being, somatic state, psychic transformation, altering of relation to the world, all. But what this account suggests is that the meaning of an emotion, its individuation as a complex of all those components, which is familiar to oneself and others in common within a culture, and often unfamiliar cross-culturally, is overlaid upon somatic and psychic substrates, while the latter lend themselves to a variety of meanings, a spectrum of variation, and even finely tuned nuances. It is this that provides for the difference of meaning emotions assume, their different roles, in different cultures. The differential of narratives that present them as socially familiar within a particular cultural framework provide for them to be experienced differently between cultures.

Thus, feelings become common (recognizable) feelings with certain significations (i.e., establish themselves as socially and individually recognized feelings at all, to be encountered and felt at moments of being caught, attacked, caressed, etc.) through socially given narratives. To undergo a feeling is already to recognize it as a common experience through a structure of double narrative that involves a real or imagined other.[20] What Sartre's account suggests (and structures) is that though one undergoes a feeling situationally, as wholly one's own, at the hands (eyes, words) of another, what it is that one thereby recognizes through a disguised narrative metanarratively attributed to the Other, through whom one recognizes (generates) it in oneself, is socially (culturally) generated. Where Heidegger poses the abstract existential question of "Being-with," and Sartre develops the existential possibility of oscillating, mutual, and perhaps balanced objectivations, the NMN-structure reveals a chiasmic relation between the ontological and the language of narrative, at the core of human interaction and human feeling itself.

Sartre has already given a certain inverse confirmation of this relation, having incorporated a similar structure in his account of the emotions. He argues that the emotions are intentional transformations of the world at moments when the world has become untenable; they become transformations of one's relation to the world that magically abandon such givens as causality or social structure in order to provide the possibility of psychic survival (*Emotions*, 58). At the moment of untenability, one renarrativizes the world in order to render it one in which the character one has to be accords with the metanarrative of surviving the way the world besets. That renarrativization becomes the non-enacted space of the emotion that transforms the relation to the world it mediates through its narrative.

> Emotion . . . is the body which, directed by consciousness, changes its relation with the world in order that the world may change its qualities. (*Emotions*, 61)

If one accedes to an emotion as a character, it is because one had already written (retold) a metanarrated transformation of the world to which to accede. If Sartre calls this transformation magical, we can now recognize his own "sleight of hand" as a separation and conjunction of metanarrator and narrated character upon the stage renarrativized, a drama one enacts through one's own authorization of the world as author of one's emotional response to it in all its particularity.

A second extension of the NMN-structure, in its narrative role and cultural specificity, is to the field of experience generally. The inability of the experience of feeling (which remains hidden) to present itself to the communal, as common experience, holds for activity as well but in an inverted manner. Where the subject's feeling is what the other cannot see, activity is what the actor/agent cannot see, in part because it is what the agent sees with. Whether it be a dance, or the way one carries on a discussion or argument, or the tenderness of interaction with a friend, one apprehends a sense of the action's meaning only through others. That is, one attributes narratives to others which then narrate one's own actions or feelings precisely in order to undergo them in the other's account as the meanings one can give one's own actions, now metanarrated through the other. As Derrida puts it, "'*experience*' has always designated the relation with a presence, whether that relationship had the form of consciousness or not."[21]

The implication of all this is that we already and originally undergo what presents itself as experience and feeling as a social reenactment whose non-origin is already represented within a doubled narrative, a doubling of narrator and character, and a double attribution. The meaning of experience is given through the "other" as a commonality, but through a "factuality" that renders its narration (within the double narrative) its actual existential origin. Not only do our feelings and actions become simulacra, but we discover and constitute our human attributes for ourselves through a configuration of narratives through others. That is, we discover our human attributes with the meanings we desire for them through a social source that blinds us to itself, leaving us to purvey and locate that source in the intentionality of the actions themselves. While narrative brings them into existence from a prior social source, intentionality becomes the way their existence is lived as an individual meaning. Though the other remains necessary to apprehend those meanings as an interweaving of narrativizations, intentionality decenters the Other to the confrontational, the subject-object interpersonal relation, as an artificial source in its separation of narrational sources.

Narrative does not engender "experience," but it is the condition for apprehending it as a familiarity in its particularity by both individuating it and constructing it as a meaning. One recognizes each experience through the individual narrativity of which it seems to be the very origin, and one experiences each narrativized experience through the familiarity it seems to have as one's own. That is, experience is both lived and constructed through a structure of narratives that both render it one's own (individuated) and bestow a prior familiarity because it is within a cultural framework (necessarily from elsewhere). And each experience appears new as well as familiar because the structure of narratives becomes very complex and overlapping, from within which a particular situation enacts its own. These narratives do not originate through the social interface of the Other but occur as the meanings of that interface in a structure of double attribution, from a common cultural source. What is thus given back to the social is always already taken from the social, in the name of familiarity generated as if "originary" by the individual.[22]

As the mediation between the lived and the constructed, narrativity constitutes the "substance," the medium for the naming of the hiddenness of experience (or feeling). That is, the narrative is not the name, but its ghost as the familiar, the participation of an other as a trace in the discernment of what is named, and which continues to reside within the recognizability of experience that allows a name, a nominative sign, to be affixed to its hiddenness. What becomes the linguistic name, by which one refers to one's experience to another who understands, is a sign that not only bespeaks the meaning given an activity or feeling but invokes the complex of narratives as the absent trace that presents as well as reengenders the familiarity of experience, the commonality of the hidden.

This can be understood in analogy to the relation (discussed earlier) between a poem which is always more than its text because it includes the many varying and variant rereadings of its text, the text of the poem as its name, and its title as a shorthand expression for the text as what names the poem that overflows and transcends its text. The linguistic name for an experience or feeling is a way of speaking about what has become "experience," the "title" that invokes its narratives without retelling its story, but which reaches through the story to the experience the story has made apprehensible. The nominal sign structures a chiasm of narrative and name, in which the name refers to the narrative experience whose narrative "names" the experience to which the name then refers. In effect, the name mediates between what narrative engenders as a knowledge (recognition, meaning, structuring) of experience, and the experience it names as the representation of the narrative (its familiarity)—between experience recognized narratively and one's ability to speak about experience through naming it as such. Thus, experience resides between the sign that engenders its familiarity as a meaning, and the signification engendered for it by the social narrative that the individual appropriates as knowledge and self-recognition.

The third point to be made about the double narrative (NMN) structure is that it finds an echo in Derrida. This is not unanticipated, given the chiasmus between narrative and ontology. Derrida argues that context is never immanent in a text (*Marg*, 316). One reads a text through a (coded) assumption of context—one that the text perhaps suggests, but to which the text will never accede without reserve or without supplement. Unequivocality is precluded by the impossibility of appeal to a definitive context. There can be no real reading of a text, only a reading given it, because what the text holds in reserve from any contextualization produces a recontextualization, disrupting definitude. Indeed, its textuality as discursive form constitutes its most immediate alternate or supplementary self-contextualization, beneath all literal readings. Meaning is disseminated (in the Derridean sense) by the impossibility of definitive contextualization; it is dispelled by the text's discursivity, its form and poetic. A text arrives at a meaning because it arrives at being given a reading. Though every text appears to present itself as having the meaning one discovers there, the assumption of that meaning by the text is a mask it puts on in response to the reader's assumption of a context.

But to pose the act of reading in this way is already to position and reenact it on the stage of the NMN-structure. A reader reads through an act of contextualization that then becomes a production of its meaning. But to construct a context in which to give a text a reading is to render the text a character for that reading through which to tell oneself its meaning. It is a narrativization, a way one comes upon the text—the act by which one discovers what the text is doing. But on the other hand, the reader is not at liberty to read arbitrarily or capriciously, to construct a context gratuitously, without the participation of the text it is about. The reader is constrained to a realm circumscribed by the text, as the text itself is similarly circumscribed by other texts, by its own textuality, and by the unreachability of non-textuality, an outside of the text (its *hors-texte*). A reader can construct a context only within those discovered constraints, if the reading that makes the discovery is to be coherent.

Insofar as the reader makes the text intelligible to him/herself within the bounds and terms that the text presents, the reader has submitted to terms that the text "imposes" on the reader—that is, terms by which the text "tells" (narrates) the reader's activity of reading, within the realm of that presentation. That is, reading is the act of discovery of what the text is doing, but in the text's terms, a narrative of discovery that the text tells through the reader by providing the terms in which the discovery is made. The reader narrates the text in the text's terms at the same time that the text invents the reader who will give the text the meaning it assumes through the reader's assumption of a context. The reader reads (regards) the text as a character in the text's metanarrative; and the reader is metanarrated by the text s/he discovers as a meaning narrated through the construction of a context. Text and reader doubly confront each other as narrated (character) and narrator. In other words, reading is homologous to the Sartrean look. This might suggest that the subject (reader) is the subject of reading, the "other-as-subject" in the structure of reading. The reader is always the Other, the one who catches the text at the semiotic keyhole, as it were, and renders it an object. And the reader does so only by becoming the means whereby the text becomes the reading it does. That is, the Sartrean NMN-structure and the Derridean sense of the dissemination of meaning through the ambiguities of context find themselves interior to each other.

This raises a number of questions. Does the text, or textuality in general (oral or written), in some fashion participate in the reader becoming a subject by being what the reader can be the Other for? Does the reader attain to subjecthood through the act of reading? If reading, before it is an encounter with a text, is already an intertextuality, because what is discovered in the look must already be a familiarity, is there also always a subject already lurking in each text? Is this subject, as a sub-subject, the means by which the reader becomes a subject, as an other-as-subject for the text?[23]

In the case of reading, of course, the look also goes the other way. The reader does not read at will. In reading, one is constrained by the words and the thread of thought they present. Following their thread becomes one's project; one's apprehension of them becomes the object of what they present. One loses mastery to them, in the sense that they lead. In one's reading, one becomes the knowledge that they already contain, that they are. One is given a nature as one who has read and followed the thread of those words, that text and its reasoning. One finds oneself elsewhere, in those words and their import. In other words, in reading, the text becomes the look, the other-as-subject for which one is the object, objectivized by the meaning of the text as one who has been given that meaning. One becomes the metanarrator of the text that then tells one's meaning in its words, a meaning as an awareness that is then still elsewhere in the other, the text. One has enacted that meaning in one's apprehension through that other, the text, that has told it in one's reading, as oneself. One is both metanarrator and character in the narrative of meaning the text presents and tells in one's reading, while the text becomes both what one narrates in reading, and the narrator of the story or meaning one apprehends as one's own in having read it.

In reading, in encountering the text as a look, one encounters a hidden, lurking sub-subject. One encounters a voice represented (or not) by the words read, a voice whose acts narrate what is enacted when the text is read. The reader loses him/herself to that voice, loses his/her autonomy and project to the text's flow, path, assumptions, goals, as a necessary way of making sense of the text. To read is always to be caught with one's ear pressed to the door, listening; it is to peep through the semiotic keyhole and encounter the eye of the hidden sub-subject, whose voice one had heard in the text, looking back. To read, to be the subject reading, is always such an intimate act. The reader becomes the object of a look that peers unseen through a voice, the voice of a real and imagined Other lurking in the text. One invents an author to give personhood to that voice, and one finds oneself under the gaze of that person.[24] If authorship is an already socially narrated role, it is a role reinvented by the reader to be an already familiar other in the text, whose voice is extended to the text's look and whose eyes are disguised as a voice. The author is "the look," and the reader the one caught in the act (of reading, of making sense of the text, of making a sense of the text that may be at variance with the "author's" sense, of imposing a context on the text in order to do so, etc.; some reprehensible in the reader's terms, and some worthy of the author's approbation, perhaps). To read, to enact the narrative told by the text's voice, is to be written by it, to become the object of its look. It may be a judging or longing look (longing to be understood), or neither; it might rather be an author-itative, explanatory, transcendent (and in all those senses, intimate) look.

In other words, there seems to be a reciprocity between the text and the reader in which each becomes the look that objectivizes the other. It is a reciprocity that is also an incommensurability between text and reader, between two forms of the look in which one or the other becomes an object for an Other-as-subject. But this implies that this reciprocity is between two forms of being metadiscursive toward the other. Each becomes the way the Other is read, an instrumentality not of a project but of becoming a subject for the other. In that sense, the renarrativization of the look represented by the NMN-structure sets out a template in which the incommensurability between Sartre and Derrida can perhaps find residence. Or rather, that incommensurability can perhaps be understood through the re-narrativized structure of the reader.

This does not define the domain of the subject; it constitutes the domain of the problematic of undefinability of the subject, of the general philosophical inability, throughout the history of philosophy, to do more than simply name it without aporia or contradiction. As writing is the realm that reveals all language, including speech, to be a form of inscription, so reading is the realm that reveals the subject to be neither text nor being.

The Form of Form

There is a chiasmic relation between text and reader, which both structures and renders inseparable the terms of their incommensurability. It is homologous to the chiasms heretofore encountered, of ontology and narrative, or individual recognition and social familiarity, or narrative and name, which similarly mark incommensurabilities. Each pertains to a different arena of discursivity, to different relations of inscription, to structures that provide no synthesis. They constitute a form, a sculpture carved by a discursive reasoning and narrativity in a medium constituted by the incommensurability itself between texts or textual elements that take shape through their inseparability. Metaphorized as sculpture, carved in the metadiscursive medium marked by incommensurability, they assume an aura of both solidity and ephemerality, like iconic forms in ancient ruins, or glyphs on a stele.

A glyph, after all, is a symbolic image or figure carved in relief on a surface, signifying a complex of meanings whose incorporation in singularity within a plural presentation the glyph is. A corporate logo, the poles and straps that mark the waiting line for the next available teller in a bank, or the position of football players at the line of scrimmage all constitute glyphs (for the public, the bank customers, and the defensive team respectively). The glyph is not iconic, in the Peircean sense. It does not present what it signifies, neither as presentation nor representation, since what it signifies is given in part by its process of construction from its medium—as a textual form, for instance, constructed as a mode of textual reasoning. Neither is it a symbol, since its domain of signification is not the text itself (nor the team in the case of the scrimmage formation, nor what the corporation does specifically in the case of a logo). If it is a category of signification, as is a team formation at the start of a play, it refers to itself as a structure rather than a depiction or portrayal.

In its discursivity, what a glyph presents is its materiality; it has no substrate other than the discursive medium from which it is constructed, and in which it resides in its role as experience (even in football, whose substrate is the rules of the game). The glyph of the chiasm has a different contour in each domain in which its doubling back upon itself occurs. As a form carved by the operations of narrativity and ontology, it signifies the ontology of narrative and the narrativity of ontology because that is what it is constituted by. But it also signifies an experience of itself as a formal relation, as well as the sociality of the common experience embedded in its readability, anterior to the incommensurability of the operations of ontology and narrativity from which it is carved. Like the double narrative of the

NMN-structure, the glyph signifies and represents the incommensurability between individual and common experience. It is a metatextual "object" that exists beyond the mere binaries of name and narrative, narrative and enactment, enactment and experience, or experience and common experience, one part of whose structure is itself metatextuality. The glyph of the NMN-structure thus refers to the structures of the social, the semiotic dynamics of reading, of feeling or enactment, of what is inexperiencible by others, hidden within subjectivity, that can then be read as NMN-structures. What it names is both individuated and social, not as a dialectic of prior things called feelings and names, but as an existential structure for the incommensurability of the name and the enactment or feeling in whose existence the name participates as a necessary condition.

The glyph is not a word, because it is a structure of discourse. As a formal structure, it must be differentiated from generalization. Generalizations about people, human feelings, or capabilities, or generalizations about who a person is, always violate the individual by their very nature. They are thus paradoxical, insofar as they emerge from an imposition of a metaphysics on people. For instance, people always present themselves as individuals. A generalization of them is thus not derivable from experience of them as individuals. To generalize people, to see them as members of a category, relies upon having defined such a category beforehand, by which the individual is then to be noticed, prior to the encounter. If the generalization must exist prior to experience with the individual then generalized, and to function as what points out a person as one to be noticed as belonging to the category to which the generalization refers, then it must be of social origin. It comes from elsewhere, other than the individual, and elsewhere than all prior individuals on whom it had previously been imposed. It is not only defined prior to encounter with those it generalizes but defines or determines what is to be experienced upon encounter with the individual categorized. It substitutes itself for experience of the individual, thereby obviating experience of anything but itself as a generalization.[25]

Like the narratives of the NMN-structure, the content of a generalization comes from social sources; but unlike the NMN-structure, it participates in an imposition rather than a chiasmus, and it imposes itself directly upon the one seen, as an object, rather than being a way the one seen apprehends the one seeing as a subject. It is in this sense that generalization becomes a discursive operation by which a person is rendered a metaphysical entity. We recognize this as the basic operation of any prejudice or chauvinism. Perhaps it seems natural to those who do it because it only carries to an unethical extreme the residence of narrative commonality at the core of human community; that is, the centrality of narrativity to common experience, enacted in a situation of hierarchy or dominance, and imposed on those whose domination and exclusion it then rationalizes.

In the operation of the glyph of the chiasmus, however, whether with respect to the structure of reading as the look or as the look itself, one remains an individual and knows oneself through what the other sees in oneself, as well as what the other (text or individual) sees fit to name about oneself, either in word or action, as what is to be seen or textually determined. In that sense, the glyph is already a deconstruction of the act of generalization. It reaffirms the dynamic of the social as the apprehensibility and preserved unknowability of the individual by another as subject, against which generalization reduces the individual to prior knowability and social unknowability.

But now, the structure of the glyph of the NMN-structure suggests that a system of narratives nestles at the core of a culture, as that culture's determination of common experience for itself. And this implies that the distinctions between cultures, their emotional and temperamental particularity, for which the absence of origin is general, would both refuse universalization and be the source of each one's self-universalization toward others. That is, as a culture, people live the content of the narratives that purvey common experience to them of each other, as what culture is. Different systems of narrative would necessarily produce alternate and equally exclusive modes of familiarity and recognition, and hence incommensurabilities of feeling, emotion, and ways of apprehending experience. Universality, and the violation of Others that is always attendant upon its imposition elsewhere, derives perhaps from a desire to traverse the incommensurability, to articulate the inarticulability contained in the disparity of narrative systems. Or, perhaps, it derives from a desire to impose one's "universality" on others.

6 The Sartre-Derrida Homology

LET US RETURN NOW to Sartre's elaboration of the look. He delineates a number of transformations that occur to the prereflective subject "at the keyhole" upon being seen by another. Three of these transformations will be of concern here. Yet the account of the look that Sartre gives has already been slightly transformed, and a number of social extensions have been articulated for it. We have shown it to have inseparable links to the cultural milieu, and that it is not free of attributions, though they be narrative. These two aspects are joined in that the source of those narratives is the specific culture and socius from which come the participants in the encounter. It is the interplay of the culturally given with the immediacy of enactment within the structure of the look that opens an interior space between the inexperienceability of another's consciousness and the social.

This space has a structure, as a narrative-metanarrative space. It participates in a multilayered structure that conjoins narrativity (the social), enactment (the immediate moment), and the name, the social nomination of individual acts, feelings, emotions, and so on. The term used for the lamination of these multidimensional discourses is the *glyph*. Eventually, we will see that the glyph constitutes a general theoretic of the sign, beyond its Saussurean duality. While both the glyph and the narrativity of the NMN-structure function as concrete discursive or narrative elements in intersubjective encounters, they are identifiable only through metadiscursive operations; in a sense analogous to the mythic, which cannot be seen from within its own cultural framework because it is the way one sees in that framework, the operation of NMN-structure narrativities and the glyph are the ways one enters into personal encounters, the look and counterlook; in other words, the content in the moment of being-for-others. Residing between the inexperienceability of another's consciousness and the specificity of the cultural to social interaction, they touch the inarticulable (or indeterminacy) at the core of both Sartre's and Derrida's discourse.

To reiterate, the three transformations that the subject undergoes under the other's look that will be of concern here are these: (1) One discovers one has a nature, an outside turned toward the world; (2) one becomes an instrumentality in the Other's project; and (3) there is a loss of autonomy, or authority, in the world. While these transformations constitute concomitant facets of a single ontological moment in Sartre's ontology, they each have their own peculiar (and proper) structural characteristics, which we can now also articulate in terms of specific narrative structures.

THE INSIDE OF THE OUTSIDE, THE SUPPLEMENT

Upon having been seen by another, whether real or imagined, the first transformation that the subject undergoes is that one ceases to be pure consciousness, pure project. No longer an "I" for oneself, one becomes a "me." When interrupted "at the keyhole" in a prereflective state, one suddenly finds oneself self-reflective, grounded and frozen in the form of what the Other has come upon. One has to be the object that one already is. One becomes a given, a determinate nature produced by a hidden elsewhere for which (whom) one's self-determinacy dissolves (*BN*, 262).

Schroeder refers to this colorfully as a fall from grace ("*ma chute originelle*") or as a loss of innocence because, in Sartre's example, it is encountered in shame (*SHP*, 184; *BN*, 263). Schroeder is, of course, playing with the term, conflating existential and moral shame, its "ontological difference." For Sartre, existential shame, is "an intimate relation of myself to myself" (*BN*, 221) that amounts to "passing judgment on myself as on an object" (*BN*, 222). If Sartre had said "questioning" instead of "passing judgment," this would almost describe the role given Dasein by Heidegger. But Sartre's concern is more complex than that.

> It is not that I perceive myself losing my freedom in order to become a thing, but my nature is over there—outside my lived freedom—as a given attribute of this being which I am for the Other. (*BN*, 263)

The Other, with no nature, no outside, is "here" at the center of one's givenness, while one becomes an outside, a nature that is "over there." Being in question is no longer a possibility; the "I" is beyond being in question because exteriorized to an interiorized other.

This attribution of a nature occurs because of the Other's look, not in it. Though one knows oneself as given, one becomes unknowable to oneself precisely because one is now given. "To be looked at is to apprehend oneself as the unknown object of unknowable appraisals—in particular, value judgments" (*BN*, 267). Unknown for oneself, and known for the Other; all one knows of that nature, that givenness, is that it is known by the other.

> I apprehend my possibilities from outside and through him at the same time that I *am* my possibilities, somewhat as we objectively apprehend our thought through language at the same time that we think it *in order to* express it in language. (*BN*, 264)

In Sartre's further elaborations of this relation, one reencounters his parametric thinking as a double non-negation. One becomes "this being for the Other" whose freedom is here (a state) at the same time that one's own freedom is shifted to an "over there" (a non-act). One provides one's own givenness metanarratively (an act), and that givenness is not oneself (a non-state). In the sense that one's loss of innocence obeys the logic of the double non-negation, it not only signifies an incommensurability but an inseparability of what is incommensurable. The Other-as-subject and self-as-object, and indeed subject and object as such, do not negate each other; they relate metadiscursively. As an object for the Other, one's "being [is] written, in and by the Other's freedom" (*BN*, 262). One gives one's givenness, in order to find it given by the other. One reads oneself as given by the unreadable other, as the condition and effect of the Other reading one's givenness for that Other. In short, one finds oneself outside oneself, and inside the Other for whom one is the outside.

One is reminded of W.E.B. DuBois's description of the double consciousness of African Americans, subjected to white supremacy and an enforced "color line."[1] For DuBois, this double consciousness emerges from having to see oneself through the eyes of another, for which one's own self-awareness is partially out of reach, together with a striving against that doubleness. "Who one is" occurs only through the "revelation of the other [white] world," but also as the "second-sight of this American world." "Race," in those terms, must be understood as a social distinction created politically and juridically by making "color" a factor of social importance. If the "color line" becomes the separation between who one is, and who one is made to be by others, then it is not color that is the foundation of race, but "race" or the social process of racialization that is the foundation of "color." That is, the term "color" is not a descriptive term, but a "racializing" term; the social process of categorization that "racializes" also racializes colors as signifiers of that social categorization. Social categorization is the outside given by the (white) racializing look, a look that is there even when not there because the entire socius is racialized already, as the interiority of living in it. The look becomes an endless act of noticing what is racial(ized) about people first and foremost, a social noticing that both produces a structure of racialization and relies upon it to predefine what is to be noticed.

This holds for whites as well, who are made white by the social structure of whiteness that gives them their own social categorization. Those who invented the color line by seeing others on the other side of it did so only in order to see themselves as well. Whites become white only by seeing (defining) others as other in a variety of ways ("black," "non-white," etc.). They do not catch African Americans at any keyhole but rather invent a keyhole to place before them in order to catch them there. The insidiousness of the "color line" is the inescable interiorization one undergoes through the absolute exteriority of that invention. Who one is made to be must reside within who one is, while who one is lives the objectivizing exteriority of who one is made to be. Consciousness is not only double but chiasmic, precisely because the line is artificial.[2]

One can trace the trajectory of the Derridean trace in DuBois's description, at the core of its political dynamic. The trace is the absent presence to a sign of what differs from it, the presence of what is absent precisely in differing, as the condition for that sign having the meaning that it has. As Derrida puts it, the trace is what must be thought before the object. To see oneself as the object of a structure of domination through which one is seen is to think that structure as the trace before the object one apprehends oneself to be for it, thus already doubling one's self-awareness as a person. For those racialized by white supremacy, there is a double bind in the sense of being aware of oneself through the trace of the other and aware of what the other is making of one through the trace of what one has been that is then dominated by the "eyes" of the other, 'the social categorizations of white society.' That double bind manifests itself insofar as being oneself as a subject (embracing the trace of one's autonomous being) means to stand in opposition, to rebel, to be seen as aggressing against the gratuitous violence of social racialization; and accepting one's objectivation (embracing the trace of the other's domination) is to betray oneself. One's situation is irremediable insofar as a counterlook must both deracialize and reracialize at the same time.

The politics of deracializing rebellion and reracializing self-appropriation is always seen by white supremacy as aggression, that is, without reciprocity. For whites as well, to the extent they identify themselves as white, the trace (of the other) must be thought before the object (self) through which it obtains its meaning (whiteness); this is the source of the obsession with race by whites, why it is the first thing to be noticed about another. The refusal of reciprocity becomes the hallmark of this obsession and continues its modes of domination.

This suggests that the reciprocity that Sartre conceived as possible, as for the returned look, was out of relation to social forms of domination; the returned look could only re-objectivize in a social situation that permitted it, that did not criminalize it as rebellion and thus turn it into something else. The reciprocating look then becomes criticial in breaking the structure of racializing domination, as well as in opening the possibility of a mode of resubjectivizing dialogue, as the basis for social deracialization.

If the trace is the absent presence to an object of what differs from it, that must be thought before that object as the necessary condition for its meaning, then the trace is the condition for the object being both individuated and recognized as having a meaning (*Gram*, 47). This implicitly constructs thought in a way that is anterior to a thought that constitutes thought; thought is doubled as both thought and the condition for thought at the same time. Sartre is more explicit about this same doubling. In Sartre's account, to apprehend oneself as an object means to apprehend oneself through the trace of one's former prereflective subjectivity. One's difference from that absent subjectivity produces one as that object. To have discerned a look of intimacy, in which one apprehends oneself as the object of a desire, one has first to have thought the trace of the absence of that look, prereflectively, into which that look intrudes—as do the footsteps that discover the peeping tom at the keyhole. The trace is doubly operative in Sartre's account: (1) as oneself as a subject in one's objectivation by the other's look; and (2) as the other, whose subjectivity remains unknown as an intrusion for which one becomes the object.

The structure of this interrelation is what Derrida investigates as the "supplement," part of his "technology" of deconstruction. The supplement is a structure involved in how the trace operates in the production of meaning. Indeed, the supplement's "role" as a critical "logic" is central to Derrida's entire critique of metaphysics. To see this, let us turn to Derrida's narrativization of Rousseau, though by way of his deconstruction of the relation between writing and speech.

Derrida argues that the foundation for metaphysics, along with its conceptualization of truth and referentiality, lies in its claim that thought and knowledge can seek to truly reflect the world; that is, in assuming that the world is in some sense autonomous of just such attempts at reflection, and thus available to be reflected on as such in its autonomy. For metaphysics, knowledge can be judged as truthful in its reflections on the world in the same way that one judges whether one's speech truly reflects or represents one's thoughts. Thought and its truth are given systematic and conceptual primacy over representation, especially that of language. Speech, in such a system, must be privileged over writing because speech is immediate to thought, to its mode of presence and its being in the present, that is, to thought's self-presentation. By extension, writing is something distant from thought, an exterior representation, an ancillary and inessential substitute for speech (*Gram*, 20). If speech purveys the signifiers for the thought it expresses, as a representation of them, writing but represents that expression; it is a representation of a representation, a signifier of a signifier. And this renders writing suspect, because it unnaturally "diverts the immediate presence of thought to speech into representation and imagination" (*Gram*, 144).

By shifting his attention to the nature of signs themselves, Derrida argues that this chain of representations, and thus the metaphysical attitude that relies on it, is on shaky ground. The signs of a language acquire meaning through their differences with other signs; it is the structure of these differences that constitutes the structure of signs one understands as a language. But as a structure, linguistic signs make reference only to themselves. The meaning of a sign is provided through its relations to other signs (as in a dictionary). That is, a sign's referentiality to objects can occur only through its anterior reference to other signs. A claim to referentiality (to the world or to thought) must rely upon an adjoined and ancillary discursive operation or code, one that inserts the assumption of referentiality into the discourse that claims to refer. In other words, the referentiality of language is given to it discursively, within and at the hands of language and its structure, and not any "natural" relation between word and world. The claim to referentiality is itself a form of self-referentiality.

But if that is the case, then representation gets indefinitely postponed. Each moment of discourse that claims to refer to the world or to thought, and thus to represent it, ends up referring to language which it then claims refers to the world or to thought (generating an infinite regress). Language presents itself, and means through itself, before it can be claimed to represent. Language cannot merely be an instrument of representation because it resists reduction to instrumentality through its self-referentiality, a self-referentiality that is inherent in its every moment of discursivity. In the face of this resistance, thought gets decentered with respect to representation and referentiality; it must share the source of what is expressed in language with what language itself generates in the process of deferring the meaning through which thought sought to express itself.

In these terms, every attempt by metaphysics to live up to its own fundamental presuppositions throws metaphysics beyond its own axiomatics to statements it does not want to make, to singularities and inconsistencies that cannot be accounted for because they are self-referential. Point of view is such a singularity because it is what sees without being able to see itself seeing. The disclosure of such inconsistencies parallels Gödel's Incompleteness Theorem for mathematical axiomatic systems. Like Gödel, who invented a set of mathematical operations to demonstrate the untenability of a bounded axiomatics, so Derrida reinvents or redeploys terms (such as trace, supplement, etc.) by which to name the aporetic discursive operations that reveal the untenability of metaphysical coherence. In a sense analogous to mathematical construction of proof techniques, Derrida's terms constitute a form of technology of critique of discursive form.

But additionally (and as mentioned briefly earlier), to understand language as a system of differences means that the meaning engendered in any sign by the multiplicity of its differences from other signs must also be understood to be multiple. Each sign brings with it connoted and alternate meanings that impinge upon what is coded or indicated by context. A sign's significations play across the expanse of this structural multiplicity, as it plays across the immateriality of its self-referentiality. In other words, language always escapes the constraints, and even the possibility, of univocal representation. It exceeds or overflows definitude or precision at every turn, as the necessary condition for presenting the possibility of definitude, or of representation itself. In Derrida's words, what makes representation possible also makes it impossible (*Gram*, 143). That is, through super-adequation, a surfeit of meaning for its task, language exiles representation and referentiality to a discursive operation that is both interior to its being and ancillary to its operation. The thought that metaphysics wishes to represent autonomously in language in its own terms (as present, at least, to itself) ends up disseminated by those very terms, and by the language upon which it relies for that autonomy and self-presence, to other self-referential meanings elsewhere.

But the rigorous disclosure of language's dissemination of meaning, as its inner dynamic, can be accomplished only through an investigation of writing. Speech goes by too fast; it is too momentary, too immediate; it obeys a linearity that disguises its structure, and which guards it against analysis, against an understanding of how language operates structurally or in nonlinear fashion. In the written sign, however, one can discern the aspects or criteria that must hold for it to function as a sign. Derrida enumerates three. To function as a sign, to become linguistic, the inscribed "object" must be repeatable, or iterable; it must be individuated or spaced from other signs; and it must belong to a structure of differences, insofar as its meaning is produced through the absent presence of the trace of other signs with which it differs. In effect, iterability, spacing, and the trace constitute the parameters by which an inscribed object becomes a sign, able to produce meaning.[3]

But what holds for writing must then also be the case for speech, which is itself a sign system. The signs of speech can be apprehended as signs only in their iterability, spacing, and the operation of the trace as well. That is, spoken signs, as elements of a structure, also defer representation and operate through a self-referentiality, a polyvalence of expression, and an inherent undecidability. On that basis, one can consider speech to be a form of writing. This is not meant in a historical or ontological sense, but because the most general portrayal of the structure of language occurs with respect to writing, all other modes of language become specific cases. Though it was to supplement speech that metaphysics conscripted writing as its representation or "diagram," speech becomes a representative case of writing, which general case Derrida calls *writing in general* (*Gram*, 9). That is, speech is to be understood through its substitute, through what supplements it.

As Being, for Heidegger, is implicit and implicated in each existent, so writing in general is implicit and implicated in each mode of signification: writing, speech, hieroglyph, graffiti, or a pathway through the forest ("writing in general is the possibility of the road"; *Gram*, 107). It is not that writing in general is ever "there" as a language, but it is "there" (here) as the logic itself of any structure of signs.

If speech is a form of inscription, structured in common with writing, then like writing, it too attains a certain independence and autonomy from the thought it is supposed to represent. That is, the operations of language, as understood through writing rather than speech, reveal thought to be not autonomous but dependent upon, and indeed extended beyond itself by, the very language it thinks it deploys in its service. The stake metaphysics has in hierarchizing speech over writing is nothing less than the autonomy of thought. Without that hierarchy, thought ceases to be autonomous of its systems of representation and becomes enmeshed and dependent upon them to be what it thinks it is. Though language is thought to be the outside, the exteriorization of thought, as writing and representation it resides at the core, interiorly central and essential to thought itself, the inside. Inside and outside change places; each is found where the other is, inside the other—the outside inside the inside. This inversion disrupts the definitude or inviolability of the distinction between thought and language, between the inside and the outside of representation.

It is this blurring of the two, of the inside and the outside of a system based on and requiring a definitive distinction between inclusion and exclusion, that Derrida characterizes as supplementarity. Where speech becomes the supplement of writing, thought becomes the supplement of language. Like the trace, such supplementarity is anterior to language, as an element of its structure; it is anterior to the specific forms that language can take as writing or speech. It structures language's mode of being and is the condition of its existence at the same time.

Derrida's inversion of writing and speech, by which he inverts the core and periphery of the metaphysical approach to thought, has been famously misinterpreted as suggesting that writing preceded speech historically or ontologically.[4] This misinterpretation misses the sense of recontextualization of the relation between speech and writing that he engenders. It is a question of inverting a hierarchy of priorities. The metaphysics of thought relies upon a priority of speech over writing, in order to preserve the sanctity and actuality of thought and reason, by which it contextualizes its description and knowledge of the world. Derrida inverts that hierarchical relation, dispelling the priority of speech over writing that metaphysics relies upon, and by dehierarchizing them, renders both instances of the more general form. It has been to conceal the reliance of thought on modes of inscription that metaphysics has insisted on its hierarchy. The actual historical relations of speech and writing are not changed, but the power relation given them by the metaphysics of representation is undone. It is what Derrida would later call, in *Spectres of Marx*, a "performative interpretation," that is, "an interpretation that transforms what it interprets."[5]

In general, the supplement is the necessary outside that must be internal to anything's existence. For a presence or definitude (a "this") to have boundaries, to be definable or articulable, there has to be an elsewhere, beyond that boundary, that is implicated by and implicit in that boundary, as essential to it. For something to be understood as "natural," for instance, the artifical must have already been apprehended.

> The supplement harbors within itself two significations . . . [it] adds itself, it is a surplus, a plenitude enriching another plenitude, the *fullest measure* of presence. . . . [A]rt, *techne*, image, representation, convention, etc. come as supplements to nature and are rich with this cumulating function. . . . It adds only to replace. . . . The supplement is exterior, outside the positivity to which it is super-added, alien to that which, in order to be replaced by it, must be other than it. (*Gram*, 145)

When the indigenous of a region are named "natives" of it, non-natives (colonialists, tourists, settlers) must have arrived and arrogated a certain interiority for themselves within and yet alien to the "native," an exteriority that is interior to the transformation of the indigenous into "natives" (and other) in their own land. The "native" is a "native" only for the foreigner. An alien arrives who substitutes him/herself for the "native" through the appropriation of the act of being on that land. The colonialist does not apprehend or intuit his own supplementarity to the "object" he has designated "native" (*Gram*, 149) and which he sees as supplemental to his own presence. But the notion of native is an indeterminate designation, an Other defined as outside the invasiveness of colonialism. The colonialist's so-called civilizing mission can define itself only through having defined the "native" as uncivilized and indeterminate. An indeterminate outside is requisite for the possibility of a determinate inside (colonialism, in this case) and must therefore contain it, as other, within itself, as its supplement.

In referring to an object, the sign is supplementary to the thing, outside, indeterminate, and the necessary condition for the determination of that thing (*Gram*, 145). The metaphysical operation in general is the attachment of a specific meaning to a sign, and through it to the object. The fact of this attachment is then concealed through a dis-apprehension, a forgetting of the polyvocality of the sign and of the act of definitude that is overlaid upon it. The object becomes part of "the way the world is."

For instance, in the Euro-American cultures, what has come to be known as a "white race" is the attachment of a specific meaning to certain people who are produced as white through a definition of others as "not white" and against which "white" people then recognize themselves as white. "Whiteness" is produced by an enforced universalization of this relation, as an imposition upon others; its enforcement, as a structure of racialization, is what constitutes white supremacy. Whites designate and racialize the non-white in order to universalize themselves as white. While "whiteness" is seen as a "thing" of the world, with a meaning that makes it an attribute of persons within a certain society, this only covers up the fact that it is constructed as a relation between groups. The term *race* does not refer to inherent aspects of persons but to social relations between people. And that relation is one of supplementarity. The racialized other is the sine qua non, the indispensible condition, for whiteness, the trace hidden within the universalization of whiteness that makes whiteness a reality for itself, with a meaning. That is, the racialized other is found at the very core of whiteness, and white identity locates its source and itself in the non-white other.[6] It is this hidden relationality of "race" that is the source of the unending attention whites must pay to the designated non-white other, the necessity to be continually "noticing" them, even in their absence (and this would include the violent discriminatory "attention" Christians have paid, and still pay, to Jews throughout European history, even in their absence).

Even antiracist whites who seek to alleviate the condition of racism's victims continue the process of othering, of differentiation and objectification of the other, and in so doing, remain blind to their dependence on that process for their own identity as white. It is a blindness to the supplementarity of the relation that today has turned into its opposite. Many whites now claim that to even raise the issue of race, as a question of resistence to the domination it imposes, is racist. While this implicitly recognizes the supplementarity, it reverses it as part of the process of domination and of self-universalization. The determinate or universal always depends upon the indeterminate, the other, to ground it, in a dependence it then hides from itself and within itself in the clothing of universalization and determinateness.

The logic of the supplement is a chiasmic relation that dissolves the metaphysical pretension to autonomy by revealing definitiveness to be self-referential and dependent. It is a logic of meaning that doubly locates itself within and withdrawn from the sign—a non-thereness within, and a thereness that is always elsewhere. It fills the void produced by the trace (the absence of meaning in the absence of the supplement), the other of that inside. Art adds itself to nature, and becomes the means whereby the concept of Nature can be produced, ideologically or descriptively, as artful representation (*Gram*, 145). The supplement is the exteriority that becomes the way a thing means from within itself.

Sartre's account of the look obeys the logic of supplementarity on the plane of human interaction for which it is a molecule. For Sartre, the Other-as-subject becomes apprehensible as such through its effect in the self-as-object. As an alien indeterminacy, the other-as-subject produces that self (in its own self-reflection) as a determinate "object," as given a "nature," to which the other-as-subject adds itself as the one for whom the self-as-object is. To be determinate with respect to the other, and indeterminate in oneself—to be the source of one's own exteriority, while at the same time finding the source of one's interiority (one's nature) in the alien other—is to evince the logic of supplementarity with respect to the other.

A structural homology emerges between them immediately. The "logic" of the supplement can be parametrically expressed. It is a state and non-act in the sense that the boundary between presence and its other is a boundary (a state) between things, plenitudes, a separation of the definitive, while the other, the supplement, becomes what finds itself within what it supplements as the necessary condition for that externality (a non-act). And conversely, the (act of) encounter with one's self-definition through the other contains an absence that precludes its plenitude being full without the presence (the trace) of the undefined, of what is both immanent and absent to the (self-)defined, to self-presence itself (a non-state).

A number of things are noteworthy about Derrida's presentation of the supplement and its "logic." He derives it through a narrative, a critique and renarrativization of Rousseau's *Confessions* in *Of Grammatology*, addressing Rousseau's own narrative use of the term *supplement*. From this, a sense of the operation of the supplement within a literary text, and in textuality in general, emerges. But one can argue that Rousseau's text as well, principally in its confessionality as seen through the Derridean "logic," constitutes itself in a way that repeats the NMN-structure homologically. And the effect of this is to braid these disparate threads in the texts of Sartre, Rousseau, and Derrida in a structural mutuality.

Derrida deploys the "logic" of the supplement in the very process of deriving and describing it. He begins his discussion of Rousseau with a disclaimer: "If we lend to the text below a paradigmatic value, it is only provisional" (*Gram*, 149); as if its narrativity were ancillary. Yet, at the same time, he affirms a certain essentiality for the narrative he is about to address: "My ambition will be to draw out of it a signification which [a] presumed future reading will not be able to dispense with." Already, Rousseau is the supplement. Derrida is doing in form what he is speaking about in content. And ironically, Rousseau's story as well, at least the part Derrida "retells," partakes of disclaimer. Rousseau's subject matter is his sexual excess; but his confession, or self-explanation, is rather to being in love with love itself. Thus, he too provides himself with paradigmatic value through renarrativization.

The scene in question, to which Derrida turns his gaze, is Rousseau's return to Geneva from Italy where he had "learned that dangerous supplement that cheats Nature" by artificially, and in the throes of all "innocence," assuages sexual appetite.[7] Rousseau recounts a series of callow romantic vignettes, all more imaginary and projective than sensual, which ostensibly testify to his sense of extravagance. Their role is to form a background to his affair with Madame de Warens, at whose house he resides in Geneva, and with whom he becomes infatuated. By his onanism and his extravangance, he considers himself to have abandoned his morality, while not having lost his bodily virginity (*pucelage*).

His onanism, he explains, is important because it made possible a distance from de Warens. She becomes a sister, a friend (*une soeur cherie, une delicieuse amie*; *Con*, 109) and finally his "*Maman*" in mock familiality (*Con*, 106). But his distance is also the proximity of proxy involvement, a secret attention to objects representing (silhouetting) her daily existence. For instance, he caresses her pillow, "fondling her image in my secret heart" (*Con*, 108). That distance gives him reassurance, not only with respect to de Warens, but in general with any woman. It "saves" him from the temptations of other's wives (*Con*, 189). It permits him "to dispose of the whole female sex at will, to make any beauty who tempts serve [his] pleasure, without first obtaining her consent." As his "fatal advantage," it affirms the supplementarity of what is closest to him, as well as his embrace of the supplement itself. His passion for "*Maman*" can continue to be expressed from afar, toward her shadow, which then presents itself to his self-affirmed "nature" as lover. Like a sign, Rousseau's supplement "by-passes the presence of the thing and the duration of being" (*Gram*, 151).

However, like the sign's difference in identity, wherein it signifies something while signifying itself, there is a difference between Derrida's account of Rousseau and Rousseau's account. When Derrida tells Rousseau's story, he focuses on Rousseau's admission to the danger of the supplement; namely that it enervates, submerges one in the imaginary, in guilt and anxiety, and even threatens madness. "In his [Rousseau's] eyes it will remain the model of vice and perversion" (*Gram*, 153).

> The supplement that cheats maternal nature . . . is dangerous to life. The danger is that of the image. Just as writing opens the crisis of the living speech in terms of its "image," its painting or its representation, so onanism announces the ruin of vitality in terms of imaginary seductions. (*Gram*, 151)

But when Rousseau tells it, it is inverted. It is the ruin of vitality that announces his onanism. He is coy, and approaches his admissions indirectly, symptomatically, as a supplement to his self-reassurance. Rousseau only theorizes his vice. What is always absent from his story is his own body, that immediate "nature" by which he cheats nature within the compass of imagined women whose stories (and consent) it is his desire to omit. "Seduced by this fatal advantage, I set about destroying the sturdy constitution which Nature had restored to me" (*Con*, 108). Rousseau is seduced by his seductions, a self-seduction that discounts "consent" at the same time that he substitutes his own consent to this seduction for the absent other's. This occurs, as well, in his *Reveries*. There, he protests that his detractors are out of mind when out of sight, yet he writes about them with subtle invective.[8] They are in fact the obsessive core of his *Reveries*, not "there" when he writes of them but wholly on his mind, represented in his text not only as a ghostly presence but as his text's addressees. And similarly, his "women" are both presence and absence; they too are effaced in everything but their (obsessive) existence as narrative. It is they who give him the ability to look narratively at himself and see another. Though fantasy women may be the object of his desire, he himself becomes the object of supplementarity itself.

But his confession is to being affected, not affecting himself. In the presence of the fantasy, Rousseau is passive, the seduced. Indeed, the fantasy that onanism (and narrative) requires and desires amounts to being alone, to immersing oneself in the absence of other "beauties" as an elsewhere, while narrating in the first person. It is an aloneness as Other, rather than a solitude. Aloneness becomes his model of the supplement, a metatext of his subterfuge. Each fantasy is both the reality of a self-presence given narratively from elsewhere and the actuality of the Other's absence given narratively in immediacy, and by which he besets himself as if from a distance. That is, narrative is his aloneness under erasure, the presence of self-absence through which he becomes an object for an absent self-presence. It is not that he becomes an object in the fantasy's look, but the many small narratives by which he constructs his obsessions constitute a presence to himself by which he besets himself and renders himself an object. That is, he himself continually catches himself at the keyhole.

But though he has given himself a nature by discovering his own seduction "to his fatal advantage," his aloneness remains more than a model (of perversion or anything else); it is his own real access to the other, that is, as his own "nature," which he tells again and again in the other's presence and absence. Indeed, the imagined presence need not be a woman; nature itself requires an invocation of solitude. For instance, though alone on his island, he dreams of the bliss of being alone on the island, and emerges "from . . . reverie, seeing myself surrounded by greenery. . . . I fused my imaginings with the charming sights, . . . [and] could not draw a line between fiction and reality" (*Reveries*, 90–91). In other words, even immersed in the presence of the idyllic, he imagines the idyllic as an "absent beauty" and awakens unable to choose. That is, he both gives himself a nature from a distance and suffers his own look from that distance, as if caught in the act by another he narrates, and who narrates him. Though he catches himself at the keyhole, he does not catch himself catching himself.

If Rousseau confuses being and fantasy, and continually objectivizes himself in his own eyes (and at his own hands), it is not only to metanarrate being caught at the keyhole; it is to preserve his own subjectivity as storyteller by telling the story of Rousseau the storyteller. In effect, each narrative fantasy is a double narrative in which he is both a character (seduced) who is caught at the keyhole, that is, a narrator of the seduction who is a self-as-other (again a character), and an onanist (metanarrator) as fantasizer, fantasizing (metanarrating) subjectivity. Thus, the story remains untold by being told through a self as Other through whose eyes he grasps his nature as the supplement of his own (other) Nature.

As a structure, Rousseau's enactment of the supplement is thus homologous to the look, or to the look's NMN-structure. Rousseau's project is to make himself other by himself by writing, and then to lay it at the other's door. That is, his interior metanarrative countermands both what his text confesses (that he does it to himself) and what his text professes (that he has risen above "all that"); it provides the arena in which Rousseau the narrator and Rousseau the character change places. In both Sartre's and Rousseau's narratives, one knows oneself through the other's knowledge, as the other's knowledge. And Rousseau, as himself the Other, thus needs still Others to constitute that Rousseau who will give him his nature, who will see him narratively, from afar, as he "is." (It is the same demand that each of Sartre's characters makes in his play *No Exit*; and it is why none can leave the room at the end of the play, knowing there are no other Others elsewhere to fulfill this function.)

Each act of fantasy, desire, narrative, or encounter induces a non-state of objecthood, a non-nature; each state of "cheated" Nature constitutes the non-act of his onanism, of giving himself a non-nature as a nature given by absent others. He supplements himself through imagining the other and representing himself in the narratives he tells; he supplements the others he is telling in his writing by re-presenting the other and imagining himself. As both the look and the supplement, Rousseau's text is a double non-negation. It is not that he has inverted the Sartrean NMN-structure; he lives within it. In Sartrean terms, he would simply be in bad faith; Rousseau, on the other hand, would probably consider Sartre to be one of those tormenting "others."

However, it is Derrida who retells the story; and in that retelling, Rousseau's body reappears and becomes writing. That is, Derrida's writing becomes Rousseau's body, the one he had omitted from his own confessions. Derrida metanarrates Rousseau's narrative and tells the story of the onanism Rousseau hides from view in his own telling, as exemplary for Rousseau.

> Rousseau will never stop having recourse to, and accusing himself of, this onanism that permits one to be himself affected by providing himself with presences, by summoning absent beauties. In his eyes, it will remain the model of vice and perversion. Affecting oneself by another presence, one corrupts oneself [makes oneself other] by oneself. (*Gram*, 153)

Hence the centrality of Rousseau's "onanism" in Derrida's critique; it is an icon for self-presence rather than sexuality. Yet, if "that dangerous supplement," and supplementarity in general, are a model for Rousseau, to which "Rousseau will never stop having recourse," it is because they are a model, an icon, for the Rousseau narrated by Derrida—that is, a model for Derrida rather than Rousseau. Where Rousseau's onanism is a substitution of himself for the representation and imagination he has already substituted for himself, Derrida substitutes his own representation and imagination, as a reader, for what Rousseau (not so) carelessly leaves absent, for what Rousseau silhouettes narratively. That is, it is Derrida who catches him catching himself at the keyhole.[9] In effect, Derrida's own critique of Rousseau parallels Sartre's account of the look. Derrida not only plays in Sartre's narrative, discovering Rousseau in the act, he provides a third-person philosophical integument to a first-person metanarrative, as an analogue to Sartre's text itself.

Like the look, the critique, or the reverie, the supplement is the form of nonpresence whereby "all begins through the intermediary" (*Gram*, 157). What mediates a relationship is what engenders it, and thus also engenders what is in relation. This is the case for Rousseau's "confession," for the Sartrean look, and for the Derridean text about Rousseau. Though these discourses diverge in history and substance, they conjoin in an interwoven congruence that permits each to be a reading of another. All are narrative and chiasmic within the form of their narrativity, and thus homologous in their textual form. Ultimately, in all three, what is known is the form of knowing: the supplement. The critique of the supplement and the confession of the supplement repeat the structure of the look. The look and the confession repeat the logic of the supplement.

What this repetition signifies is a homological individuation of a particular textual form (the discursive structure of the supplement), a similar sculpting of textuality in three disparate discursive realms. The individuation of that textual form is what gives, or renders discernible, in each instance, a boundedness, a definition, and being. Yet because this textual form only becomes discernible as a structure within and through the homological relation rather than the discourses in which it is found, it has textual rather than semiotic being, an embodied rather than signified definition, an enacted rather than defined boundedness.

It is the discourse of the supplement in its double non-negative form (rather than the "supplement" itself) that presents a structure mapped homologically onto the look (in its first transformation of the subject-as-self-as-object), and which is in turn homologous to Rousseau's self-presence as a relation of narrator and metanarrator. Both relate to the discourse of the supplement, as lamina in a complex structure of relations; both relate to each other through a homology to what Derrida has called the supplement. What is constituted by this structure of structures is again a glyph. Earlier, I used the term *glyph* to "name" a sculpting of language, the metadiscursive production of an iconic form whose medium is a homological relation of discursive structures. In the preceding case, that medium was incommensurability itself; in the present instance, the medium is the discursivity of the supplement (three instances), and the homological relation is between double non-negational configurations in that medium.

The glyph iconically presents, and thus represents in substance, the individuated textual form. As the sign of the sculptural in the text, the glyph becomes the name, the act of naming, for a textual form discerned homologically in Sartre's look, Rousseau's confession, and Derrida's text of Rousseau. It "names" them by relating these embodiments as instances of that form.[10] If the logic and discourse of the supplement function as the exemplary structure of this glyph, by which the Sartrean narrativization of the look and the Derridean narrativization of the Rousseauian confession relate, then it epitomizes the form englyphed. The glyph can be "named" the supplement glyph. Using the term *supplement* here is not intended to give it definition or transform it into a structure. It is only deployed to identify a structure that is both sculpted and already found in Derrida's account of the term, its own "infrastructure," as it were.

Because the supplement glyph becomes iconic for the logic of supplementarity itself, however, it obtains a certain objectness that is repeatable, or iterable, as the condition for that objectness. Though it has, as yet, no meaning as a sign to be read, one nevertheless reads it as the shape of the textual structures it metatextually presents and represents. To read the glyph, a non-text, means to reenact its metatextuality. Reenactment and iterability become the same, and indistinguishable as homological discernment of the glyph, the very possibility of meaning for it as a textual form. Though as yet its being resides only in its discernment, the glyph must eventually arrive at a meaning because it is always already a reading.

A Note on "Infrastructure"

This brings us to the edge of something that, while not the abyss, is perhaps a more insidious trap than the abyss. (The inarticulable is the abyss.) The sense of a glyph of the supplement, a reification of the term not in itself but as a structure of mutual reference, crosses a boundary. It is a boundary that many have crossed in attempting to philosophize Derrida's "terms" (such as différance, supplement, hymen, pharmakon, etc.). Gasché, we have already seen, had sought to theorize Derrida's deconstructive "method" under the rubric of a heterology. But he had also thought to conceptualize Derrida's deconstructive terms as signs, though they cannot as yet be read as signs, by categorizing them through the notion of "infrastructure." To understand them as signs would be to give them transcendent being despite their undefinability in Derrida's discourse.

Gasché notices that the terms mark and name places or loci in a text where they become undecidable, or reveal a singularity, a moment of self-referentiality.

A textual singularity is a moment where the text loses touch with its world and becomes self-referential, where it relies upon what it has constructed as its own expression to ground the language it depends upon for that expression. It is at those moments that all ideological discourse calls into operation a variety of presuppositions to maintain or engender discursive coherence. And Gasché's argument is that by constituting ways of naming singularities, Derrida has thus made them discernible as those places where presupposition is indispensible, thereby revealing the extent to which they are imposed upon the text from outside. In Gasché's conception, the singularities, as a text's self-referential (and chiasmic) moments, are in incommensurable (heterological) relation with the text, but that in marking such moments, Derrida produces a theorization of singularity in its textual incommensurability. Though the process of discerning them occurs in a metatext, as theorizable, Gasché then claims, Derrida's deconstructive terms constitute an infrastructure for deconstruction (*TM*, 244).

Derrida has responded that the singularities of a text are wholly particular to each text, and thus ungeneralizable; and it is precisely this ungeneralizability that he seeks to preserve by developing a panoply of such signs that do not function as a vocabulary ("neither word nor concept"). Gasché argues that the singularities can be categorized as the text's points of speculation (in its Hegelian sense of reference to a text's own self-referentiality), because they reveal a commonality of operation in pointing to where the text must pretend to establish an inherent univocality for itself. If such a categorization is possible, then a dialectical construction between the general and the particular produces precisely a theorizability for deconstruction, one whose synthetic structure will be heterological. And for Gasché, this synthetic structure will produce an interface between deconstruction and the required systematicity of philosophy.

But there is a problem with such a heterological space (*TM*, 180). The concept of an infrastructure itself overstructures the deconstructive not only by imposing a dialecticity but by giving a formal articulation to what remains anterior to language as an operation upon which language itself depends. By dialectically constructing a categorization of singularities, Gasché is forcing into the shadows the very incommensurability between singularity and text that his heterology depends upon. Furthermore, the "terms" Derrida coins point to moments of the text where it cannot be grounded. What constitutes singularity for him leaves no textual material remaining by which to situate them with respect to each other. In the absence of any such materiality, or even a common form of self-referentiality (which would have to be a priori) by which to relate them dialectically, the attempt to categorize them becomes, itself, a speculative operation. The infrastructure unfolds as a scaffolding around the text; it becomes another reading that itself must reveal singularities to which it attaches meaning in order to be the reading it is. But for Derrida, the deconstructive terms he develops function neither as substrate nor as superstructure of textuality (*LI*, 148), nor finally as a metatextual stratum for that textuality.

Derrida's own use of the term "infrastructure" in *Of Grammatology* confirms this difference (*Gram*, 164). For him, the infrastructure of text and textuality is the interplay between them. "Infrastructure" refers to "text" itself, where the term "text" signifies "all [that is] called 'real,' 'economic,' 'historical,' socio-institutional; in short, all possible referents" (*LI*, 148). It is the structuring of what is meant by "*il n'y a pas de hors-texte*" (*Gram*, 158).

In effect, considering Derrida's "terms" an infrastructure (*TM*, 244) ontologizes them, where ontologization signifies an attribution of being to something that has none (such as an interstice between things that do have being). Gasché ontologizes by transforming an approach to textuality, one that takes another text as its object and finds its own objectivity there in that other text, into an object text itself. The effect is to exchange the difference between text and metatext for a textual object that can be studied, and flattening the incommensurability between text and metatext into the definibility of a heterology, even though that definitude is heterological. Gasché could not avoid stacking the deck in his favor to produce this outcome; it was the nature of his philosophical project. And he reifies this by axiomatizing philosophy as necessarily coherent and systematic.

The question remains how Derrida's "terms" are, or can be, approached. It is an aspect of Derrida's writing that this question has produced endless fascination.[11] The attempt to find a philosophical ground for what Derrida does with them (beyond their structure as inventions) deconstructs, as an ontologization. But this presents a problem for the present essay, since the "glyph," as deployed here, already points in a number of directions, one of which is precisely such a philosophization.

Ultimately, where the notion of "infrastructure" formulates an approach to the form of language for Gasché, for Derrida, it is the very form of language that requires the unformulational, as non-definitude. In this sense of the unformulational, his "terms" do not even function as a "technology"; as instrumentalities of the undecidable, they are derived from particularity, from what is at hand. For Derrida, these instrumentalities are not structures generated by textuality, nor do they formulate textual form. Rather, they indicate operations that are the condition for generating reading itself, and the reading of textuality. What generates textual form is the text itself, apprehended metatextually–beyond and in spite of all attempts to render the text closed or univocal. "Instrumentality" might be a more appropriate notion, in the sense that the deconstructive or grammatological constitutes a "science of writing"—echoing Saussure's suggestion that semiology be a "science of signs" (*Gram*, 51)—but an unengineered one. What generates structure for Derrida's "instrumentalities" are the structures of his own discourse. Because Derrida develops his terms to speak about what is anterior to language, and what is thus not governed by the structure of language as such (yet can be seen as structured as arche-writing), he must necessarily be neologistic, and anagogic as well. Rather than meaning, it is only their operation that can get articulated. That is, in constructing the discourse of an instrumentality, Derrida does what it is he is describing, developing these terms to speak about what he is doing in the act of doing it—anterior to language, not governed by language, and available only to be silhouetted by language. The apprehension of these silhouettes is the direction in which I wish to take the notion of "glyph."

But one is drawn by such a consideration to an aspect of Derrida's discourse that overflows it, in spite of himself. The trace points to the absent presence of what differs. As such, it manifests as meaning a remembering of what differs, as if that remembering were indeed the object meant by the sign seen in its objectivity. That is, what differs is re-gathered, and already re-joined, like a homecoming, or the enactment of reunion, a performance, as if it were a nameable thing. The trace is an impresario; it administers the logistics of the performance that re-members itself, and acts in it, having called the actors, script, theater, and audience together for itself. As a yearning not for what is simply elsewhere but for the memory of what is safely elsewhere, the trace plays at remembering, at etymologizing and punning, at free associating and alienating. These are its enactments that take on real presence without recalling, without falling into the trap of being real memory. It is resistence to remembering, as the immediacy of the re-membered, the performative ensemble, while overflowing the boundaries of what only exists within a remembering, within differing.

But it does not administer blindly, in the absence of having already acted; instead, it adds its particular logic to its logistics. A remembering that re-institutes, it re-configures a memory it has never lost, re-defers it as if to the end of a performance that has always been only memory. The trace, as a performance and in its performance, is always a nostalgia and the anticipation of nostalgia. Yet, the nostalgia for which it feels nostalgic does not interfere with the attention it gives to what will have been remembered. Its re-membering, in order to once again think what differs, does not interfere with its attention to the present as performance. As memory, the trace is already the foundation for intentionality.

Separation in Immediacy, the Hymen

Where the first transformation of the self-as-object in Sartre's account of the look constitutes an apprehension of a nature (a "loss of innocence"), the second transformation is a loss of instrumental contact with the world, a loss of project. This is not isolated from the first, from one's facticity; facticity and project are mutually immanent facets of the same ontological moment. In falling from grace, in Schroeder's metaphor, one gains a body and loses its dominion. In becoming an object for the Other, one's possibilities retreat out of reach in the other; though they remain present, they become the other's possibilities, both immediate and hidden.

But along with this immediacy, there is a separation from oneself and one's possibilities in that one apprehends oneself through the Other as a project that is not one's own; and one lives oneself as the other's freedom. The Other is free to narrativize, to apprehend, to arrest one in whatever manner s/he may please. "Every act performed against the Other can on principle be for the Other an instrument which will serve him against me" (*BN*, 264). Through loss of autonomy, one becomes an instrumentality in the other's hands (*BN*, 264). "In the shock which seizes me when I apprehend the Other's look, . . . [I suddenly] experience a subtle alienation of all my possibilities, which are now associated with objects of the world, far from me in the midst of the world" (*BN*, 264). One lives oneself as the metanarrator of the Other's freedom, whose project one has become, and one lives the other's freedom as a character in the other's project; as an instrumentality, one becomes the mediation between being a metanarrator of and a character for the other. In effect, separated from oneself in an elsewhere, the self-as-object becomes an actor on a stage for which the Other is the director, performing a script one will have written that the Other then directs. And this structure suggests a strange replication of the marriage paradigm in patriarchal society; the woman is given away, to live the "other's" freedom, to be her own mediation between herself and her husband, to lose her possibilities as a body over which dominion is elsewhere.

This highlights the idea that a subtle dimension of force lurks within this second transformation. Sartre gives the example of himself hiding from a cop or a soldier who, with gun drawn, is looking in dark corners for him. In mutual anticipations, each enacts the Other: the cop by imagining which corners his quarry might hide in, transforming their remoteness into accessibility; the "I" by preempting the soldier's reasoning in order to seek places to hide that would be less accessible to that reasoning. Each becomes an instrumentality for the other in seeking their contradictory ends. This mutual preemption transcends the mere roles of cop and fugitive in the immediacy of their enactments; it is the violent commandeering of each consciousness by the other through the role each plays in the situation the other has created. The whole is a structure of their violent separation as previously defined by each in not refusing that role—after all, the cop does not have to look, and the fugitive, instead of hiding, could agree to believe he will get a fair hearing in court.

The insidiousness of the violence can be discerned in everyday events: the detaining, apprehension, or harassment of a person because of the way s/he looks. A woman wearing stylish clothes, for instance, because it is required by her job, may be attacked on the street for having dressed "suggestively." Automobile drivers of dark skin may be stopped by police for arbitrary "probable cause" through racial profiling. In the first example, one might decry the violence of society, and add, "She should have known better." What is not considered in such a response, though it recognizes the instrumentality to which she is transformed by her attacker for himself, is the reason for which he puts on his uniform (of attacker, of "teacher of lessons," of one who notices and gives import to her dress) in the sense that its familiarity advertises the project (and the ideology) for which he has "arrested" her. We recognize the uniform; it is not that of the gestapo, but of the patriarchy for whom a woman is already an instrumentality.

On the plane of street situations, the woman is being used as a sexual object and at the same time being disciplined or "arrested" as a transgressor of the man's self-definition of the human, by having been predefined as a semi-human object. She becomes the instrumentality by which he becomes definitive "man," already narrativized and self-narrativized in the masculinist paradigms he enacts. Yet in so enacting that paradigm as one of sexuality, the character of sexuality gets erased as such, canceled at the hands of a violence that nevertheless expresses itself sexually. For a woman, such an attack, rendering her an instrumentality without cause other than her mere existence as a woman, appears wholly gratuitous. Furthermore, as Sartre makes clear, the look can be either real or imagined; she suffers the attack in its gratuitousness, and herself as instrumentalized under that attack, even when she does not go out in the street, or when there is no one else there. Indeed, it is the condition for changing her mind and not going out, for deciding that she does "know better," in order not to suffer that look and for nothing to happen. Her being seen by such a man is present in its immediacy in her prior decision to "know better." Under the imagined look of the man in (masculinist) uniform looking for her, she takes evasive action and remains at home, in total real separation. Her body and its clothes have become the imposition of another's choice, preempting her as its instrument through her "internalizing" the socially given metanarratives of his look (and actions), even in his absence.

If this example reifies a particular aspect of the Sartrean look, it does so as a social structure. Its violence is not necessitated by Sartre's narrative of the transformation to instrumentality under the look, which can involve the more welcome instrumentalities of intimacy as well. On the contrary, its structure provides a way of apprehending the dynamic of violent behavior or prejudice that is all too often inexplicable. The metaphoric "uniform" is a mode of behavior based upon prior narratives that metanarrativize in turn the one encountered for the one who looks. In Sartre's account, there is a reciprocal instrumentalizing of attacker and attacked, whether street stalker and woman or cop and fugitive. The cop, for instance, when seen by someone in a certain way, will consider himself to have been seen by a fugitive, to have been instrumentalized by the narratives of his job description with respect to such a (fugitive) look. If he gives chase, it is both a mode of obeying that instrumentality, as the object of the other's look, and of returning the look, thereby reaffirming himself as a subject. The stupefying nature of the "uniform" as a system of narratives through which one is instrumentalized in its terms, though by means of the look of the other, is that one's vision of one's situation is narrowed by the pre-narrativization given anteriorly by them.

The arbitrariness of most police action against certain political activity or against people of color in the United States today escapes simple explanation or control because of its dual nature. That dual nature becomes a labyrinthine fortress against contestation of the police. Questioning the cop's instrumentality, his job description, is met by shifting to the other, the police profile, the cop's re-objectivizing (criminalizing) of the other. Those same narratives of criminalization of the other that serve to produce the cop's subjectivity as social agent then become the metanarrative of police instrumentality. While these are both aspects of what the cop would call "just doing my job" or "just following orders," the ethics of arbitrary action drop through the cracks between having been objectivized by the other, from a position of the other's already de-authorized status, and having been instrumentalized through the other by the position of his own authority. The cop's relation to the other as subject and his relation to himself as object, within the narratives of his uniform, play against each other as explanations for his transgressions of the ethical. They bury the ethical under his own ability to continually change the subject, to toss reason back and forth between them.

A similar structure can be seen for the man who attacks a woman on the street, from the man's perspective. In the uniform of masculinist consciousness, he finds himself looked at by a woman who may not even glance at him, because the narratives of the uniform have already informed him that this is what her clothes are doing. Instrumentalized by her "look," by the "way she looks," through his metanarrativization of her at the hands of the masculinist narratives, he attacks according to the scripted action given the character in those narratives, and by which narratives his moves are also attributed to her through her prescripted acts or responses. Thus, he reaffirms himself as masculine through his metanarrativization of her as a character. It is not a psychological drive or animalism he is obeying. Psychologizing the attacker provides no access to the attacker's complex reasoning concerning his own sense of his innocence in the attack he perpetrates, nor can it understand the complexity of his obedience to a semiotics that emerges as his own transformations, his own oscillation between subject and object at the hands of the metanarrativized woman. If the cop's job, as given by his job description, is to arrest those he has "probable cause" to consider fugitives, as a meaning given to himself as cop, the man's "job," as given by his masculinist uniform, is to "give the woman what she wants," what she's "looking for," again as a meaning he is given through other men.

In thus allegorizing the idea of instrumentality in Sartre's account, its differences from the first transformation he describes for the look can be seen. In both, there is a loss of autonomy; but the instrumentality of the second occurs at the site of the relation between the status of metanarrator and character in another's narrative, for the one looked at, while in the first, the loss of autonomy occurs at the site of the relation between the metanarrator and the other as narrator.

There is a moment in Derrida's text that is also a story of violence. It is one that thankfully involves the comic rather than the fearful. But it is similarly a moment of conflation of immediacy and separation, like the second transformation in Sartre's look. It occurs in the complex textual interplay that Derrida calls the "hymen."

The hymen is a textual membrane, a boundary that is wholly within the text, separating the inseparable and joining the disparate. It is a reading that always transgresses that inner boundary, but which also leaves that textual boundary still to be transgressed, preserving the sanctity of the text's newness and wholeness (*Dis*, 257). For Derrida, it is not a formal or metatextual structure, but a moment of passage from the known to the unknown, from the textually possible to the impossible.

As with the supplement, we may begin a consideration of this structure with Derrida's critique of textuality and then consider his narrativization of it. The instance of textuality to be addressed concerns the relation of a text to its preface. Derrida's discussion of the preface focuses on the fact that a preface is written after the text it introduces in order to precede it; and the text emerges (as if through gestation) from inside a preface about that text, in order to stand outside it as prefaced. The boundary between them, where the end of the beginning is the beginning, is a space across which they change places, a domain of transition that one breaks (in upon), having begun the text, and that breaks upon one as the onset of the text itself. In Derrida's image, it is like the shock of passing from reading the speech of one who is mute to the impossibility of miming intentions or causes that can only be spoken—like a mime who "while speaking upon the stage, begs forgiveness for having done so" (*Dis*, 205). The inarticulable moment of transition from the representation of a presentation to a representation as the presentation, "the hymen [is] the consummation of differends [*des différents*]" (*Dis*, 212). It names the space necessary for transition or exchange to be possible.

For Derrida, such a space extends to all writing; for every word, phrase, or textual sign, other texts have always already provided significations and referents for it; that is, they have functioned as prefaces.

> Such is writing that it only refers [*renvoie*] to itself and, *at the same time*, carries us back, in an undefinable but systematic manner, to other writing. . . . in each moment of allusive return [*renvoie*] to another text, to another determinate system, each textual entity then implicates [*renvoie*] itself as a determined structure; in other words, every text and textual element is both open and closed. (*Dis*, 202, 229; translation modified)

That is, for each sign, there is an interior difference, an interior boundary between its newness (in self-presentation) and its iteration of prior inscription elsewhere, between identity and difference. In some endless Barthesian fashion, as if organizing the reunions of an extended family, each text gathers all other texts to itself as its amassed prefaces after the fact, as antecedents to explain and introduce what the text will be about without them. Each text renders itself a self-referential textual moment already embraced as the secret subject matter, the referent of all textual elsewheres. That is, the structure of supplementarity is the content of the hymeneal structure; the hymen is the form the supplement takes.

But when Derrida arrives at discussing the preface, he has already introduced the hymen narratively: specifically, in a reading of Mallarmé's critical reading of the mime Margueritte's comic drama of Pierrot (*Pierrot Murderer of His Wife*). Pierrot plays (mimes) a scene in which he tickles his wife Columbine to death. To reenact the murder, he returns in mime to that past in which the crime was a future, a project; that is, Pierrot begins by miming, in the present, the past deliberations over how to commit the future crime (*Dis*, 200). To reenact those deliberations, he enacts the crime before the fact (and without the victim). The scene thus mimics in reenactment an act that has not yet occurred, and hence represents nothing. In it, time collapses: "I killed her, yes. . . . But how shall I go about it?" (*Dis*, 200). In addition, the crime will never occur because space collapses as well. Pierrot plays both roles, the tickled and tortured wife as well as himself as tickler and torturer; and in the role of Columbine, he dies under his own hand. If it represents an act, an event that will never take place, then it becomes a presentation whose only representation is itself. It is mimicry that has no original, that precedes what it mimics. The represented becomes the miming as itself, and the representation the mimed itself miming. In embodying in immediacy the possibility of repetition, as a representation, it only enacts the space, the separation, the difference between itself and itself. "There is no longer any textual difference between the image and the thing" (*Dis*, 209). The object (the murder) can only mimic the story told of it. The mime mimics the immediacy of non-mimicry in mime (*Dis*, 198–99).

The non-spatial space structured through these multiple textual inversions is what Derrida calls the hymen.

Like différance, the hymen is neither a concept nor a thing. An unthinkable, inconceivable effect of textuality, "the hymen only takes place when it doesn't take place, when nothing *really* happens" (*Dis*, 213). That is, it "enacts" the unrepresentability of the interrelation (the "nothing" that happens) between presentation and representation. But if what is represented by a description or narrative does not precede that representation, then the object represented represents its representation, and representation as mimesis works in reverse. It is the mimicked that must mime, the world that must copy (as a simulacrum) its "re-presentation." The textual signifier, as a narrative or description, both is (conjoins) and places at an impossible distance its always future object (its signified). In its immediacy to itself, representation engenders in its represented a presentation that will always follow it as again a representation of itself. The hymen is thus the enactment of différance on a discursive level, the level of textual unities, textual form, of textuality itself.

And, as usual, Derrida is doing what he speaks of. The hymen is a form of textuality Derrida discovers through a reading that represents it as already there, though no presentation (in Mallarmé's text) had occurred until noticed and named in Derrida's. In Derrida's text, the hymen, like Pierrot's murder of his wife, is a future presentation of what the past will then have represented.

Let us quickly note the parametric composition of this, to confirm its common textual geometry within the general structure of the look, that is, within the medium or "materiality" of the discursive relation at hand. Pierrot's performance (an act), in which time collapses, becomes other than a representation (a non-state); and the mimed content in/of that performance (a non-act), in which space collapses, becomes itself the re-presentation for which there is nothing beyond (a state).

A similar non-space between presentation and representation occurs in the second transformation of the look. By representing itself as an object for the Other, the self-as-object enacts in itself its loss of itself—not as a self, but as a subjectivity for which the self is instrumental. The loss of one's own instrumentality (of project) enacts an emptying representation whose empty represented is beyond, in another's unknown future (hands), sourceless in loss and projectless in non-enactment. It is the non-enactment of the self-as-object as both character and metanarrator who simultaneously read each other in themselves, wholly immediate, yet separated through the mediation of the other whose metanarrated look narrates the metanarrator as character. The loss of instrumentality under the other's look is not enslavement to the Other, but a dramatization of loss enacted instrumentally through an arcane source, a representation of nothing, a self representing no subject, a given representing the infinite distance of givenness between metanarrator and character. Both Pierrot and Sartre's "I" lose instrumentality by becoming an instrumentality at their own hands through another (a metanarrated character as narrator). Both enact a representation of what the narrative will have been the presentation. (Sartre would rephrase Pierrot: "I've been caught in the act . . . but how will I come upon myself?")

The woman in the previous discussion loses her autonomy through her own decision not to go out, having metanarrated herself as a character in the look of her assailant in his (masculinist) uniform, becoming the object for his uniform look in that elsewhere that is his world. And at the same time, the self-referentiality of his (masculinist) enactment of that narrative is wholly gratuitous, having no reason beyond itself and its renarrativization of her; hence, its terror in its predictable unpredictability and unforeseeability. The corresponding parametric configuration of this should by now be familiar and recognizable; its existence provides a mapping between the hymen and this dimension of Sartre's narrative. In enacting a characterization that is at once its own, its immediacy, yet over there, written by itself through another, the self-as-object has already mimed what it becomes at its own metanarrative hands.

There is a male principle to be discerned here in the confluence of supplement and hymen. It is that Man (Rousseau) takes firmly in hand his way of seeing himself as Other, as Being an Other who sees himself as self. But a "male" principle requires a female principle to differ from, in order to be. The female principle encountered here is that of an indeterminate (and inverse) gestation in which Man (Pierrot) puts an end to himself by killing woman, rendering "her" elsewhere by transgressing her (predefined) non-being here. These male and female principles are both recognizably patriarchal, not only in the source narratives from which they are derived but in the way we read them, the way we find ourselves looked at by them. Both represent dialogues between men, in which the same man plays both sides. As patriarchal, they portray the inverse of an insemination; indeed, insemination is what these prior self-de(con)structions have rendered impossible. Dissemination, as the logical extension of the inner logic of patriarchy, is the loss of this knowledge (the principle of loss of patriarchy, for which there are as yet no narratives[12]) that enables text and metatext to refuse each other, yet at the same time constitutes their textual interplay, their cross-fertilization of forms.

From this point of view, we can begin to glimpse the gender orientation in Sartre's account of the look. We cannot let Sartre off the hook here. In patriarchy, the Woman is already being looked at; a woman is seen not only as an object but as the content of an enactment in which a man is seen being with her, receiving certain attention from her, or able to tell a story of her to other men. As Simone de Beauvoir has argued, the male gaze sees each woman as image, as representation.[13] For the patriarchal mind, she is a male-generated portrait of herself, something that she as a subject must mimic as *its* object. As Hèlène Cixous puts it, men say to women, "We will paint your portrait so that you can hurry up and start imitating it."[14] A woman understands herself as other than that portrait, and at the same time through that portrait. Though this portrait is different from her identity, it is constructed as an attributed sameness for her as her representation. She thus encounters the aporia of the same in conflict with identity, incommensurably. And when she sees other women, she sees herself over there, in that object of the male other's freedom, having lost her own autonomy to that other woman's image in the male look. Other women become her mirror image, the self for which she must become the scene, the object of the male demand not that she (as subject) give up herself and her project, but that she see herself as the man's project, as the object of an enactment that is already the object of a narrative. It is because the lamination of objectifications (and objectivations) is multiple that the dehumanization of this structure remains so hidden to men and so inarticulable by women. Indeed, opposition required a political movement, a huge multiple enactment, and the generation of a community (the women's movement), through which the possibility of alternate narrativization could present itself. In the sense that Sartre described the look in terms of an other not already looked at, his account of the look is gendered masculine.[15]

The Role of Narrative

Let us return a moment to the role of narrative in the construction of feelings and emotions—that is, the relation of that mode of discursivity to the impossible fact of undergoing emotions in a certain commonality. The logic of Sartre's account suggests that the feelings one undergoes (love, fear, shame, etc.) must in some sense mime systems of socially given narratives through which they already constitute commonly recognized experiences. The structure of the hymen provides an articulation of emotion's appearance as common experience. The narrativization of emotion constitutes a representation that presents (engenders) the very thing it then seems to represent.

As was said above, what description or narrative represents does not precede that representation; instead, the object represented represents its representation—the mimicked mimes what mimicks it; the world copies (as a simulacrum) its "representation." In this sense, the metanarrator narrates through the other and the other's look what he becomes in that look, but also as a metanarrator. What he sees as himself is given to be recognized in his becoming that thing after the fact in the look. Perception, as narrated metanarratively, stands between the structure of narratives that determine it and the object it then sees, which mimicks the representations those narratives already were. To put these two accounts together, the discursive presentation of an object becomes the mode by which perception of it occurs as experience. Or, again, the textual signifier (narrative or descriptive) conjoins and defers to an impossible distance its always future object, its signified, the very "thing" it sees (the "thing" that anthropomorphically can be understood as seeing itself seen by its signifier). Representation engenders the immediacy of its represented to itself at the same time that it separates that presentation from itself as a representation of itself.

This structure provides a way of understanding the cultural specificity, the non-universality and cross-cultural difference, of human emotion.[16] If a narrative structure is what both presents and represents a structure of emotional meaning, then emotional meaning, the personal and social significance of particular kinds of somatic feelings and affective responses, and hence the role of emotion would have a specificity determined by a commonality to a cultural milieu. It would also remain unrepresented as a cultural discourse precisely because an apprehension of emotion from beyond the domain of that narrative structure would give it content from the observer's background, and not that of the observed. The role of emotion, in its particularity in community (and commonality) would be seen through the significance it had for the one apprehending it. For those undergoing emotional responses to other or to the world, there is no narrative dimension, since that is a reiterated metanarrativity in another's look, and thus undergone prereflectively. One becomes the object of the emotion. And this would mean that an outside observer of a cultural milieu in which the socially given significance of emotional responses was given by a different narrative structure would still apprehend the emotional responses s/he sees as irrevocably separate from that narrative structure, and comparable as experienced to his/her own emotional immediacy.

The cultural specificity of emotional response would be immanently indiscernible as such, because cultural specificity hides behind a framework of assumed familiarity (and assumed commonality). It only becomes discernible when one reacts in the milieu of a different culture as seems to befit the situation, and those around one react askance to that, sometimes with violence. What one confronts in such situations is an unintelligibility generated by the incommensurability of narrative structures underlying the sociality of emotional responses. Ironically, it is the assumption of familiarity that creates distance and unfamiliarity. It also produces an aura of the exotic (a familiar unfamiliarity) in another's emotional responses. Objectified difference becomes the exotic as soon as it does not belong to the ordinary, but can be absorbed into it. To apprehend something as exotic is already to appropriate it into one's own cultural framework, as different. In short, it represents a way of not granting others their unfamiliarity or difference.

In effect, the narrative that renders a feeling or emotion a common experience for a particular socius does so by inventing it as a meaning for the individual (by attaching it to the individual's relational and somatic situations) within that framework, which then presents itself as originarily individual. The narrative names what it invents as a meaning in order for that (narrative) meaning to be discovered in the individual as a somatic or social response (as a character undergoing what has been thus metanarratively named). That is, if the narrative representation is socially given originarily, then an immediately enacted emotion *is* its representation. One undergoes that emotion in the knowledge that it is a familiar (a common cultural experience) for both oneself and others with respect to whom it occurs. The "name" of the emotional experience is then the "name" given what the narrative describes and the social community accepts as its signifier, such as "fear," "anger," "desire," and so on, for which the underlying narrative is the trace. The names represent the specific experiences by pointing back to the social narratives that bestow recognizable common meanings on the emotional response, to which the name then refers—within the structure of how one as metanarrator undergoes as a character the (relational and somatic) enactment of what is named through the other to whom it is enacted as a response. Thus, what is named as an emotion is not itself a narrative; it is what turns the narrative into a "performance" (a transformation of an inner "worldly" state) which reabsorbs that narrative into individual reality as the very discernibility and familiarity to others of the (emotional) experience the narrative "names."

Where the first transformation of the look braids Sartre, Derrida, and Rousseau in a common structure of supplementarity, the second engages Sartre, Derrida, and Pierrot in parallel textual performances; a structure of performativity that, as iterated in their several texts, also presents itself as a glyph. Where the term *supplement* names the glyph of chiasmic relation between outside and inside, so the term *hymen* names a glyph for the simulacrum of all enactment (as repetition), the loss of instrumentality through the inseparability of representation and presentation (the originary as repetition, and repetition as originary). As a double non-negation, this glyph marks the identity and difference of the self-as-object as both metanarrator and character, the metanarrator that mimes a character, and a character that enacts an originary, metanarrated (distant) representation.[17]

And parenthetically, I might note that to designate these glyphs by means of Derridean deconstructive terms is again to apprehend an instrumentality for those terms (that Derrida did not intend, and even warned against; *SP*, 158), but which differs from the notion of instrumentality applied to them directly above.

The hymen marks a glyph not only for the Sartrean enactment of loss of project, of instrumentality ("The hymen only takes place when it doesn't take place, when nothing *really* happens"), but for Derrida's conjunction with and separation from Sartre. Across "the whiteness of a certain veil that is interposed or torn" (*Dis*, 179), both enact (in writing) a formal structure that cannot be seen (read) as a form in the absence of the other. Each is seen not by means of the other's text, nor as an intertextuality, but through the conjunction and separation of a homological mapping. In content, their meanings and their respective textual "ecologies" remain distant while transgressing each other homologically as form. The whiteness (blankness) of the interstitial space marks the inversion, the inverseness, rather than the refusal, that holds them apart, and which constitutes the non-spacing between them.

Imagistically (and by inversion, since the hymen is non-symbolized by loss), one could say that the hymen symbolizes the existentialist notion that "Man is alone" and that the context required to shred the fabric of aloneness is a violent one (that is, that "Man" as such is who has to be broken into, retrieved from the instrumental "he," the instrumentality "he" must lose in order to have himself). As a distanceless abyss between the self and the Other, the hymen enacts the mutual exclusiveness of being a subject or an object, and at the same time enacts the mutuality of requiring that a "you" be an "I," that there be a "you" in order that there be an "I"—a "you" which is not simply a reply but a conjunction of character and metanarrator in themselves.

Though Sartre is a phenomenologist and essentializes subjectivity, this glyph fills part of the space between him and the de-essentializing Derridean critique of the language of subjectivity; it does so by providing a language in which the Sartrean account becomes nonessentialized. It both names and incorporates into itself as a name the two significations for the term "I" in Sartre's narrative, relating them referentially in their separation and inseparability. That is, the glyph gives residence in language to the already decentered (and polyvocal) "I" in Sartre's narrative, without defining two selves. This is not a deconstructive operation; the glyph is a rebuilding of the complex construction of meaning that exists behind the unitarity of the sign, a unitarity whose assumption merely reflects the absolute familiarity signs betray within language.

This constructivity characteristic of the glyph is not foreign to Derrida. Derrida addresses narratives such as *Pierrot* (through Mallarmé) or Rousseau's confessions in order to find in narrative those elements of textuality that are at work as the ground of textuality in general (the hymen, the supplement, etc.). It would affirm his project to suggest that the structures of textuality he seeks are indeed more easily discernible in fiction than in exposition precisely because narrative (or drama) preserves particularity; fictional texts are less fettered by ancillary metadiscourses of truth and referentiality that are essential to expository generality. Though the "hymen" and the "supplement" point back to structural elements of narrativity, they are also to be found at work in all textuality to the extent that generality includes narrativity through the reinclusion of all prefatory textuality in form. What the glyph of these structures imparts is the inseparability of the particular and the general in a form that must make itself general out of what can only appear in particular. That is, if this structure is the content of what is signified by the term *hymen*, it is also its form. This repeats the sense in which the deconstructive term is the signified in its discursive structure (form) of what it signifies in its discursive disclosure (content).

THE SOCIAL TEXT OF THE GLYPH

Let us return to the issues on the social plane that have presented themselves as instances of the glyphic. These include emotions, feelings, experiences of persons, and so on. The "name" for an emotion or feeling, for instance, has been posited as representing the "name" or "title" of a narrative (or system of narratives) that presents that feeling (etc.) as common experience, for common recognition. That is, the narrative itself becomes the sign that contains within itself the aporia between the individual experience or feeling that it describes (which remains private, hidden from common apprehension), and its social commonality as the effect of its narrativity. It "names" or nominalizes itself as access to that hidden experience and its aporetic sociality.

But a "name" for a feeling (such as anger, shame, intimacy) is always of one's "own" feeling, though not a "proper name" and not a "social" feeling. As a social nominative, the narrative interiorizes the difference between the general and the specific (as well as between a narrative's double act of nominalizing itself and what it recounts). That is, the narrative itself also becomes a "name" for that aporia and for its content. Even in a system of narratives, that content individuates itself homologically as the common element of the NMN-structure in which that system is deployed. The nominalist narrative (or system), as commonality, contains the incommensurability between consciousness (intentionality, subjectivity) and narrative (its reading of itself), while at the same time singling out and presenting the content as what the name of the feeling or emotion then names. In effect, the entire structure of name, nominalist narrative, and social aporia constitutes a single signifying structure through which the feeling or experience is purveyed, recognized, known, rendered a familiarity. And in that structure, the name englyphs the system of homologies, of congruent structures in the narrative system that tell that feeling. Ultimately, it makes sense that the structure of the names for feelings and emotions would have such complexity in light of the impossibility of an emotion being and not being a common experience.

Take, for example, the system of narratives that engender feelings of loss of respectability in the disapprobation of another when that other catches one in a position one knows (assumes) the other will think reprehensible (at the keyhole, for instance). Those narratives, as a system, name the scene (eavesdropping, voyeurism, spying) that repeats them; the system tells the feeling appropriate to the reperformed scene and denotes what label (moral shame) to put on the feeling. In its multiplicity, that system is a totalization of particularities that interrelate structurally (recounting homologous situations: of spying and getting caught, for instance) and socially (as different narrativized scenes presented under the rubric of the same name). The specification of that name (the feeling of getting caught) then becomes the title ("shame") of a narrative the scene (of getting caught) repeats, and of the narrative system that names it. In being what it presents and names as narrative, the name (and the feeling named) is a text; in being named through the title of what that text presents, the name (of the feeling) is a metatext. As a glyph, containing a formal structure of aporia between these two, which signifies the feeling as a "knowledge" of it as well as a recognition of it when undergone, the name is a non-text. It is because it is a non-text, whose trace is the system of narratives that compose it, that the enactment of the feeling can occur with a sense of autonomy, for which Sartre's ontology is one of the descriptions.

There is no dialectic here. The form the performance takes (as aporia) is narrative; the form the narrative takes (as aporia) is a name; and the form the name takes (as aporia) is a performance. The confluence or lamination of all this is the glyph. When we use the term for a feeling (for the known and unknowable), it is through the glyph that the term presents itself for use.

Derrida provides a parallel example in *Dissemination*, where he intimates an awareness of how the post-structuralist critique, of which his thinking is a part, has transformed the notion of literature historically. He asks, "Why should 'literature' still designate that which already breaks away from literature?" (*Dis*, 3). The question asks, among other things, how the name disguises the space that opens between literature and what it becomes by becoming aware of itself as "literature," by naming itself as such. The name "literature" becomes a glyph that encompasses the non-text of the hiatus, a double reading and double writing of the concept of literature in the space between the name that recapitulates literature metatextually and the text that anticipates the name of what breaks away from literature (its self-awareness).

Hugh Silverman gives an account of Sartre's approach to literature that structures it in a comparable manner.[18] In a 1971 interview with Michel Rybalka, Sartre had said, "There is no more literature." And Silverman asks rhetorically what Sartre could mean by this, given that Sartre still wrote, and that literary works in general were still being produced. Silverman argues that Sartre felt that his original notion of Literature (in *What Is Literature?*), as that which brings about human freedom, had become in the contemporary era a utopian endeavor. For Sartre, by 1971, the most a writer could produce was a work, a specific totalization of aspects of the situation in which readers find themselves. But no overarching totalization, such as that contained in a "literature," could still address itself to the freedom of the reader. The ability to think freely was constantly being outflanked by the complexities of the political situation; that is, the situation continually engendered aporias between a work and a reader's totalization of it, which, for Sartre, had come to constitute the contemporary condition of the literary. To call this a glyph would recognize that the term contained and reflected Sartre's political narrativization of the literary work's inability to go beyond itself to a *literature*, as well as the possibility and impossibility of the literary itself. If the Derridean glyph represented the literary text's (literature's) going beyond itself within the incommensurability of text and metatext that this implies, the Sartrean glyph is the inverse; for one, the metatext leaves the text out of reach, and for the other, the text leaves the metatext out of reach. Because it contains the aporias underlying these possibilities, the glyph presents itself as both a contentless form (the sculptural, the iconic) and a formless content (the signified of the non-text as non-sign). Formless content is what emerges at the limit of the text, and contentless form is what emerges at the limit of the metatext. The glyph appears as the textual structure that iconizes each structure that composes it. Its form is its content; and its name refers to the subject matter that it both presents and hides, to the performance it renders at once representational and autonomous.

But if, through our narrativization of Sartre's account of the look we can conclude that the terms for feelings, emotions, those aspects of human existence not available for common experience, are named through a form of the glyphic, then we have already gone beyond the argument Sartre makes in his *Outline for a Theory of Emotions*. In that work, Sartre argues that emotions are "magical" transformations of the world that are effectively and affectively chosen, acceded to, though already proper to the individual as a human being; Sartre did not posit that they might be socially constructed, or of necessity recognizable through a certain prior narrativity. But if narrative is actually prerequisite to the constitution of individual experience as common experience in the communal arena, then emotion is already the way the world gives itself to be transformed. The emotional, or feelings and experiences, becomes the mode whereby the communal, or the cultural, as world, constitutes itself by constructing the individual experiences that will then constitute it by participating in it. This is, in general, the role of what is called the mythic; the "mythic" can be said to be that which functions in this way.

DISSEMINATION

In the look's third transformation, the subject that had been autonomous suddenly finds itself no longer self-determining; instead, its selfhood, the foundation of its "self," is discovered outside itself, lost to the Other's hidden apprehension. In the immediacy of one's separation from the world (project) and supplementary to one's apprehension of having a nature (for oneself through another), one encounters the loss of one's subjectivity and a knowledge of an unknowable Other subjectivity (*BN*, 261). This knowledge overflows beyond one's awareness of having a nature, as the loss of subjectivity transcends the loss of project.

> Beyond any knowledge which I can have, I am this self which another knows.... I am my Ego for the Other in the midst of the world which flows toward the Other. (*BN*, 261)

Losing one's own knowledge of the world to the Other's look, one's Being becomes the other's knowledge; as one's self drains into the other, one's knowledge becomes the other's being. Knowledge and Being are both erased and inversely reinscribed in the Other's Being and knowledge. There is a double knowledge and a double loss that appears in the form of a double discovery and a double hiddenness. One discovers oneself appropriated by the Other's hidden knowledge, while one's own knowledge of the world is hidden in one's discovery of the Other's Being as a subject. The loss through one's appropriation by the other's appearance is conflated with an appropriated knowledge that is lost in the other's hiddenness (a loss to appropriation and an appropriation that is lost). Thus, loss and knowledge fill one's sense of oneself as an object.

Again, this has the parametric structure of a double non-negation. The self becomes a form whose content (as knowledge) is elsewhere, and a content (a nature) whose form (as Ego) is lost. Formless content and contentless form are how the Other's freedom appears for the self-as-object. The Other is known as act (a discovering freedom to which one loses oneself) and as non-state (an unknowability), and one knows oneself in incommensurable difference to that as state (an object) and as non-act (an absent freedom).

To rephrase this, to know the Other in self-loss as the Other's knowledge is to be given twice and withheld twice. One is given by the Other as the content of the look, and given by oneself through the Other as an object (a character in a story one tells oneself the Other is telling about oneself). One is withheld by oneself from oneself in losing apprehension of one's autonomy or self-authorship through the Other, and one is withheld by the Other as the Other's hidden knowledge. In becoming the Other's knowledge through one's loss of autonomy, the loss of one's ability to determine what is to be known, one becomes the mediation of the incommensurability of character and narrator in the Other: of the character one becomes in the other's narrative as the other's knowledge, and the metanarrated narrator to whose subjectivity one loses one's own subjectivity. Where the supplement was constituted by a reading of the narrator-character relation as the "outside inside the inside," and the hymen was constituted as a conflation of the narrator-character relation in the separation of the metanarrator "I" and the character "I" in the other's look, in this third transformation, one's givenness and withheldness mediate the narrator-character relation in the other-as-subject as a freedom, as a narrator, a hidden storyteller.

In this third transformation, parametrically congruent to the other two, the double non-negation, as a mediation of incommensurability, is again far from being dialectical; indeed, it seems to reverse the dialectic. It is the dissolution of a synthesis, the look as a subject-object relation, into a complex relation of incommensurables; a movement from the dissolution of that former synthesis through the relation it synthesized to the mediation that had constituted that relation.

But to mediate an incommensurability is to in some sense realize it, to find it in the world. It is this that Sartre maps as the two poles of being looked at: shame and pride. Shame or pride represent negative and positive poles of one's visibility and objectivation, within the context of returning the look in the mode of self-resubjectivization through the objectivation of the other. "It is shame or pride which reveals to me the Other's look and myself at the end of that look. It is the shame or pride that makes me *live*, not *know* the situation of being looked at" (*BN*, 261). The difference is whether the look, as narrativized, is one of approbation or deprecation, whether the visible object one becomes in one's own narrative is to be given one or the other socially. To live the situation of one's visibility in pride as the mode whereby one's objectivation and the Other's autonomy are mediated is to grant oneself, through the other, a socially given and narrativized positivity, a positive sociality. In the realm of the social itself, in the look of others rather than a singular other, this becomes a political relationship; that is, it constitutes itself through both ontological pride (awareness of being looked at) and ontic pride (a sense of one's positivity).

Similarly, at the other pole, to live one's social narrativization of being looked at, of one's visibility, in shame (again, like pride, both an ontological shame and a socially given ontic shame) is to accept the imposition upon oneself, through the other, of a socially given and narrativized negativity, a negative sociality, again as a political relation, as a mode whereby one's objectivization and the other's autonomy are mediated. The political or religious leader feels a certain pride at being the charismatic object of attention, even in his/her own dissolution as an autonomous subject who cannot just be him/herself. S/he becomes *what* conjoins others in social solidarity through his/her visibility, through the mediation that the leadership role gives the leader within the incommensurability between individual and collective group.[19] Only the real or virtual (as speech) visibility of the leader flows out to the others as the mediation of their own dividedness as autonomous subjects, a mediation between their own narrating sociality (as narrator) and the leader as character enacting what is hidden in them. The leader thus bestows a subjectivity where that may have been withheld or even unimaginable outside the movement. In a sense, it is as a substitute narrated character (produced by the metanarrating leader) that a symbol or icon raised by a movement or religion functions as a center of coherence or coalescence, to be read by its followers as that which recapitulates the look and reconstitutes their organizational subjectivity.

At the other pole, the incommensurability contained in a role as a character in another's (or a group's) social narrative has the power to inferiorize, in the sense of generating a scapegoat. This occurs through the imposition of a narrativity on the other that the other then understands as the content of the look of those who generated the narrative. It is for this reason that all scapegoated groups have imposed on them a visible or physical trait, even where it does not or cannot exist, or makes no social or biological sense, as essential to the social narrativity of domination. It is that visibility that becomes the icon for the noticing and attention that is essential to the imposition of the narrative of deprecation previously attached to it. For the anti-Semite, the Jew looks Jewish; and for someone who does not "look Jewish," the knowledge that he is Jewish will make him "look Jewish." Homophobia performs a similar alchemy on gay men. It is in the look, under the aegis of the negative narrativity by which the scapegoat is defined, that the scapegoat feels the negativizing shame that inferiorizes and reduces him/her to objectivization. In this deployment of the visible, through which the one looked at apprehends him/herself as loss and the other's knowledge, social subjectivity becomes hegemony.

Derrida puts this conjunction of loss and knowledge a different way. "To lose one's head, no longer to know where one's head is, such is perhaps the effect of dissemination" (*Dis*, 20). Derrida's puns are distorted or lost by quoting out of context (the "loss of one's head" occurs between re*capit*ulation and anticipation, for instance); but he too is conflating loss and knowledge ("no longer to know" is a form of one's own knowledge where "not to know" can only be an Other's knowledge).

In describing his notion of dissemination (as he has invented it), Derrida again speaks of prefaces. As mentioned above, the preface follows its text in order to precede it. That is, it is already a past reading announcing in the future tense the text to be read: a recapitulation and anticipation of the text. The preface must disappear, lost in a temporal mist, since at its end, one is at the beginning; yet it does not disappear, since, having already rendered the text a subject matter for itself, it remains a knowledge of it. The preface cannot be sublated; it has no Hegelian polish. Instead, it exemplifies the meeting of non-text (prefatory form) and metatext (prefatory content) between which the text is a ghost, a mere mediation. (That is, a hymeneal structure forms the content of dissemination; dissemination is the form the hymen takes.)

In dissemination, the text engenders a metatext (an Other or allo-text) for itself, for which it becomes the object, the subject matter; that is, the text tells its own story through a preface that takes over and tells the text's story. Like the look, the preface intervenes as the text's loss of mastery, of self-determination. The origin of the preface in the text is lost to the origin of the text in the preface. But that origin is in turn also elsewhere, in the social convention that a text be prefaced. The text engenders (metanarrates) its preface as a socially given way to discover itself as an object, and for which it becomes that object. In effect, the preface is the look. Wholly outside the preface (a state), the text loses itself metatextually within it (a non-act). Wholly within the preface (a non-state), the text makes the preface part of itself, a knowledge of itself (an act). For the text, the preface is both loss and knowledge, a reading that will not have been a reading, but rather knowledge of the text that turns it into a knowledge—an objectification of the text at its own socially ordained metanarrative hands. The form of "prefacing," as a form of "dissemination," is homologous to the NMN-structure.

In addressing the form of the preface, Derrida marks the structure whereby a text becomes its own metatext with respect to its own textual forms. To the extent that a text discloses or renders discernible its own textual forms in its own operations, it plays the role of the metatext. Though the production of textual form is grounded in the text, its existence as textual form and the meaning it produces become the subject matter of a metatext that is about textual form. But the "preface" names a form whereby the text becomes metatextual to itself; and in marking this, Derrida situates the text in a field of multiplicity of metatextual levels among which meaning disseminates itself. The content of such metatextuality recapitulates and anticipates (like a preface) the way textual form arrives at signification within its own textuality. But it cannot go beyond its formulation to its arrival at being a signification.

> The gap between the empty 'form,' and the fullness of 'meaning' is structurally irremediable, and any formalism, as well as any thematicism, will be impotent to dominate that structure. (*Dis*, 21)

In other words, textual form, before it can generate meaning of its own, already escapes the textual meanings of which it is constituted, either at that level or in a critical discourse on it. The metatext of textual form is different from a literary critique; it represents a difference of textual levels that is absolute, even in their inseparability.

This gap is none other than "the incommensurability of the signifier and the signified," which it formalizes and generalizes. Textual form always already finds its signification as a signifier elsewhere than at the textual level of signification that generated it as its form in the first place. Thus, in general, the signification of signs, to the extent they transcend narrative to the definitive, or are lexiconized, depends on some metatextual operation. And this is the ground on which structuralism pointed out that reference, and the "truth" of representation, are established metatextually through codes or ancillary discourses about logic, truth, and referentiality (cf. *S/Z*). It is not the formulation of textual form but its recapitulation, its iteration elsewhere in the textual field, that exiles it—as signifier, formal structure, and sign; but in the same gesture, that recapitulation extradites form back to the text, its homeland, where it had been found metatextually in the first place. In effect, its meaning (signified) is condemned to the emptiness of what is anticipated (by the impossibility of "spelling" it out or the endlessness of the chain of signifiers) as a future aftereffect, a future recapitulation of that past anticipation.

> Dissemination interrupts the circulation that transforms into an origin what is actually an after-effect of meaning. (*Dis*, 21)

In other words, one never simply reads a text; the discernment of its forms, and of its signs, requires the reading of a reading, in which its forms (as signs) are given being beyond the text, and in which it loses itself, becoming a knowledge of what had been read. That is, the production of textual form (whether as sign, narrative, prefatory form, etc.) occurs through the recapitulation of a knowledge that is already the loss of the text that anticipates it. The interplay of anticipatory text, non-text (discernment of textual form, sign, etc.), and metatext (the articulation and recapitulation of form, the reading of a reading) is the reverberation of dissemination that strews (or broadcasts) meanings among these irreducible discursive levels.

> We know semantic saturation is impossible; the signifying precipitation introduces an excess facing ("that part of the lining which extends beyond the cloth," according to Littré) that cannot be mastered; the semantic after-effect cannot be turned back into a teleological anticipation and into the soothing order of the future perfect. (*Dis*, 20)

Thus, the discernment of form, which lifts the seige of social coding on textual meaning, reveals meaning to be a "semantic after-effect" in general. Beyond the production of significationless signs or contentless forms that Barthes sought, there is a structural lamination of text (meaning), non-text (form), and metatext (the text for which textual form is the content), which becomes, in their interplay, the generation of a place of meaning, of difference between forms. If the text is the substance of textual form as non-text, which in turn constitutes the substance of a metatext, that metatext, as the reading of a reading, bestows meaning upon the text as a reading of its form, and becomes the substance of the text, what it in fact finds itself signifying. If textual form has meaning, it is because it produces itself as a form (a reading) that becomes its meaning when interpreted metatextually and then finds itself posited in the text as the meaning of its textuality. In this lamination, for each level, the preceding is the substance, the subject matter, and the succeeding is where it posits or finds posited its meaning. It is a circle, a never-ending deferral of meaning to the constitution of forms as the ongoing constitution of meaning.

But to have deployed "reading" in this manner opens the question of reading itself, which involves the question of the production of meaning (*Gram*, 158). Though we have essentially recapitulated and deployed Derrida's sense of reading in the preceding discussion, let us return to Derrida's own terms, which had perhaps been anticipated. On the one hand, for Derrida, a reading cannot reproduce meaning, because it cannot reproduce "the conscious, voluntary, intentional relationship that the writer institutes" with his/her text and with his/her history through the language of that text. Furthermore, a reading cannot be content to simply "double the text"; it must account for the "excess of syntax over meaning" (*Dis*, 231)—that is, of form over content. "A reading should no longer be carried out as a simple table of concepts and words. . . . One must reconstitute a chain in motion, the effects of a network and the play of syntax" (*Dis*, 194). On the other hand, a reading cannot produce meaning, because a meaning is already housed in the text as a sign, and in the signs of the text as signifiers. It cannot go beyond itself; it "cannot legitimately transgress the text toward something other than it, toward a referent . . . [or a] content [that] could have taken place outside language" (*Gram*, 158). (This is in addition to the injunction that one cannot read capriciously, because the text is bound to certain signifiers and their relationships.)

> The reading must always aim at a relationship, unperceived by the writer, between what he commands and what he does not command of the patterns of the language that he uses. (*Gram*, 158)

That is, a reading must also be a metatextual account of the relationship of text to non-text, "the production of a new sign, a meaning and a form" (*Dis*, 256).

In effect, a reading, which is already the look, gives and withholds the text twice: it is given as iteration and withheld in the non-textuality that imposes itself through what is read as an effect of iteration; it gives itself in its transparency of meaning and withholds itself in opacity as difference, as a "new sign." Under the look of a reading, the text becomes a knowledge and loses itself to the metatextuality of reading. The text becomes both more and less than it is. It discloses itself as form without content (the non-text of discernment) and content without form (the reading of a reading, the aftereffect as origin). Reading has the structure of dissemination, to which it is homologous, as it is to the look.

But the reader's relation to the text evinces a reciprocity. The text invents its reader as both its character and narrator, because the reader is the look. But the reader likewise invents a voice in the text to narrate it, the narrator or "speaker" of the text, as the reader's own character. As mentioned earlier, this character is often called the "author." The text tells the reader the story of what has been read, to which narrative the reader submits under the aegis of this voice narrated by the reader through the text. The reader becomes the recipient, the addressee, of a narrative (of the authorial voice) attributed metanarratively and metatextually to the text, as the textual act of giving the reader a "nature" as reader, as addressee. If the reader metanarrates the text through the voice narrated in the text, that voice, as an authorship whose silent presence and expression the text is, emerges from the text to discover the reader listening (reading). The text objectivizes the reader. The reader becomes an object come upon, discovered, encountered by the authorial voice as what the reader has already read in it, and read into it. Thus, the narrated ("authorial") voice in the text becomes the look; the "encounter" with this voice in the text, this "regard" (concern) of the text, conjoins a context by which coherent sense is bestowed on the text. The act of having metatextually chosen context and authorial voice to which the reader then "submits" analogizes the socially given discourse by which a content is given to the Other-as-subject's knowledge in the look as a self-awareness by the one looked at. While there is a clear element of attribution to this (again), it is the attribution of a personhood to an absent author, an attribution of a subjectivity to the voice already "encountered" in the words read, rather than the attribution of a knowledge.

Reading the Imagination as Reading

But to speak of "attribution," even if just of narrative, is to speak of imagination. A brief comparison of respective approaches to imagination will perhaps fill out some of what is being done here through homology. For Sartre, imagination is understood as a mode of intentionality. Sartre addresses the question of imagination through the notion of a mental image. The mental image is a content given to something seen, by which the object seen is given meaning and rendered a representation of something, above and beyond its being as an object. The materiality of the image is not the object but the "way of surveying it" (PI, 50).

In this, the "way of surveying" plays a role analogous to the noema in Husserl's account of intentionality. It is what bestows the meaning of the general on each particular instance, the way each dog, picture of a dog, and schematic sketch of a dog is recognized as a dog. It is the way words are read. "To read is to realize *on* the signs a contact with a world of unreality" (PI, 91). But in this sense, imagination is a way of knowing, as recognition, which for Sartre is a way of going beyond consciousness's relation to an object (PI, 94). In short, the "essential characteristic of the mental image is a certain way an object has of being absent within its very presence" (PI, 104). Thus, "an imaginative comprehension is always a part of a temporal form to be described, in which consciousness takes a certain position in relation to its object" (PI, 144). Thus, if consciousness takes a standpoint on an object through its mental image, that mental image divides into what it is and what it represents (PI, 76). In this sense, the role Sartre gives the mental image is that which enables the world to be apprehended as meanings.

Derrida gives a short account of what he understands as the imagination in one of his discussions of structuralism. Structuralism concentrates "on the organization of meaning, on the autonomy and idiosyncratic balance, the completion of each moment, each form; and it is to refuse to relegate everything that is not comprehensible as an ideal type to the status of aberrational accident" (*WD*, 26). Imagination, he argues, can be understood within this, but only to the extent that it is without, beyond, outside; the concentration on the organization of meaning pushes one beyond the ability to apprehend the work of imagination. This differs from Sartre's treatment in the sense that Sartre examines imagination as a structure of consciousness, and Derrida looks at it as an operation beyond structure, something that one approaches through artifacts that become signs for its inarticulability.

For Derrida, imagination is "the power of mediation or synthesis between meaning and literality . . . the empathy between 'form and content'" (*WD*, 7). To apprehend "the operation of imagination," he goes on, "one must turn oneself toward the invisible interior of poetic freedom. One must be separated from oneself in order to be reunited with the blind origin of the work [of art] in its darkness. . . . [It] is a departure from the world toward a place which is neither a *non-place* nor an *other* world, neither a utopia not an alibi, the creation of a 'universe to be added to the universe'" (*WD*, 8). This is what Derrida refers to as "force," the "other of language without which language would not be what it is" (*WD*, 27). And here he is talking about literary language, the literary text, the formless content that Barthes would look for in the literary work. Imagination is the operation by which "the text presents itself as the metalanguage of the language that does not present itself" (*Glas*, 129); "it is the air it [the work of art that both presents and hides] causes to circulate between its screens" (*Glas*, 75). And we can see that each of Derrida's instrumentalities, such as the supplement, the hymen, différance, and so on, are attempts to point at some of the modes by which what does not present itself is in operation, the air that circulates within writing.

But Derrida then adds, through his critique of structuralism, that "force" is not form. "The force of the work, . . . of that which engenders in general is precisely that which resists geometrical metaphorization, and is the proper object of literary criticism" (*WD*, 20). On the other hand, form, which is the only possibility of articulating "force" (*WD*, 28), "fascinates when one no longer has the force to understand force from within itself" (*WD*, 4). That is, literary criticism is the philosophy of the literary that seeks through its own imagination to apprehend the operation of imagination in the literary text. And it is part of Derrida's critique of structuralism that it divided the text into "objects" that, in their stolidness, lost the ability to present the imagination, the force, of the original work. This ultimately was a realization Barthes was to come to, after the publication of *S/Z*, and which led him to write *The Pleasure of the Text*.

In sum, where Sartre addresses the ontology of imagination, Derrida looks at what the fact and work of imagination suggest about the outside, the exterior, the beyond of metaphysics. In their disparate approaches, as a structure of consciousness or intentionality that apprehends the world as meaning, and an operation of force between writing, text, and the metatext that engenders the text as form and meaning, they encapsulate their own incommensurability.

But Sartre has also been given a different relation to imagination through our derivation of the NMN-structure. If a social narrative is undergone in the look of the other, it is because one has imagined who one is in that look, and imagined the thoughts of the other, in which one has become an object. These are coherent within Sartre's phenomenological account of imagination. What is not accounted for is the role of the metanarrator as a character in his/her own narrative through the other. Both metanarration and the other as narrator are enacted without being imagined as such with respect to the content of the narrative, without recounting the story whose operation is the act of discovery. The NMN-structure is the untold telling behind the look, "the language that does not present itself" in the story of the look that does present itself, but which secretly becomes a metalanguage.

Both Sartre's and Derrida's notions of imagination are at work in the NMN-structure of reading. As metanarrator of the voice imagined in the text, the reader is encompassed within, while, as the character addressed, the reader remains wholly outside the text—as a supplementarity. Structurally, the text prefaces its reader, "speaks" as a text about what the reader will be in the act of reading this particular text and in giving meaning to it—in hymenic relation. The text surrounds its reader as the preface surrounds its text. It gives the reader a nature. The reader (thus prefaced) suffers a loss of self-determination to its Other (the text read), though through something the reader brings to it. For both the reader and Sartre's "I," the loss of autonomy, of mastery, is a repetition of something else, brought to it as a mental image of something given by a social elsewhere—a dissemination of meaning. This social elsewhere mediates the inseparability and incommensurability of text and reader, preface and text, signifier and signified, the center around which those relations revolve.

In the Derridean semiotic, the signifier is not a "materiality" whose purpose is to bring its signified into existence; rather, each iterable mark, as a recursion of an elsewhere given to a materiality, becomes a signifier through all the prefaces of prior textuality, bestowed metanarratively to be undergone as a prefaced character by a reader as the look.

Ultimately, it is as the look that every text, every sign, every encounter with signification, is apprehended as a subject, a subjectivity. But it is an ephemeral subjectivity that disappears the moment one looks for it, because that means looking at it and turning it into an object for oneself; it returns only at the moment one submits again to the sign, to one's reading, to one's metanarrated apprehension of one's self-awareness in its meaning. Every sign contains a lurking subject, hidden within itself.

A sense of belonging accrues to those who read. In the case of movements or religions, the symbols or icons function in reverse; to encounter the icon is to feel oneself seen by it, to become an object for it. What kind of lurking subject that looks at those reading its symbols is of no consequence; ultimately, it remains as unknowable as the other-as-subject, but it represents a conflation of itself with the movement or organization, to its leadership, experienced either as pride and belonging, or as shame and abhorence. Belonging is a loss and a knowledge in which one mediates the double meaning that a political movement has: the meaning it has for itself through one as a member, an objectivized metanarrator; and the meaning it has for oneself as what gives one a nature, an outside, a project that is no longer one's own, but which one is. Here we recognize the incommensurability of anticipation (metanarrative) and recapitulation (character), of the not-yet and the already, across which meaning is disseminated. As the one discovered in the look of the symbols of a political movement, one lives the dissemination of its meanings as both form and signification; one lives the social structure to which it points beyond itself and its lurking subjectivity and one lives its symbol pointing to itself as that for which one is.

This gives a sense of the power of narrative and of textuality in general. We have seen that narrative constitutes a mode of common experience. But it also renders itself a preface for its reader, an outside that mediates the reader's relation to the world, for which one becomes an object and to which one loses autonomy. The stories of a community, which render each member their object, become the preface to the member's existence. If these narratives express one's prejudices, which they cannot help but express when they are about others—negatively when they concern the exclusion of those others—then those narrativized others and the prejudices narrativized for them are lived as truth and reality respectively, and seen as such because one finds oneself seen by those narratives. The act of bestowing a sense of truth on a narrative becomes the very constitution of reality. It is ancillary to the act of reading, beyond it and metadiscursive to it. In this way, children are brought to apprehend the weight and concern of a society's assumptions (necessarily hegemonic coming from a parent, teacher, or other adult); the child discovers him/herself as object in the look of the other, and in the look of the story. This is the nature of myth, which can only be seen from elsewhere, never from within the community or culture that lives that myth as reality—in other words, beyond that reality as the foundation of its ability to see the world in the first place.

These are not psychological questions. The self-objectivization (of the reader) through the signifier constitutes a semiotic dimension of the political that precedes the psychological. For a reader to give being to a signifier, to metanarrate it as the lurking subjectivity of one's social world, is to impose its metaphysics on oneself. Propaganda, metaphysics, political assumption, one's perception of the social world, are all engendered through the imposition of a discourse that one has always already imposed upon oneself through the other who imposes it.

CONCLUSION

In sum, Derrida's notion of dissemination, an account of the reader, and the two senses of the reader produced by the look, along with their various narratives and narrativizations, conglomerate under homology as a glyph, in which a sense of the political is to be discerned. (Later, we shall reencounter these two senses of the reader as dimensions of Sartre's notion of being-for-others.) Or, put otherwise, the look becomes an allegory for the interstice between the metaphysical and what escapes the metaphysical; that is, an allegory for (1) the incommensurability of signifier and signified, (2) the dissemination by repetition of signifier and signified among a metatext (about form) and a non-text (of form), and (3) a glyphic structure whose substance is the operation of dissemination. As a structure of loss and knowledge, a structure of specificity and nonspecificity, and the interplay of narrator and character and of text and metatext, the structure of dissemination points to the impossibility of meaning (reading) ever fulfilling itself, of being more than a simulacrum, and of reading (meaning) ever not overreaching itself, of not containing or constituting what it is not. Dissemination becomes itself the abyss that mediates the boundary of the hymen and the non-boundary of supplementarity.

If the previous glyphs have iconized the play of narrative and dramatics respectively, the play of the stated and the enacted, "dissemination" names, as a glyph, the arena of textual interplay itself between different discursive levels. The dissemination glyph iconizes the incommensurability of reading as such, as the reciprocal process by which the reader is both the look and the self-as-object at the hands of the text. In effect, the three aspects of the operation of writing in general—the trace, spacing, and dissemination—have been iconized through these glyphs.[20]

In comparison to conceptualizing Derrida's instrumentalities—as transcendentals (Harvey) or as infrastructure (Gasché)—the notion of the "glyph" appears less impositional because it does not abandon the structures of textuality, nor the nontransparency of language; instead, it is the embodiment of them. If each glyph encompasses textual structures beyond its use of a Derridean instrumentality as namesake, they correlate in some fashion with the discursive structure they point out as terms; that is, they take both the textuality and the non-textuality (the infrastructure and possibility condition) of Derrida's discourse as their own conditions. As argued above, one reads the glyph as representing a textual structure metatextually; one reads it as the shape of that textual structure non-textually; and one reads the glyph as the name for that structure textually.

If the textual form represented is given in a non-text read metatextually and named in that metatext read textually, it presents a text whose form is still read non-textually. What the incorporation of the name (whether an emotion, a Derridean instrumentality, or a Sartrean category) into the glyph accomplishes is a mediation between metatext and non-text. And that returns us to a triadic circular structure, now constituted by textuality (read as structures), metatextuality (the reading of those structures), and non-textuality (the form of reading itself). These all reside internally in the glyph, giving it a circular coherence. The synthetic entityhood of the glyph absorbs each narrative content (Derridean instrumentality, etc.) into itself as what mediates the interstice between its interior metatextuality and its interior narrativity, as an interior structural act of naming. With the particular glyphs named through the terms of the Derridean primordial structure of signs, we are on the edge of a primordial consideration of language that is not a primordium of language because it contains and presupposes an interweaving and intratextualization of different modes and levels of discourse (*SP*, 67).

The glyphs do not suggest themselves as conditions of possibility, but rather as an accumulation of meaning from the many levels of operation of language, in its process of generating meaning—structures of discourse that the glyphs interiorize and carry with them. The glyph can thus be understood as the real inner structure of all linguistic signs in the sense that it incorporates within it all the aspects of what must go into the existence of a sign: not only the aporia between signifier and signified, but a narrative (social) source of signification as the common experience of what it signifies (the construction of both signifier and signified), and a name which then comes to constitute that signifier in a language that uses it while representing the entire structure that it subsumes. What the glyph then represents is an "exposition" of a word, like an iceberg that lies unseen under a surface through which only its name protrudes; and through that exposition beneath the appearance of the word (as name, sign, signifier, and glyph), it presents a theory of language.

But they are themselves circular, these glyphs named by instrumentalities. The hymen is the form the supplement takes for which it constitutes the content; the supplement is the form dissemination takes for which it constitutes the content; and dissemination is the form the hymen takes for which it constitutes the content. As a reflection of a circular relation between iteration, spacing, and trace, or text, metatext, and non-text, or character, enactment, and narrative of a reading, the circle becomes a structure of importance here.

There is no unlocking or unraveling these glyphs from one another. Like a vortex, they pull all the layers of signification toward themselves, the variations of narrative, name, and enactment that have flowed through the Sartrean structure of the look and the Derridean critique of writing. Between them, the circle has a social meaning, because it is the mediation of their interaction.

In the confluence of these glyphs, the texts of Sartre and Derrida seem to get closer, first as inversions (supplements), second as interspatializations (hymen), and third as an interplay of formal structures (dissemination). If the glyph of supplementarity deconstructs how they stand opposite each other in inversion, and the glyph of the hymen deconstructs their apparent incommensurability, the glyph of dissemination names the unfilled and overfilled space of the abyss between them, the hiatus in which each is an object at which the other is not looking.

7 Circularities and Foundations

Bringing the Incommensurable into Dialogue

The Sartrean account of the look (of another), in the form of the NMN-structure, breaks the boundary between the ineluctibly interior (consciousness) and the sociality of the narrativizing and naming of personal experience. As such, the look, with its apprehension of the Other-as-subject, becomes the elementary particle of social interaction. On the one hand, the transformations that occur to the one seen in the look structure what one undergoes in apprehending another as subject. On the other hand, these structures become alternately discernible through homological relations to the Derridean critique of narrative language and the inescapable "textuality" (*rien de hors-texte*) of the social communality of the personal. The intersections of Sartre's narrativizations with Derrida's critique of narrative discourse, of this elementary particle of the social with the anteriority of Derrida's critical instrumentalities, have interwoven a primordial intersubjectivity with a primordial intertextuality. Between the two, there emerges a threshold of access to the social as a stratum of human affectivity whose fundamental ground is the specificity of the cultural framework in which it occurs.

In serving as a mode of reading the interior transformations the look imposes on one, the process of homology has highlighted how those interior relationships reflect anterior discursive relations. Derrida's instrumentalities become readings of the NMN-structure, and the look's transformations become readings of those Derridean anterior structures. In concert, they give form to the interaction between the hidden (consciousness) and the social, the social and language, language and the hiddenness of consciousness. Within this circle, the social origin of narrative particularizes (establishes "spacings") between social enactment metanarratively; self-awareness repeats the social "enactments" narrated through the other; and one's apprehension of the other-as-subject constitutes the operation of différance between subjects. Thus, the three anterior elements of Derridean semiotics and the three of elements of Sartrean narrativity appear and interweave in the circle.

Social particle, social narrative, homology, and elementary social structures manifest by textual form amalgamate as a single entity of meaning, incorporating intersubjectivity and intertextuality in a complex multilayered structure, namely, a "glyph." The glyph laminates signification, narrativization, and the aporia between personal experience and the social. In this case, it conjoins the intersubjectivity of the NMN-structure on the semiotic plane with intertextuality on the social. It embeds the aporias of the social and the personal (interiority), the social source of narrative and the semiotic source of the social, in each other. Through it, the aporetic relations between the hiddenness of consciousness and the publicness of the social, the discursive and the performative as experiential interaction, the signifier and the signified, can be seen condensed into the sign.

If the instrumentalities that get structured in complex form as glyphs represent what is anterior to language, as the primordia of "writing in general," then the glyph too, amalgamating the significations, narratives, and aporias anterior to the "elementary social particle," would be in some sense anterior to language. Though the glyph encapsulates within itself an entire complex structure, it remains hidden from view behind representation, as anterior to it; and the sign in turn as representation serves as its name. As a proto-linguistic and hyper-linguistic social entity, a structuring of social enactments and discursive anteriorities, what the glyph represents remains primordial as a formalization of the sources of signification; in a sense, it presents itself as an iconic explanation of signification itself. The sign encapsulates what the glyph encompasses as both culturally given and individually experienced.

The glyph can only be read through the reading of discursive form, whether as textual or social. The reader of form reads metadiscursively by homology and metanarratively in the allegorical enactments of the socially given. Such a reader is both an object of the production of meaning and a producer in the act of reading of the look of an Other, of the social particle. But this means that, while the linguistic sign names the glyph it represents, the glyph in turn mediates between persons who read it in each other by rewriting the two as a molecular social interaction of such elementary particles—in other words, the dialogic as social molecule.

What the investigation of textual form has constructed through homology and the glyph, with respect to Sartre and Derrida, is not a mode of conceptual connection between them. They remain conceptually and discursively incommensurable. Neither does it represent a path or bridge from one to the other across which one could walk. The bridge would be circular and go nowhere. The construction of forms implies a system of relations of forms across which meanings could represent each other, not as a sign system, nor as a translation procedure, nor as a common language, but as an anterior context, a matrix for writing each in the text of the other. What the concept of the glyph represents is a context in which incommensurability makes social sense, and hence in which it becomes itself a signifier in a narrative milieu in which signification can occur in interaction. It opens to view a certain intimate, undisclosed complexity of human experience as the (social) condition for signifying the non-experiential, for repeating the unrepeatable, as the very enactment of aporia.

Ultimately, two theoretical operations have been interwoven, the transference of meaning homologically between Sartre and Derrida, and a general exposition of the glyph. The confluence of these operations suggests at once a theory of language and a theory of the social. Because the construction of the glyph is inseparable from a theorization of reading in a primordial sense (for instance, one reads the signs along a deer trail in the forest for what had passed recently, and thus differentiates the forest from what it had been before while dividing each "place" from elsewhere), it laminates the many dimensions of reading (in particular, the two incommensurable accounts of reading in the texts of Sartre and Derrida) into a single structure, a kind of "reading in general."

Rather than a common language, the glyph points instead to a mode of uncommon listening; in other words, reading the speech of another in its application of anterior interactions or the comprehension of "this" reading as an interaction. The glyphs then signify and engender an uncommon realm or space of speaking-to-the-other and responding-to-the-speech-of-the-other that would constitute a structure of "reading-each-other" glyphically in social interaction. If the text is the look for a reader, then each text expressed in speaking-to-the-other becomes a subject for the other who listens, and the listener becomes a reader who apprehends and responds to the subjectivity of that textual Other.

The glyph opens on the realm of anteriority of dialogue, as an interaction of textual subjectivities whose condition is the structure of reading in general. If we follow a Sartrean path from reading to the subject and to dialogue, we will at the same time be following a Derridean path from writing to the "text" and to what Derrida calls "conversation."

THE READER

Let us examine this first-person life-form called the reader more closely. As we have seen, the reader is the look; but the text is also the look. In the NMN structure, the reader becomes a character told by the text in the process of reading (and thinking) that text, as an object in the text's look. The text narrates the reader and the reader's thinking from its textual elsewhere, as metanarrated by the reader's reading. The reader finds his/her foundation in the text read as one whose project has become the text's project through the text. The meaning (content) of the reader's reading (in the text's look) is contingent upon that outside (text) that is interior to reading as such (the supplement). But in form, the reader as character is separated from the text read in its immediacy, acted upon (by the text) and thus enacting the text in thinking what the text says. That is, the reader as character takes the form of the hymen. As a non-text (hymen), the reader enacts the text as the character, the supplement to and in the text. In effect, to read is to enact the hymen, where the hymen is the form the supplement takes.

But the reader does not simply read; s/he interprets and teases meaning out of the text, in the sense that the text presents "a guide to a transcendence," that is, co-opts the reader's interpretive autonomy. While reading thus appears as an instrumentality, the reader in the act of reading loses instrumentality to the text both literally and interpretively. That is, reading absorbs the reader in a double process, a loss of instrumentality to writing and an awareness of writing as an instrumentality. In other words, conscious (thetic) interpretation distances the text metatextually as a double writing, an apprehension of its form, and a metanarrativization of its content. The reader enacts a double reading as a double writing. The reader is an enactment, through which (as Derrida says) the text yields and withholds its meaning. That is, the reader is in content the otherness of the text, its immediacy and separation, and in form is a renarrativization, a dissemination of the text's meaning among its modes of yielding and withholding, its telling and being told. The reader enacts the hymen in content and dissemination in form. That is, to read is to disseminate the meaning of the text, where dissemination is the form the hymen takes.

Finally, reading becomes a sign for the text and for itself as well, telling the text to the reader and telling the reader through the text. The reader signifies (narrates) his/her own reading (as an enactment) at the moment of reading and becomes a character come upon in that particular moment. Narrated by this enactment of reading, the reader will have already lost mastery to the text's knowledge, a loss of autonomy to the text as narrated by the text, though metanarrated by the reader reading. The reader becomes a text, a narrative that disseminates the text's meaning and finds him/herself inside the text's knowledge. The reader loses autonomy to an interiority, the text's prior narrativization of the reader as its narrated character, for which the reader, outside the text, is the supplement whose enactment of a reading signifies a dissemination of the text's meaning. In other words, the reader enacts dissemination in content and the supplement in form. To read is to supplement the text, where the supplement is the form dissemination takes.

Thus, we reencounter the circularity of instrumentalities: the hymen is the form the supplement takes, for which it constitutes the content; the supplement is the form dissemination takes, for which it constitutes the content; and dissemination is the form the hymen takes, for which it constitutes the content. Insofar as the reader is at once character, enactment, and narrative of a reading, reading constitutes itself as a circle that is at the same time a structuring of the glyphs of the NMN-structure as homologies of Derrida's discursive anteriorities.

In an earlier discussion, we saw how a mode of chauvinist domination by one group over another proceeded by dividing the elements of a subject's encounter with others against themselves through self-referential acts of reification and instrumentalizing. In the sense that instrumentalization constitutes prior narrativization, and thus obviates a returned look and a retrieval of subjectivity from the instrumentalizing look, it manifests a dehumanization. The inverse occurs with reading. The interweaving of elements involved in encountering an Other as subject, in their structure as a circle, preserves the personhood of the reader in which subjectivity, as a possibility in the interaction, is also preserved. The act of reading becomes a rehumanizing act by preserving the circle of character, enactment, and narrative, as constituted by a reading.

The circle, we recall, is the structure of generalized mediation; and with respect to the NMN-structure, what is mediated is social interaction. The circle is self-grounding in form rather than self-referential in social content. It is self-generating in form, in an endlessly mediated way, rather than self-defining through an instrumentalized Other. When social self-referentiality unravels the circle's interwovenness, it reveals the circle to have been a symbolic or topological mode of reading the Other, grounded in a confluence of intersubjectivity and intertextuality—which a structure of domination can never be. The structure of domination separates the elements of the circle; it separates the glyphic elements of reading from each other, obviating the interactivity of reading. Only the unknowability of the other is produced; and domination must then pretend to a knowledge it invents self-referentially to conceal its ignorance. The concealment of unknowability behind an invented knowledge, as a characteristic of domination, has found itself philosophized and codified in Western metaphysics. Indeed, it appears in the text of Hegel and Heidegger in their theorizing knowing the other as subject through an extension of oneself, by attribution.

Against the dehumanization, the death by reification, signified by the sundered circle, the intact circle takes on a life of its own. The supplement is a reading founded on a mode of narrative, a narrativization of différance that names a mode of coming upon the world coming upon itself, a way in which the world is discerned through itself as other. The hymen is a reading founded on enactment, a mode of representation of différance that represents the world as representation, a simulacrum in which one's actual situation becomes an instrumentality that represents a prior reenactment. And dissemination is a reading founded on a double writing, a rereading of différance, a loss of knowledge as a character in another's narrative, and a knowledge of loss as a memory of having been the narrator of oneself as a project—a loss of autonomy and a character in a conscripted narrative. Thus, not only is reading, as the NMN-structure, a restructuring of the Derridean glyphs, but the NMN-structure itself becomes articulable through the glyphs that name the moments of its structure. The glyphs become signs for the NMN-structure, signifying its different elements of narrativity—narrative, enactment, and character.[1] The components constituting a glyph—signification, narrative, and an aporetic structure of the social/personal—are transposed to the NMN-structure itself and the interweaving of form and content as the circle of reading becomes its interior meaning.

The elements of narrative can homologously be given the same circular structure. Character is the form a narrative takes; narrative is the form enactment takes; enactment is the form a character takes. These need no elaboration. They can be read in the reverse order: character is the content of enactment; enactment is the content of narrative; narrative is the content of character. This is not just an entextualization of the existential subject; it is also a description of the literary critical object.[2]

Earlier, this triadic circularity was referred to as an ecological structure. This can now be given a technical sense as characterizing the energy of such a circle. Each element of form obtains its content from another part of the ecology and bestows it on a third. It reveals an inner dynamic, a "life." Founded on both indeterminacy and the derangement (separation and deferral) of form and content, it is self-powering.[3] As the form of mediation in general, it is the smallest, simplest model of what Derrida means by an endless system of displacement. Behind it, one discerns an echoing circularity of iteration, trace, and spacing—the components of writing in general. Spacing, the quantization and individuation of the sign, is the condition for, the form of, iteration, the possibility of repeating only what has a certain individuation elsewhere. Iterability, and the fact that no occurrence is ever the first, is the condition for, the form of, the trace, the presence of what is absent in its precedence, the differing of the subsequent and the possibility of a subsequent differing. And the trace, the presence whose precedence ensures the individuation of its repetition, is the condition for, the form of, spacing, of each occurrence having spatial and temporal boundaries in its differing from what precedes it.[4] If this form of the circle formalizes the notion that writing in general has no origin, it renders "writing in general" the name of an ecology of anteriority.

Against the woven unification of the circle's moments, its inherent wholeness, division of those moments into separate entities or reifications would necessitate redefinition, rendering them metaphysical as redefined. This would suggest that the circularity, as a social ecology, is a site from which an understanding of social reification (of others, of events, of modes of hierarchical relation) can be pursued. And this possibility suggests that consciousness, sociality, and language have no self-referential origins, nor can they be conceived as individually self-generating. They appear, and condition each other, but not at their own hands; it is within an ecology that constitutes the social. In other words, referentiality itself, or an appeal to prior foundations, plays no originary part in either language, consciousness, or sociality. Foundations become important only to thinking the division of the ecological (the human) into reified (de-ecologized) components. In counterposing itself to reification, the circle becomes more than a conjunction of elements; it becomes the site where the process of systematic separation and reification can be named, a place of critique.

For instance, a separation of the moments of the narrative circle (narrative, character, and enactment) into autonomous elements reveals what is lost. First, a sense of the text as the look, as a lurking subject, disappears. By extension, encounter with others in subject-subject relations, which presupposes the subject read as the look, gets crystallized (perhaps as a clash of rote readings). The incommensurable elements of narrative that are mediated around the circle become categories of analysis that only counterpose each other, reducing "literary criticism" to the textual but obviating a sense of the cultural, social, and political that are names for the "human ecology." What is finally lost, then, is the sense of narrative as common experience, as the matrix in which to embrace (rather than objectify or use against) others, to embrace the existential unknowability of the other.[5] In effect, it is the sociality of the subject, of consciousness, and of the ontological difference of Sartrean freedom that is signified by a narrative or glyphic circle, by its ecology as signifier.

Through this circular dynamics, the subject (the operation of néantisation) and writing in general (the operation of différance), the intersubjective narrativity of Sartre's look, and the intertextual narrativity of the Derridean glyphs have been brought into interaction, a circling around the difference between the structure of narrative and the narrativization of structure, between semiotics and ontology. Sartre narrates the subject in order to maintain its particularity—which Derrida deconstructs to show how its textuality in its particularities subverts such purposes. Derrida deconstructs textuality and its narrativities, and turns them against themselves, in order to reveal the operation of anterior inarticulable structures through which meaning is constituted—which Sartre would ontologize as the inarticulability of a freedom that chooses itself and its projects as a reading of the world. What the homologies make explicit is that there is no need to prioritize either of these operations. Still founded on particularity and inarticulability, they confront each other as incommensurable, yet interweave and overlap in a way that only a construction of circularity can articulate. Sartre moves from néantization to narrative, and from narrative structure to the glyphic structure of the reader; Derrida moves from narrative to différance, and from the operations of différance to the glyphic structure of the reader. The glyphic structure of the reader is already beyond the grammatological account of reading and contains it; and it is beyond the ontological account of reading and contains it.

Reading becomes a primordium of interaction. The circles of "Derridean" glyphs and "Sartrean" narrative moments present themselves as a foundationless ground for writing in general and the apprehension of the Other. The ontology of narrative interweaves itself with the semiotics of inarticulability, and the ontology of the inarticulable enmeshes itself in the semiotics of narrative. The circle mediates and presents its own meaning as mediation (in general). It has thus become a signifier for what is being brought together here.

THE CIRCLE

This recalls Heidegger's dance with the circle, which will bear briefly revisiting. In his complex topology of the triadic circle, Heidegger attempts to do three things at once: transcend the metaphysical account of understanding in order to turn toward the meaning of Being, avoid the phenomenological account of intentionality, and provide an articulation for the categories of existence (ek-sistence), such as understanding, signification, and so on, in a way that does not reconstitute a subject-object relation. His particular configuration of triads does not imply an attraction to trinities. It is instead an artifact of his forward and backward method and movement, a way of articulating the meaning of Being without articulating Being. The gathering together of each triad transforms the separate instances of his "forward and backward" movement by giving them continuity and "endlessness," for which the circle is the natural figure. The triad is the minimum set from which an analytic can construct a circle and an endlessness.

Wrested from his circular structure, each element becomes a metaphysical entity, a fish out of water, as it were, for which definitions must be invented both as foundations and to clothe the violence involved in dividing them from each other. In constructing circles, Heidegger appears to be reversing processes that had previously torn asunder an inner coherence. Concepts or metaphysical categories (recognition, perception, significance, etc.) that had been given independent status he welds back together in a form of anterior analysand. Heidegger's deconstruction of metaphysics, in moving forward to the circle, moves back toward a prior structure that precedes what gets encircled.

In other words, Heidegger does not construct circles to be or to generalize a process of mediation. His purpose is to generate a text that evades the assumptions and presuppositions of metaphysics, but in which "the meaning of Being" will still make sense. That is, it is to generate an intelligible signifier that will contain and yet leave unarticulated its signified. His triads are not designed to constitute circles as such; rather the circle as form is used to constitute the foundation of what

Heidegger is looking at, in order to avoid defining foundations. The circle becomes his substitute for philosophical ground. Investigating the being of philosophical ground, one finds only what is grounded, equiprimordially, in itself. (Thus, Being is the basis for the meaning of Being; the meaning of Being is the basis for the unknowability of Being; the unknowability of Being is the basis for Being.) Beyond metaphysics, only the circle is ground. And thus, it is for accounts of consciousness, language, theories of intentionality or narrativity; each will encounter the same circularity in itself.

Having brought these triadic circles churning deep in Heidegger's philosophical machinery into the open, we now see them go freewheeling into the space between Sartre's existentialism and Derrida's semiotics, the space between the social and the individual, and the space between anteriority and meaning. It is ineluctably a social space, the more so if it is to be the arena of interaction between these two thinkers.

But Heidegger will not get us to the social. For him, the "others," the Anyone, the "they" may be the source of significance that composes the world, but not as interacting subjects. For Heidegger, such interactions will have always already been there, and thus not be there as other than juxtapositions of the "I" and the "they." The possibility of interaction between Sartre and Derrida is already more than juxtaposition; however, it still requires a socius of at least two. Hence, it requires a theoretic of the social, the construction of a space of the social.

In that space, the foundations of their respective texts have become circular, structurally positioned in the same philosophical arena, though inverse at the level of content or presuppositionality. That is, they sit facing each other at the same (circular) café table, as it were. To create the possibility of dialogue between them, it is not a common language that is needed, since that would lose itself in the labyrinth of their incommensurability. Sartre would sit down facing a subject who looks and sees him, and to whom he would return the look. Derrida would sit down giving the text of Sartre a reading, and returning that text to him with its presuppositions and pretensions to subjectivity and identity deconstructed. For Sartre, for whom the foundation of ontology is the inarticulable freedom of the subject, the question would become, What happens when the inarticulable is cast into a social space that is its own foundation, where the very notion of foundation is recast? And for Derrida, for whom the text (and the world as text) is already foundationless because foundations are metadiscursive and belong to the self-referential functionality of an elswhere, the question would become, What befalls anteriority in a social space that is already anterior?

To engage each other through such homologically generated questions, Sartre and Derrida would be left to approach each other through the effects of their respective critiques of Heidegger, their emergence from his circles, and the metadiscursive reconstitution of their own. For both, the subject-object relation disappears in such a space, leaving a duality of critiques of the subject, each of which may be deconstructive, yet incommensurably so. Their interaction, as the unfolding of this dialogue, must venture into the space of their respective deconstructions of the subject.

DERRIDA'S DECONSTRUCTION OF THE SUBJECT

In an essay on Paul Valéry, Derrida addresses Valéry's meditation on the "I," which is articulated and metaphorized as the source, the "place" where identity, thinking, the essence of human being, comes from. Valéry, of course, is naming the central questions of Western (Euro-American) metaphysics, the concepts (identity, thinking, and human being) that the "subject" is designed to explain. For Derrida, the question of the "place" of the subject raises the question of the ideational or discursive source of this "source," with its foreseeable logical regress. Derrida argues that the "I" (to which Valéry refers as "the subject" and Derrida only sardonically as "pure consciousness") cannot simply be the identity it is "designed" to be. Beyond referring to the autonomy and uniqueness of a person, it must also refer to the autonomy of the sign, precisely in its non-uniqueness (*Marg*, 280).

For Valéry, the "I" (*le moi*]) is "the fundamental permanence of consciousness, that depends on nothing." In Valéry's metaphor, the "I" fulfills this sense of origin by connoting a spring, or headwaters, as the "source" of origin itself. The "I" is not a cause, as the spring is not the cause of the water that flows from it, but it is the source of presence, of the meaning of things—of "everything that is not I." Derrida paraphrases this as follows:

> The non-I [*non-moi*] is *for* the I [*moi*], appears as non-I for an I and on the basis of an I. Everything: which is to say that the I, the exception to and condition for everything that appears, does not appear. (*Marg*, 281)

Or, as Derrida puts it later, Valéry's metaphorics "place on view that which has no *figure*" (M, 284ff.). In Derrida's paraphrase (and his use of the objective pronoun *moi*, which the translator Alan Bass transforms to the subjective "I"), we hear an interesting echo of the Sartrean structure for consciousness (that it is what it is not and is not what it is). The difference between "source" and "nothingness" marks a conceptual distinction (between Valéry and Sartre) on the Cartesian field, but not a structurally different approach.

It is the abstraction of the "I," however, that is the first problem; in its universality, the "I" stands for no particular person or name. It is the singular universal. As a source, it is not present to itself, is "there for no one," has "no name or history" (*Marg*, 281). ("An unnamable, 'unqualified' source, in effect it has no determinable character since it is not in the world and never presents itself.") It is no more tangible than "the center of gravity of a ring" (quoted by Derrida). In effect, the source is the result, then, of the (w)hole; it is reduced to an "abstract point, to a pure form," the center of a circle.

Thus, its abstraction deconstructs it. Without predicate or property, it pertains to no particular individual, nor even to a consciousness; that is, it is not an "I" either. In its existence, it does not exist. That is, the "I" deflects itself, finds itself displaced by its metaphors (as "source"/"spring") to the place where it is itself only a metaphor, a discursivity. As "a source that names itself I" (*Marg*, 281) and that substitutes itself for the metaphor of the "I," it is both "within and without language."

Sartre escapes the discursive trap of the abstract "I" by positing a "for-itself" whose self-objectivization the "I" is; he escapes the conceptual aporia of the abstract "I" through an insistence on narrativization, a reparticularization by means of narrative structure that confirms at every turn the subject's (non)being in the first person. It is the nominalism of narrative that allows Sartre to preserve the inarticulability of the non-particular, of ontological freedom. Derrida, however, insists on the aporia as a reflection of the aporia of the sign. It remains implicit even in the representation of the general "I" by a specific narrator in a specific speaking event, to the extent that the event itself is made possible by that aporia in the first place; that is, the aporia implies a supplementarity that structures it. (In fact, Derrida's insistence is homological to Sartre's reasoning that one can be unfree situationally only if, as a subject, one is absolutely free ontologically.)

As a source out in the world (a supplement to the personal "I"), the abstract "I" is unable to be self-conscious because separated from the self (the "I") to which it is immediate (the form of the hymen); it is "always disseminated far from itself, [with] no relation to itself as source" (*Marg*, 283). As a space between source and enactment, it is again a space between narrator and character—a dissemination of metanarrator ("I") and narrator (abstract "I").

And in that space between source and enactment, Derrida opens the barest glimpse, a shadowy suggestion of a narrative between his and Valéry's text. If, for Valéry, the source (the "I") is always elsewhere, alone, then it presents, from that distance, the most real absence (like the disappearing point at the center of a circle). And Derrida invites the reader to "imagine the God of a negative theology attempting by himself to describe himself, to catch himself in the grid of a determining discourse" (*Marg*, 282). It hints at a "relationship [that] is barely a relation," a whisper of common experience that one might tell oneself in solitude, as an "I" that seeks to generate its own individuation by speaking as not-"I" (like Descartes at the moment of carrying his skepticism to its limit). Though (barely) suggesting a narrative, it must, like the socially given narratives of emotion or experience, engender itself as common experience in order to appear and be named on the individual level. The narrative of the negative god seeking an outside in (his) aloneness names how the "I" generates itself as abstraction by being first the individual generated by that abstraction. In naming itself, the "I" names the aporia of its being itself and not being itself.

For Valéry, however, aloneness is a problem of abstraction but not of speech, from which nevertheless the "I" cannot be dissociated. Speech is of the essence. For Benveniste, for example, the "I" is always the one who is speaking. Valéry inverts this; "I is an element of language [and/or linguistics] linked to speech itself. All speech has its source which is an I" (*Marg*, 288, translation modified). Yet, for Derrida, this invocation of the act of speech does not reach into the fact of speech, to what is said in language. And there the inverse of abstraction occurs: the undifferentiable. He points out that no sentence spoken can be differentiated, "either in the form or in the content," from that same sentence heard by oneself or any other, either silently to oneself or out loud. If they are separate, it is ungraspably so (a differentiation as formless content). And so with "I," as Derrida's paraphrase of Valéry continues:

> This I is [mine if/that of X if] X [hears it/gives and receives] this speech, and in receiving it recognizes himself as source, i.e. simultaneously an object and a non-object, a space or world of objects. (*Marg*, 288; translation modified)

The aporia that Derrida is revealing or teasing out of this paraphrase of Valéry is the notion that both my "I" and that of another, the two first persons, each depend on the one or the other recognizing him/herself as the source of what is spoken. It cannot be the source of anything to the extent it depends on a question of recognition that precedes it—in general.

Sartre embraces a similar aporia in his treatment of one's being-for-others, of one's being both "an object and a non-object" for the Other. For Sartre, the for-itself sets the self, the "I" as ego, off in a reflective distance (proximity) as an object that is present only when not a presence (*BN*, 103). He thus inverts Valéry in yet a different way. Where Valéry transforms narrative into aporia, Sartre transforms aporia into narrative.

If, for Derrida, the aporia marks a contentless form, then form also appears as a circle. Valéry says, "I, You, Him, this triangle—Trinity! The three roles of the same, in relation to the verb, Mouth, ear, thing." To which Derrida responds, "In the return of the phonic circle, the source appears as . . . a moment," an interruption and saturation of circulation, where "everything comes to be explained . . . in this circle similar to the snake biting its tail" (*Marg*, 288). And of course, Valéry's "I," with its triadic character and its hint of narrativity, recalls the abstract NMN-structure, in which "I, you, him" become the metanarrated character, storytelling character, and Other-as-subject narrator.

The source that Valéry wishes to preserve as contentless form is one that is both elsewhere and an iteration that is here and sourceless (a circularity). These are the two forms of "I" that Derrida locates in Valéry. That "I," the "one" that is both this "I" there (a point) in space, and that other "I" here that is always a repetition of another, has a meaning; that meaning is the pure narrativity of being the spoken, the heard, and the object that is here because elsewhere.

But what is this moment, this source of the circle? It is not only the center, in its intangibility. It is any point on the circle, coming from the preceding and endlessly generating the next, whose discernment interrupts it, yet saturates it with the circularity it represents. In both senses, it is an intangible point that is elsewhere, that engenders and is engendered by a circularity that has no origin. It is a source that has no source, that exists and does not exist, a double absence of a point that is elsewhere in space, and a circumference that originates in iteration, in circulation itself.[6] The source becomes a momentary significationless sign, which insists on "resisting meaning" (*Marg*, 304). And for Valéry, it presents a "critical formalism" that attracts him because it reflects his desire to preserve something from interpretation, to know that there is something that resists interpretation.[7] That something discloses itself as the most insouciant meaning, a formless content produced by a contentless form (a double reading and a double writing). The structure that Derrida is discerning here is the structure of a glyph; it is a lamination of an abstract circularity and an inherent narrativization, a name for that narrativization and an enactment of that name as the content of its narrativization. The subject is a glyph, a concrete structuring of discursive moments from which that most abstract of meanings, the subject, emerges.

Derrida's deconstruction of Valéry's notion of the subject parallels Sartre's critique of the Heideggerian relation between the "I" and the "me." For Sartre, Heidegger's concept of the "I" is too abstract to incorporate itself as that "me," and too specific in its every use, especially at the social level, to be the abstract "I" at any particular time. Heidegger is content to conflate Dasein and the "me" that walks among the "they" across the ontological difference, whereby the "me" becomes the way in which Dasein attains to its social being, its identity through others. But Sartre argues that for a "me" to be in the world, there would already have to be a subject that is both granted its subjectivity at the ontological level by others and attains that ontological being through an ontic "I" that is given by others. If Heidegger's "me" works at the abstract level of Dasein's existentials, it does not work at the real level of the individual walking down the streets of a city. And Derrida has pointed out a similar disparity and conflation in Valéry. Where Sartre couches his critique of Heidegger in terms of consciousness, the interplay of the for-itself with its being an object for another as the implicate possibility of intersubjectivity, Derrida couches his critique of Valéry in the operation of the supplement, and the unraveling of Valéry's conflation of "this 'I' and that" as positing an impossibility of location for the "I" in the social world.

Sartre's Deconstruction of the Subject

For Sartre, the question is the subject, beneath the many lamina and blankets of self, ego, "I," and their pretensions to intersubjectivity. While Sartre's "nothingness" does not differ structurally from Valéry's "source," Sartre nevertheless escapes the aporia of the "abstract I" through nominalist narration. Not only does Sartre's notion of the subject differ from Valéry's "I," but the glyphs built upon the NMN-structure imply a restructuring of the social in which the subject enacts itself—a restructuring not in the sense of changing its political and institutional relations as such, but in changing the way they are lived, how they are understood.

To grasp this restructuring, for which the subject is foundational, one may begin by noting a problem in Sartre concerning subject-object and subject-subject relations. In *Being and Nothingness*, Sartre engages the subject-object relation first, in the form of a relation between the for-itself and the in-itself. He does so as well in his discussion of the look, where he begins with a preliminary articulation of the Other-as-object. An aegis of alleged priority of the subject-object relation over the subject-subject relation is generated, one that seems to accord with Sartre's alleged Cartesianism. This sense of priority has been generally accepted in most Sartre scholarship.[8] The works of Dominick LaCapra or Denis Hollier are notable exceptions; for them, the textuality of Sartre's thinking is primary, and they perform their deconstructions by revealing where Sartre has to secretly think so too. But even Christina Howells accepts the "standard" topical hierarchy and works with it.

But it constitutes a stumbling block. Sartre's account of one's apprehension of the Other-as-subject passes through a sequence of object modes (Other-as-object, self-as-object, being-for-others) that assume a sense of the object and its difference from the subject. Yet when Sartre opens his account of the look with the Other-as-object, though his argument appears Cartesian, he proceeds as though the concept of a subject were tacitly or pragmatically understood on a different basis.[9] That is, he assumes it is already apprehensible, as that which is other to the object, without specifying the basis on which it might be. It could be the Cartesian assumption of the object's existence as perceived, an assumption to be negated through doubt. Or it could be the assumption that the object is derivative from the subject, with a certain immediacy, and thus unavailable to the subject's path toward understanding itself (the second moment of the Hegelian dialectic). Or an assumed "sense of the object" could be an apprehension that generates the object and a subjectivity immediate to it.

Sartre himself critiques the Cartesian duality. Because Descartes formally posits consciousness of an object as a substance, it is different yet on a par with the object (*BN*, lvi). This makes it difficult to say what an object is—that is, whether it be an object perceived or the content of one's awareness of it, an object thought or the thought of the object (*BN*, 83). The subject that apprehends this object both disappears in a labyrinth of partial existences and becomes a hyper-reality over-determining it (*BN*, 84). Thus, it makes it difficult to say what existence and thinking are. Sartre rejects the duality. If a subject's relation to the world (of objects) and to itself generates both a labyrinth and a hyper-reality, Sartre reasons, then the subject itself is nothing, an interstice at best. Though the object depends on the subject at the same time that the subject depends on its object, consciousness of the object is not the object, and not the content of which one is conscious. Thus, consciousness is itself nothing, non-being. And this suggests that perhaps Sartre's invocation of a Cartesian subject-object duality (for-itself and in-itself) at the beginning of *Being and Nothingness* is simply obeisance to the philosophical tradition that surrounds him. Yet there is a closure in his critique of Descartes that presents a problem with respect to other subjects.

To apprehend another as object, one must not only already understand what an object is but apprehend the difference between an inert object and an Other-as-object as an object that (who) "sees what I see." If one's apprehension of an Other-as-object preserves him/her as a person (seeing), it implies that one already has a differential understanding of others; one must already have been in relation to Others. In the logic of Sartre's account, the subject-object relation could not be the foundation of a subject-subject relation because the other-as-object, as a subject-object relation, already depends upon or refers to subject-subject relations (toward one who sees).

But this inversion of priorities is more complex than that. Phenomenology understands objects to be apprehended as meanings. But an apprehension of an object as a meaning must already involve some interaction with others with whom an exchange of meanings was a relevant component (*BN*, 427). This "exchange" of meanings with others already presupposes an engenderment of meaning with respect to them, and a lived meaning given to meaning itself in terms of those others. Heidegger had made this point, but in an inadequate manner for Sartre. It is insufficient to simply invoke the connection, the commonality of "exchange." As Sartre mentions, one enters the human order of meanings, as an apprehension of the world, by "setting up a dialogue with the Other." And this would hold a fortiori for the other-as-object who sees, as well as for subject-subject relations.

On the other hand, dialogue, as pertaining to subject-subject relations, points to the impossibility of a true ontological intersubjectivity. For Sartre, ontological intersubjectivity does not exist, because it would close the separation between for-itselfs, a separation that is a necessary condition for dialogue in the first place, and for which dialogue is itself one of the necessities. Yet intersubjectivity cannot be posited as simply ontic either, as one "they" (*das Man*) to another "they." As one solution to this problem, Sartre considers a structure of two others-as-objects, seen by a third, acting in concert, as a form of intersubjectivity, which he calls an "us-object" (*BN*, 415 ff). And this constitutes a form of sociality, or interpersonality, rather than intersubjectivity for him. Yet it is the necessity of the third to this schema of (subject-subject) sociality that renders it inadequate to the Other-as-object.

Thus, the question of the basis for apprehending the Other-as-object lies somewhere between an impossible ontological intersubjectivity and an us-object sociality, yet which recognizes that objects, subject-object relations, and the Other-as-object all depend in some essential way on prior subject-subject relations. If subject-object relations refer to subject-subject relations as a trace, then objects become one of the ways subject-subject relations express themselves, or establish existence for themselves as such. This implies that objects and subject-object relations constitute a system of significations by which subject-subject relations articulate and name themselves beyond themselves. Subject-subject relations are mediated by a sense of the object. In other words, subject-subject relations, as well as apprehension of the other as subject, take subject-object relations as part of their content, as a mode of connection, that is, as a language. Objects constitute a mode of articulation for subject-subject relations. Not only would subject-subject relations be necessarily primary to the possibility of subject-object relations, but they would be metadiscursive to them in the sense of generating subject-object relations as articulations or mediations for themselves.

This of course disrupts the traditional hierarchy of subject-subject and subject-object relations, because it absorbs and deploys objects as instrumentalities in the unfolding of subject-subject relations. It raises the question, Do objects have meaning, or being, other than as the instrumentalities of subject-subject relations? And this would extend to the question of whether social relations, as "objects" of study, have objective reality as well. Let us revisit Sartre's argument from the vantage point of the glyphic circles.

In the look, the notion of objecthood is metaphoric. The self-as-object remains different from an object; it is a moment within an interpersonal interaction, in which one never loses one's "character" as metanarrator. This differential is implicit in the Other-as-object (which is not a metaphoric object but a real object, yet different from an inert object as such); and it is explicit in the metaphoricity of the self, in that the (metaphoric) object one becomes when seen remains predicated upon an apprehension of the Other as one who sees.

In the look, the Other (as Other) is one who "sees what I see," which is central to the Other's essential role as one who "sees what I do not see," that is, one's own exterior appearance to the world. One is aware of this appearance, given that one is the source of the Other's narration of it, yet without "seeing" it as such. One's awareness of one's appearance is a trace for the look of the Other. The entire structure of the look is predicated on this entity that "I do not see" and that is seen—the "I that does not appear," as Derrida says of Valéry. The implication is that the look of the Other, and the metaphoricity of the self, are what express themselves ontically as the differential between the Other-as-object and an inert object (that does not see what I see). Thus, the logic of Sartre's narrativizations require us to move from the look to the "one who sees," inverting the order of his argument.

In Sartre's account of the Other-as-object, the Other is seen as both an object and more-than-an-object, and bestows on one a distance from the world that establishes epistemological objectivity. The (unknowable) Other seen is the condition for that distance through which objecthood as such (rather than objects-as-world) can be grasped. Seeing an objective, nonmetaphoric object then contains the experience of seeing the Other who sees as a trace, a prior narrativization. The Other-as-object in effect allegorizes the generation of objectivity as a knowledge, through the unrelinquished narrative of the Other who "sees what I see." When an object in its objectivity is grasped through the Other-who-sees, it concretizes the allegory in which the Other is the trace for the object perceived. But then, the metaphoricity of one's being an object in the look, of being able to take that narrative perspective on one's outside as seen, implies this prior notion of an objective object, distanced or deferred now through its very metaphoricity. The Other who is the look, as an Other-who-sees, re-allegorizes both the object and oneself as object. (It is this re-allegorization that is renarrativized in the relation of narrator to metanarrator.) The object, or oneself as object, as well as one's distance from these, contains the moment of coming upon the Other-as-object as its trace.

The tropic narratives that condition an awareness of objectivity occur only in a non-thetic mode, however, since the trace as trace can only effect itself non-thetically. To apprehend an object thetically reverses the allegory, since it takes objectivity itself as a trace, and becomes the ground for apprehending another as an object. This sets in motion the inverse structure, encountered in our brief consideration of racism and masculinism. If one comes upon another through an objectifying allegory, objectivity becomes the content of the narrative, and the other, as its form, is reified. Reification represents the inversion of all the tropic narratives encountered here.

But in that case, the allegoricity of another who sees becomes generalized. It is not only the condition for apprehending oneself as object, the Other-as-object, and through that objectivity itself, but also for perception as well. The awareness of not-being the object that, for Sartre, resides at the heart of one's apprehension of an object, or its perception, is inseparable from the object's being seen by another, and that Other not-being that object. In that sense, perception itself of an object is inseparable from the Other who sees and is thus grounded in the existence of Others. All forms of subject-object relation—perception, objectivity, the Other-as-object, and the self-as-object—become metaphoric expressions for prior involvement in an Other who sees. And to perceive an object (through whichever sense: touch, hearing, etc.) is to grasp it as that object insofar as it already metaphorizes a narrative involvement with an Other that it symbolically represents. There is a doubling of meaning. The Other as allegory and the Other as trace render the object (always already) different. For the object, in its being to-be-seen, the Other-as-object who sees it is a trace, but a trace of another who must not-be-the-object, and thus already not an object.

Perception becomes doubly allegorical. In perceiving the relation of the Other seeing the object, one perceives the object as what the Other is not. The Other thus represents one's own not-being the object. But second, because it is in principle unknowable which object the Other is looking at, and thus which object the Other is not, the Other is thus not all objects. The other seen as seeing represents a situation prior to an object apprehended as an object, as well as to objectivity. That is, the Other, insofar as the Other-as-object is not an object, allegorizes the priority of one's relation to Others to one's relation to one's world and its particular objects.

This double allegory represents, or presents, the subject-subject relation itself, through the object as a sign. That sign (object) obtains its meaning through the Other-as-object, which it attaches to its objectivity as an allegory (meaning), and it signifies itself as a sign (object) through the priority of the subject-subject relation to its individuation as an object (a sign). One's relation to the Other is what is represented by objects. That is, objects become a sign system for subject-subject encounters, as the way subjectivity brings interpersonal encounter into being as such. It is not objects that are present to the Other-as-object; one's relations to Others are instead the presentation of objects to the Other, because they have already been the presentation of objects to oneself through Others. If the object presents itself, it does so as a simulacrum, a representation of what represents it; but that representation represents it as something wholly other, a system of relations to Others that the object allegorizes.

This wholly post-Cartesian structure of subject to object implicit in Sartre's account cannot be mapped into the NMN-structure; it is essentially incommensurable with it.[10] It is not just that the narrative and metanarrative of enactment in the latter is incommensurable with the double allegorical character of the former. In the former, the other is looking at the world, performing an act that distinguishes the other's subjectivity from his/her being an object, without providing an apprehension of him/herself as a subject. Instead, it is the worldly object seen that returns a subjectivity to the Other seen as an object. In other words, the one who sees the Other (as object) seeing takes a third-person point of view on that act, though it is apprehended in the first person (only to be drained away as that first person's loss of world). Nevertheless, it follows the NMN-structure's logic, as a logic. If, mapping the two analogically, the self-as-object in the look corresponds to the object seen in the former, and the other-as-object to the other-as-object, and the other-as-subject in the look, then the narratives of the NMN-structure would correspond to the meanings by which the world is mutually apprehended.

If objects, and the world, are the product of subject-subject relations, then to posit subject-object relations as such means to transform a representation into the represented. It is to literalize the metaphoricity of the representation. The objecthood of the object as simulacrum, what one recognizes as the object as such, is an object that literalizes an allegory; it constitutes a literalized metaphor that presents itself as literal.[11] It is as a literalized metaphor that the object enters into a subject-object relation and at the same time expresses or mediates subject-subject relations.

In sum, if the object as such, and one's not-being-the-object, literalize a metaphor for prior relations to others, then subject-subject relations not only precede subject-object relations, they constitute their foundation. Subject-subject relations are anterior, supplementary, and inarticulable with respect to the Cartesian subject-object binary. The latter can only function as a language for the former. And this is consistent with Sartre's claim that subject-subject relations, and in particular being-for-others, are not ontological categories of the for-itself; it is also consistent with his notion that the for-itself itself is "relation" (*BN*, 362).

Ultimately, the inner narrative logic of Sartre's text produces a fundamental inversion in what is traditionally understood as Cartesian. Sartre himself, at one point, subtly suggests that he recognizes he has superseded traditional ontology by putting his subject-object account in the past tense, as if to confirm a historicity for it.

> When consciousness realized itself as not being a particular *this* in the world, the negative relation was not reciprocal. The *this* confronted did not make itself not-be consciousness; it was determined in and through consciousness not to be consciousness; its relation to consciousness remained that of pure indifferent exteriority. . . . With regard to the Other, on the contrary, the internal negative relation is a relation of reciprocity. The being which consciousness has to not-be is defined as a being which has to not-be this consciousness. (*BN*, 284)

Here too, the object seems to present itself as a metaphor that literalizes the notion that consciousness makes itself not-be the Other.

On the other hand, Sartre's inversion of subject-subject and subject-object relations does not imply that the Other is ontologically prior to the for-itself. That the Other must not-be "this" for-itself at the same time that the for-itself must not-be the Other implies, instead, that nihilation and alterity are foundational, rather than the for-itself and subjectivity (just as différance and iteration are fundamental in the Derridean semiotics, and not language or writing). Thus, the most fundamental level of Sartre's discussion is not the duality of for-itself and in-itself, but their incommensurability as act and state (nihilation and alterity), their (ir)relation as incommensurable. Sartre does not assume the primordiality of the object, but only of one's freedom and the structure of néantisation, to which the world appears through a number of mediations. And this confirms the notion that one cannot consider Sartre a Cartesian thinker.

Let us follow the logic of Sartre's narrativizations one more step. If objects are literalizations of a metaphoricity for the way they are come upon (socially) and become the articulation of subject-subject relations as such, then what becomes of the meanings of such terms as *referentiality* or *truth*? How are we to understand them if they depend on, or are produced by, the literalization of metaphor? (Nietzsche's entire project is recalled here; he is, perhaps, looking.) What does it imply about language that subject-subject relations can give rise to an apprehension of the world through which the world becomes their language? What happens to Sartre's desire for a language that says what it means and means what it says?

The question of referentiality is not separable from the question of truth. But within subject-subject relations, and the look in particular, truth is not a concern. One encounters being looked at with a certainty that one is oneself an object, even if the other is not "there." (And here we see the fulfillment of Sartre's separation of the cogito from its Cartesian form, his transformation of it from metaphysical principle to simply first certainty.) The truth of one's objectivization, as the content of that certainty, is only existential, relational, the facticity of one's being-for-others in the apprehended look. But toward an object, there can be no such certainty; appearance is apprehended only within a probability (PI, 124ff.). It is toward the object that truth becomes relevant and hence, also, metaphysical. Metaphysics valorizes truth in order to judge the veridicality of its representations of appearance. The discourse of metaphysics begins with the object as such, rather than a system of literalized representations, and in which it includes subject-subject relations (as objects). It is metaphysics, then, that had inverted the priority of subject-subject and subject-object relations; and Sartre simply reversed them back. Metaphysics does not begin with the social but with objectivity which, from the point of view of the look and its logic, hides both its own social nature and the metaphoric nature of the object. Thus, it presumes a reified (and rarified) objectivity. The associated notion of reference hides the process of literalization, upon which metaphysical truth depends, and substitutes itself for the subject-subject relation from which the object is derived as representation. In other words, while metaphysics considers its project to start from the real world, it can do so only by rendering subject-subject relations ancillary to referentiality, supplementary to objects, outside objectivity, while necessarily leaving them at the core of objecthood as a trace all at the same time.

Thus, more than an inversion of subject-subject and subject-object relations is at stake in Sartre's text. If the self-as-object forms the ground on which there are objects and for which coming upon the object is allegorical, and if the object come upon as metaphoric becomes the language by which one articulates relations to other subjectivities, to be metaphorized in turn by that objectivity, then objectivity, the materialization of perceptual distance to the world, only names a sign system constituted through a social allegory, as well as through the Other-as-object (who sees). And objectivity then forms the ground on which the subject is grasped as a self, an object for itself, which the self then metaphorizes as a repetition of the Other's look—the self-as-object seen through one's own eyes.

Each aspect (object, objectivity, self) is a literalization of a metaphor for subject-subject relations and a means by which subject-subject relations manifest or preserve themselves. But they also constitute the elements of a circle. The self requires objectivity to be apprehensible, and thus takes objectivity as its form. Objectivity requires objects through which to constitute itself, and thus takes the object as its form. The object requires the self through which to be come upon, and toward which to be constituted, and thus takes the self (the self-as-object in its self-object relation) as its form. This circle of literalized metaphors subsumes all the forms of objectness that subject-subject relations generate in Sartre's ontology: namely, the object itself, objectivity, and the self. Each is the content of the next while taking the preceding as its form. The content of each object is its objectivity; the content of objectivity is the self; and the content of the self is its being an object (for the for-itself).

But what characterizes this circle is attribution; the objecthood of the self is an attribution of repetition; the objecthood of the object is an attribution of social encounter (its trace); and the concreteness of objectivity is an attribution of distance from another, of space. Each evinces an aspect of the Derridean structure of writing in general. And the circle itself becomes the foundation for this process of attribution, in the manner in which the Heideggerian circles became foundational, as a substitute for foundations themselves.

This circle is not a description of the metaphysical object; rather, it is recognizable as a Sartrean description of the complex, many-layered moments of how the for-itself encounters the world.[12] It displaces the metaphysical entityhood of the object; indeed, it inverts the metaphysical—or rather, the metaphysical is an inversion of all this. For metaphysics, the object is a prior autonomy, a plenitude that is already objective and ready to be looked at and appropriated, whereas on the circle, autonomy exists only in its circularity. Sociality, experience, and emotion exist for metaphysics as part of the world, named by language deployed socially for the purpose; language is barred from being what constitutes the existence of these "things." Metaphysics gives the object objectness, objectivity, and selfhood from elsewhere (through attribution) and buries the system of social encounters along with the system of differences that produce both the object and its meaning. The object is the assumption of an object itself, coiled within the assumptions of an autonomous existence that produce its objectness/entityhood in order to be seen as autonomous. But like autonomy, language and social encounter are brought out of hiding and given representation on the circle, as its circularity, as the intermediary moments that connect and are metaphorized by object, objectivity, and the self.

To the extent that entityhood, objectivity, and autonomy become metaphysical categories of perception, they represent reifications produced by dividing the circle's interwoven moments from each other and separating them from the subject-subject interaction that generated the circle in the first place. Constituted socially, the circle is a reading of meanings generated by the text(ile) of its interwoven elements. When metaphysics sunders this circle, it transforms these elements into categories that become presuppositional. Having broken the circle, it then claims one must see the object rather than read those meanings.

It is for this reason that the metaphysical object is aporetic; and philosophy divides over whether it is assumed to be there or assumed to be constituted by consciousness or through an awareness of it. Though considered fundamental, objective, and "there," the "object" cannot itself be accounted for except through a certain axiomatics. It has, on this account, lost its connection with where its individuation and its thereness come from.[13] The metaphysical object ceases to be the form for anything because it is stipulated to have autonomous objectivity and assumed significance; in thus becoming its own (self-referential) content, it becomes meaningless.

Ultimately, if what is to be recognized as an object has to be given not only content but form first, then something that functions socially has to be the means toward that givenness. In the case of emotions, for instance, it is not the complexity of human emotion that necessitates a complexity of linguistic representations to articulate it. Rather, it is the complexity of social interaction, which invokes a plurality of structures of form and description that generate as sociality the complex concepts and forms of human emotions, through which each individual comes upon them—both as autonomous individuality and common experience. The circle, then, is both a representation and a schematic explanation of that social involvement in the individual. As an involvement, it is not a determinism; but as we shall see later, it offers an explanation for the possibility of a variety of social determinisms, as ideational systems.

The object-circle is not a phenomenological or semiotic account of the object, since it does not include the production of meaning either as the apprehension of the object or in its function as a sign. What is this circle, then? One of its meanings can be grasped from its relatedness to the Derridean notion of writing in general. It constitutes the structure of anteriority of the object, upon which foundation the object can function as a sign in subject-subject relations, and upon which the object can be apprehended as a meaning phenomenologically. It is more complex than the Sartrean in-itself; it serves to structure the domain he names by that term, which reproduces the self-referentiality by which he characterizes it (as "never anything but what it is," *BN*, lxvi). As a circle, it is the foundationless foundation of the object, produced incommensurably by subject-subject relations, while structuring the hiatus between the sociality of subjects and the ontology of objects.

Ultimately, it is as the movement of this circle that the object is come upon (cognitively) through perception, having already been given meaning through a renarrativization and named through a literalization process. The circularity represents the metanarrativity of the object perceived. As a circle, it is a weaving of narrative (allegory), ontology (the subject who sees), and the social (subject-subject relations), which together constitute the object. That is, it is a glyph of the object, a hyperdiscursive structure whereby the object is generated (socially narrated), found in the world (a semiotic enactment), and given a priori status (named) all at once. In effect, the circle articulates the dynamic process, linked to the social, by which worldly objects are individuated from a background, given situatedness in their gestalt, and rendered the repository of meanings. To the extent an object constituted in this way absorbs and metaphorizes common experience on a social level, it becomes a repository of narrative, meaning, and name that bestow seemingly eternal independence upon it.

In effect, along with emotion, feeling, and experience, the perception of objects, and perception as such, can be understood as a complex glyphic structure, including narrativizations, aporias, and names—and which are likewise culturally specific in how they are generated. What the glyphs perform is an attention to this complexity. If they place the social at the center by deploying textual forms, they mediate the relation of textuality, language, and the social through homologous circular operations in which writing, narrative, reading, naming, enactment, and discursive form all intertwine, structuring the incommensurability of the individual and the social, and at the same time giving content to the subject and human feeling.[14]

In a sense, all meaning can be said to come to us glyphically, as the social manifestation of a conflation of narrative (common specific experience and its social engenderment), enactment (specific experience and its individual echo of social narrativity), and name (social generalization of the specific, and specific individuation of the socially given). The glyphs become the detemporal objects by which we think in communication or interaction, the interface between the personal aspect of the social and the social aspect of the personal.

WHAT THEN IS the structure of the subject that emerges from these structures as they proceed into the space between Sartre and Derrida? The subject is a reader of the world who becomes a consciousness, a for-itself in the world by metanarrating the world, telling how it will tell him/herself as a reader in the look of the world. As a reader, the subject's primary relation with the world is with the others who taught him/her how to read and who reappear endlessly in the world as the narrators metanarrated in the world's look. The triad of relationships of the subject with him/herself and the narrativity of the world are named character, narrator, and metanarrator, each relation is a double non-negation, and all are in a circular relation with each other as the foundation of the structure of reading by which the reader becomes a consciousness whose name is the "subject." Between character (I) and (other as) narrator, there is a relation named by the supplement as a glyph. Between character (I) and metanarrator (I), there is a relation named by the hymen as a glyph. And between the metanarrator of the (other as) character and the (other as) narrator of the character (I), there is a relation named by dissemination as a glyph.

In effect, the two deconstructions to which Derrida and Sartre submit the subject of Western philosophical thought render it the construction of an intimate, doubled, narrated and self-narrated, culturally specific, ontological notion in a world to which no dialectical connection exists, but within which an endless circulation of social renarrativizations and narrative enactments conjures a sense of being.

The circle of Derridean glyphs is interwoven as mediations in the circle of narrativity that constitutes the structure of the ontological subject, whose elements themselves become the mediations between the Derridean glyphs. What lies at the center of the Sartrean elements of this double circle is the inarticulable of freedom that, through the circle, grants the other freedom and subjectivity. What lies at the center of the Derridean elements of this double circle is the inarticulable of textual and discursive form, the non-text that inhabits every text and generates a metatext within each text as the mode of reading it. Each moment of this double circle is a double non-negation. Together they constitute an interweaving of the double nature of reading, of the reader as the look and as the one seen by the subject lurking in the text. This is the case for reading a text, reading another's eyes or facial expressions, or reading the world as one passes through it. These circles structure the relations that serve as foundation, as a structure of reading, by which the reader not only becomes a consciousness in the world, but does so through others whose modes of consciousness (feelings, emotions, experiences) are familiar through the common narrativities of their cultural milieu.

The subject is itself a glyph, bringing together all these elements. The glyph of the subject is homologous to the circle of Derridean glyphs. It contains not only the trace of the philosophical subject but the site of its hiddenness and its inarticulability. This inarticulability has traditionally led philosophy to consider the subject fundamental, since it cannot be traced to anterior underlying concepts within philosophical discourse (philosophy caught in its own logical circularity). But if the glyphs have any substance, as the lamination of narratives and textual forms, that substance becomes the silhouette, the outline of the inarticulable content that is known as emotion, social interaction, and the subject itself—the unportrayable space which it surrounds at its center. It is that fundamental unportrayability, outlined as a silhouette by a circular discursivity filled and made concrete by the narratives and forms that give it existence, that enables emotional states and feelings to vary considerably from culture to culture.

But what, now, of dialogue? This summation has set up a situation in which a dialogue must occur between two readers, in the context of two speakers speaking. The act of speaking "to each other" becomes a metaphysical assumption, a doubled objectivity for which the meaning spoken and the hearing of the meaning as communication are given material reality rather than contingent enactment. It is, in its presuppositions, outside the dynamic of the circle of the subject or of the NMN-structure. But with these circles, we are already beyond that simple metaphysical notion of the social. The speaking subject, as a glyph, is already interwoven in the social, a reader, and an enactment of narrativities all at once. Each reader is a double reading and a double writing, a glyph that already includes the other a priori. What then is the process of pulling them apart again, so they can speak to each other?

This is important since, in the background, there sit both the metaphysical categories that result from pulling any circle apart, sundering and reifying its ecology of elements, and the dispersal of the NMN-structure accomplished by chauvinism, masculinism, or racism in reifying the narratives and rendering the look non-reciprocal. To differentiate the structure of subject interacting with subject in its dialogic ethics from these various forms of destruction of the glyph is the task of the rest of this essay.

8 A Theory of Dialogue

IN PREVIOUS CHAPTERS, we have looked at forms of hierarchical objectification of people and modes of domination. Part of what structures domination is a discourse of nonparity, an incommensurability of language and being that is imposed and reified through the practice of such a discourse. Specifically, to articulate one's sense of people or personhood through the notions of subject-object relations fostered by hierarchy, one's interpersonal relations will take the forms of metaphysical propositions. When such imposition of incommensurability becomes part of the cultural fabric of a society, it not only buttresses the forms of domination that produce it, but obstructs all attempts from within to resist or dismantle them socially or politically. Something must first break the incommensurabilities and open a domain of dialogue in the thinking of both those who seek to resist or change their situation and those who need to let go of it. Dismantling the discourses of hierarchy to establish a sense of parity, the possibility of a practical equality and autonomy that would transcend the metaphysics of social status becomes a critical social and cultural question. What is at stake in this is a concept of dialogue, the ability of people to speak to each other in a way that grants autonomy and subjectivity to each other. Dialogue necessitates a concept of the social that escapes the modes of silencing that inhabit every form of social domination.

In part, the incommensurable discourses of Sartre and Derrida have been addressed to examine the question of what dialogue between them would entail, with an eye toward possible conceptual extension to other social incommensurabilities. In engineering this encounter between Sartre and Derrida, a formal matrix has been framed in which an elemental and primordial sense of the social wells up from within the interstice between the archaic privacy of consciousness and the archaic sociality of writing ("writing in general"). It has not sought to resolve their incommensurability but to render it the foundation of a multifaceted interaction. In an elemental form, social interaction erupts within the personal insofar as: (1) enactment is always with respect to others, narrativized in social terms; and (2) the narratives that render enactments and projects familiar in their particularity are social narratives. In the Sartrean deconstruction of subject-subject and subject-object relations there is a primacy of the social over the concept of an object. It moves toward how a sense of the social would construct itself with a sense of interpersonal parity and reside between intersubjectivity and intertextuality.

Indeed, in examining the space between intersubjectivity and intertextuality, a complex structure of laminated language, narrative, and enactment has begun to emerge as a kind of discursive fluid from which individuals, texts, states of affairs, and the apprehension of experience seem to crystallize. If the structures of this crystallization are articulable—for instance, as glyphs, double non-negations, circles, or chiasmuses—they present signifying structures interwoven between intersubjectivity and intertextuality, between the ontological and the semiotic, that map the social, and for which the aporias of consciousness and social narrative, the inexperienceable and common experience, are the signified. This suggests that, as subject-object relations constitute the mediating language in which subject-subject relations articulate themselves, so the aporias between the individual and the social, structured as glyphs, present the possibility of a mediating language in which dialogic relations could be articulated.

An Elementary Particle of the Social

Sartre's account of being-for-others is of being in the situation of responding to the look of the other. In the look, one obtains a nature, an outside, and one loses one's own sense of a project or autonomy by becoming an object, a knowledge for the other who one thereby apprehends as a subject. In the look, the for-itself finds itself in a bilateral relation of being-for-the-Other and being for itself. While the other besets as a freedom that remains unknowable as such, one knows oneself to be still a subjectivity, but structured and objectivized with respect to the other.

> The appearance of the look is apprehended by me as an ekstatic relation of being, of which one term is the 'me' as for-itself which is what it is not and which is not what it is, and of which the other term is still the 'me' but outside my reach, outside my action, outside my knowledge. (*BN*, 268)

One does not gain a knowledge of the other as subject; it is not the other that one sees or encounters, but rather the look of the other that one apprehends. If, as a loss of autonomy, the look incurs what Sartre calls a form of bondage (*BN*, 267), it also constitutes a form of belonging to the extent one understands that one exists for all other people (*BN*, 280).

For Sartre, the look constitutes the "original relation with the Other" (*BN*, 361), but as "original" it is already double, not only in the mode in which one apprehends it (as a double "me"), but in one's response to it. One's two possible responses are:

> To transcend the Other's transcendence, or, on the contrary, to incorporate that transcendence within me without removing from it its character as transcendence—such are the two primitive attitudes which I assume confronting the Other. (*BN*, 363)

The first is that one retrieves one's subjectivity by returning the look, turning the other into an object for oneself. The second possibility is that one enacts a form of subject-subject relation by seeking, in returning the look, to remain an object for the other in order to maintain the other as a subject for oneself. In the first possibility, one recaptures one's autonomy and project, but at the expense of the other's subjectivity. One leaves the other the possibility of likewise returning the look and reobjectivizing in turn, implying a potentially endless oscillation of objectivizations, with an eventual concomitant hostility or sense of social alienation.

For many Sartre commentators, this is the primary aspect of the look, imparting an essentiality to the aura of separation, aloneness, and social conflict for the human condition. There is a decided narrative violence in returning the look to objectivize the other that Sartre recognizes. It involves "wrenching oneself away" from thrall to the Other (*BN*, 287). "Insofar as I am the object of values which come to qualify me without my being able to act on this qualification or even know it, I am enslaved. By the same token insofar as I am the instrument of possibilities which are not my possibilities, . . . [that] I can not even glimpse, and which . . . constitute me as a means to [another's] ends . . . I am *in danger*" (*BN*, 267–8). And conversely, if one's objectivization by the other binds in violence, one's breaking those bonds through a returned look is just as violent. The possible endlessness of this violence has convinced many commentators that no sense of social solidarity can emerge in principle from Sartre's ontology.[1]

This might be an understandable interpretation if one had not pursued the deconstruction of subject-object relations in Sartre's inversion of the Cartesian paradigm. But if a social metaphysics is involved in the prioritizing of subject-object relations, as the alienation theorists hold, then that cannot be the essential nature of either the look or of one's response to it. And thus it behooves us to examine carefully the second possibility, in which one enacts a "subject-subject" attitude toward the other in responding to the look.

To maintain the other as a subject for oneself, one must turn toward the other in a way that does not reobjectivize the other. That is, one must adopt (not) doing so as a project. It means abjuring the reobjectivizing look by adopting a mediating stance toward the other as a "self-as-object." One accepts one's objectivation, one's having been appropriated and given a nature by the other, in order to accept the other as the subject who is the condition of that objectivation.[2] Though one recaptures one's autonomy, it is as a subject that apprehends itself as that former object in order to preserve the other as a subject for oneself. The self-as-object, "in order to be would have to experience itself as made-to-be by and for a consciousness which it has to not be if it wishes to be" (*BN*, 300). One becomes the situation in which there was another one must refuse to be (*BN*, 283).

The effect is to place the other at the center of one's being. To return the look in this way assimilates the other as a presence in the form of an Other-as-a-look (*BN*, 272),[3] and it makes the Other be an object in which one is nevertheless engaged (*BN*, 291). The other's freedom (consciousness) becomes a property of his/her being, something interior to him/her that has oneself as an image in it, namely, that image seen by the Other's prior look, the trace through which one now apprehends the Other, and to whom one relates as a freedom that chooses itself as a self-as-object for which the Other-as-subject is the trace.

In sum, one shifts one's apprehension of being looked at to the situation of the Other being-a-look seeing oneself, in order to grasp the Other as the center of an alternate, reintegrated world (*BN*, 272). This being-for-others is a choice of being, a choice to embrace the other as subject and to assimilate that subjectivity into one's own being.[4] The "me" remains doubled; but that doubled "me" now becomes I-and-the-other and I-and-my-recaptured-self (*BN*, 299). One is no longer out of relationship as a "me." One's assimilation of the other becomes part of what one is as an object for the other, as part of being-for the other.

One's being-for-others is thus also double. It remains self-referential, apprehending the other as a subject through reference to oneself; and it instills a sense of mutuality. For the other to return the look now would not be to catch one at the keyhole or in the throes of a companionable non-thetic personalization. The activity one is caught at is that of looking at the other through the trace of the other-as-a-look, that is, in the enactment of the project of being-for-the-other through looking at him/her. It would be to catch one in the act not of seeing the other as a subject, which one cannot do, nor of seeing the Other as an object, which would cancel one's project, but of having accepted the other in the act of having looked at oneself (*BN*, 301). This mutuality does not establish equality of ontological standing between the two, but it creates a reciprocity of possibility in the moment for both. It is a mutuality that is incommensurable with that of mutual objectivation. One remains the nature one had been given but becomes, at the same time, an unrevealed subjectivity face-to-face with the Other, who is in turn given a nature, that of being the one who has given a nature (to oneself). The Other does not become knowable; rather, the Other is preserved in unknowability as the condition for an "inexhaustible synthesis of unrevealed properties" in oneself (*BN*, 268).

It must be emphasized, however, that this mutuality is not an ontological intersubjectivity. That is not possible in the Sartrean ontology. It would mean relating as a subject to the Other as subject. But that would eliminate the separation between for-itselfs, canceling their being as freedom. One either retrieves one's subjectivity through objectivation of the other, or one seeks to relate to the Other as subject, requiring one to remain an object for the Other. In the latter, there is a mutuality that accompanies their mutual incommensurability; and this (familiar) structure represents a means of seeing into the social.

The doubled "me" reflects this structure in residing between I-and-the-other and I-and-my-recaptured-self. On the one hand, the "recaptured self" is a re-subjectivized for-itself (non-act) that apprehends itself as a "self-as-object" (a state); and I-and-the-other is a project (an act) toward the other who is objectivized (nihilated as a subject, a non-state). The "I" (which for Sartre is not a sense of self, but a project of the for-itself from which a sense of self emerges through self-objectification) is incommensurable with, yet inseparable from, the "I" of formerly having been objectivized by the other. This doubled "me," as a doubled "I," constitutes an ontological difference: The "I" as a for-itself is the trace for the objectivized "I" for-the-other, and the latter is always a representation of the possibilities of the former.

The space opened by this doubled "me" brings with it a social role. It highlights an aspect of the Other that does not belong to the Other, his/her character as "Other."

> The only consciousness which exists without apprehending me or refusing me and which I myself can conceive is not a consciousness isolated somewhere outside the world; it is my own. Thus the Other whom I recognize in order to refuse to be him is

> before all else *the one for whom my for-itself is*. Not only do I make myself not-be this other being by denying that he is me, I make myself not-be a being who is making himself not-be me. (*BN*, 284–5)

One must be a being that has to not-be the other. If, in preserving the other as subject, one becomes the being through whom the other is, it is in a place of mutuality of negativations, of each not-being-the-other. What resides at the core of otherness, a reciprocity of otherness, is a responsibility for it. This social moment, in its reciprocity, is more than merely an interaction. One apprehends the Other as a being-in-situation, for which one is, oneself, the situation. And in that "face-to-face" encounter (an interiority: I-and-the-other, rather than an external relation), the Other's otherness becomes one's unavoidable contribution to the other. "I am the one who makes the Other be" (*BN*, 285). That is, one makes the Other be in one's world as a subject. One makes oneself responsible for making the Other be as a subject. "It is I who by the very affirmation of my free spontaneity cause there to be an Other and not simply an infinite reference of consciousness to itself" (*BN*, 287). That is, one grants the Other their subjectivity, while at the same time being responsible for the existence thus granted. It is a double responsibility. There is a responsibility for the Other in one's existence as facticity, as "self-as-other"; and there is a responsibility to the Other that one lives as a "oneself."

Set apart from all other subject-object relations, this double not-being-the-other becomes the atom, the primordial relation of sociality, because it is a structure of mutual responsibility. Herein it echoes the mutual conditioning of "response" and "responsibility," not as an atomization of sociality, but as a recursivity of mutual autonomy, doubly granted and doubly projected, as social interaction.

What is critical in Sartre's account is that "the Other and myself cannot come to one another from the outside" (*BN*, 299). That is, one can come to the Other only through the effect of the Other on oneself. One is not responsible for having been objectivized or having been rendered a metanarrator of the situation, even though its narrative content is one's own. But one is responsible for the project of assimilating the Other, as the content of that narrative, as a being-in-situation as such. One is responsible for there being another, and thus to that Other, as a transformation of one's interior responsiveness, as responsibility, to that other.

In producing this double responsibility, one's self-deployed assimilation of the Other-as-subject becomes a boundary between the Other as limiting and the for-itself as limited. The Other is limiting in presenting a freedom that remains unrevealed and unknown. And one is limited in now being one with an outside, an outside totalization that leaves one detotalized and indefinite because still a freedom. These limits do not functions as impositions, but rather like a dance, a sense of mutuality in something the Other does for which one is responsible and which one does oneself for which the Other is responsible.

It must be noted that, in both cases of the returned look, there is an assumption of certain social conditions, an assumption that some form of reciprocity is possible. One can recapture one's subjectivity, autonomy, and project with respect to the other only in a milieu that permits social parity in the sense of admitting a common narrativization of social values. The other's look has to permit a response; it has to be recognizable as an effect on oneself that makes response possible. This does not happen when the implicit narrative in the look is not one of present objectivization, but one of prior objectification. The encounter has to leave the one looked at a metanarrator who can be recognized as narrativizing. If not, then one cannot leave the "me" alienated in the Other's look with the Other, since it would not have existed as such for the Other. In certain hierarchical situations (white supremacy, for instance), recognition is not reciprocal; there is only a narrative of imposition obviating such recognition. One is already pre-narrativized in the white supremacist eye as something else. And a response to that look will be pre-narrativized as the impossible act of an object, uncountenanced as such, to be interpreted most often as rebellion or arrogance.[5] (Because Sartre does not investigate those possibilities in the general discourse of the look that he presents, in the context of European patriarchy, his discourse must be seen and understood as gendered male, and racialized as white and European. I shall return to this below.)

Being-for-Others as a Microsocius

The project to assimilate the Other as a freedom, a subjectivity, a knowledge, means to transform one's apprehension of the Other as a subject into the situation one in turn discovers in one's responding look. If one bestows upon the Other a nature, through a knowledge of having apprehended the other-as-subject, it is as a preserved (narrated) subjectivity rather than strictly an Other-as-object. Yet one cannot apprehend how the Other apprehends one's look. The nature bestowed (the preserved subjectivity) and the knowledge of the Other (as apprehending one's alienated "me") are both the memory, the trace, of what one had been in the Other's look. The returned look has a past. The Other-as-subject retains subjectivity (in one's apprehension) through the trace of having been a subject, as a meaning implicit in the trace of one's former objecthood, but assimilated as a meaning in one's present project.[6] The returned look thus becomes a narrative structure whose trace is a self-referential (narrative or memory of) intersubjectivity.

Let us recapitulate a moment. Though it unfolds as a narrative of intersubjectivity with a past, the returned look nevertheless remains non-temporal, a lamination of transformations. First, in an awareness of having been an object for the Other, one reaffirms an ontological precedence of the for-itself in refusing to be that object and refusing to be the Other in the face of having lost one's autonomy to him/her. Second, one refuses to relinquish that "me" made to be through the Other, in order to have the Other remain an Other as subject for oneself. And third, one transforms the "me" as an object for the Other into an object for oneself.

In the first step, one takes on the role of the metanarrated character, the one narrated by the metanarrated narrator (Other), and renarrates oneself metanarratively. In the second, one adopts the narrative of the first step, owning it as one's own character, but transforming that character into a narrator of the Other as narrator, the one whose subjectivity is inseparable from being a storyteller in whose story one is that character. Thus, the Other is preserved as subject by being given the character of storyteller (narrator). And third, one affirms oneself as subject by bestowing on oneself the characteristic of storyteller as well, narrating the character of the Other as storyteller.

The returned look transforms the NMN-structure from a structure of apprehension in which two narrators, a metanarrator and a metanarrated narrator, also appear as two characters in a single interaction. It becomes an interaction of two characters who appear face-to-face as subjects because they are both narrators—the interaction metanarrated by the for-itself who is looked at and who returns the look. The prior socially given narratives that had constituted the content of the original look for the metanarrator become reified in those characters (for the for-itself) in the returned look; and the content now metanarrated is no longer those narratives but the narrative/experience of the prior look one is returning.

The narrative center of the structure shifts from the sociohistorical given to one's own interaction with the other. While the counteracting (reobjectivizing) look would transform the NMN-structure from the point of view of the Other, setting oneself in the position of seeing the Other in the distance as an Other-as-object, the returned look (non-counteracting) preserves the precedent NMN-structure through an engagement in it, as an engagement in the Other-as-subject through it. If a social narrative provided the content for the prior look that the one seen metanarrates, and that former NMN-structure becomes the narrative content for the returned look, one inscribes in the content of the returned look the entire NMN-structure that constituted one's awareness of being an object. The narrator of the "me" that one leaves in the Other's hands face-to-face with oneself is no longer the metanarrated Other, but now the metanarrator of both "me"s, each of which signifies the former NMN-structure. The returned look is a form of meta-NMN-structure.

The inner incommensurability in the returned look is now not between subject and object, but between discourse and metadiscourse.[7] That is, the structure of the returned look becomes a form in the space between an impossible ontological intersubjectivity and a subject-subject interaction at the level of facticity, of two characters as storytellers. Because the narrative that the meta-NMN-structure provides for them is the common narrative/experience of the prior look, this interaction is constituted as a proto-socius, a social molecule compounding two elementary particles of the social. It becomes a form of proto-socius because it engenders the possibility of both repetititon and commonality of narrative.[8] But it is neither of those yet; the returned look first has to be returned again, in its own terms.

For Derrida, "The possibility of re-petition in its most general form [is] the constitution of the trace in the most universal sense" (*SP*, 67). This is the essential structure of the possibility of meaning. The sign can be posited only as something that is repeatable, and which not only points back to a former instance from which it differs as the same, but which also resides in a structure of differences, obtaining its singularity through the trace of other signs from which it differs. The returned look, which does not repeat the Other's look of discovery, takes the NMN-structure generated in the Other's look of discovery as its trace, as what it repeats—the trace "in its most general form," a sign metadiscursive to itself as a trace, giving itself meaning as different.

This meaning, preserved in repetition and appearing in the form of a narrative, does not require thetic awareness. It still takes narrative form as the reappearance of the anterior NMN-structure that constitutes the meaning of the returned look. Whether thetic or not, the anterior NMN-structure is metanarrated self-referentially as the meaning of the returned look. The Other-as-object exists as a subject through reference to oneself, but not as a repetition of oneself.

Rather, one affirms one's own existence as a self-for-others, whose trace is the Self-as-object; and one embraces the existence of the second person, the Other-as-subject, whose trace is the Other's being-as-a-look. Together, as a doubly metanarrated narrative, these condition the reaffirmation of the for-itself, the Self-as-subject, and the granting of subjectivity as a narrator to the Other. One grants oneself subjectivity in the sense that one has been granted subjectivity by granting subjectivity to the Other.

This raises a question of mediation. In the look, the Other is apprehended as a subject in his/her being-as-a-look whose content is as a storyteller in a metanarrative of the self being discovered. There is no name for the Other's existence, and the Other need not speak. The Other's being a narrator becomes a metaphor for what is unknowable, yet metanarratively known. In returning the look, the Other's being apprehended as a subject is assimilated as a project, as a nature given the Other, while one's knowledge is not of the Other's subjectivity but that the Other is a subject. Given that what is known is the possibility of being rendered an object again, the question becomes what mediates between the first, the NMN-structure as form (signifier) for which the social narratives (of experience and common experience) are the content, and the returned look for which the NMN-structure is a trace from which the returned look (as meta-NMN-structure) attains meaning as a signifier.

In the first instance, the Other-as-the-look is rendered metaphoric through the nature given oneself as a character in the Other's narrative. It is a tale told within an act of metanarration, and in which the Other's knowledge and one's own nature become metaphors for character positions. But, in addition, the characters are metaphors for narrators. The two narrators are not the meanings of the character's metaphoricity; it is their concomitant modes of non-being, the unrevealed and the unknowable, that constitute the content of the metaphors. These elements of non-being are concretized in the relations of narrators and characters in the NMN-structure. Subjectivity, which is allegorized through narrative (whether Sartre's narration of his ontological subject or the Other-as-subject narrated as narrator by the one seen), is the meaning of the interaction of these characters (metaphorizing the unrevealed and the unknowable). The double metanarrativity of those metaphoric characters becomes an enactment of the production of subjectivity in social interaction. This still constitutes facticity for each, but it is interactive as a microsocius.

Sartre, of course, dispenses with such metaphoricity and deals directly with the ontological as categories; but these simply literalize the narrative metaphors (in the sense that if narrative allegorizes subjectivity, the subject becomes a trope for narrative). Rather than present the subject as metaphoric, his ontology takes the elements of enactment and character position literally. In other words, Sartre's account of being-for-others, in reference to the social, is already a literalization of the metaphors of its molecular narrativization of subject-subject encounter. The fact that what each character enacts toward the other, as an experience of face-to-face encounter, is in fact two character positions that are incommensurable and inseparable remains unseen and unarticulated in his text. Yet the enactments of those interacting subjects, in their mutual narrativizations, must be metaphoric of some form of anterior social narrativization. It is that anteriority that is both effaced through literalization of the interaction's metaphoricity, and reinscribed in the returned look as a meta-NMN-structure.

Thus, there is a double structure of signs structuring mutually delimiting subjectivities, for which the form is the trace (of the NMN-structure) and the content is a mutually delimiting subject-subject encounter as an event whose domain is metadiscursive to the look. In turning to the Other (returning the look), reiterating the event of the look, the event takes itself as its trace. But as a self-referential event, the double narrator-character relation of the NMN-structure replaces itself non-narratively as pure reiteration, in which the Other-as-subject becomes the double condition for reapprehending oneself as subject. The "oneself" that returns the look is no longer the one given a nature in a story told through the Other, but the name of the event that the Other has become. The Other, granted subjectivity by the returned look, takes the form of an event whose content is a metanarrative structure, but as a trace. It is an event whose form is "oneself" as name for a content that is the Other as non-narrative for the event. It is an event that is diacritically represented by the hyphen in the notion of a "subject-subject" relation.[9] The three moments of one's returned look, the other as subject assimilated and the doubled "me," which constitutes the totality of "I-and-the-other" (a totality to which the "I-and-my-recaptured-self" is skew), is for Sartre a totality that is non-totalized insofar as it is a boundary between oneself and the other, a boundary from which the double narrative structure between them differs as signs, a boundary without narrative.

In sum, this double relation to the Other, as the first moment of the operation of microsociality, the most elementary molecule composed of the atoms of the NMN-structure, has no foundation in the Other, nor in any anterior narrative of social relation. Its foundation is the triad of subjectivities (narrator positions) that emerge from the iterations and transformations of the NMN-structure, for which the prior social narratives that render common experience possible are the first-order sign system.

> Being-for-others can be only if it is made-to-be by a totality which is lost so that being-for-others may arise, a position which would lead us to postulate the existence and directing power of the mind [*esprit*]. But on the other hand, this being-for-others can exist only if it involves an inapprehensible and external non-being which no totality, not even the mind, can produce or found. (*BN*, 301)

This means that it can take no point of view on itself. The externality of non-being is not an outside but another subjectivity, a "totality that is non-totalized."

In Sartre's thinking, this dispenses with the metaphysical concept of mind (*esprit*) as meaningless. The notion of the mind cannot be nominative, nor spoken of as a thing. In deconstructing the metaphysical concept of mind, the structure of being-for-others also deconstructs the boundary between subjectivities. They become inseparable, while remaining separate, incommensurable, because unknowable to each other.

The Boundary between Subjectivities

If a form of boundary ("I-and-the-other") has been constructed between individuals, it does not assume isolation or alien being but continguity, the inseparability of the incommensurable. The three subjectivities of the returned look contain that boundary as an essential structure that they generate.

But this boundary also has a concreteness, the body of the Other that one sees through the "me" of one's recaptured self, as a body through which one is given a nature. The body does not relate to others as a thing; it marks a facticity. It is the site of enactment of the narratives whereby one's nature is apprehended. Those narratives become a clothing that one wears as a body, which give it social meaning and recognizability. It is on the body of the Other that one discerns the difference between a look of intimacy or a stance of accusation, depending on how one is discovered by the Other's look. However much desire or belief may appear autonomous, as expressions of the sovereign individual, their recognizability signifies the social narratives they represent in a state of reiteration, while their enactment in movement or articulation presents their recognizability. The intentionalities and motivations of one individual toward another, which are incommensurable in principle with the other, become recognizable because they are enacted in terms of prior experience, of feelings and emotions that are culturally generated, pursuant to discursive structures within the social. The body thus concretely reflects the double non-negational logic that Sartre had used to describe the look in the first place.

At the level of the body, the returned look self-referentially enacts an encounter that renders its reenactment a possibility. It becomes a sign that refers to itself (as a project), points to itself as its (now) embodied meaning, re-members that meaning whose trace is the NMN-structure with a memory that is both metaphoric and self-referential, and metaphorizes that signified as self-difference, as the other of the interaction, the event, all at the same time. It separates trace and repetition, its trace being the antecedent look and its repetition being its recognition in reenactment.

When Derrida says that the trace is what must be thought before the entity, he is recognizing that recognition is anterior to cognition. Yet memory cannot be an activity; it is precisely what consciousness can never fathom because it is what thinking as well as enactment depends upon at all times. As the foundation for all thinking and enactment, memory is anteriority itself. Thinking and enactment proceed only because they "know" what they are doing, which means they already recognize it. If the meaning of "I-and-the-other" is of having returned the look, of its having presented itself for recognition prior to its having a social content (that it would have to self-referentially generate) for cognition, it presents itself as anteriority as well as that which makes possible the repetition of returned looks that sustain a subject-subject encounter. This is what, in special circumstances, will constitute dialogue.

If the transformation of the Other into a sign for one's remembered objectivation is a sign for différance itself, that sign repeats the antecedent look it differs from, in the Other now being looked at. As opposed to the difference between one's project and one's former subjectivity, where there is neither signified nor referent, but only a self-referential metaphoric signifier (the indeterminacy of the other as subject), the Other now becomes a signifier for oneself. And one becomes a name for the iterable event that is not a repetition, for which the Other's look (the NMN-structure) is the trace of what differs. Rather than a metaphoricity, there is a naming; and the boundary of I-and-the-other becomes a boundary between the disappearance of meaning toward the Other and the bestowal of meaning on oneself, between signified and signifier, respectively.

In returning the look, one transforms oneself from a signified whose signifier is hidden to a signifier whose signified is one's own transformation; and one transforms the Other from a signifier that signifies itself and metaphorizes oneself into a signifier for oneself. These transformations are all skew relations, between a signifier without signified and a signified without signifier, between semiotic and ontological narratives, between text and consciousness. One is, in granting subjectivity to the Other, both sides of the boundary, of the encounter; that is, both a trope for the Other-as-subject and what literalizes that trope as a sign for oneself. Being-for-others becomes both a narratable encounter between the unknowable and the unrevealed, for which one is oneself the metaphor, and an inarticulable non-narrative text whose trace is a narrative structure of encounter, the separation and inseparability of a name and a metaphor.

To separate this into two forms of discourse, one would have the following: in Sartrean terms, the for-itself and the oneself are not negations of each other; they are not the same, and they are not different; and in Derridean terms, each is the trace of the other, both the same and different. In both languages, they constitute non-intersecting, non-parallel non-negations between a metaphoric meaning and a literalized sign, a literalized meaning and a metaphoric sign. If the returned look constitutes itself through its difference from the look it iterates, and as deferral of the Other (subjectivity as meaning) to one's own project of granting that subjectivity, then being-for-others becomes the play of différance at the level of the ontological subject. In effect, being-for-others, as a structure of the space between consciousness and writing, is both the literalization of two self-referential metaphors and the metaphorization of an interrelation of a signifier without a signified and a signified without a signifier. Its content is the subject-subject encounter, for which it becomes a name, and for which the subject-subject encounter becomes a metaphoric enactment.

The Ontological Structure of Dialogue (Sartrean Conversation)

Now, how does this relate to conversation, to that situation in which the events in question are spoken?

In a conversation, one speaks in order to be heard. But it is more than simply "being heard." One speaks, and in speaking, one comports oneself in a way to be discovered "in the act" of speech. The act of speech calls attention to one, so that one is looked at, in order to become the object of the Other's look, to be discovered in that look. The fact that the one who speaks is seen and rendered an object by the one who listens is, in fact, the purpose of speaking. It is to be beheld and heard. One's words are the situation in which one seeks to be beheld by the Other, as a matrix for their meaning. While the Other who sees is discovering, the discovery has been set up by the speaker. It is not a case of being surprised at the keyhole. The structure is the same as the look, except that one acts to be discovered; the discovery is purposeful rather than inadvertent. In having set up the "discovery," one is no less an object of it, but the tenor of the discovery then inherently includes an intimacy, a guise given the look's objectivization that presents it as one to be returned in kind. As in Sartre's original narrative, the Other does not actually have to be there for one to be "discovered," to be seen and heard in the act of speech. The act will nevertheless have an aura of intimacy about it, as speech.

In this variation of the look, one becomes a character expressing (metanarrating) a meaning through an act of speech to which another is listening—or rather, to which the Other is (meta)narrativized by the speaker as listening. The Other's act of listening is as a character in the speaker's narrative of the Other, and the meaning expressed in speech is an attribute (or nature) given the speaker as character in the Other's narrative of discovery (listening) as metanarrated by the speaker. For the speaker, the listener (a character) acts (discovers) according to what is spoken. One's expression in speech is the act of the character the Other discovers and narrates, and through which one acquires a nature, that of what one had spoken.

On the other hand, the knowledge that one's speech is, one's nature as having said what one did, is hidden from the one speaking, yet metanarrated for the other by the speaker. But if the meaning of one's speech is a nature given by the Other, then one's meaning as such is given by the Other who hears it. One speaks to be looked at (heard), to become the object of a look of "listening" and a knowledge (of what is said), thinking that one is expressing a meaning, while that meaning has yet to be engendered by the one who hears (sees, listens), as their knowledge of one's speech as their object, which is metanarrated for them by the speaker. One may assume that the knowledge the Other has of one's nature, albeit hidden, is the meaning one intended for one's speech, but this assumption is part of how one metanarrates the Other in speaking.

One speaks, therefore, as a double project: to express a meaning, to be discovered in the act of expressing a meaning, and to defer that meaning to the Other, ultimately to discover one's meaning as deferred. It is in this sense that the act of speech invokes the look as a look to be returned. It is to that returned look that meaning is deferred. This is a project fraught with counterfinalities, of course. But it is this doubleness that ultimately allows a dialogue to have a character all its own, independent of the desires of the participants.

When one speaks, one does it to apprehend the Other as a subject, insofar as the Other's listening objectivizes one as heard (looked at). As in the look, in which it is not the Other that one sees but the look of the Other that one apprehends, when speaking it is not the Other as listener that one encounters, but the attention of the Other that one apprehends. That the Other is listening is a social narrative through which one (meta)narrates the nature one acquires, as the meaning of one's speech.

One returns the look by listening to the response. After having finished speaking, the speaker turns to the Other to listen. A "returned look" is always in the offing as soon as a speaker finishes speaking, stops to listen to what the listener might then have to say. It is, perhaps, the primordial act of reciprocity. The returned look, as a dialogic turn toward the Other's response, reiterates the prior interaction as its trace. It seeks to preserve the other's apprehended subjectivity in the double memory of having been an object (heard) and a subject discovered by the Other in the act of speaking. But it is also the primordial act concretizing the granting of subjectivity to the Other. In listening to the one who had listened, one makes the Other's subjectivity one's own project. If one speaks in order to turn to the Other and listen, it is to grant the Other the subjectivity one had apprehended in the Other in speaking to be heard. In Sartre's schema, to respond to listening by listening is not just to return the look but to step into the other's look, to act in order to bring the other to be-a-returned-look. For the Other to then speak does not just reverse the look; the look is already reversed. And what the first speaker sees, in listening, is not just a simple iteration of the first encounter but a response. It is speech by an Other-as-object toward which one is a subjectivity, and for whom the world is objective and referential.

Thus the granting of subjectivity becomes mutual. One grants subjectivity to the Other by speaking in order to listen, and one becomes a subjectivity by being spoken to in order to be heard as a response. With each response, the NMN-structure ceases to be the same, yet remains the same. Each instance has a different narrative, and a different meaning, because it makes reference to those that preceded without repeating them. As in the returned look, each response transforms the preceding NMN-structure. While the formal narrative of listening remains the same, its content as a knowledge changes. And when one then responds in turn to the response, it is in light of that content having changed; one's nature as seen by the Other in one's response is continually becoming different. Thus, one's nature changes with each addition to the dialogue. Each time one speaks to be seen (heard), it is in an NMN-structure that is again transformed, while taking the preceding act of speaking as its trace.

Modes of listening vary from culture to culture, because their overtness or covertness can vary through gestures and silences. But the metanarrative is the same for each reversal of the NMN-structure. In the response (in one's returned look), one discovers what it was that the Other had in part understood, what knowledge of oneself the Other had acquired by listening. In dialogue, one discovers what one's nature is not in being discovered, nor in the meaning of one's statement as heard by the Other, but in the content of the response. One's nature is deferred to that response. And it differs from what it will have been after the Other's next response to one's own response. Thus, people become. And what one discovers in the becoming of responses to responses is the structure of dialogue. If the possibility of misunderstanding is built into this, it is immaterial in the sense that the only "objective" meaning in question is that which forms in the space between responses, rather than to anyone's extant speech as such.

In sum, one speaks to apprehend another as a subject. One listens to grant them their subjectivity. One engages in an encounter of subject to subject in adopting listening, and thus the subjectivity of the other, as a project. One loses oneself as a project in speaking, by becoming the Other's knowledge, without knowing in any immediate sense what that is. And one discovers the meaning of one's own nature, as given to one by the Other, in listening to the Other's response. That meaning, as concretized in participatory statements, is given to one in the confluence of responses. It is not in the intended meaning that one sought to enact in speaking; it is the other who provides one with the meaning of what one had said. As Sartre puts it, dialogue is "a plural thought," one with a meaning that "each person approaches in his/her own manner" and produces on "different bases, premises, and preoccupations".[10]

What a speaker (metanarrator) says thus becomes the possibility of common meaning (a possibility contingent on whether the mutuality of listening in dialogue actually develops). Like a socially generated narrative, by which feelings and experiences in subject-subject interactions can be recognized communally as familiar, what the listener constitutes in listening is a form of discovery of what is not socially narrativized but is narrativized socially in the exchange. And what the listener enacts in responding constitutes a content that, because it comes from elsewhere (the Other), is already social—and a form (or narrative) of common experience in that sense. Though each response gets its meaning from the next response it elicits from the previous speaker, the accumulation of responses constitutes a discourse that is in itself a common experience and thus bestows that commonality on all its remembered components. What each response arrives at providing, along with the possibility of common meaning, is the mutuality of having been apprehended as a subject and the ongoing discovery not of what each speaker wanted to say ("meant" in the sense of *vouloir-dire*) but of a system of narrative traces in which the accumulation of responses is embedded and becomes a common meaning.

Thus dialogue is not primarily a question of communication from one person to another; communication is a different unilateral intention or activity and involves a different set of assumptions, such as a prior socially given common language and a necessity to communicate. Communication does not need the response of the other to give it meaning. What conversation does is construct meaning and common language in the space between its participants. It does not answer that infamous question that so often obstructs communication: How has the other understood what I have said? Nor does it render it unanswerable. What it reveals is that dialogue is a relation.

In this sense, what Heidegger called "small talk" is the inverse of communication, in that one speaks small talk simply in order to become a presence for the Other, to inform them that one is "there," rather than to communicate anything of content beyond that, or to construct common meaning.

In dialogue, each participant contributes content as part of presenting him/herself to be seen (heard) and to grant the Other more than presence, that is, subjectivity. Each participant determines only a share of a dialogue's substance; and each participant determines the linkage between his/her own contribution and the statement to which it is a response. If this provides the meaning the antecedent statement will have for itself, it is nevertheless only in the ensemble and for the ensemble. The dialogue develops its own meaning, in its own language, objectively, as an ensemble beyond the desires of each participant. In short, it acquires a character all its own, independent of the intentionalities of the participants. Each participant must read the common meaning as it develops in the repeated and exchanged NMN-structures that fill the space between them, and respond to both the statement heard and the ensemble that the statement has changed. That ensemble of meaning is both already constructed and purveyed as such, and at the same time always in progress. It is not a spoken communication but a confluence of meanings given to both listeners by both speakers. Hence, a participant must coordinate three disparate simultaneous moments, his/her own thought, the thought represented by (read in) the speech of the Other, and the substance of the dialogic ensemble itself. The plurality of the thought is not the dialogue itself but the process emerging from each relinquishing control over their meanings.

Thus, even from its first moments, a dialogue constitutes the formation of a microsocius, with its own self-narrativization and its own self-engendered elements of language.[11] Each speaker's speech takes the form of a double kind of metaspeech, spoken to elicit a response and thus spoken to metanarrate what is to be responded (to metanarrate each reversal of the NMN-structure), as well as to reinterpret the antecedent ensemble through what is added to it. Like a metanarrative, in the NMN-structure, one's speech is made a sign for itself through the Other. Where the metanarrative remains unspoken in the look, the speaker's speech metanarrates the response in the open, between the two participants, grounded in narrativities that come from a temporal elsewhere, in the antecedent dialogue. In effect, each listener's response (to an act of speaking) presents itself as a sign of what represents it, and which it names in return. Each response provides speech not only with the meaning it has for both through the content of the response, but with a chain of recursive metanarratives that constitute the matrix of that microsocius.

In short, dialogue occurs in glyphs. Each step of a dialogue, insofar as it takes the antecedent meta-NMN-structures as its narrative of content, is the name for a microsocial relation, a common language, and each meta-NMN-structure is the establishment of common narratives that render the individual intentions of the participants forms of common experience—not as the participant envisions, but as the ensemble constitutes and contextualizes them. The dialogic becomes an ongoing creation of language, meaning, and experience, structured through a lamination of its three discursive elements. It is not the language spoken or created between the participants in their interaction that occurs in glyphs. The glyphic nature of the dialogue lies in its creation of meaning as a structure, as a recursive structure endlessly inverting and reinventing itself as speech passed back and forth. It is each statement in that passing back and forth that becomes glyphic in what it takes as its past, and what it relies on as its future in the response of the listener.

The Semiotic Structure of Dialogue (Derridean Conversation)

Derrida articulates the notion of dialogue quite differently. He conceptualizes conversation as "a communication between two absolute origins that auto-affect reciprocally, repeating as immediate echo the auto-affection produced by the other" (*Gram*, 166). In other words, he begins with a reciprocal pair that extends itself immediately to four points of a structure constituted by auto-affection and echo, that is, self-referentially and iteratively, like a sign. The aporia in this is obvious; it produces an anti-dialectic in which the act of speaking to another effects itself only as auto-affect, as speaking to oneself.

But what does Derrida mean by "auto-affection"? The notion of auto-affection derives from his critique of Husserl in *Speech and Phenomena*. Derrida argues that speech is not only expression but indication. The act of indicating, of pointing to, is not itself expressive. It is a gesture that points to what is expressed, through the means of expression, that is, through the words spoken (*SP*, 37). But though it ostensibly points to what is expressed, what is expressed remains internal to the speaker, an intention, a feeling, an emotion, a story. None of this is present to the "communication" (understanding "communication" here in the broad sense of an avenue of access for moving, walking, or transmitting meaning from one point to another; cf. "Signature Event Context," in *Marg*). The signs of the communication can only point to them. Because the spoken signs attempt to express something that is in principle inexperienceable by the listener, they do so incompletely and remain a combination of expression and indication.

For Derrida, all signs express incompletely in general (even in the presence of common meanings or narratives) because, as signifiers, their signifieds are absent, elsewhere, deferred to other signs. Thus all discursive communication is incomplete in principle, because it is mediated by signs. The signs of any communication must indicate something to which the one hearing (reading) must give a meaning. The hearer must read (the spoken words) and interpret. To be complete, a communication would have to dispense with the space between itself and the other to whom it addresses itself (*SP*, 40). (That is, complete communication would be analogous to the ontological intersubjectivity to which Sartre denied possibility.) Complete communication could occur only with oneself. Auto-affection, hearing oneself speak and knowing what one seeks to communicate, marks the moment and site of the most complete communication, of the most complete coincidence of expression and indication, and thus of the most complete expression. When one speaks, one hears oneself with immediacy: "Speech . . . requires that it be heard and understood immediately by whoever emits it" (*Gram*, 166). The speaker hears himself speak; and for him, there is no difference between the expressed communication and its indication of intended meaning.

Yet even for the speaker, Derrida suggests, that coincidence of expressions and indication is still not absolute. The speaker knows the other hears and auto-affects what is spoken, and that the meaning the hearer gives it differs. That difference remains hidden, unknowable, yet present to the speaker in its absence. While the speech is heard by the speaker in its immediacy, the speaker also monitors it in its transmission to the other. While the voice is the place where auto-affection and the meaning of a spoken act come together, as the moment of access for the hearer to the sign of the speaker, in its expressiveness, it defers to what is not expressed but indicated in what is spoken (*SP*, 70). Its immediacy is supplemented by that difference, by what the speaker monitors through the other to him/herself.

Because voice is "produced as pure auto-affection" (*SP*, 79), it is different from other experiences, and from writing. In speech, through the voice, "the possibility of auto-affection manifests itself as such: it leaves a trace of itself in the world. The worldly residence of a signifier becomes impregnable. That which is written remains, and the experience of touching-touched admits the world as a third party" (*Gram*, 165). That is, voice differs from those most public or private of acts, writing, touching, and so on that go beyond themselves and involve the other in themselves. "The operation of touching-touched [that one cannot touch another without them touching one back in that same act] receives the other" (*Gram*, 165); it includes the other in its being in the world, in its materiality. But voice leaves only itself as a trace, to be heard or not—and always heard at a distance (physical, social, and semiotic) from where it is heard auto-affectively by the speaker.

For the one to whom one speaks, hearing speech is a different mode of experience, which is also the same. "To speak is [also] to make him [the listener] repeat immediately to himself the hearing-oneself-speak in the very form in which I [the speaker] effectuate it" (*SP*, 80). The other hears it in the same way that the speaker does, and echoes it auto-affectively as well. And the speaker hears not only what s/he has spoken, but in hearing it hears what the other will also have heard. Thus, the words spoken are auto-affected on both sides, as the same repetition of the words spoken. Where Sartre characterizes the Other as "the one who sees what I see," for Derrida, the other is one who "hears what I hear." But there is a difference.

The act of speaking implies the fact of auto-affection repeated by the one who hears as a fact of hearing that implies (indicates) an iterated act of auto-affection. Where the first is a total correspondence between expression and indication, the second is an appearing of a sound, which is repeated as speech, as an auto-affecting iteration, whose "appearing" as sound is not yet a signifier. For Saussure, the sound heard is the sound image that functions as a signifier. Derrida suggests that this misses the mark. "The sound-image is what is heard; not the sound heard but the being-heard of the sound. Being-heard is structurally phenomenal" (*Gram*, 63). That is, Derrida moves the spoken sign beyond the sound itself, where

Saussure had posited the signifier-image, to the apprehension of the sound, its being-heard. While the sound is only heard in its particularity as sound, it is the phenomenal being-heard of the sound, its repetition as the same and different, that produces it as a signifier image, the possibility of its having a meaning for the other who hears. Yet its existence as a signifier is still not automatic. "Without a retention in the minimal unit of temporal experience, without a trace retaining the other as other in the same, no difference would do its work and no meaning would appear" (*Gram*, 62).

The sound-image, "the being-heard of the sound," in being a repetition of the sound heard, in that "temporal experience of repetition," is thus not only heard, but also opens itself to be read. It can be read only through its trace in the world of the fact that the other spoke, through the difference between its appearing and its appearance. "The unheard difference between the appearing and the appearance (between the "world" and "lived experience") is the condition of all other differences, of all other traces, and *it is already the trace*" (*Gram*, 65).

In phenomenological terms, without the auto-affective echo of the other's words, the phenomenal would not be transcended toward meaning, because the entity of speech would not form itself into a sign, neither as indication nor as expression. Indeed, Derrida generalizes this process to all experience.

> Only a being capable of symbolizing, that is to say of auto-affecting, may let itself be affected by the other in general. Auto-affection is the condition of an experience in general. (*Gram*, 165)

In effect, writing (in general), as the ongoing repetition of the sign (in whatever form, whether inscription, speech, the look, or a pathway), as symbolization, is involved in, is significative for, and is significant to, all experience in the world. Because speech, in its iterability, is auto-affective and can render itself a mode of inscription of signs, those signs can then be read in another's voice. The sign always already comes from elsewhere, even in the originality of doing something wholly interior, in oneself as such; its auto-affective iteration is the condition for it being read.

Moreover, though the spoken word heard becomes the ostensible source of meaning through a reading of its repetition, the "being-heard" of the sound seemingly requires an origin for itself, a place from which it came. One hears the sound spoken, but that sound-heard then disappears behind the being-heard of the sound, which then seemingly becomes both itself and the sound of the voice. It generates itself as the origin of its meaning in the guise of the disguised sound heard. Though the trace is gone in the being-heard of the sound, it is rematerialized as the source of meaning in the voice. The effect of the origin is the origin of seeing it (the effect) as an origin.

> The trace is not only the disappearance of origin. . . . [It means] that the origin did not even disappear, that it was never constituted except reciprocally by a non-origin, the trace, which thus becomes the origin of the origin. (*Gram*, 61)

The speaker's speech heard by the hearer is not the origin. The sound heard "did not even disappear"; it was never apprehended as such. It is heard as sound and apprehended as the being heard of the sound. Yet neither is the auto-affected being-heard of the sound the origin, since it repeats, or echoes, the sound heard. In form, as a repetition, it is the origin of the origin. But the origin of meaning lies neither in the spoken words heard nor the repeated words that point back to the sound heard from which they came; it lies in their difference, whose condition is their iterability and the fact of iteration. What is beyond the articulable is only retrievable through the articulable. The sign apprehended (in the speaker's speech) is the difference between what the speaker produces as a sign hidden behind a sound and the being-heard behind which the sound itself hides. "The plenitude that is called sensible would not appear as such without the difference or opposition which gives [it] *form*" (*Gram*, 62). Thus, the auto-affection of the hearer of the speech supplements the auto-affection of the speaker. That is, the fact of auto-affection in the act of speaking repeats itself (as an echo) in the hearer, and the hearer's act of auto-affection becomes the speaker's fact of speaking echoed in and by the hearer. For Derrida, a conversation occurs through the endless process of such double auto-affections.

But before looking at Derrida's account of the response, of speech returned as conversational reciprocity, let us look at what still remains unsaid in the difference between the sound heard and the being-heard of the sound, that is, at an ineradicable presence of the inarticulable, of an unpresentable presence.

In the difference between the sound heard and the being-heard of the sound, the sound heard constitutes an anterior element that functions as the trace for the being-heard of the sound—for both the speaker and the hearer. Its appearance, which the being-heard of the sound repeats, becomes the trace from which the phenomenological being-heard differs, yet holds inside itself. For Derrida, "the (pure) trace, . . . although it does not exist, although it is never a being-present outside of all plenitude, its possibility is by rights anterior to all that one calls sign" (*Gram*, 62). But the spoken sound is real, an event, an occurrence albeit lost, occluded and included, behind the being-heard of the sound. It presents itself with a certain singularity, though in that singularity it remains devoid of having a signified to point to, and even of a repetition to enable that pointing, since its character as iteration and as iterable resides in its apprehension as a sign, as the being-heard of the sound. But in its singularity, "neither in the world nor in 'another world'" (*Gram*, 65), the sound heard remains anterior to its presence as anteriority itself.

This anteriority is not the source of significance, but the possibility of signifying. It is a non-origin named as origin by the origin to which it gives rise as effect. In the sound heard, one is given anteriority (rather than a hidden lurking subjectivity, as in a text). Yet even as anterior, constituting the trace for the act of listening (the being-heard of the sound), it does not constitute, as the fact of speech, a narrative by which the speaker becomes a metanarrator; nor does the sound heard function within an NMN-structure. It is only an act of speech in which the hearer (both of them) recognizes the speech as the possibility of signifying, and a fact of speech for which the inarticulable as anterior to what the speech articulates is the trace. A different difference opens up. There is not only a difference between the sound heard and the being-heard of the sound, but in their being transmitted from one to the other, the auto-affection of the words experienced by the speaker as total communication is experienced by the listener as an echo to him/herself echoing that speech. The anterior singularity, in becoming a fact of speech, loses its character as pure indication; in pointing back to the act of speech as such, it becomes a linguistic sign.

But what then is the relation between the moment of pure indication and the functionality of the sign? As an incommensurate relation between anteriority and signification, it is analogous to the difference between Being and beings for Heidegger, the ontological difference. Anteriority is in general a way of referring to inarticulability, to the anterior condition for articulation itself, the necessary condition for the structure of meaning. It cannot be signified in the system of meaning it engenders.

Derrida allegorizes this anteriority in his consideration of the proper name. The proper name is what names something (a particular person or thing) in its singularity. It belongs to an individual without mediation or ambiguity. To be a proper name as such, it must belong to the person it names and no other, and constitute unmediated reference to that person. Yet to belong only to the person it names, it could not be a sign; otherwise it would have already lost its unmediatedness as an element in a system of signs, a structure of differences. Thus, it could not be what the individual is called, even as an individual. To call a person by that ("proper") name would remove it from the realm of "proper names," from the realm of the unmediated, and transform it into a sign among other signs. Within a structure of signifiers, it would then obtain a meaning, but from the signifying system and not from what it "properly" names. The proper name, to remain "proper," must remain hidden, untouched, nonexistent as a sign. It cannot be "used." Hence, the "actual" name that is in use in social discourse is no longer a proper name. Though its use points back to its condition of anteriority, once produced as a "proper name" within a linguistic system, it is no longer a proper name; "[its] production is [its] obliteration" (*Gram*, 109).

Essentially, a "literal [proper] meaning does not exist," though it is a necessary function in any language (*Gram*, 89). It is "the myth of a transparent legibility present under the obliteration" of the proper (*Gram*, 109). The proper name, in becoming a "proper name," undergoes an act of violence, an immediate violation of its properness and its immediacy, its "belonging to" in its singularity, and ceases to be proper. Henceforth, it refers. It loses its singularity and its uniterability. It becomes abstract and general; it is given a nature.

Thus, there is a seemingly ineluctable moment of violence in language, one that is fundamental to personal contact and to speech. "Writing cannot be thought outside the horizon of intersubjective violence" (*Gram*, 127). Where, for Sartre, this occurs in the threat of the reobjectivizing look of autonomous subjectivity, in first-person retaliation for objectivization in the Other's look, for Derrida that violence resides not in what is generative of the social, of intersubjective relations, but as inseparable within them. That is, the "inter-" of intersubjectivity and intertextuality assumes the character of an articulation and generalization of what is singular and specific, a violation of its inarticulability.

If violence accompanies the transformation of the inarticulable into the articulable or the semiotic, it is a violence that then resides in the difference between the sound heard and the being-heard of the sound. In repeating to oneself the sound heard, the hearer transforms the absolute indicative singularity of the speech (which is a complete communication, momentarily and singularly, for the speaker) into a sign that is now part indication of a meaning referred to, part indication of the fact of having been spoken, and part expression. It is wrenched from its being immediate and proper to the speaker and rendered social, a sign, an elsewhere. For the speaker, the fact of speech names the thought or intention spoken in absolute properness; but this is a properness that is obliterated in being heard, and in becoming the being-heard as a sign. The trace of having spoken has the structure of the proper name, and the difference between hearing that speech as a proper name and listening to it as the other's speech is an act of violence that transforms speech into something else, the erasure of its particularity and the attribution of meaning to it as a sign.

If the sound heard bespeaks what the speaker speaks, the listener's repetition presents the sign that represents it, that names it, that reenacts in some characterological sense what the speaker had inscribed in sound. And that repeated speech thus becomes the name for the enacted sign, the proper name for the name transformed into a sign, the name that names the sign.

But now this difference, as an act of violation of the properness of speech for the speaker by a listener, presents a certain congruence to the NMN-structure. In the Derridean account, the absolute communication of the speaker, what unquestionably indicates what the speaker seeks to communicate, in the self-engrossment of auto-affection, is caught at the keyhole of semiosis and given a nature in the form of expression. Whether the speaker knows how the listener hears his/her speech as expression (and one may assume it to be different), it occurs across a violation of its properness to the speaker, simply in having been spoken and heard. And this recapitulates the structure of the look, in that the act of speech becomes the metanarrator, who is then given characterhood, or discursivity, or a name as a thingness or nature or meaning. It is the NMN-structure undergone from the perspective of the Other, the one who looks, the one who commits an act of discovery. Caught at the keyhole of semiosis, the act of speech is seized in apprehension of its act and violently transformed into a fact, forced to abandon its coincidence of expression and indication. Speaker and hearer hear the same thing differently, the first thinking something that becomes interior to the act of speech, and the second interpreting something exterior to it in the fact of speech. They differ in the first being the trace, that from which the second differs, and for whom the meaning is deferred to an elsewhere, neither to an anteriority nor to a subjectivity, but to the operation of the NMN-structure itself.

In this congruence with the NMN-structure, Derrida's notion of the act of auto-affection is mapped into a narrative, and the experience of auto-affection is mapped into a character. It is as différance that this difference separates the metanarrator from the narrator who is a character in the metanarrated narrative. Différance, in the NMN-structure, becomes the relation between the speaker as metanarrator and the listener as narrator. It collates the operations of supplement (between speaker as metanarrated self and listener as narrator-other), hymen (between speaker as metanarrating narrator and speaker as metanarrated character), and dissemination (between speaker as character and listener as narrator). Both the act of speech as the trace and the fact of speech as NMN-structure are prior moments that themselves represent anterior enacted structures (metanarrator and character, anterior non-origin and the being-heard of the sound).

These enacted anteriorities, the fact of speech and the act of speech, recapitulate the two inarticulables in Derrida's account of the conversation. That is, the Derridean notion of conversation places inarticulability and anteriority in a semiotic frame, in a manner congruent to Sartre's phenomenological framing of being-for-others in terms of the unknowability of the other and the anteriority of freedom. It is via the inarticulables in Derrida's notion of the conversation that a mapping back to Sartre's molecule of social interaction becomes possible, as a mapping between inarticulability and anteriority on the one hand, and unknowability and anteriority on the other.

Where, for Sartre, the returned look structures the dialogic response, the saying that responds in dialogue to the Other who had spoken, reversing the hiddenness of knowledge and the unknowability of the listener, for Derrida, it is the repetition of immediacy, of absolute indication in speech, that is, the repetition of anteriority and inarticulability (of absolute indication) that sets in motion the possibility of a response to the first speaker's words. Between reversal and repetition, these present inverse portraits of the social molecule; they invert each speaker's relation (albeit homologous) to the structures of the inarticulable or the unknown. In both, two people arrive at granting each other either phenomenological or semiological being. Where in one nihilation and alterity are primary, in the other it is différance and iterability.

The Derridean Moment of the Social

Let us look at the other side of the violence in listening to the spoken. Though one can say that for the speaker, the listener is the "one who 'hears' what I 'hear,'" this ignores that violence. For the hearer, the being-heard of the sound spoken is the production of expression out of that sound, the production of a reading. At the same time, it is the production of an indication that points back to the trace, the sound heard, which is a different indication from that of the speaker, whose speech points back to his/her immediate thought. The hearer's own repetition of the sound heard, as an auto-affective act for which the fact of hearing is the trace, creates the difference between the sound's being-heard as expression and its being an indication pointing to the fact of the speaker's speech as expression. The fact of speaking is the signified of the act of hearing as a signifier, and the fact of the being-heard of the sound is the signified of the act of speech as the trace of the act of hearing. There is a signifier whose signified is hidden and out of reach, and a signified whose signifier disappears as a trace. This is homologous to one's nature in the look, which is a signifier whose signified resides elsewhere with another as subject, and a signified whose signifier is the trace of one's lost autonomy.

In sum, in generating an expression out of the being-heard (the fact of hearing) of the sound, the hearer generates an indication of the content of that act of auto-affection which is given to the speaker—the fact of having spoken transformed into an expression (self-referentiality and signification). There are two moments of meaning, each of which is the trace of the other; one is a repetition of the speaker's speech that transforms it into an expression, and the other is an indication that points back to that expression as if it were the speaker's own meaning. In other words, the speaker's speech is renarrativized as both the expression the hearer has engendered out of it and the origin of the expression indicated by the indication of the renarrativization. This chiasmus generated by the hearer's double act of auto-affection renders hearing the speaker's speech homologous to the NMN-structure. There are two moments of expression and two moments of indication, reflecting the pairs of narrators and characters in the latter.

But the two moments of meaning that are the trace for each other are bestowed upon the speaker who is then considered their origin—even in the event of the grossest misunderstanding of what had been said. This attribution, if transferred to the NMN-structure, would be an attribution by the discoverer to the one discovered. This inversion of perspective on the speaker's speech becomes the source of the hearer's response, that to which the hearer can respond, for which that double transformation of indication and expression would be the trace. Both are prior to the possibility of specifying whatever content can be given socially (as common experience) to either the speech being-heard as signs or meaning given to the speaker's speech by the listener articulated as response. In both cases, from the Sartrean and the Derridean perspectives, even though those perspectives are not the same within the homology, the interaction between speaker and hearer is chiasmic, and the meaning of each moment emerges through the operation of that chiasmus in the next. It is not that each account of dialogue can be mapped into the NMN-structure. The NMN-structure is a form of chiasmus, which takes a different form in Derrida; it is the chiasmatic structure in each that functions homologously in both.

We are at the threshold of a homology of dialogue between Sartre's and Derrida's account of spoken interaction, within their inverted perspectives on the interaction. What brings the two together, to relate their accounts of dialogue, is the presence of misunderstanding. For both, the possibility of "misunderstanding" is not only built-in, ineluctable, but essentially inevitable—so inevitable that the term *misunderstanding* loses its meaning. It is not that there are two different languages, but that within the same language, two expressions are always generated. For Derrida, this is through the same sound heard, because the accompanying moment of indication is necessarily different for speaker and listener. What the hearer cannot apprehend in the expression, what remains indication in the speaker's words, points back to a meaning that is hidden in principle. And what the hearer does apprehend as expression points back to a different auto-affection (his/her own) than does that of the speaker. For Sartre, rather than a difference of indication and hence expression, there is a deferral of meaning to the response. And this difference between them occurs because Sartre's account of the look centers the one seen, the speaker, while Derrida's account of speech centers the reader, the listener.

If, in both cases, the hearer renarrativizes the speaker's words from a multiplicity of contexts, not all of which are given in common, and some of which come from past dialogue, past experience of the speaker, social narrativities, and so on, and others from the present encounter, that renarrativization becomes the moment of creativity of the dialogue. Because the possibility of misunderstanding is built in, it embraces the reality of human interaction as creative. Yet it must remain creative in a manner independent of each participant, and thus assimilative.

In Derrida's account, the NMN-structure in its guise of two moments of indication and two moments of expression occurs as hidden, as the operation of the trace and the confluence of a significationless sign with an inarticulable signified. Regardless of context, speech provides the listener with the ability to perform the semiotic act—as auto-affection, as echo, as the assignment of meaning, and as the immediacy of repetition, of immediacy itself, in a response; that is, the listener becomes the site of production of absolute meaning within the context of the speech given as context. It provides the opportunity to become the provider of meaning to what, for the speaker, is itself immediate indication, to write for the first speaker to read, as different from self-contextualization. It is one's returned speech in its many facets that is the semiotic act, which, as in Sartre, provides the speech of the initial speaker with its meaning for that other.

However, while the being-heard of the sound dissolves into and disguises the sound heard as its origin, the meaning read in the sound-being-heard has nowhere to go to find itself; it is always in part deferred to an elsewhere, to the vast context of other meanings that somehow attempt (auto-affectively) to point to the speaker's speech as expression. The response is what transforms what is immediate and absolute indication for the first speaker into an expression in dialogue, and into the trace for what must be given meaning in turn to the respondant. This then constitutes the molecule of the social within Derrida's semiotic account.

In both accounts, there is a difference between the act of listening and the apprehension of what the speaker has said. The first implies accepting the subjectivity, or the absolute indication in hidden auto-affection, that the speaker is granting or initiating by speaking; the second consists of turning the speech into a sign, both expression and indication, to which a meaning is given by the listener, and then conveyed in recontextualized or renarrativized form to the first speaker by responding. If the response in part gives a meaning to what the first speaker had said that the speaker does not recognize, it is not a reflection of the incompleteness of the expression in the sound's being-heard nor the hiddenness of the other's characterhood as narrator/storyteller; rather, it is a function of the deferral of meaning of the listener's response as a sign to the future context of the dialogue as an ensemble of enacted responses. A difference in meaning occurs in deferral for which "misunderstanding" is the metaphysical name, the name for a unilateral suppression of reciprocity by a speaker who defines for both a category of "being understood."

Ultimately, for Derrida, the possibility of misunderstanding (or rather, its inevitability) is itself the site of the social; it is his molecule of sociality. For Sartre, it is the social that marks the space of the possibility of misunderstanding. If the metamarrator (speaker) chooses (non-thetically) the meaning of the look as listening for the encounter in question, in terms of what is spoken, while having to defer meaning to the other (the response), then misunderstanding itself is deferred to the unfolding of the social (the response) in the interaction. Again, between them, the operation of différance is inverted, but surpasses its inversion in subsuming the whole of the interaction. For both, dialogue is the site of the social, and all dialogue is always creative, because hearing the speech of another is beyond the determination of the speaker, either as absolute indication or loss of autonomy.

But what is created in dialogue, because all speech is doubly based on inarticulability, resides in its own self-contextualization, as the "social" overlap of the contextualizations of each contribution. A dialogue cannot exist as the speech of either but only as the accumulated amalgamation of spokennesses (plural) that contextualizes itself. It is creative not only in the deferral of meaning but in that amalgamation, in the invention of itself as a context out of the different moments of narrativization (the fact of speech) and character enactment (the act of speech) that seek to continue the prior narrativizations (as an ensemble) generated within the encounter. Thus, they take on a different value than culturally given narratives. If one comes to understand one's "nature" in that recontextualized look (listening) of the other, it is a nature that is different from that which is socially given in the narrativizations of communal experientiality. That is, what the speakers (metanarrators) have said becomes the possibility not of social meaning but of a common meaning—like socially generated narratives, but enacted in repetition (discovery) as personal interaction.

In sum, we have a speaker whose speech becomes the name for a meaning given in response, a narrativity of transformations of meanings between the hidden and the overt, the unknowable and the known, and a chiasmic relation that sets meaning up ahead, yet amalgamates it to a discursive mediation between participants that becomes both creative in being referential and autonomous as self-referential. In other words, dialogue is structured as glyphic, perhaps the primordial glyph of the social.

We can fill this in with the circle of glyphs that identify the moments of the NMN-structure itself. To listen is to fulfill the structure of the supplement for speech. But it also discloses the structure of the hymen between oneself and one's generation of meaning as semiotically separate from the absolute indication of the speaker. Finally, it constitutes separation and loss in the sense that the act of speaking constitutes itself as a text for the other, for the listener's transformation of absolute indication into two expressions. To listen is to engage the structure of dissemination.

At this point, we have these incommensurable thought systems named "Sartre" and "Derrida" seated at the same glyphic table in the same café, looking at each other. If one of them should speak such that the other could respond (which is not, strictly speaking, possible between discourse and metadiscourse, as we have seen), a conversation would begin, and the two would find themselves in dialogue. One of them speaks; it is Derrida.

> Auto-affection, the as-for-itself or for-itself—subjectivity—gains in power and in its mastery of the other to the extent that its power of repetition idealizes itself. Here idealization is the movement by which sensory exteriority, that which affects me or serves me as signifier, submits itself to my power of repetition. (*Gram*, 165–6)

What is he saying? Is auto-affection just a sign for the subject? Is this just a return to the boundary or interface between the semiotic and the phenomenological? It is an unusual passage, a place where the Derridean critique of language seems to caress phenomenology. Indeed, Derrida avails himself of the first person, as if narrativizing in a Sartrean manner a moment of the subject's being. On the other hand, to say "Auto-affection . . . gains . . . in its mastery of the other" seems oxymoronic.

Auto-affection is the power of repetition. An idealization of the power of repetition includes the sign's referring to itself as a sign. It is the sign's ability to signify, transformed into an unignorable meaning (mastery). The power of repetition is the existentiality of the sign.[12] The sign does not simply participate in meaning through the totality of its differential relations with other signs, it *is*. It has being as such, insofar as it signifies itself as a sign. That being, and the lexicality it derives from its metaphysical detour through a system of signification, are alienations from expressed meaning. Its alienation constitutes its being as heard by another (the "me" in Derrida's passage).

In other words, the sign has a different being for the speaker and the hearer. Beyond marking the difference between expression and indication, the difference in existentiality of the sign bestows upon the hearer the power to express what the other had only indicated, to supplement it from outside the sign's lexicality.

> Speech and the consciousness of speech—that is to say consciousness simply as self-presence—are the phenomena of an auto-affection lived as suppression of différance. That *phenomenon*, that presumed suppression of différance, that reduction of the opacity of the signifier, are the origin of what is called presence. (*Gram*, 166)

Presence, the concealment of difference and of temporality's difference from itself, means that the gap between the trace and enactment has been given existence and rendered a thing. In conversation, the voice becomes the location of that ontologization, the boundary between the semiotic and the phenomenological, between writing and consciousness, between différance and mastery. But this is also to say that the voice resides at the place of incommensurability between Sartre and Derrida, between a discourse founded on the visible and one founded on the discursive, between ontology and writing.

> This auto-affection [voice] is no doubt the possibility for what is called subjectivity or the for-itself; without it, no world as such would appear. . . . The unity of sound and voice which allows the voice to be produced in the world as pure auto-affection, is the sole case to escape the distinction between what is worldly and what is transcendental; by the same token, it makes that distinction possible. . . . No consciousness is possible without the voice. (*SP*, 79)

This is not only the moment of the subject, but the point of generation of the world itself. Where for Sartre the look manifests the possibility of consciousness of another as consciousness, for Derrida it is the voice. For Sartre, the look reflects the subject narrativizing itself and the Other through the Other, deploying socially given narratives to tell itself and the Other through the Other; and for Derrida, the voice reflects this sociality, the sign giving itself to be read and reading itself as well, as the appearance of the world.

The voice becomes the bridge between a double auto-affection and the NMN-structure. It conjoins the two versions of reading: writing apprehended as the representation of speech, and speech discovered as a representation of writing—that is, the subject as reader and the subject lurking in the text—in the guise of the one who "hears what I hear." It is the difference between the subjectivity of repetition as the mastery of subjectivity, and the other as subject through the différance of repetition. It is the materiality of the molecule of the social for Derrida.

But for Sartre as well, the voice spoken to be beheld as speaking, heard as in a look, constitutes the molecule of sociality as the place of self-generated narratives. The voice is the place of true reciprocity in the returned look because it occurs within the same self-generated narrativity. The Sartrean look as listening represents the speechless speech spoken only to oneself and the Other in the common apprehension of the emerging narrativity of each participant speaking to this particular other person. The Derridean notion of conversation is the reading by oneself and the other, as coincident repetitions, of what is in immediacy a common transformation from pure indication to signification. Across the boundary of the voice, the incommensurable discourses of Sartre and Derrida have come closer than homology and become the same. They see each other from different perspectives, across a gap, but the gap is internal to both, between the fact of speaking and the act of speaking.

Here is their common ground, the voice. It is their being-for-each-other to the extent that each contains approaches to the other that can be articulated as homological structures, mappings, glyphs, and the double non-negational logic that each uses. The double non-negational logic is itself the logic of the voice, the way in which the voice is understood (an act as non-statement, a non-act as statement). Across the fact of the voice, they enact a form of dialogue, because their languages have become *engagé*, interweaving without losing their character as "proper" languages. Being-for-others, as the discursivity of the NMN-structure, becomes the form in which the auto-affection of the voice takes place between two people; and the double auto-affection of speech and returned speech is the form the NMN-structure takes when the look becomes listening to a speaker. No longer homologous, they each simply take the form of the other, though under the aegis of an amalgamation of name, narrative, and interior glyphic circles.

LISTENING AND (RE)CONSTRUCTION

Now let us go one more step. The listener is the reader, the look, the one granted subjectivity. If a certain expression is addressed to a reader/listener, that reader/listener's iteration of it bestows upon it an expressiveness and an indicativeness that belongs to the listener's repetition, to a specific operation of différance. But the listener's repetition is the reader's look; and as a text read, the speech heard becomes a text that looks at the reader in turn, becoming a look (as speech and not as speaker), the moreso in being addressed to "this" listener specifically (second person). For the one addressed, there is a lurking subject in the text read in the spoken words heard. This lurking subject is not the speaker but a subject hidden in the text, the author of the words apprehended who becomes the source (author) not of the sound heard (speaker) but of the being-heard of the sound. To apprehend the words of the other as the look is not only to grant the speaker subjectivity but to transform the other discovered in the act of speaking into an apprehension of the fact of subjectivity in the words. The speaker is not reduced to an object but is transformed into an author, a meaning in a narrative told about the text read through the words heard.

To narrativize the act of speaking in this way discloses a distinction between one's speech being a fact of one's existence and it being an act. As a fact, it is echoed by the hearer auto-affectively and read in that auto-affection; as an act, it produces the apprehension of a subjectivity while at the same time granting it. The hearer becomes different from him/herself in the process, between the fact of listening and the act of listening, between reading the being-heard of the sound and encountering the expression of the other's speech as a subjectivity in its textuality, because the hearer is no longer the look but one looked at, no longer a respondent but a reader. The third subjectivity, the subject discovered in the text of expression by the hearer as looked at by that textual subjectivity, is not the source of meaning to which the hearer then responds, but the other to which the hearer speaks. This mediating subjectivity forms the foundation of dialogue, the "consciousness" that transforms dialogue into an independent discourse in itself between two listeners as readers and two speakers addressing a mediating subjectivity.

These three moments of expression in this hybrid account of dialogue are homologous to the three moments of thought that must be coordinated by each participant in the Sartrean account of dialogue at each moment: one's own thought, the thought expressed by the other, and the composite thought of the dialogue itself as it constructs itself in the space between them.

In being spoken, the response expresses itself, its connection to the first speech, and its interaction with the mediating subjectivity in the speaker's expression. If the third is the narrative through which the respondent has heard the speech as text of the first speaker (the look in the text of the speaker's expression) and the second is the meaning given the actual speech of the first speaker (the Other-as-object who hears what I hear) by the listener, the first is the respondent's participation as a subjectivity granted by the other two subjectivities. This traverses the differences contained in those three dimensions of speech; the absolute indication for the speaker in speaking, the look of the first speaker as listener, and the metanarrated narrative of the antecedent act of speaking, in which the other responds. In responding to the subjectivity of the text heard/read, and in granting the first speaker his/her subjectivity by responding, one is also providing both the social and the microsocial meaning of what the first speaker said from within the difference between the sound heard and its being-heard.

This is the structure of the special quality some dialogues have in developing their own system of narrativizations, so that the third (textual) speaker that becomes the look for each participant as reader is the same third subjectivity. This approaches what is often referred to as a "common language." And it reaffirms the notion that because misunderstanding is built into dialogue, it is not understanding on the part of each participant of what the other is saying that is paramount; instead, it is understanding the meaning being constructed between them, as the creative and independent entityhood of the dialogue itself. It is between understanding and misunderstanding what the other has said that one's response becomes an addition to the construction, not a reiteration of it, nor an affirmation of the mere fact that one has understood, nor a misunderstanding that abandons or erodes the construction.

To insist that the other understand what one is saying as such is to bring the process of construction, and thus the dynamic of the dialogue, to a halt. In some cases, that turns it into an interrogation; in others, into a banal attempt to merely convey information (even if just about one's own inner thoughts). If the fact of understanding represents an ontologization of this process, its metaphysical name, then the act of misunderstanding is itself the site of the power of creativity of the act of dialogue, the domain where the process of creating or construction beyond the facts of expression becomes possible—as does its destruction.

In sum, as a doubling of the NMN-structure, each dialogue manifests the creative difference between narrator and character within the differences between narrative and metanarrative that are given by the speech of the participants. Each molecular component of that endlessly repeated microsocius thus contains: (1) a narrative structure in which an act (of speech) is told (enacted) in order to be recounted by another (story) teller to him/herself, and whose content is returned to that discovered original act (of speech) from elsewhere, through a different act of discovery; (2) speaker/listeners, each of whom is discovered in the look of the listening other, and who then discovers the meaning of what s/he has said in the response of that other, at which time that speaker becomes the look (listening); and (3) a textual subjectivity embraced in each listening as a reading, which is then projected back and forth through respective responses, as the independently creative element of the common textual unfolding in its movement toward constituting a common language between and for the participants.

Because each moment takes the overall form of the look, it also homologously presents itself as a circle of Derridean glyphs. That is, the phenomenality of hearing the words of another, which signify through a complex system of differences that constitute the space between the act and the fact of listening, is mediated across the absolute abyss between its two forms of auto-affection by a glyphic structure. The communication of meaning, then, must be understood as the creation of meaning after the fact, reflecting the incommensurability between speaker and listener, between speaking and listening, that constitutes an essential part of this glyphic structure.

What this incommensurability manifests is the fact that each dialogic sign spoken between people, because contextualized by the dialogic ensemble, takes on the character of a glyph, a structure that amalgamates or laminates in itself all the different discursive processes by which the sign obtains the meaning given it in and as speech and response. For each sign, there is a lamination of the NMN-structure of being spoken to, the narrativity of the spoken enactment to which the response makes reference, and the fact of the spoken expression naming a meaning that emerges from that complex structure of narrativizations. What is ultimately expressed as the content of the dialogue is what is given it by the mediating glyphs that structure themselves between the participants as the dialogic discourse. It is the structure of the third subject as a glyph that encapsulates all this; the interactivity of the look, the NMN-structure, its narrativities, the naming of a meaning structurally by the spoken expression, and the mutual granting of subjectivity as engagement in the dialogue through that third subject.[13]

A dialogue conjoins its two participants by structurally establishing its independence from them, while subsuming their interaction. In entering into this mode of sociality, each participant is following something that is not them. It is only the "dialogue" itself that "knows what it is doing" in its directedness and autonomy. It is an untotalizable totality, constituting itself as an entity and dispelling that entityhood in the disparate experiences of its participants. If it is considered a sign in that entityhood, its signified, the meaning that emerges from the totality of what is being said is itself the signifier for the dialogue as a structure (of interaction) (its cohesion, its connectionality, its common language, its autonomy as the social itself). Like the instrumentalities, it is a signifier whose content is its form. It is what it is not (a signifier), and it is not what it is (a weaving of discourses on a shifting subject matter). In conjoining self-generation as a structure with the autonomy of the constituent meanings provided by its participants, dialogue constitutes a glyph that is homologous to Sartre's notion of the for-itself and to the structure of Derrida's instrumentalities. Thus, it presents the totality of the structure that becomes the phenomenological subject when projected on the plane of ontology, and becomes in turn the Derridean notion of writing when projected on the plane of semiotics.

Conclusion

The inversion between Sartre and Derrida in their respective accounts of dialogue, in lining up on oppposite sides of the exchange—the structures of acting in speaking and the structures of meaning in the spoken—also transcends them toward different levels of generalization: semiotic anteriority and ontological anteriority, différance and freedom. If there is a transcendent meaning to this, it attaches not to an original incommensurability but to the ability to set incommensurability in conversation around a homological commonality, a commonality of form. In form, each grants the other being, both as textuality and as subjectivity. They interact (or converse) at a level anterior to their subject matters; and if the glyphs make this possible, then it is the glyphs that constitute anteriority.

The glyph provides a common domain between Sartre and Derrida by homologically linking structures of social anteriority (the social narrative of the sign/name and the social sign/name of the narrative) that generate the sign with the specificities of subjectivity. The glyphs suggest not a sameness between writing and consciousness, but an equivalence—an equivalence that is not a common language between semiotics and ontology but a dialogue.[14]

What is engendered by conversation is language itself. Language is not primordial, nor is it genetic. Those who are not taught language do not acquire it. Those who undergo more than five days of sensory deprivation begin to forget it. How could there be aphasia if language were not learned, that is, continually invented and reinvented? The source of language, its realm of anteriority, is not with the human being (or brain) but in the space between people who interact in speech. (And I might note, since I am speaking of learning language in fact, that in the use of gestural sign systems by those who do not speak, speech is movement, and listening is indeed the look.) In these interactions, those who speak also teach it to themselves, through the response of the Other, in each microsocius.

But if language comes to be through the activity of speaking to another, that other, the listener who responds, becomes both essential and what is brought into existence (contingently) by speech. Conversation constitutes itself as language, at the same time that it constitutes language for itself. It is not through the deployment of language that conversation comes into existence; it is through the engaging in conversation, the unfolding of glyphic interaction, that language comes into being.

Writing is the form that language takes; language is the form conversation takes; and conversation is the form the arrival at social inscription takes, as the creative and independent arrival at textuality, the social process of arriving at the inscribed (in other words, conversation is the form writing takes). We have a circle of semiosis that parallels Sartre's circle of subjectivity. But they interweave, like intertextuality and intersubjectivity. The for-itself maps onto the mediation between language and writing; the Other-as-subject maps onto the mediation between writing and conversation; and being-for-others maps onto the mediation between conversation and language.

9 A Theory of Language

SOMETHING NEW NOW spans the space between the Derridean discourse of textuality and the Sartrean discourse of the subject. Across the homological space between the Derridean instrumentalities and the Sartrean narrativities, between semiotics and ontology, between writing and consciousness, Sartre and Derrida have been brought into a form of conversation with each other on the basis of interwoven glyphs. Elicited by the homologies between them, the glyph marks where a theory of dialogue between incommensurable texts can be broached. The word *glyph* signifies a complex structure combining several dimensions of meaning, discursive form, and narrative. It can be understood as the anteriority, the "proper name" of signification, arrived at through enactment that combines two levels of narrative: a coming upon the world and a social production of meaning. The glyph envelops these disparate dimensions of the discursive and amalgamates them into a single structure that becomes iconic for meaning, reference, objectivity, definitude. Composed of signs, it structures what is anterior to the sign (spaced specificity, iterability, and difference) and thus constitutes anteriority for the sign.

The structure of dialogue is itself glyphic in the sense that it amalgamates a process of signification, a narrativity and an entityhood of its own in a form of microsocius. One of its effects is the germination of a common language for that microsocius based upon its specific development as an interactivity. In dialogue, the three dimensions of the glyph bring into complex structural conjunction the sociohistorical (as given language) and the molecular (the creation of language).

For Sartre and Derrida, it is a conjunction of their being-for-each-other, their disparate discourses and their coincident discursive forms, for which the voice is the common zero point. Though they move inversely and photonegatively away from that zero point in their thinking, the glyphic mechanics of dialogue open a space where their respective languages interact and speak in common about the same things.

These mechanics enable the glyphs to transcend the structural production of meaning of specific systems (in this case, ontology and semiotics) and contain it homologically as anteriority. In other words, the glyphs structure the very process of the production of meaning in its inscriptive and social complexity (as human interaction, the act of coming upon the world, the act of naming) and represent structurally how the production of meaning would have presented itself had that productivity been articulable. As a structuring of anteriority, the glyphs suggest that all signs, in some geological manner, are glyphs reduced to the familiarity of signs. That is, the complex lamination of discursive form, social narrativity, and name gets reduced to the name as sign, much as an iceberg is apprehended as that which floats above the surface. The sign, in its social use (as word, signal, text, gesture, discourse, etc.), is thus the concretion of this metonymic process whose automaticity renders it invisible. It is haunted by the ghosts of the narratives, homologies, and microsociuses that disappear beneath it, but they are the artifacts, the "technologies" of a meaning's social recognizability. In order that signs for "fear" or "intimacy" signify commonly recognizable experiences, the words that name them (*fear* and *intimacy*) must attach to non-textual structures (forms) which abstract and dissolve the narrativities that present fear or intimacy as recognizable within a cultural framework.

This confluence of anteriority and disappearance raises a question of the relation between the glyphs and language, or sign systems in general. Because the glyphs already place the social at the center of what language is, while language places itself at the center of the social through dialogue, the glyphs become the question of the social that lurks within any semiotics (whether Saussurean or Derridean) and within all ontology.

The glyphs are not signs; they do not function as signs. We have encountered them in the space between ontology and semiotics, between consciousness and writing, where they evince a general structure derivative of that space. Each glyph emerges metatextually from a double reading of a sign (word, sentence, discourse, experience, narrative) both as signifying and as textual form. And it is doubly written, like dissemination, by the NMN-structure as narrative and as about social narrative. Each forms a foundation for the other. The sign, on the other hand, must evince inscription in the world within a repeatable, spaced, and differential system, through which it signifies a meaning and signifies itself as a sign. Each sign surrounds itself with absence—the absence of an inscriber (author), a reader, its referent, its context, other signs that differ, and the meaning it defers to other signs. It becomes a form that coalesces absences, rather than an absence that coalesces forms.

The glyph is anterior to all these ("coming upon" is anterior to reference; social narrative is anterior to the reader; common experience is anterior to context, etc.). The sign appears in the presence of narrative, form, and name, while the glyph disappears as a multiple absence (in narrative, form, and name) that reduces itself to the sign. The glyph articulates an anteriority to what articulates it in reduced form, and to the metatextuality of the homological through which it can be discerned. Thus, unlike the sign, the glyph is a non-mark; that is, it is not "material" in the sense of a sign. It cannot be discerned as iterable except through metatextual processes. The glyph is non-textual while the sign is textual.

Finally, the absences that characterize the glyph and the sign are incommensurable and inverse. The referent of the glyph is not absent because it is nonexistent. The content of the glyph is never absent because it is the glyphic form itself, its lamination of narratives and forms in their particularity. Both the referent and the content (signified) of the sign are brought to it metadiscursively, though absent to the sign through deferral in its system of signs. The sign separates the reader from the writer at the moment of inscription. But if a reader must construct the glyph through a metatext that has already read and discerned its textual form, then, in turning to the sign's anteriority, reader and writer become one. Where they coincide is that each can be read through the other.

Herein the glyph represents in its most essential way the incommensurability between Sartre and Derrida. One reads the form of Sartrean discourse through one's narrativization of it, and one reads a Derridean narrativity through one's disclosure of its discursive form. In the Derridean text, each glyph contains a socially given narrative; in the Sartrean text, each narrative constitutes a social glyph (revealing the hidden particularities of consciousness as common experience). Each can be read through the other in an inverse manner; and each writes that inversion as what is to be read.

The glyph names this the formal inversion by structuring the anteriority of the social to language (as coming upon the world, common experience, etc.) and the anteriority of language to the social (social narrative, the creativity of dialogue, etc.). Like ontology and semiotics, each is the foundation of the other. The glyph is the encapsulating of this chiasmus, an unpresented entityhood that surfaces in its particularity as the ability to name things in social interaction, and to produce an aboutness that goes beyond the self-engendered entityhood of dialogue. Naming, by which things are known and subjects speak to each other, cannot escape the lamination of narrativities from which the act of naming arises, nor the dialogic interaction that constructs the name as a sign for its signification as a name.

In its ability to name, dialogue becomes more than glyphic, insofar as it pretends to communication, reference, and description, and invents modes of naming that take on those meanings for the dialogue. But prior to that, the glyph is the way dialogue names itself, as the self-naming that reflects the glyph's anteriority to the sign. Spanning the difference between the social and the sign, the glyph structures the mutual conditioning of the sign by its social production and the discursive production of the social by the sign. The discourse of the glyph provides a language through which to understand the complexity of all this.[1]

But this implies that the glyphs will not function as a common language between incommensurable discourses; instead, they represent the operation of discursive form such that common meanings can be constructed across homologies of those forms. It is in this sense, and not that of common language, that a conversation has been elicited between the texts of Sartre and Derrida.

But what does this mean? For a sign system to function as a common language for dialogic participants, it must name things in commensurable ways. The name, as a sign, before it refers to the content of the englyphed narratives it metonymically abstracts, refers to the glyph as an abstraction of a process of homological relation that renders its constituent narratives and forms discernible. The glyph is an act of naming that names itself through the chiasmus between sociality and language that it amalgamates into itself. But on a social level, if an event is recognized as having a particular meaning, it is because it is given that meaning interpretively by one who sees it (or looks back on it in an effort to comprehend what happened, or what one had done); namely, by a reader of the event. Such a reader structures the event as a double recognition; a narrative socially recognized as a form, and a form homologically related to others for which a meaning is recognizable. The event's particularity as an entity, that is, its boundedness as a form (having a beginning and an ending provided by its narrativization) is the product of the interpretative act ("totalizing," as Sartre would say), which is one's metanarrativization of its relation to oneself in reading it. Its particularity is as the look. In effect, there is an NMN-structure, a narrative of social origin, a metatextual iterability and an individual recognizability; event perception is a glyphic structure. And it is precisely in its glyphic structure, through which the event can be named (either through a name or a narrative), that the event reveals the glyph as particular and not a common language.

The Sartrean discourse of objects parallels this, as we have seen, insofar as objects float upon a socio-discursive anteriority. This anteriority includes an individuation of the object through one's specific project (its "totalization" as a particular meaning) and the choice of project within a cultural framework, that is, a framework of social and dialogic relations that renders a project socially understandable in the first place. Like the glyph, the project is doubly immaterial yet material as act and social relatedness (the entityhood of the glyph). It expresses who a person is within a framework of relations, and what s/he is intending to do within it, as a person, an identity. It evades conceptualization by signifying itself as its own content (like Derrida's instrumentalities) yet nevertheless retains an objectivity that the person's acts then represent as signs. Like the glyph, the Sartrean project reflects itself as its own anteriority. Thus, within the space between the glyph and the sign, an entire stratum of particularity lurks and, through its glyphics, resists the generalities that are often idealized as common language. The essence of a "common language" lies elsewhere, in interaction itself.

Shifts in Social Semiosis

With the glyph, we are beyond semiotics, and beyond ontology. Once even perception (of an object or an event) can be articulated as socially dimensioned (along with feeling, emotion, experience, etc.), it escapes categorization as either individual or social, ontological or semiotic. A different sense of perception and a different notion of the social are implied, necessitating a shift in how we understand the social and how we understand language.

This shift began through understanding the social with respect to narrativities, and its relation to the individual as mediated by complex systems of narrative. This implies that language is narrative expression first, from which language as descriptive, communicative, or expository derives. This is not a proposition concerning the origin of language, which is lost in paleontological shadows, but of the ongoing origin of meaning, the invention of meaning. The interiority of narrative to language, as a constituent of the glyph, imparts to the sign its ability to designate specificity and generality at once, given the level at which the glyph is abstracted.

The ability of the sign to signify the general is an amalgamation of the specific (events, acts of naming, acts of pointing out, etc.), each of which takes a plurality of narratives (the many modes of "coming upon" its meaning) as its trace. Not only does use occur in renewed specificities that get absorbed into the generality in turn, in an ongoing accretion, but a participant is never irrelevant to each addition, as enacting the narrative. Narrative is the form enactment takes. Narrative will always be a signifier for an enactment as its meaning, the telling or intuiting of an unfolding in temporality. If enactment is the form that character takes, while narrative is the content of character, then it is the person as character (as per the NMN-structure) who cannot escape mediating between enactment (as event, dialogue, speech, or any other social act) and social narrative. Because social or cultural narratives, as the signifiers given from elsewhere by which experience is recognized as a particular meaning, constitute the source of individual experience, they bestow meaning as social on the temporality of individual experience and on one's acts. A person, a subjectivity generated through activity in the world, becomes who s/he is through that bestowal. In one's acts, through the system of social narratives that condition and delimit them as social meanings, one confronts oneself subjectively as produced by those meanings. Personhood inhabits the glyph; one experiences the world from within it.[2]

This may seem to smack of a determinism, because it both delimits what will count as social meaning and conditions what forms of experience will be recognized as such. Even the desire to determine autonomously an unequivocal meaning for one's activity, to be the source of the meaning one produces, is derailed or predetermined as already a relation to another who sees and recognizes one's act through meanings that are socially given (and valorized) in advance. But it is recognizability that is in question here, not determination. At the extreme, the desire to be wholly autonomous means to perform an act that escapes all prior narrativizations; at that point, one ends by performing something meaningless to everyone else. The only experience such an act will generate, in the dialogue between one's act and others' apprehension, will be that of the possibility of meaningless enactment as such. Though that possibility remains, it also remains meaningless. On the other hand, insofar as such an effort becomes the narrativization of absolute autonomy beyond social meaning, it opens a space of difference between determinism and common experience. To that extent, it establishes a possibility (and even perhaps a desire) for absolute autonomy from prior social narrative as a "prior" social narrative. The complexity of interactions at work between a desire for autonomy and "prior social narratives," or the incommensurability between autonomy and recognizability, which condition each other within a cultural space, requires something like a glyph to describe it.

This becomes important for social thought and for sociological thinking. And one could inquire if it was possible to "think" in glyphic terms at the sociological level. I would argue that it is. For example, Aaron Gresson, in his book *The Dialectics of Betrayal*, in describing how an individual arrives at social or group priorities, paints a schematic portrait of the glyph.[3] For "Man" to be deceived into seeing his own actions made normative, he must have accepted such a norm, and even a concept of "norm," from elsewhere. But to do so, he must reify his personal reality as a structure of "beliefs and practices" by which to communicate with the social. Gresson understands this as "suppression" of creativity with respect to social interaction, while we could also understand it as a recognition of the need for recognizability. For Gresson, the suppression of the "creator" role engenders an aporia between the social and the individual.[4] But the necessity to have one's actions and intentions recognizable and recognized is a confluence of the individual possibility of recognition and the enactment of social recognizability, a recognizability whose "name" is the "social."

The structure of suppression that Gresson describes as sociological absorbs the content of daily personal enactment into social meaning, rather than semiotizing it; if this preserves the social aporia between creator and norm, as an interplay of form and content, it is reified within specific descriptions of social reality and deception. Thus, it contains all the lamina of a glyph, a real aporetic relation between the individual and the social whose social generation is subliminal, and whose enactment is undergone, but in the unarticulated terms of narratives of deception and acquiescence. One discovers oneself in narratives of suppression, which one renames, and the naming of the normative, which one enacts. The implication is that, though the glyphs do not function as signs with respect to each other, they structure a social space of common unarticulated experience, of "what goes without saying" culturally.

In effect, a third form of inarticulability lurks beyond what is anterior to the subject (the inarticulability of freedom as such) and anterior to writing (the inarticulability of différance as such) in the social matrix of the glyphs. The systems of social narratives that engender the content of feelings, emotions, or experience as common experience remain in unspoken form, subliminal, generalized, abstracted, and are thus lived as "what goes without saying." Only the name represents what the subliminal engenders, as the sign for what is "summed up" in the form of a name. "What goes without saying," as the cultural systematicity of the unsaid, is what constitutes the anteriority of the social matrix. The unsaidness of the system and structure of narrativity underlies how a commonality of experience accrues to itself without reverting from its generalization for all members of a cultural community to individual specificity, and thus to its many particular component experiences and enactments.

But does the ability to negate or escape the narrative system exist? Would one still live in a system of social relations? Would that constitute real autonomy? Or is it only within the narrative system that one can even think of escape? Sartre would argue that within any given social system, which not only represents the social bestowal of meaning on enactment but engenders what counts as enactment in the name of that meaning, the possibility of a negative mode of reading opens itself (he also approaches this question throughout the second volume of the *Critique of Dialectical Reason*). All narratives imply their negation; that is, enactment can be iterated in the negative, or unraveled, even under the aegis of a meaning given antecedently, though in counterposition to it. One not only lives the meanings that social narratives give to one's actions but lives the possibility, at every turn, of denying them, of rejecting those meanings and their constraints. The positive enactment is not negated; but the negative enactment is positively undertaken, as possibility. Indeed, the two forms are incommensurable: act and non-state, state and non-act. Social meanings would then become norms only against the possibility of denial or negation and their suppression. But this implies that self-enactment, as a presentation of autonomy outside the determinism of cultural narratives, could still not exist beyond the purview of their normativity, but would instead become metadiscursive to them, transforming them into the very medium of refusal, sculpting them to one's own account. One's act would necessarily constitute a complex and distorted deployment of the system of given narratives, but recognizable as such.[5]

All civil disobedience takes this form. So too does nonconformity to the extent that it is socially recognizable. What the metadiscursivity of nonconformity implies is the antecedent existence of social narratives of nonconformity that name the non-enactment of norms in rendering itself nonconformist. But should one's actions remain unintelligible to others, they would not even be recognizable as nonconformity. In other words, there is a conformation to nonconformity, outside which it loses its ability to be. To render oneself unrecognizable, to effectively break the mold, to feel what is not a commonly recognized feeling, to transcend morality as a moral position, is to enter a realm of inarticulability whose trace is the entire system of normative narratives. It is for this reason that the normative system appears as determining or totalitarian.

The problem of rebellion falls into this space. Implicit in Sartre's derivation of his existential ethics is the notion that, in facing institutional, socially generated discursive structures such as morality, etiquette, tact, political ideologies, and power structures, one continually confronts the choice to acquiesce or to rebel, and in what manner. One always has the ability to negate social narrative by enacting its inverse in response to its givenness (taking into consideration the reaction of power structures, for instance, to doing so). The autonomy of the strike, the sit-down, the silence, is one pole of an entire spectrum of modes of rejection. To reject or deny the meanings generated by those structures constitutes a mode of rebellion, whether in enactment, word, or style. But it is one thing to say "no" to such structures individually, to act to countermand their demand or their power, and another to have this be recognizable to others, especially those not involved. The narrative of the negation of a narrative is a new narrative; its terms may be the terms of the old, but its narrativity, because the form of narrativity is enactment, will be in different terms. A complex hiatus opens between one's own meaning of rejection, the rejection of a social meaning, and the social meaning of that rejection. None of these are immediately recognizable in each other's terms.

Ultimately, it is perhaps the truly political role of art to create modes of articulating unrecognizable meaning in a manner that can be repeated and thus rendered common experience ("art" as a word does stand for "articulation," after all, and not "artifact"). As supplementary to social norm, art becomes a critique of social norm and recognizable as such. And as an articulation beyond and in contravention of social norm, it often presents a source of signs and signification where rebellion is either bereft or linguistically co-opted.[6]

Yet this is too simple a view. Norm and rejection of norm are not opposites in contradiction, but chiasmically related. Within a rejection of the socially given, an alternate social givenness becomes requisite. There is social pressure for individual deference to group institutionality as an alternate social norm; it is different in many ways, but nevertheless a norm. The call for solidarity is a demand to accede to group cohesion, to defer and conform to its standards of common comportment. As soon as political activity involves a group, it accepts the traditional narratives of solidarity. In this layering of meaning, standards get played against each other and identities redefined, which become intelligible because constituted through systems of recognizable narratives. Conversely, accession to social standards of comportment can be exaggerated to the point of satire: for instance, untactful tact, or social connection as alienation. Even individualism is a narrative system that ranges over a spectrum of possibilities. In its enactments outside the norms, individualism often functions as a rationale and thus a norm.

This shifts the aporia between the individual and the social to a different dimension. The NMN-structure operates in two registers, the enactment of social narrative and the microrecreation of narrative systems in a dialogic encounter. The social molecule of dialogue serves as machinery that creatively resculpts the system of social narratives as it unfolds its operation on the dynamic plane of personal interactions. While individuals think experientially in modes that render them recognizable to others in terms of common sociocultural meanings, the dialogic process creates alternate autonomous systems that transform this. The individual inhabits two categories of socius and thus a multiplicity of socialities, between the overarching and those that emerge from multifarious dialogues. The dialogic situation marks the site of both alternate narrative systems and critique of the overarching social system, of what constitutes the cultural for them. To submit the cultural to critique is to speak of "what goes without saying," to say it, to interrupt its presuppositionality. Indeed, the new narrativities of dialogue may function to render the presuppositional unrecognizable or alien by articulating it, distorting its conformity to who the dialogic participants have become in their dialogue. Both registers are beyond the simplistic binary of acceptance and rejection, acquiescence or rebellion.

In these terms, the category of social norm that "goes without saying" also takes on a dual character. On the one hand, it represents that which resides so deeply in a culture that its narrativity is lost in social automaticity. On the other, "what goes without saying" signifies a social pretense to unquestionable universality, an overweening ideological totalization it renders unquestionable by so signifying. This conjunction of a narrative of social comportment and a subnarrative of nonrejectability is rendered unquestionable as unspoken. To speak it, to disrupt its disguise of silence, is to subvert its social institutedness. In this regard, the category of "what goes without saying" becomes a rejection of the openness of dialogue. In that sense, what "goes without saying" always points subliminally toward sites of social domination or hierarchy.

The Circle and the Social

Thus far, the concept of the glyph has served two functions: it has encapsulated or synthesized a complex laminar confluence of incommensurable discursive modes, and it has iconized the anterior substrates of the social production of meaning; indeed, it has iconized anteriority itself. In bringing together intersubjectivity and intertextuality in the form of a relationship between social narrative and individual experience, positioned between historical sociality and creative microsociality, the glyph presents both a theory of language and a theory of the social. It is a link between the individual and the social.

The glyphs and their circularities emerge from narratives of interaction, homologically mapping fields of mediation between the individual and the social. What semiotics locates synchronically as a structure of differences, the glyph brings together with a cultural historicity as an ecology of disparate levels of social discourse, bridging the abyss between discourse and metadiscourse, between the individual and common experience. As icons of social anteriority, one might expect the glyphs to function as carriers of common meaning for all dialogue. But this would not be the case. Between incommensurable discourses, the glyphs do not function as translation procedures; if they enable the reconstruction of the meanings in one discourse in terms of another, it requires homology procedures. The glyph is anterior to content insofar as it structures the anteriority of textuality, as well as of subjectivity; its anteriority to the sign is a condition for microsocially generated meanings. What the glyphs do provide is a possible interweaving of incommensurable discourses in a third discourse that locates itself in the space of that incommensurability.

There is a third function that the glyph performs; it incorporates the circle in the social. Three points have already been made about the circle. First, it functions as a foundation for its elements where a foundation for each singly would fall into metaphysical speculation on presupposed foundations. Such presupposition most often effects itself as an ideological imposition upon interpersonal relations: a metaphysics concerning human nature, the imposition of structures of racialization, the hypothesis of a social contract, and so on. These speculations have analytic force, which I examine below; suffice it to suggest here a relation between this force and their extraction from the ecologies of which they are components.

Second, the circle manifests an ecology of its terms in the sense that they condition the existence of each other around the circle, interweaving form and content. Without origin or logical necessity, the circle completes the mediation of relations between its elements, such as of narrative, character, and enactment, or text, nontext (discursive form), and metatext, expressing the meaning of social narrativity without having to postulate a source for it. As an ecology, it points back to a distant wilderness. In their ecological relations, for instance, the Derridean instrumentalities have a certain wildness about them, which differs from the urban or urbane aporias of Sartre's account of the for-itself. That has been part of their attractiveness to many. The wildness of the instrumentalities results from contentlessness, their anteriority to imposed or assumed ideological meanings, and their liberation of textuality from the pretense that meaning is inherent. It recalls Roquentin's experience with the "brute existence" of the elm tree root. The "subject" becomes a domestic (and domesticating) word for a similar wildness that persists in ourselves, beyond the confines of social narrativity. Philosophy fights over whether to keep it caged or let it out, or even if it exists or not; it provides modes of defense or denial, uncertain about whether to run away or run wild. When Derrida claims that the trace must be thought before the entity, the secret narratives in his account inject a subject that does that thinking, not as a metaphysical entity but as narrative character out in the underbrush of polyvocality.

Doxa, on the other hand, as the assumed sociality of meanings, claims to have already tamed that wildness. Yet it has only divided it up into analytic parts that still evince, through the aporias to which they are subject, an undying nostalgia for that anterior completeness, sourcelessness, and belonging that the circle provides. As an ecology, the circle accuses the force that individuates its elements, transforming them into analytic categories or concepts (activity, intentionality, or objectivity, for instance), of rendering them entities in alien environments. That is, it highlights the "violence" that constitutes the metaphysical, the attempt to define an origin after having kidnapped the category from its "original" absence of origin.

Third, the circle has a logic. Its chain of braided interaction between form and content is dynamic, while its circularity gives its systematicity entityhood. As an entity, the circle signifies the mutual mediation of disparate elements. Rather than signify as a form, however, the triadic circle presents a character or style of being in the world. Like the instrumentalities, its meaning is its form. In the Derridean text, paradox, parable, and aporia continually resurge, preventing the instrumentalities from becoming a new doxa when momentarily isolated from the circle. The circle rescues them from us rather than us from them. As wild beings, the instrumentalities abjure ritual or metaphysical training. They are always "out there," just out of sight in the underbrush of the textual field. They invade at night and disrupt the corral of what we take for granted.

To think in terms of the circle transforms how the social is to be understood. And it transforms how the subject is understood. The glyph of the subject is a confluence of two circles, the Sartrean circle of the NMN-structure and the Derridean instrumentalities, which mediate the NMN-structure's internal relations and are mediated by them, as a confluence of intersubjectivity and intertextuality. This does not mean that human experience becomes less ephemeral or more dependent on discourse. But the circularity of narrative, enactment, and character becomes embedded in discursive form, as ground, that puts a different spin on human experience altogether. Its logic is the condition, as a social circularity, for mediating the individual and social, or dialogue as microsocius.

But the relation of the ecological, the logical functions of the circles as social anteriority to their component concepts, presents an historical or perhaps an archaeological problem. These circles have been constructed out of concepts and categories of discursivity given by history and the cultural productions of Western Euro-American societies (such as the subject, Being, objectivity, etc.). I have reconstituted them from components presented within that tradition as separate, individuated philosophical and textual notions. If those components actually refer back to an analytic sundering of those circles as anterior ecologies of concepts, what was the process of breaking them? And what has made their reconstruction possible? What social process renders the definitions and conceptualizations of these elements intelligible to us (as fish out of water)?

Metaphysics speaks of objects and selves in the sense of their being recognizable "objectively" rather than ecologically. Yet when objectivity is taken as axiomatic, outside the circle of object, objectivity, and self, then objecthood becomes an assumption rather than something come upon, a reified literalization of a metaphor rather than as metaphoric. The literalizations of metaphors for subject-subject relations outside the ecological—the self as character, the object as narrative, and objectivity as the mediation of inscription, a non-act of enactment—occurs only through a bestowal of axiomatic status. One effect is that personhood gets fragmented into presupposed psychological pieces. How does this happen? What occurs socially, either as machinery or as institution, that breaks the circle?

The Colonial Principle

Let us revisit the discussion of chauvinism that has threaded itself through this essay. Various forms, such masculinism, white supremacy, and nationalism have been touched on. Each is characterized by a structure of derogation, overt or covert forms of social exclusion, and instituted practices of gratuitous violence and impunity against the derogated by which domination is preserved. The attempt to dominate another group as a source of self-superiorization and social identity, for economic and political benefit, through systematic and gratuitous violence characterizes the structure of colonialism. The conceptualization of oneself and the other that makes this seem like ethical behavior constitutes what could be called the "colonial principle." (It is a companion principle to the "male principle" and its patriarchal ideologies.) In the United States, white supremacy, racism, patriarchy, and heterosexism are all forms of the colonial principle.

If subjectivity obeys a cultural specificity, then the narrative framework by which one lives individuation or subjectivity in one culture will not be the same as that of another; the narrative structures that produce forms of subjectivity as common experience will be different. And this will also be true for those on opposite sides of a hierarchical boundary, in which the subjected must live within an unneeded system of imposition, survival, defense against assault, and possible retaliation—which the dominating do not. The very fact of hierarchy, of the violence of self-superiorization through inferiorization of another, produces different subjectivities that live the hierarchical boundaries within necessarily different cultural frameworks, because the boundary is hierarchical. This boundary is the structure that obviates the reciprocity of the look between people hierarchically situated.

But if no common value standard can be derived across the disparity of narratives engendered by hierarchy, then no self-superiorization over another can have common conceptual validity. The operation of the colonial principle then depends on forceful social imposition. That is, in any social framework, either there is simple coexistence, a system of agreement creating mutual cultural values, or there is colonialism (even between men and women). And this is not an abstract or academic consideration. The force of imposition of hierarchy, regardless of how subliminal or traditional, is not a matter of indifference to those who suffer from it.

A recognition of the cultural disparity as well as the specificity of cultural forms engendered by the colonial principle is at all times necessary. The structures to be discussed here may be seen with a certain abstraction, but they are always specific acts against real people. It is the commonality of their structures, insofar as those structures underlie the particularities of various forms, that is of interest. While "chauvinism" constitutes the individual form that an instituted colonial principle takes, it also names different modes of coloniality, which differ with respect to form or historical development. To understand its structure, it is in the space between chauvinism and the colonial principle that we must start.

All chauvinisms rely structurally on an act of generalization. A generalization about people is always something imposed on them from elsewhere, a system of assumption that is of social origin, in which those generalized do not themselves participate. People only present themselves as individuals in social encounters; to see them through a generalization is to have brought that generalization from elsewhere and to have thus accepted it in advance. If all generalizations about people are a priori, originating with those who generalize, then they essentially express the power to impose a generalization in the first place, rather than anything extant or perceivable about those generalized. Once the generalization is in place, however, everything it describes becomes discoverable in those it causes to be noticed in that way.

One imposes a generalization on an individual in order to see the individual as an example of it. The other becomes abstract at the very moment of particular encounter and unrepresentable because represented in advance. It does not matter what kind of human or cultural difference is defined and characterized through the generalization; that difference (real or imaginary) is then apprehended and perceived as real. The effect is that generalizations render the people they are allegedly about unknowable because the generalization substitutes itself for encounter with the individual it is about.[7] And because the generalizations are assumed in order to disparage the other's individuality, they are necessarily negative valuations, even when they pretend to extoll a cultural virtue allegedly embodied in the individual encountered (the "compliments" paid to a so-called model minority, for instance).

Ultimately, generalization is indistinguishable from renarrativization. To be renarrativized means to be made other than one is, in terms that are not one's own. It is to be displaced and replaced by a system of imposed narratives—narratives by which hierarchy defines, manifests, and maintains itself.[8] And here a distinction must be made. Across the boundary of domination, the act of generalization can take a reciprocal though incommensurable form. For the subordinated, the dominant are often generalized as dominant, because of the structure of domination through which they appear. On the one hand, what gets generalized is the fact that the other imposes as a group, which appears in the form of the dominant group member. The dominant as a structure appears to the dominated in the form of an individual, while the dominated as an individual appears to the dominant in the form of a structure (generalization, stereotype). On the other hand, the ability to generalize the dominant occurs in the presence of potential force and gratuitous violence; thus, the dominated have to take careful account of what each individual of the dominant group is about. Indeed, the generalization of the dominant is in fact a generalization of the potential encounter with gratuitous violence, which is real.

In short, the narrative systems that generalize in any hierarchical situation essentially reflect the needs of domination; as such, they provide the generalizing group with a language for itself between its members. Membership is judged through the deployment of that language. Its compulsive reexpression, in order to denigrate and inferiorize the other, becomes a way the dominant performs his/her membership in and for the dominant group. The derogations and inferiorizations of others form an essential (and inescapable) aspect of group identity, a social identity of denigration.[9]

But, in addition, chauvinism constitutes a mode of common experience. Because it relies on the self-generated discursivity of social generalization, chauvinism exists only in the imagination of the dominant. Its system of narratives, as renarrativizations of another, become the social narratives by which each apprehends the membership activity of the others. Thus, it renders the violence of domination a monitored "common experience." Conjoined to identity, chauvinism constitutes, through that system of narratives and the language it generates, a group cultural commonality whose language is precisely that of the narrativization of the other. The effect is the paradox that members of the dominant group find their social identity in the dominant group, while the core of their selfhood, the focus of their enacted subjectivity, is elsewhere in the dominated.[10] The individual becomes divided between owing allegiance to a group that manifests his/her identity while situating the center of that identity elsewhere in an excluded other. This is the source of obsession with the other that one finds in all relations of domination. It is also the source of the demand for absolute allegiance and identification of those in the chauvinist or colonialist group. Their dues must be kept up to date.

For any system of oppression, however, what abstracts the derogatory narrative generalizations that render the other unknowable is the visible. It is by means of the visible, of noticing and of conceptual inventions of what is visible, that generalizations get applied in situations of encounter. One encounters a person to be generalized through what is already given to be noticed by the generalizations; one encounters the generalized through the eyes first. The negative valuations of chauvinism attach to what can be seen of another person (and what cannot be seen becomes "visible" as soon as it is named, such as "looking Jewish," or "looking gay"). For example, one cannot tell if a man is gay by looking at him, unless he makes this known by signifying it in some way. Once the homophobic man discovers this fact, his whole attitude changes. His conceptualization of the gay man changes the latter's "appearance" for him.

In sum, the dominant see the dominated as objects, but of a special kind. They are not others-as-objects who "see what I see." They are tools by which the dominant create, concretize, and preserve their relations with each other. What is unknowable about the dominated is rendered a priori knowledge, not of the other, but of oneself.

For the dominated, the look of the dominant is not a Sartrean look. The nature one is given is given in advance by the structure of oppression. It is an a priori determination of one's visibility as such. The one seen through the focus on one's "visibility" is apprehended as generalized, that is, "caught in the act" of simply being what is determined/defined by the generalization. And herein lies the continual possibility of violence, not in what the one seen, the one subjected to the look, does but what is determined in advance as required or permissible violence in the generalizations.[11]

One social implication of this is that, while despising the dominated, chauvinism will always seek to deploy the other as a spectacle. Spectacle reaffirms and reifies the initial arbitrary definition of the visible that iconizes the pre-narrativizing system through which the other is seen. The spectacle is expected to be a performance of those narratives, failure in which will be counted as rebellion. The spectacle is an expression of the non-reciprocity of the look and the impossibility of dialogue between the dominant and the dominated.

While the colonial (or chauvinist) process is a gratuitous imposition of inferiorizing power that demands the spectacle, the spectacle establishes that the other is inferiorized by nature and not by the colonial principle. What is given visibility by the chauvinist narratives thus gets interpreted as real.[12] Spectacle, the "naturalization" of the reduction of people to instrumental objects, thus places the onus for its oppressiveness on its victims. It makes its victims "disappear" in order to appear as the "seen."[13] And the purpose of this invisibilization is the construction of a self-universalization and a self-superiorization for the chauvinist.

Ultimately, in the colonial look, one no longer apprehends a subject but a power, a mode of hyper-subject,[14] apprehended as the subject of a structure. The colonializing narratives that give content to the colonial look do not produce a sense of recognition for the colonized, the one looked at; nor is there self-recognition as having a nature in common with the other. The colonized person is not the one metanarrating the encounter. What the colonized metanarrates in the look of the colonizer is the other's presence, the conquest that has brought that other there, the already experienced imposition of the other, against which a returned look is punishable. In the colonial or chauvinist look, one apprehends oneself as subjected to that structure. It is not the colonized who narrate their being seen; their domination, which is instituted by a force hidden and enforcing acceptance, and the narrative of that force, becomes the primary aspect of the look. When the narratives of the look are narratives of force, the look has the force of those narratives. And a returned look becomes dangerous. In the structure of domination, the dominated is always already looked at.

The other who looks (the dominant who is always there) no longer discovers one at a keyhole but places one there, at a keyhole of subordination. The NMN-structure is no longer intact for the colonized. The narratives are not those of personal or cultural experience but of past force, of conquest and political defeat. The colonizer looks from a situation of conquest, while the colonized experiences the objectivizing look as inferiority and defeat, continuing rather than engendering a loss of autonomy. It is the prior loss of autonomy that constitutes the keyhole at which one is discovered. For racialization, masculinism, or class hierarchy, it does not matter what the subordinated do, or how they comport themselves; they will always be discovered at the keyhole of subordination and generalization. Rather than a structure of difference, there is a social ontologization of difference that reduces the look to an act of reification.

But the look is no longer intact for the colonizer either. Because of the demand for absolute allegiance to the conquest and its hierarchy, the colonizer, even when encountering the colonized, is the one looked at by other colonizers. Through the narratives of social allegiance, each member of the dominant group no longer apprehends the others as subjects, because the other who looks is also the entire socius of domination, watching to ascertain that the person is relating to the dominated in the proper manner. Attempts at true friendship, a recognition of autonomy, or simply a sense of fairness will often lead to punishment or ostracism by the colonizing socius. The charges range from being "soft" to being a "traitor." Thus, the NMN-structure ceases to function among the dominant as well. A member of the dominant group becomes part of a machinery of domination, a socius cemented by membership in the look of other members.

In other words, subjectivity is predefined for both the dominated and the dominant. It is given in the narratives of force prior to the look. While the dominant are dependent on the dominated for their own subjectivity, it is not as granted but taken (and the threat of loss to a returned look as rebellion is great). Yet they remain incommensurable; each obeys different narratives of who they must be within the hierarchical relation. Neither are metanarrators; both are doubly metanarrated characters. Neither has the possibility of returning the look to engender a subject-subject situation. The circle of the subject, as a circle in dialogue, has been sundered for both, and thus the glyph of dialogue has been shattered as well. (Dialogue is only possible between hierarchs, who recognize each other through the common language that the other is, and among the subordinated who speak to each other from within their common situation, as a community of resistance, since such discussion is already in contravention of their renarrativization.[15])

The situation of women in the male gaze is of this nature, though women are dispersed among men, rather than subject to group segregating practices. A woman seen is not the metanarrator of the look. That metanarrative is given anteriorly by the patriarchal paradigm. For both men and women, the look comes from elsewhere, the system of masculinist narratives that determine the relation of men to women. Men enact the narratives (in order to be masculinist men), feeling watched by other men with respect to their comportment (enforcement of the narratives) toward women, while women undergo the male gaze as the instrumentality of that comportment, under the shadow of enforcement as the spectacle engendered by it. Both men and women apprehend themselves as seen. A woman undergoes the male look as having already been uncontestably given. A woman may choose how she is to be discovered (by the male look), but whether she is or not is already decided. Her givenness juxtaposes itself to her self-awareness. Her discovery of herself in the look is of someone who had already been given a nature, an instrumentality, an abbreviated autonomy, of which the male look seeks to avail itself rather than discovering the other as a person.

While women see men seeing them, the masculinist man remains non-thetically aware of being watched in the act of looking. He obeys what has established the standard of his gaze, the standard of attention that has already narrativized what he is doing; and he turns to other men in his vicinity, even strangers, to make mention of women, as a constantly relevant non sequitur, as if to inform them that he is on the job, assuming that they had been watching. In enacting the masculinist narrative, which is what "goes without saying" in patriarchal society, each man is eternally caught at the keyhole of "acting like a man" by other men who are for the most part not in evidence. And the primary thing each woman is discovered doing, in the male hierarchical look, is being a woman.[16] Under the patriarchal look, the relation of narrator to character gets transformed into a political relation.

In such a circumstance, to speak in order to be seen is to place oneself in a situation in which one will not be heard, as a political condition. The dominant speaks, but the other hears only the force of hierarchy speaking. The subordinate speaks, but the other, the dominant, hears through the prior generalizing narratives, speaking for the subordinate and ventriloquizing what the subordinate is permitted to say. When one speaks for another, one has stopped listening; one presupposes what the generalized could have said. And one then responds to that. The dominated are reduced to a mere extension of the dominant. In a real sense, each is merely talking to himself. Where dialogue depends on a hymeneal boundary, on the unity and separation of statement and meaning, the arrival of meaning for one's own statement through the other, chauvinism dispenses with this by speaking for the other. The exchange is reduced to a monologue.

In short, the ability to speak in dialogue has been shattered; a returned look can no longer facilitate itself against the overarching double metanarrativization of both parties. In the situation of dialogue, the returned look takes the form of being able to speak with as much authority and autonomy as the original speaker. In a situation of force and domination, it is precisely the autonomy to respond that is abrogated. If one speaks for another, one has already adopted a dominating stance. And if one dominates another or participates in a social structure that does so, one not only speaks for the other but apprehends them as having accepted and agreed to their domination, whether they have or not. Thus, the acts of generalizing another and dominating them mutually condition each other.

Yet the dominated look back. To look at the dominant in a way that contests force and reobjectivizes, in which the dominant apprehends a subject in the one who looks, changes the relation of domination. A refusal is enacted, a refusal to recognize the dominant's own self-superiorization and a recognition of the dependence of the dominant on oneself. In the look of the colonized, the colonizer can no longer see himself as universal. He is given a nature, and it is as a colonizer, as one that has evoked rebellion. It is because one becomes a knowledge in the look of rebellion that rebellion is always crushed so violently (though with a different violence than the gratuitous violence that preserves domination). If the dominant cannot countenance rebellion, and repress it, it is in the name of an identity that is wholly dependent on nonresistance (although much racist violence is initiated to provoke resistance, so that it can be suppressed).

On the other hand, to reconstitute an NMN-structure, to reconstitute the rehumanizing function of narrative as common experience, or to reweave intersubjectivity and intertextuality, an act of rebellion is necessary. Against the colonizing narratives, it is necessary to de-narrativize oneself. And for this, the look of the other colonized is invoked as a look of solidarity and resistance. That solidarity becomes essential; it provides a counter-renarrativization that de-inferiorizes. Rebellion becomes a hidden look, a look given to others of the rebelling group. Whether one calls it rebellion or not, one must escape the terms of power to engender oneself as one who can return the look, to grant and be granted subjectivity. (This is not an option open to the colonizer, or the dominant, since the look among themselves reifies membership; to rehumanize themselves, the dominant must escape that socius altogether.[17]) By extension, all modes of rebellion become narratives that establish a countersociality.

In sum, a sense of how the chauvinist paradigm relates to the circle of subjectivity, the cycles of dialogue, emerges. Insofar as the colonial paradigm means renarrativization, displacement and replacement by a system of narratives, it effects a supplementarity at the hands of a group. The colonizing look displaces the colonized to the spectacle. They remain inseparable from who they have been, yet absolutely separated by the alien terms of their renarrativization, and the imposed force behind it; they are, in effect, "hymenized," yet as a political act. Ultimately, the colonized disappear socially under replacement by renarrativization (or "disappear" in reality if they should attempt to reject those alien terms), and they lose their being through internalization of what is not them; no longer known as who they are, they are transformed into a priori knowledge for the colonizer; in other words, they materialize dissemination, not of their own story but of the sign system of the colonizer, the white or male supremacist.

In an alchemical way, each of the Derridean glyphs becomes itself a separate descriptor of the incommensurability contained in the colonial principle, a "name" for a dimension of colonialist or racializing imposition.[18] In the colonial look, the intertextual relations "named" by the Derridean glyphs become separate from each other, reified across a hiatus of power, oppression, and conquest. Thus, the circle of Derridean instrumentalities is sundered as well. In the patriarchal socius, the supplementarity of the masculinist narratives, the hymeneal inseparability of metanarrator and the narrative of "all other men," and the dissemination of the male gaze to all other men are thus specific, reified aspects of any relation of a masculinist man to a woman, not as facets of an intimate personal relation but as components of an oppressive political relation that pretends to intimacy. Each glyph becomes corrupted, reduced to a political analogue for part of a social structure of domination—just as the NMN-structure had been corrupted. The weave of subjectivity and signification is broken. The instrumentalities no longer interweave through the NMN-structure.

Supplementarity, hymenization, and dissemination have become reified as the three major terms of the colonial principle (of racialization or chauvinism): renarrativization, inferiorization, and spectacle. The NMN-structure, having been sundered, is rendered political machinery. As the effect of power, this is all a catastrophic political reality for those placed in its realm. They cease to be human in the name of an abstract humanity defined for itself by conquest. Both the overtness of sociality and the hiddenness of individual feelings are thrust aside in the name of race, gender, citizenship, sexuality, and so on. Those dominated under the hierarchical aegis of these terms' reifications are granted no unknowability by the structures of domination; and the dominant are granted no subjectivity since they cannot return the look of the colonialized or the racialized and thus find themselves figures of a metaphysics of "human nature."

Chauvinism and the Sundering of the Circle

To connect the chauvinist paradigm with a sundering of the circle, let us return to the circle of the subject a moment, as the glyph of the subject. It is a doubly woven circle of the NMN-structure (metanarrator, narrator, and character) for which the instrumental (Derridean) glyphs function as mediations. It iconizes, as a structure, the inarticulability of the subject, setting all the articulable elements of intersubjectivity and intertextuality around itself, a textile in which it is clothed, and within which its outline can be discerned. The circle structures dialogue, social interaction with others, the granting to others of their subjectivity, the recognition of others partaking in common emotional experiences; and it mediates the aporias between the individual and the social. But the circle is predicated on there being reciprocity between persons and on there being no social definitions of personhood that would supersede or co-opt the process of recognition of social narratives in another.

It is this last condition that is broken by chauvinism or colonialism, in pre-narrativizing those they dominate in a way that does not permit or countenance autonomous thought, action, or dialogue, as a reification of the other as character. The chauvinist mind cannot listen because it thinks it already knows what is going to be said. It cannot recognize the social in the other because it has already cognized the other as of a different socius. It grants no subjectivity to the other because the aporias of the individual are obviated by objectification; the hiddenness of the other is pre-narrativized under the pretense of being known. Under such a circumstance, for the other to claim subjectivity, to live the aporias of the social, to give recognition to the chauvinist (as a chauvinist), to demand to be listened to—in short, to return the look as a mode of being in parity—is also pre-narrativized and reified (as rebellion). The sundering of the circle of subjectivity (and its glyph of the subject) begins here with this break in human relations, with the chauvinist imposition on the other of conditions of non-recognition.

Chauvinism begins with an abrogation of the other's autonomy, as part and parcel of the other's oppression, a predetermination of the other as subordinate, and his/her further enthrallment to gratuitous renarrativization. There is force involved in imposing a pre-narrativized character and preventing participation in a common socius. It is not the iconization of the subjected through generalization and the reification of their pre-narrativization that makes oppression and domination possible; it is oppression that forces social acceptance of narratives that reify character and thereby sunders the circle. Generalization is the logical extension of that process, an extension which in some cases becomes so socially habitual that it ceases to be discernible to those who do it. It becomes a moment in the effective production of an identity of domination for the dominant grounded in renarrativization of the subjected.

When the circle of narrative is broken through the a priori imposition of a "nature," a "character," or a social givenness on the other, the one seen sees him/herself seen through this prior "nature" and is left with no recognized metanarrative of a common social experience through which to apprehend the look of the dominant. In the circle of narrative, character, and enactment, enactment and character have been pre-narrated, as form and content. Enactment does not take the form of narrative but only remains an icon for the "character" of the subjected. Character still takes the form of enactment, but each enactment is prescripted and thus represents predefinition rather than social recognition. The ability to return the look is the ability to act within a metanarrative of common apprehension of feelings, while the a priori narratives imposed on the subordinated do not extend that ability.

Or, to put this in different terms, on the circle of reading, as text, metatext, and non-text, the break occurs at the level of metatext. One imposes a form on the "text" of the other a priori, which one then reads as the reality, the enactments, the predispositions of the other. But it is no longer a metatext that one is reading in and as the other, whereby the other's own "textual form" can be discerned. The person, as the text, loses autonomy and becomes an instrumentality for the reader (the dominant) to be rewritten through the metatext.

For members of the dominant group, the sundering of the circle is necessary to render the other unrecognizable in exclusion from their cultural framework. Once the victims of their actions have been excluded from the possibility of dialogue, their own personal stories barred, their very exclusion becomes the rationale for gratuitous violence. That violence, which succeeds only when its perpetrators overwhelmingly outnumber their victims (in size or technology), leaving the victims no chance of counteraction or defense, becomes the material foundation for inferiorization. And inferiorization of the other (disguising the dependence of the dominant on them) becomes the rationale for exclusion from dialogue, for renarrativization. The violence deepens the dependence; dependence deepens renarrativization; and renarrativization invents new forms of violence. Thus the identity of domination is produced in self-superiorization; and its essential characteristic is impunity.

Violence, dependence, and renarrativization form a self-referential circle. The latter, in turn, constitutes the foundation for patriarchy, masculinism, white supremacy, nationalism, colonialism, and so on. There is no extant human reason for any of these forms of chauvinism; they are gratuitous in their self-referentiality.

Their self-referentiality substitutes itself for a sundered subject circle. And it is the self-referentiality of the circle, as a circle, that becomes the foundation for the categories by which imposition and non-recognition of the other are articulated. Where the circle of subjectivity mediates the aporias between the individual and the social, this circle generates an insularity that mediates the dehumanization of others and locks the dominant into a hermetic self-recognition to which no external reality can make an appearance.

On Metaphysics

If chauvinism sunders the subject circle by reifying the character of the other, disrupting the possibility of dialogue, what would result from breaking the circle at other places?

We have seen that the subject circle (as a glyph) mediates the hidden nature of individual feelings and emotions and the culturality of social commonality. What the NMN-structure has revealed is the process whereby the social functions in personal interaction and the hidden is metanarrated for society's members. It responds to the question of how one is to speak about what cannot be seen. Mind, consciousness, and fear, not to mention elementary particles in physics, the electron, the internal composition of matter, or enzymatic action, for instance, are beyond direct perception. If we think we see them, it is because we read what we consider to be evidence of them on meters, like electrons, or the effect of tests for material hardness, or facial expressions in the case of fear. In each case, we learn or construct the mode of inscription by which we read evidence of the unseen. But what we perceive pragmatically in the face or on instrument dials is not the thing. How is one to make statements about it? And how is one to know that it is "that thing" about which one is in fact speaking?

In order to speak about something that is not empirical, neither describable perceptually nor available for direct common experience, one must have recourse to metaphor. That is, to speak of the non-experiential, its inarticulability must be transformed into an articulation, along with a sense of factuality in place of nonreference. The metaphor may derive from mathematics or art, literature or fantasy; it derives from the known or recognizable. Metaphor is an enactment toward something conceptual, or toward something that requires conceptuality, whose function is reference. Reference transforms the metaphor into a name for what it metaphorizes—metaphor names in terms of other things, objects or signifiers.[19] This transforms the "referent" from the non-experiential to the experiential. One reads a number on a spectrometer and says that the wavelength (a metaphor) of the light being measured is that number (a double metaphor, first for measurability and second for the choice of scale or units to use in measuring). By this signifying act, the non-experiential becomes a referential object. As the name for that act of reference, the metaphor becomes the name for the referent; it literalizes itself. One really does read the "wave length."

But the metaphor literalizes itself at the very moment when its metaphoricity is critical with respect to the nature of its "referent." Because as metaphoric it refers to something non-experiential, its literalization becomes presuppositional for the objectivity its bestows upon that referent. This presupposition may take the form of a philosophical account (e.g., of consciousness) or of an assumption (e.g., of the particulate nature of atomic particles) or a description (e.g., of a personal state of anxiety). In each case, a signifier is produced for a concept upon which discussion relies.

What lies at the core of this process is the act of generalization, the ability to make general reference to phenomena, such as anxiety or electrons. But the need to make general reference comes from beyond the object referenced. Generalization, in the realm of factual reference to the world, is a function of logic. The world presents itself as a collection of particularities; objects are differentiated from background in their peculiarity; people present themselves in full individuality. But logic operates at a different discursive level than the strictly particular. To reason about things, to arrive at truth values about them, or to address them instrumentally, objects and actions in the world must be cast in terms sufficiently general for logic or teleology to be applicable. Objects are conceptualized or given general meaning through a recognition of qualities. Classification is a selection process among recognizable attributes. It is performed and imposed on objects to meet the needs of reasoning processes, rather than as inherent in the objects. In other words, a generalization constitutes a form of presupposition about things that is imposed for the purposes of reasoning and interpretation. For metaphysics, the presuppositions are necessary as the site of definition of what will constitute truth.

But this act of creation of presuppositions breaks the circle of the subject, though in a different way than chauvinism does. Rather than break it at the level of character whose ability to respond, to grant subjectivity, to be a for-itself in a subject-subject interaction is preempted, presupposition breaks the circle of dialogue at the level of the name, of the enactment. The name ceases to be the way the world is come upon, and becomes referential. It no longer refers to coming upon the world, to reading the world in the world's look; that look is buried in the concreteness of an imposed objectivity in the name of logic and truth value, and the name becomes a sign. Where chauvinism generalizes and objectifies the other, the operation of presuppositions objectifies the language of discussion, of interchange. Where chauvinism breaks the circle at the level of metatext, presupposition breaks it at the level of the text. Where the metatext is reified in chauvinism, it is the text that is reified by presupposition. The conversation is no longer an intertextuality and thus no longer an intersubjectivity. It is an imprisonment in an imposed language, in a reified text.

For Derrida, the operation of presupposition is the fundamental operation of metaphysics. It establishes prior axiomatics from which the nature of the world is reasoned and understood. In one such, all objects were created by God "in the beginning." In another, social reality is objective, and the meaning of things and relations is "out there" and not inscribed by investigation itself. The presuppositions that ground a metaphysics establish transcendental meaning to which all other signifiers can be related; and generalization is an extension of this. It becomes a filter through which the world is both perceived and experienced. It imposes a logic upon the world which it then experiences through that logic. In effect, generalization and presupposition are a system of derivation and theorization about the world, each form of which centers a different concept of truth about the world based upon its presuppositions. The question is not whether it is possible not to do that; it may not be. The point is that the truth of the interpretation refers to the presuppositions rather than to the world. The seeming naturalness of the metaphysical operation does not put in question what it means that a wide variety of interpretations all claim validity. It is part of the metaphysical operation that the multiplicity and diversity of metaphysical structures does not call into question that operation for each metaphysics. Metaphysics simply accepts a priori the logic of its operation and its teleological dependence upon the act of generalization.

The core of Derrida's critique of metaphysics is that any system of presuppositions on which it grounds itself is itself derived from the truth value requirements of its particular interpretation of the world. That is, what is derivative in a thought system is the source of what constitutes the origin of derivation; that is, the presuppositions that ground metaphysical thought arise as the effect of that metaphysics. The effect becomes the origin of the origin. When its interpretation of "nature" (*physis*) becomes the source of its presuppositions, they become naturalized, not as presuppositions but as the nature of the world being interpreted.

The central implication of this critique of metaphysical truth is that metaphysics is essentially self-referential. That is, *metaphysics* names an interpretive framework that attributes meaning to the world through a system of truth values, in order to discover that truth no longer as a value but as an objective aspect of the world. (Sartre eventually came to understand "ideology" as a similar structure, which he describes in his large work on Flaubert, *The Family Idiot*.) The purpose of both metaphysics and ideology is to construct a naturalization of the ideas and interpretive frameworks that arise in cultural thinking and are imposed upon the world; it is to locate them in the world rather than as human theorization itself.

In Derrida's critique of metaphysics, one confronts a double bind—not the same double bind as that found in chauvinism, but a double bind nevertheless. Presupposition does not dehumanize or generalize people. But in constructing a prior reification of a truth value it imposes on the world and thereby naturalizes, what it finds in the world interpretively becomes a generalized mode of knowing through reasoning on generalizations. It is a reification, not of narrative but of enactment, in the sense that the world is no longer enacted ("come upon") but known derivatively.

Ironically, the quotidian (banal) source of the need to generalize, to apply reasoning, to systematize an axiomatic interpretive structure, is all just for the sake of discussion with others. One metaphorizes or generalizes the particular, in order to deploy reason or logic with respect to truth values, for others. A cultural reliance on the centrality of truth value, or a need for factual veracity, requires presuppositions about the world that produce truth values and explanations of human actions that reveal the validity of theorizations of "human nature." The cultural specificity of this approach should be recognized. There are cultural traditions in which narrative particularity is primary over metaphysical generality, and in which philosophical wisdom is primary over truth. In such traditions, description and interpretation enact different interpersonal relations than they do in a society dependent on metaphysical reasoning.

In this (Western) society, metaphysical thinking (dependence on the existence of presuppositions and of transcendent meaning in the world) predominates. In the event that truth values become unattainable, discussion often becomes difficult. New metaphoricities and generalizations, new presuppositions and truth-centered propositions from which one can reason, are continually invented or derived in order to satisfy this cultural necessity. Metaphysics continually reproduces itself in multiple forms from acts of generalization; the imposition of literalized metaphors, constructed to provide the presuppositions from which truth values can be derived, becomes part of society's philosophical and political tradition.

But if that is the case, then with respect to dialogue and the NMN-structure, the imposition of presupposition is not upon conversation as such but upon the other. Though one deploys logic formally to convince the other of certain necessary truths about the matter under discussion, it is the establishment of the foundation upon which logic will be deployed that is crucial. The determination of what is factual, what constitutes a fact, is not simply a matter of description but an establishment of what is the case for everyone, what is fundamental and derived from the same instrumentality for everyone.[20] The one who first determines the terms of a subject matter (literalizes the metaphors) has partially determined both what will be true of it and the possible terms of dialogic response. Once the presuppositions of an argument have been established, one must, in order to follow the argument, accept the literalized metaphors and generalizations assumed by it. That is, to make sense of a speaker's logic, one has to make the same assumptions as the speaker, whether one agrees with these assumptions or not. For instance, one would have to accept the idea that there is a "human nature" in order to follow what is then derived from it as an argument. If a response is to participate in the logic of the discussion, it must deploy the same generalizations, even if one does not think they constitute real presuppositions for the subject matter. Failure to do so implies contesting the speaker's assumptions, which is to change the subject.

Thus, there is a double bind for the respondent; one's response is curtailed, sometimes insidiously, by the preemption of presupposed generalizations.[21] To contest its truth values means to accept the presuppositions from which they were derived. To disagree with the conclusions means to accept and agree with the presuppositions. To contest the generalizations on which they are based, their very language must be contested. To disagree with the presuppositions means to opt out of the discussion.

The power of metaphysics, or all presuppositional thinking, is that it procedurally renders its language beyond the domain of discourse. Metaphysics places its language in brackets. The truth derived from its presuppositions, logically and discursively, cannot be allowed to be dependent upon the medium in which it is expressed, but only on the world described (*Gram*, 43). Language must be transparent, transitory, a mere mode of revealing the truth of the discourse for which it is an instrumentality. Once one posits truth values, one's means of representing them must immediately get out of the way. It is the pretense to transparency that is facilitated by the act of generalization, the literalization of metaphor.

In short, dialogue that does not proceed at the level of particularity becomes possible only between people who make commensurate metaphysical assumptions. Otherwise, there is an imposition of a metaphysics by one on the other. While dialogue depends on supplementarity, in which both speakers find in the other an external character inside themselves through their own narrativization of what the other discovers, metaphysics dismisses the supplement as unimportant in the face of the coherence of validity and truth to be derived from its presuppositions. Under such an operation, the autonomy of participation upon which dialogue relies would break down; attempts to reconstitute it would change the subject to that of language itself and thus would not be attempts to reconstitute that autonomy with respect to the previous subject matter. Yet not to do so would amount to accepting the imposition, in order to follow its logic and make its conceptualizations intelligible.

In sum, the circle of dialogue is broken by metaphysics in a different way than chauvinism—at the point of enactment rather than character, of supplement rather than hymen, of text rather than metatext.

Insofar as metaphysics and chauvinism represent different dimensions of imposition, they exemplify different projects and different desires. Where metaphysics is a desire to treat a subject matter in terms of truth structure, chauvinism applies truth to desire itself, the desire to denigrate and inferiorize another in order to superiorize oneself. Where metaphysics metaphorizes and generalizes the inarticulable in order to speak and reason about it, chauvinism imposes a reasoning on another in order to generalize the other by speaking for the other. The first imposes on the content of the conversation in order to arrive at a truth, and the other imposes on the participant in order to arrive at an identity. While both speak to another, metaphysics defines the world for those to whom it speaks (text), and chauvinism defines the other to whom it speaks (metatext).

Can one be played against the other? Chauvinism remains beyond metaphysics. It starts where metaphysics ends. No language will interrupt its assumption about the other, since there is no prior logic through which to test its metaphysical truth value. In imposing an assumed preemptive truth, it circumvents reason and abjures experience. Because all narratives of experience (empirical considerations, personal interactions, etc.) can be recast in the language of its assumptions, no experience will contest it. Conversely, all language will appear to it as the language of experience, whereby it renders itself inaccessible to language as well. Thus chauvinism cannot be approached through a critique of metaphysics, since no critique of discursivity will undermine it. No metaphysics, which relies on language, will succeed in being either descriptive or contestatory toward chauvinism. That is one of the secrets of its tenacity.

A Third Domain?

If chauvinism emerges from a reification of the metatextual dimension of conversation, and if metaphysics can be understood as a reification of the textual dimension, what would a reification of the non-textual (formal) dimension look like? What discourses would represent that kind of phenomenon? Where chauvinism is a reduction of character to object, and metaphysics is a reduction of enactment to presupposition, what would manifest the reduction or reification of narrative?

To reify non-textuality would be to objectify inarticulability, to set it above and apart from any metatextual ability to make that non-text (textual form) its subject matter. It would be a transformation of narrativity into an absolute. And that takes on a religious hue. Transcendental narrative would establish a character (the content of the narrative) that was beyond comprehension or apprehension in its absoluteness. Such an objectified narrative could not be deployed in granting a subjectivity to another; it would already be beyond that, referring to a being to which subjectivity was a priori. In other words, it would refer to or project onto some form of ideal or supreme being. One might surmise, without rigor, that the dimension of social discourse produced by a reification of the non-textual, an objectification of narrative, would be the religious. Indeed, mysticism often exemplifies discursive form raised to the absolute and objectified in narrative; and that would include the mystical dimension found in the faith-oriented dimension of religious thinking.

In general, the mystical dimension of religious thinking is driven by the desire for a background sameness, a generalization of context, a oneness or identity in the world. Rather than generalizing the mode of reasoning about the world, or the other against one's own world, thinking that reified the non-textual (as an assumed context) within a text or within the world as text would generalize that world, at once given and unapprehensible in its essence.

But this is merely a suggestion, arrived at criteriologically, without extensive investigation. It fills in the space left by the circle's dissolution, which could be summed up as follows. Metaphysics is an imposition of the general on the particular, in order to establish the centrality of logical truth. Chauvinism is an imposition of oneself on another, through whose domination and derogation one defines one's own identity. And what I have labeled (perhaps hastily) "religious thinking" is an imposition of a single transcendent meaning on all difference. Where metaphysics derives transcendent meaning through inclusive logic, and chauvinism derives transcendent logic through inclusive identity, the religious derives transcendent identity through inclusive meaning.

These three forms of discourse, as ideational forms, are specific repositories of cultural thinking, marking different dimensions of social givenness. In each, there is a different mode of silencing. For metaphysics, particularity is silenced in the name of logic; for chauvinism, the other is silenced in the name of power; and for the third form, difference is silenced in the name of knowledge. But if each ideational form is self-valorizing through a mode of self-referentiality, then each is non-referential. Each refers only to a self-defined object that it has engendered for itself through its respective reification operation, by which it breaks the circle. Yet each purports to refer to a truth. What adjoins itself to this notion of truth and problematizes it is its specific form of cancellation of the NMN-structure. And each performs this self-referential operation in a different dimension of human existence.

While there are many types of chauvinism, they are all structurally similar in oppressing, speaking for, and objectifying an other as a group. And while there are many kinds of metaphysics, they are all similar in relying on an axiomatics and a logic system by which truth values are derived for the world. And similarly, there are many forms of religious thinking, but they are all similar in imposing a singular context in the face of which ideational difference is reduced to unimportance.

Dialogue depends on supplementarity, and metaphysics suppresses this by imposing presuppositions and logic; dialogue depends on hymeneal boundaries, and chauvinism suppresses them by imposing identity and the silencing of "speaking for"; and dialogue depends on difference, and the third ("religious") mode of thinking would dismiss difference as unimportant in the face of an inarticulable context that implicitly renders all meanings the same. Where the supplement, the hymen, and dissemination are the structures that mediate the elements of the subject circle, these respective reductions or suppressions of these structures each constitute a different form of sundering the circle.

The circles we have been investigating, such as those of reading, or of writing in general, form ecologies that are self-generating and not dependent on foundations. The ecologies constitute anteriority for their components, analytically separated and categorized by the discursive operations of the ideational forms. The sundering of these circles reifies their elements, leaving these social categories of thought on the landscape to be studied like objects. Against the woven unity of the circle's wholeness, the fracturing of the ecologies requires redefinition, implying that circularity is itself a site from which processes of social reification can be addressed and interpreted. It suggests that the ecological (circle) is where those reifications were born, perhaps through some form of violence.

On the other hand, this ecological notion implicitly opens to the construction of a more human order, an order grounded in the indeterminacy and creativity of dialogue. As Sartre says, to adapt oneself to the human order (the order of meanings), one "set[s] up a dialogue with the Other" (*BN*, 499). If political theory has generally been insufficient for that task, it is because it already accepts the reified social categories of thought that reflect a sundering of the human (dialogic) ecology. It is the creativity of the dialogic and the circular that appears in the resistance of communities that seek to reconstitute themselves against their reifications and attempt to think outside and against the discourses and hierarchies of domination. In generating subjectivities peculiar to themselves, they mark a (re)beginning of this process.

THE CIRCLE AS ANALYSAND

From the point of view of political thought and critique, such banal concepts as meaning, language, narrative, or the individual are already understood. But if something is anterior to the social that provides a basis upon which the individual, as well as experience and perception, are constituted, the apprehension of this social anteriority is no longer banal; nor is the experience by which to gain a perspective on it. Though we produce the social in the ways we speak to each other, we are also produced by the social in ways that remain inarticulable because anterior to our speaking to each other.

The glyphs engender this question by constituting what appear to be representations of this anteriority. Formed of laminated articulations—narrative, discursive form, and name—they iconize what underlies the ontological and the semiotic. If they are articulations in structure of an anteriority that is unarticulable in language, they overturn the essential assumption of language as the fundamental realm of articulation by residing anterior to language. They neither replace language nor constitute a protolanguage, but they construct it with modes of discursivity. The glyphs signify that their strata of construction (narrative, discursive form, and name) are enactments rather than categories of the linguistic—that is, components of the act of coming upon the world and upon others.

The glyphs are the historicity of language, the trace of having come upon meaning in the place come upon. Memorializing the immemorial, they are history itself, the inscription of what would be unrepresented without them. As the history of language, they tell the history of the inscription of their historicity. As historicity, they are simulacral. They structure how the human world is socially generated and mediated.

The circle has been essential to every stage of articulation of the glyph—as circularities in and of the glyphs. The circle represents the nonfoundation of the categories constituted by the circles, the nonfoundation to which only the glyphs are anterior, the nonfoundation that signifies the essential self-referentiality of all human affairs.

All the triadic circles encountered—of Being, the for-itself, the NMN-structure, writing in general, reading and the "I"—as "geometric" locations, all reveal a weaving of form and content that constitute the circle's ecology in being separated from each other. It is the ecological that is central to the circle's structuring of endless mediation. Its endlessness structures an undecidability of meaning wherein each element becomes a moment of its own immersion in and separation from the ecological. Each ecology of meaning suggests that all meaning is ecological. (In real ecological terms, the "meaning" of a living organism is the total ecology in which it participates, whose meaning in turn is each organism that supports and requires it.)

Separated from the circle, each element becomes something dealt with in traditional philosophy. But categorical meaning reveals itself to be a mirage, an artifact of a cessation of form, a replacement for what signifies itself as its content. The categorical naturalizes itself as evidence that the component had always been separated, that the fish is more "natural" out of water, the bird more "natural" in Audubon's paintings. It makes meaning appear inherent in the component, far from the braiding of the circle, the weaving of form. Without an autonomy of category, how is one to think of them? But the components do not lose their (alleged) autonomy in the circle; the ecology has autonomy, and the autonomy of its components becomes part of that. Only in terms of categories, with their conceptual autonomy, do the ecological meanings appear to be a loss of autonomy.

But even to see autonomy as lost implies a certain nostalgia for that to which loss occurs. Each separate categorical meaning becomes a sort of nostalgia for the whole. A nostalgia for the circle lurks in the discursive existence of aporia, the possibility of anteriority, a need for mediation. If both subject and object lose their being to each other (as they do in Sartre's ontology), while each remains the condition for the other, a mediation must exist. It is the thinking of subject and object without mediation that generates the aporias of any account of consciousness. Such is the plight of metaphysical thinking that Derrida's critique elucidates. In other words, certain aporias represent the effects of being components in isolation, of being exiled to philosophical categoriality, torn from their natural conceptual ecology. It suggests a semiotic violence. To include the mediations that lurk within the aporias is to reconstitute the circle, to accede to that nostalgia as a memory of original wholeness.

Between objecthood (determinacy) and the indeterminacy of process, the circle itself is a mediation. It becomes a form of origin in iconizing the non-originary. The circle obviates the need for foundations, since it provides it in structure as an interweaving of form and content. But then it signifies the artificiality of any transcendental foundations.

A sense of foundations becomes conceivable and necessary in being defined, but it becomes inconceivable (and unnecessary) in being endlessly redefined. Indeed, one symptom of the problem of foundations is the endlessness of redefinition in the face of the infinite regression they make unavoidable. For instance, what phenomenological temporality could ground consciousness if all temporality depends on consciousness? It is the circular nature of foundations that is foundational.

When the circle is broken, giving separate entityhood to its elements, the question of foundations (re)emerges. When objectivity looks toward objects to find its foundation, it finds only what it had itself generated; when the self looks to objectivity to comprehend itself, it finds only what it had itself already assumed. Be it difference or objectivity, enactment or dissemination, an object or its recognition, each component in isolation seems passive yet definitive, incomplete yet individuated. In passivity and separation, these reified concepts refer back to their conjunction in the ecological by the very discomfort they exude sitting alone in their conceptuality. Wondering where they had come from, they require redefinition that tells them on what ground they reside. Thus, their conceptual need for foundations makes them appear out of their element. They are truly fish out of water. The metaphysician and the chauvinist, as fishermen, neither throw them back nor consume them; they photograph them and mount them over their mantlepiece or flash them as identity cards.

In effect, the trace of the circle (lurking behind philosophical reification) bestows upon the immemorial circle the aspect of an analysand. As anteriority, it reveals itself to be the landscape rather than the source from which its components are analytically torn. This analysand has no "existence" other than as the effect of what "will have been" the source (namely, the trace). In its entityhood, the circle appears as a kind of "natural" context, but as the trace of a form of anterior movement, it recalls itself anteriorly as an analysand. The circle is not a Platonic notion; it is not remembered. In its metatextuality, as a reading of textual form performed on the discursive plane of categorical meaning, it presents an aura of symbiosis, prior to a violent wrenching, to an artificial dissection. Text, metatext, and non-text are one, yet always critically set in opposition to each other.

This then is the true nature of the glyph: a nostalgic trace of an archaic ecology, an anagogic ur-state in which reified components retain a secret membership. The glyph's narrative soul lives its elemental nostalgia for that archaic circle, while its iconicity corporealizes the machinery of signification that continually raises the problem of origin. In the space at the center of the circle, there lurks an "I," or the "eye," the subject or the look, which refuses to name itself, except as sketched out by the surrounding forms through which it comes into view. This aura or landscape becomes the (iconic) name for the sourceless "I," or the lurking, Cheshire "eye," ensconced in the ephemerality of endless ongoing narratives.

From the space the circle weaves for itself, as its mask of names and stories, it engenders the co-conditioning of the individual and the social. All the events, objects, feelings, and subjectivities that name themselves through narratives and enactments in the look, return to a textuality of disparate concepts and events that find their form and content woven together. The circle, in mediating and reuniting character, narrative, and enactment, both remembers and anticipates the (triadic) cyclic relations of text, metatext, and non-text, or of supplement, hymen, and dissemination, or of for-itself, self-as-object, and being-for-others. Beyond difference, within difference and with indifference, a space of language that is constituted by endless abbreviations of iconicity, as non-textuality, looks back on itself from its own future, and feels the nostalgia that language will invent and then discover as though it had always existed.

But where are these memories and anticipations to be found? Who does them, if they are discovered by language? Where do they dwell if they are invented by language? Is it the trace, or dissemination, in which nostalgia is to be found? Does a word remember and anticipate through the narratives it englyphs? Is memory located in an unknowable other who narrates through a metanarrative that already anticipates it? To think that we, as readers, as subjects, are the ones who remember or anticipate ignores the textual center of reading, forgets the look that looks from the text and the world read, neglects the writing that is written as the self through the embrace of the other who looks.

Derrida's instrumentalities and Sartre's narrativities only pose again the question of language. To read each in juxtaposition to the other is to enter a realm in which language is the abyss. It is an abyss that is constituted by consciousness and writing: by the existence of subjectivity and the operation of inscription, by the operation of subjectivity and the existence of inscription. It is this abyss that is represented by the difference between the intact circle and the broken one, between the ecology and a conceptual environment of categories and components. In that space, *structured* by glyphs, structured *as* glyphic, language must find itself in absence and négatité. This is where the metanarrated non-relation between Sartre and Derrida, between the subject and writing, resides. Derrida has not posed but deposed a theory of subjectivity (as a process of inscriptive cultural construction); and Sartre has not posed but deposed a theory of writing (as a process of engagement in the world). Subjectivity does not manifest itself as writing in the Derridean sense, any more than writing manifests itself as subjectivity in the Sartrean sense. One can no more say that consciousness produces writing as its thought than that writing produces consciousness as its text. They are homological, which means these are not oppositions between Sartre and Derrida. For neither the subject nor writing in general does the circle reduce itself. They are both already prior analysands that serve to render each other a possibility. In the formal (homological) parity of text and Other, writing and consciousness, there is a stereoscopy of real vision for which two "I"s, two eyes, these two, are required.

Notes

CHAPTER 1

1. A fully reasoned argument for the noninclusion of Freudian psychoanalysis on this list would require another book. I will briefly give two reasons for its exclusion. First, it has been argued by many that Freudian psychoanalysis belongs to "institutional ideology." One could mention Gilles Deleuze and Félix Guattari, *Anti-Oedipus* (Minneapolis: University of Minnesota Press, 1983), and Judith Butler, *Gender Trouble: Feminism and the Subversion of Identity* (New York: Routledge, 1990). For the former, the Oedipus narrative and structure serves as a disguise for, and a naturalization of, capitalist power; and for the latter, it serves the same function for heterosexist power. Second, Sartre gives a compelling argument that the Freudian notion of the unconscious is unintelligible, and hence a priori. Cf. Jean-Paul Sartre, *Being and Nothingness* (New York: Philosophical Library, 1956), p. 50ff.; hereafter cited in the text as *BN*. If Sartre is able to develop a psychoanalytic discourse that is rich enough to include Freud's major questions, and grounded enough to choose for itself between what Freud developed and what he rejected (as Sartre did in *The Freud Scenario*), then from Sartre's point of view as well, Freud would belong to that realm of apriorist discourse that existentialism operated against. For an interesting review of the relation and interaction between Sartre's and Freud's texts, as well as a careful and insightful extension of existential psychoanalysis to post-Freudian thought, see Betty Cannon, *Sartre and Psychoanalysis* (Lawrence: University Press of Kansas, 1991).

2. A re-axiomatizing of Marxism occurred during this period not only because an ideology free of the national and structural interests of the USSR was necessary for movements in the industrial West, but because the class nature of capitalism had changed; the center of working-class struggle had shifted to the neo-colonial relation and expressed itself mainly through third world national liberation revolutions.

3. Instead, more critical effort has gone into attempts to map the possible interfaces between Marxism and post-structuralism. One might mention the following: Michael Ryan, *Marxism and Deconstruction* (Baltimore: Johns Hopkins University Press, 1982); Douglas Kellner, *Critical Theory, Marxism, and Modernity* (Baltimore: Johns Hopkins University Press, 1989); Iris M. Young, *Justice and the Politics of Difference* (Princeton: Princeton University Press, 1990); Theodor Adorno, *Negative Dialectics* (New York: Continuum, 1973). Many others have sought to operate in the space between; in particular, the post-Marxist and postcolonial theorists, such as he Subaltern Studies group; Gayatri Spivak and Ranajit Guha, eds., *Subaltern Studies* (New York: Oxford University Press, 1988); Gayatri Spivak, *In Other Worlds* (New York: Routledge, 1988); Stuart Hall, *The Hard Road to Renewal* (London: Verso, 1988); Ernesto Laclau and Chantal Mouffe, *Hegemony and Socialist Strategy* (London: Verso, 1985); Mark Poster, *Critical Theory and Post-structuralism: In Search of a Context* (Ithaca: Cornell University Press); Barry Hindess and Paul Hirst, *Mode of Production and Social Formation* (London: Macmillan, 1977).

Michael Ryan, in *Marxism and Deconstruction*, is perhaps the most evenhanded. Ryan is not as interested in the philosophical challenge of deconstruction as he is in its potential politics. His project is twofold: first, procedurally, to bring Marx to deconstruction's gate in order to provide deconstruction with a political vehicle, a political ministry for itself; and second, politically, to regenerate a liberatory Marxism out and away from the ideological and logical stasis of "scientific" Marxism. Although he is an excellent reader of Derrida, and he avoids absorbing Derrida's text into Marxism or Marxist politics as a metaphilosophical rearticulation, he nevertheless ends by embedding his intention to develop a deconstructive politics in a (Marxian) programmatic structure.

There is a school of Sartre criticism that sees him as already Marxist, as having sought to produce an existentialist Marxism under the rubric of a Marxist existentialism: Mark Poster, *Sartre's Marxism* (London: Pluto Press, 1977); Ronald Aronson, *Jean-Paul Sartre: Philosophy in the World* (London: NLB, 1980); Thomas Flynn, *Sartre and Marxist Existentialism* (Chicago: University of Chicago Press, 1984).

4. The Marxists would say that the police and state were the main (and material) forms of political control. But police rule, so often expressed through modes of brutality and impunity, would be nonexistent if not publicized. It is the story, rendered by journalism, that accomplishes that of which the acts of police control are only simulacra. When police rule gets too heinous, movements form against it to curtail it. But these movements only signify that the police are the focus of popular attention, which is the goal of political administration in the first place—to set the police in place as the pole through which people relate to each other. At this level of political movements, the police only become more of a meaning, a symbology, as problem, enemy, antisocial ideology, and so on, all set at the center of political understanding and structure. The materiality of political control comes into existence through the operation of language at all of its levels.

5. Philip R. Wood, "Derrida Engagé and Post-structuralist Sartre: A Redefinition of Shifts in Recent French Philosophy," *MLN* 104, no. 4 (1989): 861–62. The following might be added to what Wood provides. There was a brief exchange (not quite a debate) between Sartre and Michel Foucault in the papers of *L'Arc*, a special issue titled "Sartre aujourd'hisi (no. 30, Oct. 1996, pp. 87–96), to which Foucault responded in *La Quinzaine Littéraire* (May 16, 1966; October 15, 1966; March 1, 1968). Denis Hollier (*The Politics of Prose*, Minneapolis: University of Minnesota Press, 1986) gives a rather personal, even intimate view of a kind of tacit "politics of rejection" toward Sartre among French intellectuals in the early 1980s. Deleuze pays singular homage to Sartre in *Dialogues* (Gilles Deluze and Claire Parnet, *Dialogues*, New York: Columbia University Press, 1987), as does Roland Barthes in *La chambre claire: Note sur la photographie* (Paris: Cahiers du Cinema, 1980; translated as *Camera Lucida*).

6. Cf. Jacques Derrida, "The Ends of Man," in *Margins of Philosophy* (Chicago: University of Chicago Press, 1982). Marg in *Glas* (Lincoln: University of Nebraska Press, 1986), Derrida thrusts Sartre's phenomenology away, as a "misontology," which he wishes to differentiate himself from in his own deconstructive immersion in Genet's text—though without actually engaging Sartre. His mention is more or less a critique by innuendo (*Glas*, 14b) or in passing (*Glas*, 161b). As in "The Ends of Man," he accuses Sartre of mistranslating, of going only skin-deep into Genet's words (*Glas*, 28b). Derrida develops his "attitude" toward Sartre at greater depth in an extended interview with Catherine David, published in *Le Nouvel Observateur* 983 (September 9, 1983): 84–90. This interview is discussed at length later in this chapter. Finally, Derrida engages Sartre in a concentrated manner in an interview with the Japanese journal *Gendai Shiso*, called "Pourquoi pas Sartre?" (vol. 15, 1987: 58–80). In this interview, he brings together many of the critical notions and polemics given in the above-cited works, together with some autobiographical material and a brief engagement with Sartre's anticolonialism and antiracism. My thanks to David Yum for translating this article for me.

7. Jean-Paul Sartre, "*Existentialism Is a Humanism*" in *Existentialism and Human Emotions*, trans. Bernard Fruchtman (New York: Philosophical Library, 1957), p. 39, hereafter cited in the text as *EH*.

8. Jean-Paul Sartre, *What Is Literature?* (New York: Washington Square Press, 1966); hereafter cited in the text as *WL*. In the first chapter of *What Is Literature?*, Sartre says, "Prose is, in essence, utilitarian. I would readily define the prose-writer as a man who makes use of words.... The writer is a speaker; he designates, demonstrates, orders, refuses, interpolates, begs, insults, persuades, insinuates. If he does so without any effect, he does not therefore become a poet; he is a writer who is talking and saying nothing.... [The] substance [of prose] is by nature significative; that is, the words are first of all not objects but designations for objects" (pp. 13–14). For Sartre, however, there is a distinction that a writer must recognize between representing one's intuition in the words written down, and deciding to reveal those words to others, which amounts to representing them in turn as what one has thought. Furthermore, since "to speak is to act" (*WL*, 16), it is implicitly permissible to ask of the writer, "What of the world do you want to disclose?" (*WL*, 17). Thus, the action (by disclosure) of writing is already a social act. In general, in this chapter, Sartre polemicizes a literary criticism that seeks to imprison writing in the corral of literature, in "belles lettres," and his contention is that writers must engage their world and their moment as an enterprise.

9. In this connection, one could mention the major works of Barthes, Foucault, and Derrida. See, in particular, Roland Barthes's essays: "To Write: An Intransitive Verb?" in *The Structuralist Controversy*, eds. Richard Macksey and Eugenio Donato (Baltimore: Johns Hopkins University Press, 1972) and "The Death of the Author," in *Image, Music, Text*, trans. Stephen Heath (New York: Hill and Wang, 1977). See also Jacques Derrida, *Of Grammatology*, trans. Gayatri Spivak (Baltimore: Johns Hopkins University Press, 1974), Part 1.1, 1.2, hereafter abbreviated in the text as *Gram*; and Jacques Derrida, *Limited, Inc.*, ed. Gerald Graff (Evanston: Northwestern University Press, 1988), hereafter abbreviated in the text as LI; and Michel Foucault, "What Is an Author?" in Josu V. Harari (ed.), *Textual Strategies: Perspectives in Post-structuralist Criticism* (Ithaca: Cornell University Press, 1979).

10. Gayatri Spivak, *The Post-Colonial Critic: Interviews, Strategies, Dialogues* (London: Routledge, 1990), p. 20.

11. Jacques Derrida, "Il courait mort," *Les Temps Modernes* (March–May 1996): 7–54.

12. Jacques Derrida, *Speech and Phenomena* (trans. David Allison, Evanston: Northwestern University Press, 1973), pp. 146–47; hereafter cited in the text as *SP*.

13. By and large, Sartre scholars do not address Derrida. I think there is a historical reason for this. Since Sartre's death, there have been several important posthumous publications, not all of which have been consistent with his published work. Though this has given Sartre scholarship a shot in the arm, it has tended to direct its attention backward toward the earlier work, and beyond to Sartre's more traditional precursors. Thus, most commentary on Sartre tends to speak, in general, from traditions already in place (Marxist, analytic, or phenomenological). The major contributions to this renaissance would include, as exemplary: Thomas Flynn on collective responsibility, Linda Bell on Sartre's ethics, William McBride and Ronald Aronson on Sartrean politics, David Detmer on Sartre's notion of freedom, and Betty Cannon on Sartre's relation to psychoanalysis. Christina Howells is the only thinker from within Sartre studies who attempts to relate Sartre, through his own mode of paradoxical logic, to Derrida. I mention these as highlights, and it is not meant to be exclusive. Hazel Barnes, whose seminal work on existential

philosophy and ethics antedates them all, remained active until the end of the century. There have been a number of interesting explicatory volumes, from such authors as Arthur Danto, Joseph Catalano, Marjorie Grene, Germaine Bree, Wilfrid Desan, Philip Wood, and Steve Hendley. These are by and large ancillary to the central issue in question here. There are also a number of recent biographies (by John Gerassi, Annie Cohen-Solal, and others) which hardly pertain.

Some Sartre commentary has been historical; Mark Poster, for instance, focuses on the transition from Sartre's hegemony in France to his eclipse at the hands of post-structuralism, in *Marxist Existentialism in Post-War France: From Sartre to Althusser* (Princeton: Princeton University Press, 1975). Feminist readings of Sartre are scarce. Cf. Margary Collins and Christine Pierce, "Holes and Slime: Sexism in Sartre's Psychoanalysis," *Philosophical Forum* 5 (1973); Hazel Barnes, "Sartre and Sexism," *Philosophy and Literature* 14, no. 2 (1990); and Constance Mui, "Sartre's Sexism Reconsidered," *Auslegung* 16, no. 1 (1990). The texts that include a certain existential dimension (Butler, Hartsock, or Wittig) generally attempt to separate themselves from Sartre. Recently, a volume edited by Julien Murphy has appeared called *Feminist Interpretations of Sartre* (University Park: Pennsylvania State University Press, 1999), in which the usefulness of Sartrean existential thinking to feminist thought is explored; in it, Derrida barely escapes total absence. Finally, Dominick LaCapra, in his interesting Derridean reading of Sartre, *A Preface to Sartre* (Ithaca: Cornell University Press, 1978), does not discuss any affinities between the two. Hereafter abbreviated in the text as *PS*.

14. Hugh Silverman, *Inscriptions: Between Phenomenology and Structuralism* (New York: Routledge & Kegan Paul, 1987).

15. Christina Howells, "Sartre and Derrida: Qui Perd Gagne," *Journal of the British Society of Phenomenology* 13, no. 1 (1982): 26–34.

16. Christina Howells, *Sartre: The Necessity of Freedom* (New York: Cambridge University Press, 1988).

17. Sebastian Gardner, "Splitting the Subject," *Auslegung* 13, no. 2 (1983): 186–92; Noreen Keohane-O'Connor, "Intentionality, Analysis, and the Self and Others," *Journal of the British Society of Phenomenology* 13, no. 2 (1982): 186–92. Gardner addresses the split subject in both Sartre and Derrida (roughly on a Lacanian model) and, in particular, the production of the split subject from a unified and coherent cogito. He argues that both Sartre and Derrida see the cogito as already split, or divided against itself. And he points out that Sartre offers a critique of self-presence that is paralleled by Derrida. Interestingly, Gardner claims that Lacan can be made more intelligible through Derrida's notion of différance, which he applies to Lacan's notion of the bar.

18. Jacques Derrida, *Margins of Philosophy*, trans. Alan Bass (Chicago: University of Chicago Press, 1982), pp. 116, 137; hereafter abbreviated in the text as *Marg*.

19. LaCapra suggests that Sartre is ethnocentric. If Sartre posits the project of becoming an in-itself-for-itself (i.e., God) for all people, irrespective of cultural background, he is universalizing a project that should be situated by Sartre only within his own tradition of Western metaphysics (*PS*, 128). LaCapra has posed the central question of many critiques of Sartre: To what extent is Sartre's attack on domination dispelled or weakened by his use of an analytic that supports domination (cf. Aronson, *Jean-Paul Sartre: Philosophy in the World*)? For LaCapra, once identity and difference constitute an analytic binary, reified and hierarchized as in-itself versus for-itself, one ends in a form of "species imperialism," of the domination of the for-itself over the world, which must undermine Sartre's liberatory project.

20. Jean-Paul Sartre, *The Psychology of Imagination* (Seacaucus: Citadel Press, 1972), p. 20. Hereafter abbreviated in the text as PI.

21. Cf. in PI; Part 4, Section 1, and the conclusion.

22. Ironically, Claude Evans, who is an analytic philosopher, does a similar thing with Derrida. He attempts to impose an analytic divisibility upon inseparable aspects of signification. Claude Evans, *Strategies of Deconstruction*. Derrida and The Myth of The Voice (Minneapolis: University of Minnesota Press, 1991). Evans, who is a good reader of Derrida, offers another critique of Derrida's rigor, toward which he asks of the early texts if they "measure up"—that is, to "classical logical rigor," which Derrida himself invokes (in *Limited, Inc.*), and to which he therefore can be held (Evans, *Strategies of Deconstruction*, p. 169). But what Evans ends up meaning by rigor is a univocity of terms. In discussing Derrida's critique of Husserl, he argues that Derrida, by including ancillary or implicit meanings to the terms Husserl uses, works against Husserl's "express intentions" and by thus enlarging Husserl's meaning "deliberately" misreads Husserl—implying that Derrida is stacking the deck. What Evans is ignoring is that Husserl's "express intentions" are indicated in a language in which ancillary and implicit meanings reside. If Evans can pretend to narrow Husserl's intention, it can only be from a position outside Husserl's language, through a confrontation with a panoply of English terms, which are also polyvocal.

Evans uses a logic diametrically opposed to Derrida's. Evans wishes to submit the sign to a logic; logic itself is the demand that language (words) have (univocal) meanings upon which one can reason. Derrida, on the other hand, submits logic to the sign, to the inner dynamic of language, in which logic occurs. What separates these two thinkers is the difference between classical logical rigor, which Evans claims as a standard, and the logic of classical rigor, by which Derrida carries classical rigor to its logical conclusion, revealing what the acceptance of a standard logic implies in the first place. What Derrida engages as discourse and what Evans engages are at odds precisely in where they respectively locate logic and rigor textually.

23. Some analytic philosophers cannot read Derrida at all. One who cannot, for instance, is John Ellis (*Against Deconstruction*, Princeton: Princeton University Press, 1989). At one point, he quotes Derrida (p. 23) as saying: "If 'writing' signifies inscription and especially the durable institution of a sign [. . .], writing in general covers the entire field of linguistic signs. . . . Instituted signifiers may then appear, 'graphic' in the narrow sense . . . , ordered by a certain relationship with other instituted—hence 'written,' even if they are 'phonic'—signifiers." Ellis then says, "Derrida's assertion that the idea of the institution of signs . . . is unthinkable before the possibility of writing . . . [, t]o assert that as soon as speech arises, writing it down is possible . . . is not support for Derrida's claim that writing is prior to speech." Derrida's notion that even the phonic can be considered writing, and why, passed him by completely. Ellis has literalized the notion of "writing in general" to mean "writing it down."

24. Richard Rorty, *Philosophy and the Mirror of Nature* (Princeton: Princeton University Press, 1979), p. 347; hereafter abbreviated in the text as *MN*. I will also be looking at his article, "Is Derrida a Transcendental Philosopher?" *Yale Journal of Criticism* 2, no. 2 (1989); abbreviated in the text as DTP.

25. Rorty divides opinion on Derrida into two camps: those who admire his audacity and newness of style, and those who admire his philosophical rigor; the first emphasizes playfulness, and the second critique and discovery. For Rorty, this is a political division between a Derrida who is a private, artistic, individualistic writer, versus a Derrida who purveys new antiinstitutional weaponry (DTP, 208). Rorty places himself in the first

category because he considers philosophical rigor irrelevant to what Derrida is doing. For Rorty, rigor means "problem-solving."

26. A case in point is precisely Rorty's own taxonomic propensities, schematizing thinkers (not texts) according to common lexicalities and conceptualities. Though Derrida has never ceased showing this to be founded upon an idle assumption, Rorty at no time addresses Derrida's arguments.

27. Jean-Paul Sartre, *Mallarmé: The Poet of Nothingness*, trans. Ernest Sturm (University Park: Pennsylvania State University Press, 1988).

28. Joseph Fell, *Heidegger and Sartre* (New York: Columbia University Press, 1979), p. 277; hereafter abbreviated as *HS*.

29. Martin Heidegger, *Being and Time*, trans. John Macquarrie and Edward Robinson (New York: Harper and Row, 1962); 41, 193ff.; hereafter abbreviated in the text as *BT*. *Gram*, 23.

30. Hollier, *The Politics of Prose*; hereafter abbreviated in the text as *Prose*.

31. He plays with the "For whom?" in Sartre's question "For whom does one write?" in the same way he plays with tense in *Nausea*. A dramatic play, for instance, pertains to the past by recounting it, as a fiction, but it is already a past that does not exist, because in a play, only the present does (*Prose*, 86). But, though Hollier credits Sartre with not writing the promised endings to his works, he does not credit him with avoiding beginnings by entering his subjects *in medias res* (*Prose*, 172) as in *L'imaginaire*, which begins with an example of perception, though perception will, in a fundamental way, be shown to depend on imagination, to belong to the "outcome."

32. Sartre would not disagree that a text's beginning often points in a different direction than the process it sets in motion, nor that the end of a work always lives in the future. But in those terms, Hollier catches himself in his own play. He criticizes Sartre for totalizing, without ceasing to narrativize him; yet his subject, the character Sartre who totalizes, becomes Hollier's own totalization of Sartre the person. In the character of Sartre as a consciousness, Hollier is showing how totalization is possible—which duplicates Sartre's project. Hollier becomes an example, among Sartre's many, of how consciousness totalizes. To deconstruct Sartre, Hollier must narrativize himself, as well as his character Sartre. In his deconstruction of Sartre, Hollier himself becomes Sartre's character. Hollier further catches himself in suggesting that Sartre is inconsistent. Sartre criticizes Blanchot for being neither within nor outside his language (cf. Sartre's article on Blanchot, "Aminadab, or the Fantastic Considered as a Language," in *Literary and Philosophical Essays*, trans. Annette Michelson, New York: Collier Books, 1962) and Dos Passos for writing a character who is both wholly inside his time and wholly outside it. But Hollier must adopt a standard of consistency to see Sartre as inconsistent, a standard that then must both detotalize and retotalize the inconsistent Sartre. And we should notice that Sartre's critique of Blanchot is about language, while that of Dos Passos is about Being-for-others (*Prose*, 15, 31). The question Hollier does not ask is, Which is the medium for which? Does Being-for-others embed language in itself as non-being, or is it the other way around? Either way, Sartre becomes the one who reveals how totalizing happens, rather than being the one who totalizes.

33. According to Joseph Fell, Heidegger too operated within a nominalism, which Fell describes as follows: a tree, "part of it literally in the soil, part of it literally in the air," is "this for us only when identified in language as what it is. This identification understands the tree as more than the identification. . . . this identification also finds the tree identifiable, intelligible, knowable because the 'entity' has 'accepted' our name-and-notion of it—it is

'a tree' and 'an oak'" (*HS*, 231). And he quotes Heidegger: "When we walk through the forest, we are always already walking through the word 'forest'" (*HS*, 176).

Sartre has understood his own nominalism in a different sense: "Nominalism prohibits classifications: it is necessary to understand . . . all projects . . . on the basis of a complex situation, irreducible to the sum of its elements, which qualifies them by its complexity in the very moment when these projects surpass that situation toward their ends" Sartre, *L'Idiot de la Famille* (Paris: Gallimard, 1971), vol. 1, p. 686; quoted in Fell, p. 269. But furthermore, for Sartre, "We are in language as we are in our bodies" (*HS*, 273). That is, the subject is its body, and is a language, for others, in relation to others, though as a for-itself it surpasses both body and language. This being-in-language becomes an interrelation of projects across the activity of speech (or, indeed, of writing), in the sense that speech is spoken pursuant to a project, but apprehended by another pursuant to the other's project. One surpasses speech to its meaning in this divergent, ambiguous manner. What remains is that the speech, the sentence, the story all become a common experience, and indeed, the archetypal common experience. In this sense, the common experience of the word becomes the way in which the object is surpassed to an apprehension that includes the other. This dialectic of dialogue is developed further in *Critique of Dialectical Reason* as a form of dialectical nominalism. Translated by Alan Sheridan (London: Verso, 1982).

34. Thanks to Hazel Barnes for this quote.

35. For instance, Foucault proclaimed the necessity to escape the "subject," to bracket it out in order to discern how discourse and discursive formation produced our social existence and our cultural practices. But he engaged in activities with Sartre. Cf. Michael Foucault, "Truth and Power," in *Power/Knowledge: Selected Interviews*, trans. Colin Gordon et al. (New York: Pantheon, 1980), p. 117.

36. David Wood and Robert Bernasconi, *Derrida and Différance* (Evanston: Northwestern University Press, 1988), hereafter cited in the text as *DD*. The original interview of Derrida with Catherine David was published in *Le Nouvel Observateur* 983 (September 9, 1983): 84–90, hereafter cited in the text as *Nouvel Obs*. It was translated by the Contemporary Texts Seminar at the State University of New York at Stony Brook.

37. *Gram*, 158; "Ousia and Gramme" is in *Marg*, 65. I might note that, as Linda Hutcheons argues, one always produces another reading beyond the literal content of the text by critiquing the language of the text. This is, for her, the very heart of postmodernism. Linda Hutcheons, *The Politics of Postmodernism* (London: Routledge, 1989), p. 6ff.

38. Jacques Derrida, *Writing and Difference*, trans. Alan Bass (Chicago: University of Chicago Press, 1978), p. 280; hereafter cited in the text as *WD*.

39. *WD*, 280; see also Jacques Derrida, *Positions*, trans. Alan Bass (Chicago: University of Chicago Press, 1981), p. 10; hereafter cited in the text as *Pos*.

40. A deconstructive reading regards the difference between what a text claims to represent and what it can be seen to present through displacement of that claim, as the disclosure of its blind spots. The textual "objects" that reveal its blind spots are necessarily encountered (generated) at the text's margins because they are at the edge of its "eye's" construction, where it opens a space between the text's claim of self-mastery and the compromise of such a claim with its structure. Derrida also points out that what resides close to the margins, at the edge of the text, becomes symptomatic of what cannot be presented within its axiomatics, and escape their determination (*Pos*, 7). Indeed, one of the thematic threads of "Ousia and Gramme" is the unravelling of Heidegger's account of time through the interruption of his text by a footnote whose import could not be included in the flow of his central argument. Cf. Alexander Gelley, "Form as Force," *Diacritics* 2, no. 1

(Spring 1972): 10. Also see *Gram*, 161ff., on the logic of supplementarity and the exorbitant and its relation to the blind spot.

41. It has been predominantly male. If what I am calling the existential evolution is a questioning of metaphysical presuppositions, that questioning occurred from within patriarchal assumptions that generally remained unseen. The many women who have joined, rejoindered, adjourned, and abjured this "movement" have also generally done so through a rebellion against the forms of domination resulting from patriarchal presuppositions. It is Simone de Beauvoir's distinction to have emerged from within the "movement," rather than joining it from outside, and then to have gone on to question those patriarchal presuppositions. And she did so at a time when there was no place of outside perspective such as was later provided by the women's movements.

42. For an interesting exposition of Sartre's overall project as it relates to both Heidegger and Hegel, see William R. Schroeder, *Sartre and His Predecessors* (Boston: Routledge, 1984), p. 185ff; hereafter cited in the text as *SHP.* He expands and elucidates the list just given. Schroeder's book is interesting in terms of the dialogue he carries on with Sartre. Often he asserts that Sartre is not exhaustive in his treatment and seeks to supplement it. At times, however, he forces the issues he finds; at others, the supplementation he provides is already implicit in Sartre's argument. Indeed, Sartre himself is often supplementary to Schroeder's critique. Though Schroeder does not discuss a relation between Sartre and Derrida, it is his book that provided the initial stimulus for this project.

43. Sixteenth-century colonialism, for instance, transformed the obvious fact that indigenous people of the Americas or Africa were not European, first through a definition of ethnic difference, then through its racialization, and finally by the assertion that such peoples could not attain European social norms, though they should already have done so; they were then understood to be subhuman for that inability.

44. To construct such a bridge may appear to be a fairly straightforward enterprise. But one must be careful of philosophical bridges, as Derrida suggests twice in his critique of Kant, in *The Truth in Painting*. Kant opposes two irreducible discourses, and places a bridge across the gap by fiat. In the first case, the bridge seems to rest upon an analogy between the sensible (nature) and the supersensible (freedom), but is itself the analogy. Derrida argues that such a bridge is impossible since the two shores to be bridged are on different levels of discourse. In the second case, the bridge spans the beautiful and the sublime, comparison and the incomparable as a comparison, and thus contains within it the very gap to be bridged. Bridges reflect their intention as structures as much as they do their extension between shores. Cf. Jacques Derrida, *The Truth in Painting*, trans. Geoff Bennington and Ian McLeod (Chicago: University of Chicago Press, 1987), pp. 35–36, 137–38.

45. This is not an abstract or academic point. It makes reference to some real political problems that remained unsolved in the course in which they ran. In particular, many feminists understood the power of the post-structuralist discourses to break open the standards and tenets of the patriarchy that maintained itself by being what "goes without saying." To have been able to deconstruct it, to show that its assumptions and historicity were simply assumptions and historicity, had great critical power. But when the power of deconstruction was turned upon feminism itself, as a critique of the limitations of identity politics, or of ideologies of confrontation and class, it seemed that the critique was taking the wrong side in the political struggle. And the dialogue between those who thought ideologically and those who thought deconstructively, though both had positive energy and power to offer to their common movements, broke down.

CHAPTER 2

1. Ironically, analytic philosophy has itself been involved in a historical incommensurability throughout the twentieth century. Neither phenomenology nor analytic philosophy have ever been able to bridge their disparity of reasoning structures and styles sufficiently to enter a dialogue that was not instead an attempt to appropriate the other into their own language by rewriting it.

2. For various accounts of this critique, see Geoffrey Bennington, *Jacques Derrida* (Chicago: University of Chicago Press, 1993); Jonathan Culler, *On Deconstruction: Theory and Criticism after Structuralism* (Ithaca: Cornell University Press, 1982). Derrida himself sums it up in various places; e.g., *Limited, Inc.*

3. In *The Chips Are Down* (*Les Jeux Sont Faits*), the two main characters have projects that have misfired and resulted in their death. The twist in the play is that they get a second chance; they return to life with the knowledge they gained in death to try again. But it turns out that the outcome is again undermined by the form of desire; their knowledge does not save them. Desire simply recontextualizes itself beyond and through the new knowledge that each brings to it. Even in the context of their new knowledge, the meanings of their actions remain analogous in the new context, and hence formally unchanged, or changed in a correlative fashion, and they again die. In effect, each project is deconstructed by its form, which is the form of the desire, in the context of the world in which that desire is expressed. Its relation to that context determines its outcome. Its literal content, as a strategized action in that world, is superseded by its form as desire, and its form as desire is superseded by the world's response, which is again fatal, because the world assumed by that desire is changed again by the existence of the desire's enactment in that world. Thus, the outcome is the same. Sartre presents the notion that a certain fate awaits the subjectivity that chooses itself as that particular subjectivity through what it desires of the world.

4. Derrida develops the notion of the trace to signify the retention of difference within the structure of reference. For the sign, there is the remnant of difference, which forms an integral part of it. The trace is, as Spivak puts it, an absent presence inside the sign, the presence of difference marking the absence of what differs. It is that sense of where the sign comes from that can never be an origin, since that would only be another (absent) sign. "The trace is the absolute origin of sense in general. Which amounts to saying once again that there is no absolute origin of sense in general. The trace is the différance which opens appearance and signification" (*Gram*, 65).

5. Rodolphe Gasché, *The Tain of the Mirror* (Cambridge, MA: Harvard University Press, 1986); hereafter abbreviated in the text as *TM*.

6. Gasché investigates five forms of reflections in a more or less historicized manner, including empirical reflection (Locke), logical reflection on objective relations (Leibniz), transcendental reflection (Kant), noematic reflection (Husserl), and absolute reflection, reflection on reflection itself (Hegel). In reflecting on the subject-object relation, speculation predicates the subject, which at the same time renders its object the subject for that predicate. Thus, in the speculative proposition, subject and predicate invert themselves, engendering an identity between themselves which is the copula of the proposition. The copula becomes identity, the real subject of the speculative proposition, of the subject-predicate relation. "The copula of the proposition thus becomes the real subject of the speculative proposition" (*TM*, 48). In effect, the content of the speculative proposition is the identity of self-determining thought itself. In this sense, speculation is the

overthrow of the empirical or reflective propositions, since speculation cannot be expressed as a subject-predicate relation. It is the thinking of that which transcends experience (*TM*, 55).

7. For Derrida, the moment of speculation of the text, of reflection on its reflectivity itself, reveals the metaphysics to which a text submits itself, while pretending to pose it from itself. To the extent that assumptions or presuppositions are always self-referential, posing as the origin of a discursive process, while being the foundation of a metaphysics that determines that origin, they constitute a self-reflective moment, the moment of speculation. Derrida metaphorizes speculation as part of the economy of signs. It is the moment of "non-productive investment of value," the moment in which there is nothing that cannot be made to make sense. In effect, within any pretense to truth (which constitutes the core of any metaphysics) there lies an aspect of the arbitrary, of the gratuitous, namely, truth's self-referentiality.

8. Jacques Derrida, *Dissemination*, trans. Barbara Johnson (Chicago: University of Chicago Press, 1981), p. 11; hereafter cited in the text as *Dis*. We encounter this inseparable incommensurability in the difference between signifier and signified, and again, throughout Derrida's text as a relation between stasis and enactment without self-reflection, between difference and deferral. It is the condition of contextualization itself, as in the Jacobsonian poetic, where the words of a poem establish the poem as a sign through their meanings, while the poem in turn contextualizes them as signs within the poem pursuant to its meaning (the text bequeathing meaning to its words through contextualization, and the words generating a context for themselves as the text). See, for instance, the account of writing in "Freud and the Scene of Writing" (*WD*, 217ff.) or of sovereignty in "From Restricted to General Economy: a Hegelianism without Reserve" (*WD*, 265ff.).

9. The post-structuralist critique, and deconstruction, have attracted philosophization precisely because they critique philosophy. But the attempt must assume that critique and deconstruction are philosophical ideas rather than activities or practices toward philosophy. The first would permit a generalizable sense that was not necessarily methodological. But what cannot be represented is the way the metatextual critique known as deconstruction insists on individuating the text it addresses.

10. Hazel Barnes translates *néantisation* as "nihilation," and gives the following explanation in her glossary: "Nihilate (*néantir*): A word coined by Sartre. Consciousness exists as consciousness by making a nothingness arise between it and the object of which it is consciousness. Thus, nihilation is that by which consciousness exists. To nihilate is to encase in a shell of non-being. The English word 'nihilate' was first used by Helmut Kuhn in his *Encounter with Nothingness*" (*BN*, 632). It is interesting to note that in the same year that Kuhn published *Encounter with Nothingness* (1949), R.F.C. Hull and Alan Crick claim to have coined the term *nihilate* to translate Heidegger's term *die Nichtung* in their translation of "What Is Metaphysics," published in *Existence and Being* (p. 339 and note 29). They also use the term to translate Heidegger's verb forms for the same idea: *nichten* and *nichtet*.

11. Sartre invents the notion of *négatité* not to name but to explain the presence of negation, the possibility of absence. For Sartre, the négatités, relations of negation, are conditions for the relations of instrumentality, rather than being themselves instrumental; negation "rises up" not as a thing but in the "rubric of a category" that presides over things (*BN*, 24). The négatités are the relations that express the nothingness or absence in being itself (as opposed to the nothingness in consciousness). The distance between two points, for instance, is the negation of being, still within being, between those two points, a negation that is the basis for any idea of measurement. One grasps the absence of something, or its

distance, through a project that expected it, or that seeks to traverse it. Thus, the négatité of distance is both the negation of being and the presence of absence within being. Analogous to Derrida's trace, négatité is a dual negation that does not belong to negativity but to absence: an absence in plenitude, and a plenitude that is absence. It is the avenue whereby negation is describable in Being, as the trace is the avenue whereby absent difference is inscribed in presence.

12. Interestingly, Derrida's original exposition of différance, in an article of that name, contains articulations that can only be called, because of their fame if for no other reason, Sartrean terminology. For instance, he says, différance does not invoke presence because "différance is not" (*SP*, 153); furthermore, it invokes a game in which the "loser wins" (*SP*, 151).

13. Franz Boas, "The Origins of Totemism," *American Anthropologist* 18 (1916): 319–26. "The homology of distinguishing marks of social divisions of a tribe pertains to a classificatory tendency" (p. 326). The totem is a signifier for an intentional link between the man-nature relation and the social characterization of groups. It names a homological relationship. For Levi-Strauss, Boas's approach necessarily involves a Eurocentric imposition, because it assumes what the terms mean in accord with anthropological notions of myth, rather than in terms of their own internal structure as language. Levi-Strauss rejects the idea of totemism in general, as anthropology has put it forth, but admits that something is there which anthropology calls a totem, and which anthropology is seeking to understand through homology; it is either (1) a relation between the relations of totems and the relations of groups, (2) a relation of individual to totem and others to the individual, or (3) a relation of clan to totem and of other clans to that clan (the designation of human relations to other natural beings and the designation of human kinship relations). In effect, for Levi-Strauss, it is the relation of man to nature and to the relation between social groups. Claude Levi-Strauss, *Totemism*, trans. Rodney Needham (Boston: Beacon Press, 1963), p. 11. That is, the relations of oppositions and differences in particular myths or rituals provide structural modes of interrelation irrespective of role or specific content for rituals or sacred procedures. One thus approaches the immanent cultural meaning of a particular ritual, rather than its apparent meaning as given to an anthropologist's reading of its literal terms. Claude Levi-Strauss, *Structural Anthropology*, trans. Claire Jacobson and Brooke Grundfest Schoepf (Garden City: Basic Books, 1963), p. 232ff. "A structural analysis of the myth content . . . furnishes rules of transformation which enable us to shift from one variant to another by means of operations similar to those of algebra," (p. 235). For Levi-Strauss, totems provide ways of naming clans that provide for distinction rather than distinctiveness (*Totemism*, 90). He claims Boas's system is empty because it abstracts from the act of designation rather than from systematicity.

14. Lucien Goldmann, *Toward a Sociology of the Novel*, trans. Alan Sheridan (London: Tavistock, 1975), p. 162. For Goldmann, the central problems of the novel are (1) that the hero and the world are insurmountably separate, (2) that the novelist's ethic becomes an esthetic problem for the novel, and (3) that if there is to be a sociology of the novel, it must center itself in the relation between the novelistic form and the social environment (p. 6). For him, a homology can be constituted between a character and market society that is of "one and the same structure manifesting itself on two different planes" (p. 8). And if such homologies are possible, then a sociology of a novel can be defined, and a history of the fictional form itself becomes possible. Goldmann thus joins Barthes in seeking to ground a history of literature, and of the literary, in a certain discursive concreteness. But they find it in very disparate directions. For Goldmann, homological critique becomes an instituted relation that embeds a history of fiction in social historicity, and provides a

way of understanding, for instance, the development of novelistic realism and representation (p. 149). Goldmann centers his history on the notion of character values, of the unexchangeable in a character's interaction with his/her world. Barthes positions concreteness in the givenness of language and style. He argues that a form of writing is peculiar to each social group, each ruling class, whereas Goldmann sees the novel as a particular form of cultural creation within a social and historical situation in general. For Goldmann, there is a homology between two relations: between that of a cultural creation (novel) and a social group, and of a novel's elements (character, event structure, etc.) and the work (the novel) as a whole (as world; p. 158)—that is, between the structure of the world of a novel and the mental (ideological) structures of a social group. Barthes is somewhat less constrained.

15. For instance, Barthes mentions that a "discourse is a long 'sentence,' just as a sentence . . . is a short 'discourse'"; Roland Barthes, *Image, Music, Text*, trans. Stephen Heath (New York: Hill and Wang, 1977), p. 83); hereafter abbreviated in the text as *IMT*. The effect of such a structural relation of the global to the detail sets discourse always in the realm of self-multiplying systems (such as tools used to make tools), systems whose relation to themselves is always a second-order relation. This forms the basis of a theory of narrative, in the sense that a narrative is another form of long sentence, while conversely, "every constative sentence is in a way the rough outline of a short narrative" (*IMT*, 84). Barthes hypothesizes, after Greimas, a grammatical mode of understanding narrative structure, within which the "multitude of narrative characters [represent] the elementary functions of grammatical analysis." That is, the moments of grammatical analysis have their analogues within the realm of narrative analysis, because narrative (as relations of acts, subject-object relations, and endless troping of intentionality) presents itself with the internal relations, the complexities, and the configurations of a grammar. Also, an exchange of communication between characters in narrative finds its homologue in the relation of narrative and reader. For instance, in narrative, the appearance of an "I" presupposes the existence of a "you" to whom the "I" speaks. Similarly, "there can be no narrative without a narrator and a listener (reader)" (*IMT*, 109).

16. In the *Oxford English Dictionary*, the first use of the term "homology" is located in the eighteenth century and meant "agreement." In the nineteenth century, it was used to signify "proportion," and included the rule that like must be compared to like. This was applied to biology, chemistry, and mathematics. In biology, the term was used to refer to comparable structures of organisms, such as a horse's front "knee" and a human wrist. In chemistry, it referred to series of compounds with common substituent structures, such as the paraffins, or the simple alcohols (saturated carbon chains with one alcohol group).

17. Homological relations are already familiar to the way we read and make sense of textuality. The recognition of a plot structure in one novel as previously encountered in another, or the recognition of an iconography common to the painting of two different periods, or simply the act of quoting in art, all involve a homological understanding as an act of recognition.

18. I would distinguish this homological form of "iteration" (as a relation of form) from a typology of narrative function, such as Barthes constructs in *Image, Music, Text* (79ff.). For instance, in Edgar Allan Poe's *Purloined Letter*, the prefect is able to hide the letter twice through the same device, that of leaving it open to view. In the first instance, by picking the letter up off the table boldly in the king's sight, he thus hides the letter itself as compromising from all but the queen, for whom his action is the grossest violation of privacy. In the

second, he hides the letter in his rooms by leaving it out in plain sight. In both cases, the narrative element of his manipulation of the letter has the same typological (functional) characteristic in the narrative, as narrative moments, but they are not homologous because they function differently as structures of meaning in their respective scenes. However, both instances of "hiding in the open" form part of two cycles through which the letter travels; and those two cycles are structurally homologous. Typology structures by means of critical (metatextual) categories, while homology relates and hence categorizes by means of textual structures.

19. Derrida, *Dissemination*, p. 5. The projection of a necessity of communication (with another or a reader) returns even deconstructed language to a determination that resituates it in the metaphysical (*Marg*, 314). It is in describing and deconstructing this process in language, whether writing or speech, that Derrida can be seen as carrying on, or narrativizing an extended struggle, or guerrilla campaign, of dissemination against metaphysics, snagging what metaphysics opens, untying what it ties down, tearing up what it conjoins, and unleashing what it had arrested (*Dis*, 26).

20. Robert Bernasconi, *The Question of Language in Heidegger's History of Being* (Atlantic Highlands, NJ: Humanities Press, 1985), p. 4; hereafter cited in the text as *QLH*. Also see *BT*, 41ff., 154ff.

21. It is the problem of translating Anaximander that Heidegger uses to raise the issue of the necessity to critique language to return to that past. Anaximander's language is hidden and unrecoverable, precisely because it has been translated, or transformed into the language that now returns to it Herman Rappaport, (*Heidegger and Derrida*, p. 27) (Lincoln: University of Nebraska Press, 1989); hereafter cited in the text as *HD*.

22. This is generally referred to as Heidegger's "Turn," after an article by that name (*Kehre*); but a development of the ideas contained in this "turn" will be found most extensively described in his essay, "The End of Philosophy and The Task of Thinking," in *Basic Writings*, ed. David Krell (New York: Harper & Row, 1997), pp. 369–392. Heidegger would object to this use of the terms *form* and *content*; for him, they reflect a duality that is at the very core of traditional metaphysics; or, as Husserl would reflect it, form is "mental being" and matter (or content) is "natural being" (*HS*, 20). Heidegger argues in "The Thing" that such a metaphysical approach to an object treats only with what the thing is, rather than what it does, or what it bears upon, or what it is concerned with; Martin Heidegger, *Poetry, Language, Thought*, trans. Albert Hofstadter (New York: Harper, 1971). It signifies an object "without reference to the human act of representing it" (p. 177). Instead, form should be already understood as its content, beyond which the object becomes presence and instrumentality. But at one point in the "Letter on Humanism," Heidegger makes the following statement: "Die Ek-sistenz, ekstatisch gedacht, deckt sich weder inhaltlich noch der Form nach mit der existentia"; Martin Heidegger, *Wegmarken* (Frankfurt am Main: Vittorio Klostermann, 1967), p. 158. The translation (by Frank Capuzzi and J. Glenn Gray) is: "Ek-sistence, thought in terms of ecstasis, does not coincide with existentia in either form or content." Martin Heidegger, "Letter on Humanism," in *Basic Writings*, p. 206; hereafter cited in the text as LH. The German word *Form* refers to shape, appearance, or outward presentation, and *inhalt* signifies content in the sense of subject matter, the addressed rather than the contained; it is the term for a table of contents, and would include that for which there is concern, or that for which an object or subject matter is concerned. Heidegger is signifying, in these terms, that neither form nor content is alien to the ek-sistentiality of Man. And it will be around this sense of these terms that I will be using the notions of form and content. In particular, I shall be using the

notion of form to signify something constructed, or structural, and not an essence. It will not have "mental being" because it will not exist outside the metatextual construct that articulates it.

23. For Derrida, différance is the operation of the trace, the production of difference as the trace of the trace (*SP*, 153). But in the circle of the "Being of writing" suggested here, each is the trace of the trace with respect to the other.

24. *BN*, 79. Steve Martinot, "Sartre's Being-for-Heidegger; Heidegger's Being-for-Sartre," *Man and World* 24 (1991): 63–74.

25. *BN*, 73–74. In this passage, Sartre is referring to a preceding discussion of bad faith. It is the operation of certainty that makes bad faith possible, as one of the ways of living the instant. As Nietzsche says to Josef Breuer, in Yalom's novel, "It is not what you may tell others. . . . What matters is what you will tell yourself." It is there that certainty becomes the unavoidable, the crux, and the problem. Irvin D. Yalom, *When Nietzsche Wept* (New York: Basic Books, 1992), p. 110.

26. *BT*, 72; *HS*, 42, 48ff. Fell is an interesting reader of Heidegger, not in the sense of paraphrastic correctness, but through a distance that enables him to "compile" Heidegger's thought in an instructive manner. I think he is a better reader of Heidegger than of Sartre, however, with the result that Sartre often gets viewed through a Heideggerian lens.

27. The issue of Dasein and consciousness invokes the brief critique given Sartre by Derrida in "The Ends of Man." When *Being and Time* was translated into French by Corbin, Dasein translated as "human reality" (*realité humaine*). To understand Dasein as "human reality" is to redefine it within a metaphysical framework, and thus to distort Heidegger's purpose and thinking. Derrida charges that Sartre accepted this mistranslation and thus valorized it, in spite of his familiarity with Heidegger's work. Derrida recognizes that Sartre employed the notion of "human reality" in order to think of "man" on "a new basis"; that is, to escape metaphysics, "to suspend all the presuppositions which had always constituted the concept of the unity of man" (*Marg*, 115). But Sartre had left "the unity of human-reality" itself unquestioned. While the term is deployed as part of a project of rethinking, as a translation of Dasein it leads back to the old thinking. And in accepting the term, Sartre participated in a more general marginalization and misinterpretation of Heidegger's text in France.

But Derrida is giving Sartre short shrift here. In *Being and Nothingness*, Sartre speaks of both Dasein and "human reality" and differentiates them. In his first mention of "human reality," which does occur in association with Heidegger, he places it in quotes to indicate that with respect to Heidegger, it comes from elsewhere (*BN*, xlviii). Sartre pointedly argues that Heidegger presented Dasein in wholly positive terms (*BN*, 18) while, for him, "human reality" is an emergence of a being from non-being. For Sartre, human reality emerges in nothingness and is everywhere associated with negativity, while, as Sartre notes, this is not the case for Dasein. Dasein can find itself face-to-face with nothingness (*BN*, 17), but human reality establishes itself in nothingness (*BN*, 18). Sartre affirms that Heidegger's account of Dasein has "deprived it of the dimension of consciousness" (*BN*, 73), while for Sartre human reality is consciousness. And Sartre says outright that for him, Dasein is an impoverished notion. In effect, "human reality" does not translate Dasein; at best, it transforms it. And Sartre's contiguous use of both terms indicates that he is preserving Dasein as an element of the Heideggerian discourse, while reserving "human reality" for his own.

28. For Heidegger, logos, derived from *legein*, which means gathering or "laying out," signifies discourse in the sense of "letting something be seen" by pulling it together and

pointing it out (*BT*, 56). And Bernasconi argues that Heidegger later addresses it as signifying both "the word," in the sense of a definitude of discourse, and the Being of language as recuperated from metaphysics (*QLH*, 61).

29. Sartre says, "I am not the self which I will be," but "I am the self that I will be in the mode of not being it." In that sense, nothing as the nothingness that separates him from that chosen possibility of traversing the cliff prevents him from leaping into the abyss. His conduct "emanates from a self [he] is not yet" (*BN*, 32).

30. Herman Rappaport notes that, when Derrida develops his notion of différance from the Saussurean analytic of sign systems as a structure of differences, différance is itself analogous to temporality. To the extent that presence exists only in relation to what it is not, différance presents itself as an inarticulable between elsewhere and postponement. If meaning emerges from a system of elsewheres and produces itself endlessly through its structure of differing signs that are always not yet their meaning, then the sign means through a double displacement to an already as elsewhere and a not-yet as later. It is a homologue to the absence between past and future. Deferral is the becoming space of time, and difference is the becoming time of space (*HD*, 60–61). As Derrida puts it, différance "points to the irreducibility of temporalizing (which is also temporalization—in transcendental language, which is no longer adequate here, . . . the constitution of primordial temporality . . .)" (*SP*, 130). If this again exemplifies Derrida's transformations of the form of Heidegger's account (this time of temporality) to the terms of his critique of language, it also suggests a configurational relation between Derridean différance and Sartrean being-for-itself. And indeed, it was to just such a conjunction that Howells was making reference.

31. With Fell, we may summarize the main differences in philosophical "doctrine" between Heidegger and Sartre as follows (*HS*, 364ff.). Sartre is man-centered, while Heidegger is Being-centered. For Sartre, consciousness is a surpassing of the world, of the object, a transcendence; for Heidegger, Dasein is that being for which the world, and Being, are a question. For Sartre, the world is oriented in relation to consciousness (as transcendence); for Heidegger, man is oriented in relation to the world, to gathering the world, in the sense that events, names, or objects constitute networks of other objects, events, or meanings. For Heidegger, language is the upsurge of Being, what manifests Being in the world; for Sartre, language is an instrumentality that participates in a circularity in which one discovers the language to express one's thinking in the very process of discovering what one thinks in language. Where, for Heidegger, instrumentalities are socially given or contextualized, though personalized through care or involvement, for Sartre, instrumentality is not given, but determined by a project, and at all times conditioned by one's fundamental choice of oneself. That is, if one finds in the object a certain meaning, or a certain use, or if one rejects an object as being beyond or negative to one's meanings, in so doing one has chosen oneself in having chosen the object's meaning. Finally, if Heidegger's project is to go behind metaphysics, to dismantle it, Sartre's is to reveal how metaphysics is a possibility for thought, for consciousness, as a praxis.

CHAPTER 3

1. This notion is the central thrust of Derrida's article "Signature Event Context," in *Margins of Philosophy*; it appears in reexplained form in *Limited, Inc.*, pp. 115 and 209, for instance.

2. For an example of how incommensurability and dialectic work against each other, one has only to turn to Plato's *Euthyphro*. In this "dialogue," no dialogue occurs, because

Socrates and Euthyphro are speaking different languages. Euthyphro speaks a narrative-based language, which takes its referentiality from the system of mythic narratives. Thus, he speaks in specificities, concretenesses. Socrates, on the other hand, is attempting to recast language, give words meanings in themselves, from within their role in quotidian speech, as general notions whose specificities are given contextually in the moment, as presence. If this identifies Plato's philosophical and political project, to transform the old (myth-oriented) language into this new (lexicalized) one, with Euthyphro, he gets nowhere. No dialectic is possible.

3. It is a configuration that Derrida alludes to in several different contexts. Cf. Jacques Derrida and Christie McDonald, "Choreographies," *Diacritics* 12 (1982): 72; *LI*, 203. The entire essay "'Genesis and Structure' in Phenomenology," in *Writing and Difference* is an investigation in terms of the skew structure. In speaking about the preface as being both "impossible and inescapable," Derrida refers to it as hybrid and two-faced, a relation of separation and inseparability: a slant without a straight up-and-down, which Barbara Johnson translates as "skew" (*Dis*, 11).

4. Parametrics, as a mode of criteriological argument, it should be pointed out, is not foreign to Derrida. It is, indeed, one of the few ways that even he can address the terms he invents within his grammatology. For instance, he gives a criteriological argument for the trace being the same as différance (*Gram*, 62).

5. There is a danger of reification here, which would semiotize the structure of nihilation. Sartre's phenomenological description cannot be reduced to a semiotic relation through this double non-negation. Sartre uses a fundamental negativity to invent a style of reasoning, —as well as to encompass the inarticulable precisely because it precedes articulation ontologically. The semiotic anteriority that Derrida provides would have no meaning for it.

6. Many commentators hold Sartre to his often-suggested deployment of the dialectic. One might mention Joseph Fell, Mark Poster, Ronald Aronson, Linda Bell (*Sartre's Ethics of Authenticity*), all of whom characterize the way he thinks as dialectical, even at the time of writing *Being and Nothingness*. Sartre does make reference to such deployment for himself, as in the instance of describing the cogito as a "dialectical instrument" (*BN*, 74). And indeed, his characterization of the for-itself (that it is what it is not, and is not what it is) has classically been interpreted as a dialectical formulation. The thesis of the present argument is that though it appears to be a dialectical formula, its underlying ontological reasoning is not.

7. They are not, however, conceptually alien to Derrida's own writing: Speaking of the trace, for instance, he says, "The immotivation of the trace ought now to be understood as an operation and not as a state, as an active movement, a demotivation, and not as a given structure" (*Gram*, 51).

8. I reproduce the original version of the passage in its entirety, since it will play a central role throughout this chapter. One of the ellipses (in the translation) is an entire sentence, omitted because it appeared to me only as an appositive elaboration of the sentence that follows and recapitulates it. For this French text, I am using *L'etre et le néant* (Paris: Gallimard, 1943), p. 308.

> Tout d'abord, il est l'être vers qui je ne tourne pas mon attention. Il est celui qui me regarde et que je ne regarde pas encore, celui qui me livre moi-même comme non-révélé, mais sans se révéler lui-même, celui qui m'est présent en tant qu'il me vise et non pas en tant qu'il est visé; il est le pôle concret et hors d'atteinte de ma fuite, de

> l'aliénation de mes possibles et de l'écoulement du monde vers un autre monde qui est le même et pourtant incommunicable avec celui-ci.
>
> Tout d'abord, le regard d'autrui, comme condition nécessaire de mon objectivité, est destruction de toute objectivité pour moi. Le regard d'autrui m'atteint à travers le monde et n'est pas seulement transformative de moi-même, mais métamorphose totale du monde. Je suis regardé dans un monde regardé. En particulier, le regard d'autrui—qui est regard-regardant et non regard-regard—nie mes distances aux objets et déplie ses distances propres. Ce regard d'autrui se donne immédiatement comme ce par quoi la distance vient au monde au sein d'une présence sans distance.

Though I have omitted the last sentential phrase of the first paragraph from my discussion of Sartre's reasoning structure, it is interesting as an invocation of the incommensurability that the skew relation structurally codifies at the heart of what it is used to describe.

9. Fredric Jameson, *Sartre: The Origin of a Style* (New Haven: Yale University Press, 1961); hereafter cited in the text as *OS*.

10. John Llewelyn, *Derrida on the Threshold of Sense* (New York: St. Martin's Press, 1982); hereafter abbreviated in the text as *DTS*; and Rodolphe Gasché, *The Tain of the Mirror*.

11. Llewelyn develops an extensive argument from Derrida's reference to the middle voice here, looking for a way to articulate a space between the active and the passive. Reasoning from Hegel, he discusses the sign as a middle ground between the sensible and the intelligible, or between the image and intuition. For Llewelyn, the image, as more universal, surpasses itself as idea, which in turn finds itself in the image between its sensibility and its intelligibility. Similarly, the absence of meaning in Derrida's deconstruction of the sign carries itself beyond the opposition of meaningful and meaningless. Llewelyn characterizes it as a chiasmus. The middle voice, for Llewelyn, is what a speaker would own, yet which would also speak from an exterior to the speaker, speak the exterior for the speaker.

12. Thanks to Harry Berger for this example.

13. Derrida uses just such an articulation to characterize the spacing of signs that "constitutes the origin of signification." And he quotes Saussure: "Language is a form and not a substance," because "in language, there are only differences." To which he adds, "Spacing (. . . the becoming-space of time and the becoming-time of space) is always the unperceived, the nonpresent, and the unconscious" (*Gram*, 68).

14. It is interesting that what Julia Kristeva calls the *chora*, though it has nothing to do with the notion of textual form being developed here, is nevertheless described by her in terms that are analogous: "The chora is not yet a position that represents something for someone (i.e., it is not a sign); it is not yet a signifier either; it is, however, generated in order to attain to this signifying position. . . . The chora is a modality of signifiance in which the linguistic sign is not yet articulated as the absence of an object and as the distinction between real and symbolic" (cf. *The Kristeva Reader*, ed. Teril Moi) (New York: Columbia University Press, 1986), p. 94. Thus, the chora represents, in this description, the beginning of a differentiation between the sign and its referent, rather than the beginning of an object becoming a sign; and textual form is the process of a textual object becoming a sign. Furthermore, Kristeva argues that the chora, in underlying figuration, is analgous to "vocal and kinetic rhythms." For textual form, this would be "discursive and tropic contours." But where the chora is barely discernible, if textual form is to be apprehended at all, it must be rendered discernible beyond that level, as what could potentially be a sign system in its own right.

15. Jacques Derrida, "La facteur de la verité," in *La carte postale: De Socrate à Freud et au-delà* (Paris: Flammarion, 1980), p. 441.

16. For the purposes of this essay, I will capitalize Always Already when I am using it as the name for a formal (rhetorical) structure.

17. Martin Heidegger, *Identity and Difference*, trans. Joan Stambaugh (New York: Harper and Row, 1969), p. 63; hereafter cited in the text as *ID*.

18. Martin Heidegger, *The Metaphysical Foundations of Logic*, trans. Michael Heim (Bloomington: Indiana University Press, 1984), p. 126. Heidegger uses the Always Already as a form of logic. For instance, in speaking of the "meaning of care," he says, "Meaning signifies the 'upon-which' [the already] of a primary projection in terms of which something can be conceived in its possibility as [always] that which it is" (*BT*, 371). We can take this further. The structure of care unfolds upon the three structures of existentiality, facticity, and fallenness (*BT*, 364). But these three components are given through implied stories about Being in the world in relation to itself: how it founds itself (existentiality), how it comports itself in its own eyes in being-in-the-world (facticity), and how it comports itself in the world in the world's eyes (fallenness). In other words, Heidegger recounts how the world narrates the form, and the narrative becomes what provides for the precondition for that form; the meaning of care, as narrativized, is what makes possible the structure of care. Form (structure) implies narrative which implies meaning which implies in turn form again. It is a circle, in which the ontic (form implies narrative) and the ontological (meaning implies form) are connected through the Always Already. What Heidegger leaves out, in an omission I shall critique further on, is a certain priority of narrative as the necessary implication of this circle. In Heidegger's text, it is the hidden, unrecognized ontological foundation. Narrative is the "What is . . . ?," the *es gibt*.

19. "The trace is not only the disappearance of origin . . . it means that the origin did not even disappear, that it was never constituted except reciprocally by a non-origin, the trace, which thus becomes the origin of the origin (*Gram*, 61).

20. Jacques Derrida, *De la grammatologie* (Paris: Editions de Minuit, 1967), p. 16; my translation.

21. Thanks to Hazel Barnes for pointing this out, in one of her lectures, in Boulder, Colorado, 1984.

Chapter 4

1. The main works of Roland Barthes to which I shall refer are: *Writing Degree Zero*, trans. Annette Lavers and Colin Smith (1967), hereafter cited in the text as *DZ*; *Elements of Semiology*, trans. Annette Lavers and Colin Smith (1967), hereafter cited in the text as *ES*; *Mythologies*, trans. Annette Lavers (1972), hereafter cited in the text as *Myth*; *Image, Music, Text*, trans. Stephen Heath (1977), cited as *IMT*; *S/Z*, trans. Richard Miller (1974), hereafter cited in the text as *S/Z*. All published by Hill and Wang, New York.

Barthes, in a manner that sets him apart from the other post-structuralists, engaged Sartre's thinking and debated him on the plane of the literary. *Writing Degree Zero* is his initial response to *What Is Literature?*, though he does not mention it in his text. Specifically, he challenges Sartre on the question of the nature of writing and on the possibility of a history of literature. Barthes offered a significantly different way of understanding discourse and the languages of writing from Sartre, but not in such a way as to negate the social thrust of what Sartre was attempting. Sartre took to heart much of what Barthes said, while contesting the general structuralist project, as I will argue in Chapter 6. Cf. an address Sartre gave in 1964, which is reprinted in *Que peut le litterature?*, ed. Yves Buin, Series L'Herne 10/18 (Paris:

L'inedit, 1966), pp. 107–27. On this subject, see also Silverman, *Inscriptions*; and Annette Lavers, *Roland Barthes: Structuralism and After* (Cambridge, MA: Harvard University Press, 1982).

2. One example is "zero degree writing" itself; this is writing that is wholly denotative, without connotation, or second-order significations. It is a hypothetical possibility, in which the text, in the process of being constituted by its purely denotational sentences, would have already exhausted its meaning. To the extent to which sentences become wholly transparent, the textuality that they constitute, which is itself a sign, becomes contentless, a mere integument; hence, an example of a significationless sign. Other examples are Barthes's notion of the "obtuse meaning" of a photographic image, and of the *punctum* (*IMT*, 60ff.); also the circularity of codes in the fashion system (cf. Barthes, *The Fashion System*, trans. Matthew Ward and Richard Howard, New York: Hill and Wang, 1983); finally, there is a moment of the operation of myth, which we shall look at below.

3. There are modes of discursive form that appear in writing as part of a poetic and function as a way of structuring the work. For instance, in her novel *Zami* (Watertown: Persephone Press, 1982), Audre Lorde deploys a form of preemption, of giving away the punch lines for each chapter early in the chapter. The effect is to fold her narratives in upon themselves, and delinearize them. It is a way of making the structure of the story, the interweaving of character and the communities described, more important than the outcome of the plot.

4. Eric Gould, *Mythical Intentions in Modern Literature* (Princeton: Princeton University Press, 1981).

5. *S/Z*, 139.

Balzac: "He had expected a dim room, his mistress seated by the fire, some jealous person nearby, death and love, an exchange of confidences in low voices, heart to heart."

Barthes: "In saying that Sarrasine '*had expected a dim room, some jealous person, death and love*,' etc. the discourse mingles three disconnected codes (each absorbing the others) from three different sources. The Code of Passion establishes what Sarrasine is supposed to be feeling. The Novelistic Code transforms this 'feeling' into literature: it is the code of an author in good faith, an author who has no doubt that the novelistic is a *just* (natural) expression of passion (Who, after all, contrary to Dante, does not know that passion comes from books?). The Ironic Code absorbs the 'naiveté' of the first two codes: as the novelist undertakes to speak of the character, the ironist undertakes to speak of the novelist."

6. A concomitant distinction exists between myth and fiction. In reading myth, one has a number of options. One can focus on the ideological concept, and on the emptiness of the signifier, in which case one resides in the myth, in its appropriation of the signifieds of the African soldier flattened into the background as form. One can focus on the fullness of the (first-order) meaning and see the concept as a detour, an alibi. Or one can focus on the dual role of the signifier, understanding its ambiguity, its fullness and emptiness, in which case one becomes a mythologist (*Myth*, 128). In reading fiction, a second level of possibility occurs. One can immerse oneself in the effect, which entails remaining within the first reading, the place where the braid appropriates the narrative, falling prey to its fictional spell. Or one can immerse oneself in a second reading, seeing the first as naive and grasping the fullness of the multilayered text. And finally, one can step back and study the codes in operation, distilling the essential differences between readings, the interplay of their fullness and emptiness. But in fiction, it is the codes that produce literal narrative meaning, on which narrativity itself operates as a unification, thereby constituting Barthesian mythification. Thus, the operation of myth constitutes the literal for reading fiction as fiction. And the role Barthes assigns to ideology (in myth) is formally inverted.

7. The notion of the "chiasmus" or "chiasm" seems to first appear, within the existentialist tradition, in Maurice Merleau-Ponty, for whom it also means an intertwining; *The Visible and the Invisible*, trans. Alphonso Lingus (Evanston, IL: Northwestern University Press, 1968), pp. 130–55; hereafter cited as *VI*. He uses it as a way of describing perception, a crossing into each other of vision and the visible.

> As though our vision were formed at the heart of the visible (VI, 130) . . . [and] the act of interrogating [the visible were] according to its own wishes. (VI, 133)

> There are not things first identical with themselves, which would offer themselves to the seer, nor is there a seer who is first empty and who, afterward, would open himself to them—but something to which we could not be closer . . . the gaze itself [that] envelops them. (VI, 131)

> What begins as a thing ends as consciousness of the thing; what begins as a "state of consciousness" ends as a thing. (VI, 215)

8. Jacques Derrida, *Marges de la philosophie* (Paris: Editions de Minuit, 1972), p. 188; my translation.

9. The terms "Man" and "he" are used by Heidegger, Sartre, and Derrida in their own texts to refer to humanity in general. This traditional usage is a rationalism that is both chauvinist and inseparable from metaphysical humanism. It needs to be dealt with as such. Where appropriate, I will put the term "man" in quotes, when discussing or critiquing these texts. It will not be used by me when presenting my own ideas. To have attempted to find a non-sexist term for humanity with respect to these texts would have been to ignore that tradition by rewriting it and thus not to deal with it even in the tangential manner done here. I will at times use the double articulation "his/her" or "s/he" to surpass and make mention of the male bias of humanism and of the English language. Some aspects of the sexism this represents are addressed later on.

10. A phenomenological version of this circle would read: Consciousness must be in order to define itself; it can only define itself for itself; it must define itself for itself in order to be. It is the attempt to solve this circularity, to straighten it out, that characterizes analytic philosophy.

11. Jean-Paul Sartre, *Existentialism and Human Emotions* (New York: Philosophical Library, 1957), p. 13; hereafter cited in the text as *EH*.

12. See John D. Caputo, *The Mystical Element in Heidegger's Thought* (Athens: Ohio University Press, 1978), for a discussion of Heidegger's notion of gelassenheit.

13. See also Fredric Jameson, *Sartre: The Origins of a Style*, pp. 114–16. Jameson gives a traditional reading to Sartre's use of the cogito, yet recognizes that there are inarticulable structures that lie beneath it. "The merely named cogito is the wordless, unexplained center of Sartre's philosophy." That Heidegger would overlook this is consistent with his account of the other (*BN*, 244–50).

14. *A Preface to Sartre*, 51–52. See also Jean-Paul Sartre, *The Transcendence of the Ego*, trans. Forrest Williams (New York: Noonday Press, 1957).

15. Ironically, Heidegger warns of inevitable misinterpretations of his own writing (LH, 225–26). In misinterpreting Sartre on the issue of terminology, he has done the same. Heidegger does not say that the question of Being precedes anything, but rather that it is more fundamental, and that ontology is blind until it has "clarified the meaning of Being . . . as its fundamental task" (*BT*, 31). He thus calls on "man" to return to Being as Sartre calls for a return to freedom's responsibility. But we can ask, is there such a thing as

a misreading? Differing readings emerge because the polyvalence of signs make alternative readings possible. Any reading, in striving for its own coherence of organization or thematic, will appear to have "misread" from the point of view of any other reading with a variant coherence. There are nothing but "misreadings" because all other readings are "other" readings (cf. *Gram*, 158). In fact, rereading a text a second time is a case in point. A second reading is always different from the first because one "knows the ending." The first and second readings are each misreadings in terms of the other. If a reading is always a "misreading," then there can be no "misreading," since there is no non-misreading from which to judge it as such (cf. *S/Z*).

16. Though Heidegger argues with this statement in "Letter on Humanism," his argument is gratuitous. He would change it to "we are on a plane where there is principally Being." But he argues that "plane" and Being are the same thing, and his sentence crumbles to "we are" and "Being"—or "in our Being, we are what there principally is." In effect, his dispute with Sartre on this idea devolves to the issue of including beings; that is, it is a difference concerning objectivity.

17. The correspondence of Being and Being-in-itself has been generally assumed. Fell, *Heidegger and Sartre*, makes extensive use of this correspondence. And Aronson, *Jean-Paul Sartre: Philosophy in the World*, refers to it without reference or comment.

18. Cf. for instance, Wilfrid Desan, *The Tragic Finale* (New York: Harper, 1957); and Aronson, *Jean-Paul Sartre: Philosophy in the World*, p. 92. Two notable attempts to resolve this question are Flynn, *Sartre and Marxist Existentialism*; and David Detmer, *Freedom as a Value* (LaSalle: Open Court Press, 1986).

19. Cf. *Marg*, 20 (note 23, Alan Bass). This is a notion that Derrida posits in the form of an economy (oikos, home, residence), differing between a metaphysical economy and a general economy, where economy is a metaphor for the profitable (fertile) or for profiteering without substantial investment (*WD*, 251ff.). In metaphysics, or a "restricted economy" of speculation, there is nothing that cannot be made to make sense (cents, percentage, profit), in the sense of getting something for nothing out of a discursive structure. For Derrida, this is the ultimate achievement of metaphysics. Beyond its limit, in a general economy that affirms that which exceeds meaning, there is a realm where there can be no speculative profit to be gained. Passing to that economy, by exceeding meaning and refusing speculation, is Derrida's goal, or the tenor of the deconstructive, toward which Heidegger's inquiry took the first steps.

20. We recall that the "Always Already," for both Heidegger and Derrida, is a double non-negation, a double skew relation. For Heidegger, the "always already" is inseparable from the "we" that understands, and imparts an internal difference to the "we" as a mode of ontological difference. And similarly for Sartre: the double non-negation structures the relation of the for-itself's situational freedom in its project and its freedom as absolute. It names the congruence between the first-person singular of Sartre's narrativized subject and the third-person singular of Heideggerian Dasein, the congruence between "syntactical persons" and the doubled (and fractured) "we."

21. For a more complete analysis of the circles in Heidegger's text, see Steve Martinot, "A Cyclo-analysis of 'Being and Time,'" *Auslegung* 16, no. 1 (Winter 1990).

22. Martin Heidegger, "Building Dwelling Thinking," in *Poetry, Language, Thought*, trans. Albert Hofstadter (New York: Harper, 1971). "When I go toward the door of the lecture hall, I am already there, and I could not go to it at all if I were not such that I am there. I am never here only, . . . rather, I am there, that is, I already pervade the room, and only thus can I go through it" (p. 157). See also Martin Heidegger, *On the Way to Language*,

trans. Peter D. Hertz (New York: Harper, 1971), p. 12. Heidegger says, "Only the way back will lead us forward." It is important to notice that the forward and backward analytic remains central to both early and later writings.

23. In *Being and Time*, Heidegger affirms the circle in three different ways. He defends his "interrogation of Being" against a rationalist charge of logical circularity in having stipulated that a Being is required whose mode of Being is to question Being, and which "gets its essential character from what is inquired about—namely, Being" (*BT*, 27). His argument does not lend itself to logical linearity because each premise is already the essential condition for the others. He further extricates this "method" from the realm of method by reiterating that Dasein's subject matter and its mode of inquiry are the same thing, rendering "circle" descriptive rather than "logical." "If we must first define an entity *in its Being*, and if we want to formulate the question of Being only on this basis, what is this but going in a circle?" (*BT*, 27). Heidegger's third use of circularity, which extends his sense of formalist structure, is exemplified by his discussion of "understanding" (*BT*, 194), which I address here.

24. Again, many will argue that Heidegger would object to this use of the terms "form and content" with respect to his text. And it is true that for Heidegger, "form and content" reflect a duality that has since Plato been at the core of metaphysics. For Heidegger, in general, the notions of form and content represent a false separation between subject and object (cf. Chapter 2, note 23). Instead, form should be already understood as its content, beyond which the object becomes presence and instrumentality. "Form" would function as location or structure, and the meaning that structure gives to what it is "about," to what it concerns or to what concerns itself with it. Such a rendition would be especially germane here; form emerges here not as an ontological but a structural relation.

25. Heidegger constructs circles of this braided form again and again in *Being and Time*. For instance, in his discussion of understanding, Heidegger discerns three elements, possibility, projection, and transparency (*BT*, 184ff.), which structure the way interpretation makes the implicit explicit. "Understanding" names the way Dasein confronts its possibilities, which functions as familiarity. It projects its possibilities ahead of itself and encounters the world in transparency as unconcealed in itself. Projection becomes the form possibility takes; transparency becomes the form projection takes; and possibility becomes the form that transparency takes. It is this form of interrelation that Heidegger refers to as equiprimordiality. Possibility provides the content for projection, projection provides the content for transparency, and transparency provides the content for possibility. Out of this, interpretation constitutes the explicit.

It remains to add (in this case) that these three elements—possibility, projection, and transparency—each have a traditional meaning that Heidegger projects upon a metaphor (understanding) whose content in turn is left unarticulated. They structure themselves as a form whose source of meaning is what that metaphor signifies. In leaving it unarticulated, Heidegger renders that structural form the source of its meaning, the ground of understanding itself. This "understanding triad" structures the way meaning arrives in the world and is attributed to it. The "aboutness" or "object" that bodies forth toward understanding is eclipsed; possibility, projection, and transparency provide themselves with their own content. The object is already understood as the past of understanding (recognition) and always up ahead, deferred by the endlessness and cohesion of the circle.

A similar triad is constructed for objects (actions or events), which appear or are discovered as an instrumentality for something in which one is involved (*BT*, 121). "Involvement" names the way one's relatedness to the object is grasped as the object itself. Through involvement, the object will have an "objective" quality. And the two are mediated by an "assignment" of significance. "Assignment," in assigning the "thing" its significance, clothes it in objectivity and purpose. If objectivity is already an assignment of significance, it relates backward to that assignment that lets something be an involvement and forward to its instrumentality. For each, there is a backward and forward movement. They are equiprimordial. Involvement is constitutive of assignment based on objectivity; assignment is constitutive of objectivity based on involvement; objectivity is constitutive of involvement based on assignment.

Interpretation is composed of three structures, which he designates as an as-structure, a fore-structure, and Meaning (*Sinn*), each of which is in turn a triadic circle (*BT,* 189ff.). For instance, the fore-structure is a triad of fore-having, fore-sight, and fore-conception, each of which represents a different relation to what exists "in advance." In its "entityhood" (textually) as a circular structure, the fore-structure of the apprehension of the object provides the form for the projected explicitness of the as-structure; Meaning similarly provides the form for the fore-structure, its expression in understanding; and the as-structure provides the form for Meaning, its relatedness to recognition.

It is worth noting that because understanding is already an assignment of significance, it appears as prior familiarity with the object. That is, understanding reveals itself as primordial recognition, a recognition constituted by an unrecognized past. This reveals something crucial for understanding consciousness; namely, that recognition precedes cognition. The mediation of "attention to" renders this reversal coherent in understanding the world as meanings, which is implicit in the way Heidegger restructures the dimensions of attention, of being "there," as Meaning, an as-structure, and a fore-structure.

Many other circularities are demonstrable in Heidegger as a form of his logic. They are part of Heidegger's process of refusing the (false) definitiveness of metaphysics. They represent, in his text, a composite of literal, poetic, and structural exposition. He does not present them as literal circles; they are implicit as "instructions" for their construction in his expositions.

26. And we might note that this gives a different aura to Heidegger's disclaimer about the German language in his discussion of Holderlin. For Holderlin, German is to be understood as the world-historical language. Heidegger argues that Holderlin is not being nationalistic but seeing the German language in its "nearness to the source" of Being, as destinal rather than regional (LH, 218). But we now see that there are more ways than the regional to be chauvinist with respect to language.

27. A case in point is Sartre's attack on anti-Semitism. Sartre argues in *Anti-Semite and Jew* (trans. George Becker, New York: Grove Press, 1948) that the choice to acquiesce or rebel against anti-Semitism is never simple nor absent. But Elizabeth Grosz, in a talk on Jewish exile and marginalization (UCSC, 1989) points out that Sartre understands the Jew as created by the anti-Semite, and as one who seeks to assimilate through emphasizing the universal; but, she adds, he leaves out the positive existence of Judaism itself for Jews, and objectifies them in their situation, as only effects of anti-Semitism. The title of her lecture was "Judaism and Exile: The Ethics of Otherness." It was published in *New Formations* 12 (Winter), pp. 77–88.

But for Sartre, to say that the Jew is created by the anti-Semite is only to say that the Jew is a person in the situation of an anti-Semitic society, as given, and given to him/herself by that society. That is, there is a difference between the essence of Judaism as a culture and the situation of the Jew in anti-Semitic society. Also, the Jew does not create that person in that situation because the Jew does not participate in creating that situation. Grosz herself says that otherness cannot be self-chosen because it is always the result of a power relation. On Grosz's second point, Sartre is speaking of the "inauthentic Jew," the person who accepts the anti-Semitic characterizations and humanistically seeks to universalize himself in order to escape them. For Sartre, both the authentic and inauthentic are in relation to anti-Semitism, for that is where the relevance of the question arises—and thus is neither objective nor subjective. A person's relation to Judaism is relevant to the choice of authenticity or inauthenticity, which Sartre merely says each Jew confronts. It is the choice Derrida confronted as a philosopher (and as an ethical being) in critically addressing the ethnocentric universalization of the philosophical colloquium at which he spoke.

28. Victor Farias, *Heidegger and Nazism*, trans. Paul Burrell (Philadelphia: Temple University Press, 1989). Cf. Thomas Sheehan, review of *Heidegger and the Nazis*, by Victor Farias, *New York Review of Books*, June 16, 1988. See also Gunther Neske and Emil Kettering, eds., *Martin Heidegger and National Socialism* (New York: Paragon, 1990), for an overview of the issue.

29. Sartre is noteworthy for his continual deployment of narrative in his ontological writing, beyond the merely exemplary. Narrative preserves the particularity of the subject within a generalizing exposition. Sartre explains, in an interview with Alain Koehler (*Perspectives du Theatre* no. 3, March 1960: 18–23; no. 4, April 1960: 5–9), that philosophy misses the singular, what transpires for or happens to the individual. Narrative remedies this by reasserting the specificity of the subject, while complementing it by signifying that what is generalizable is precisely the necessity to preserve specificity. Thus, Sartre has often turned to drama and fiction to resolve or investigate questions that could not be sufficiently explored at the level of philosophical generality. In "The Itinerary of a Thought," in *Between Existentialism and Marxism* (New York: Morrow, 1974, p. 49), Sartre says, "I use fiction—guided and controlled, but nonetheless fiction—to explore why, let us say, Flaubert wrote one thing on the 15th March and the exact opposite on the 21st March, to the same correspondent, without worrying about the contradiction. My hypotheses are in this sense a sort of invention of the personage." See also "The Purposes of Writing" in the same volume.

CHAPTER 5

1. Hazel Barnes translates *le regard* as the "look." In recent years, others have used the term "the gaze" to name the situation that Sartre describes as *le regard* (in particular, some Lacanian and feminist thinkers). I use Barnes's translation; for me, "to look" connotes greater directedness and activity than "to gaze" and thus is more consistent with Sartre's phenomenological focus. But also, the discourses that have brought "the gaze" to contemporary prominence have done so more in terms of ideological structures and political discourses. As ideological, the notion of "the gaze" announces a sense of third-person account, rather than the first-person perspective of the one looked at, as in Sartre's account. (It appears that "le look" has recently become a Franglais term in France, though referring to fashion rather than ontology.)

2. There are extensive commentaries on the look: for instance, Hazel Barnes, *An Existentialist Ethics* (Chicago: University of Chicago Press, 1967); Linda Bell, *Sartre's Ethics of Authenticity* (Tuscaloosa: University of Alabama Press, 1989); Marjorie Grene, *Sartre* (Washington, DC: University Press of America, 1983); Thomas Flynn, *Sartre and Marxist Existentialism* (Chicago: University of Chicago Press, 1984); and Schroeder, *Sartre and His Predecessors*. Linda Bell focuses on the relation between the look and bad faith, and describes how each plays out in terms of the other; she considers it mostly from the perspective of the objectivizing nature of being seen. Marjorie Grene complains about the

bad (philosophical) faith of the look. Flynn and Schroeder, in particular, recognize the philosophical importance of what Sartre has done within the problematic of other subjectivities.

3. Heidegger seems more Manichean when he claims that in "the encountering of *Others*, one is oriented by the Dasein which is in each case one's *own*." For instance, Heidegger says, "Everyday Being-with-one-another maintains itself between the two extremes of positive solicitude—that which leaps in and dominates, and that which leaps forth and liberates" (*BT*, 159). For Heidegger, "solicitude" is the form "concern" takes in one's being-with-others (rather than "care"; *BT*, 157). The other is encountered because Dasein is always Being-with, and the other is "encountered in his Dasein-with in the world" (*BT*, 156). By "Dasein-with," Heidegger means "that Being for which the Others who are, are freed within-the-world." That is, Being-with characterizes one's own Dasein, while Dasein-with characterizes the Other's Dasein "freed by its world for a Being-with" (*BT*, 159). Solicitude pertains to helping "the Other to become transparent to himself *in* his care and to become *free for* it" (*BT*, 159). Sartre argues that the "'with' [of Dasein-with] does not intend the reciprocal relation of recognition and of conflict" (*BN*, 245); it is an "oblique interdependence." That is, for Heidegger, others are encountered "from out of the world" or "environmentally" (*BT*, 155) and, as such, they are encountered existentially in a "sameness of Being" (*BT*, 154). The negative sense of this sameness, a "not of one's choosing," Sartre suggests, gets lost in the positivity of the "sameness" centered in Dasein's own, which constitutes its solipsism.

4. Cf. Gayatri Spivak's introduction to *Of Grammatology*, from which this formulation for the sign is borrowed (*Gram*, xvii). The other's difference from an object is what is contained in its being an object, and its difference from being an other as subject is what is contained in its otherness. This recalls the Derridean trace: "The pure trace is différance . . . the différance which opens appearance and signification" (*Gram*, 62, 65).

5. Sartre's terms for becoming an object for another are "objectivize" and "objectivation"; he reserves "objectification" for one's own material expression or reification in the material world, or representation by one's objects; and "alienation" for him is subsumption by one's objects through a social structure (including interpersonal relationships)—e.g., in the sense that the worker is alienated in his/her product.

6. This notion makes reference to the mutual exclusion between perception and imagination that Sartre theorizes; cf. *The Psychology of the Imagination*. One cannot perceive the other looking, and imagine oneself looked at, at the same time. The other's eyes behold me without distance, while I can perceive them only in the distance as objects. To intend oneself as looked at causes one's perception of the eyes that are looking to "pass into the background" (*BN*, 258).

7. Schroeder dissects and analyzes the look and its transformations most clearly (*SHP*). In his discussion, he delineates five transformations that the subject undergoes in the other's look. The three I will consider are in reverse order from Schroeder's. The fourth transformation for Schroeder is that one becomes an organizer of the world in terms of the Other, that a sense of objectivity arises from the possibility of the other as subject. And the fifth is that one falls into enslavement to the situation; one becomes "dependent at the center of a freedom which is not mine and which is the very condition of my being" (*BN*, 267). Both of these transformations, though closely connected to the first three, have a greater proximity to Sartre's ontological discussion of Being-for-Others than to the structure being addressed here. Schroeder's dissection of the moments and minutiae of Sartre's discussion is quite meticulous. He even partially anticipates the double non-negation as a structure; for him,

however, it only constitutes an irrational stylistic element of Sartre's writing. Schroeder argues in an analytic vein, which I think often leads him toward an empiricism (a "commonsense" approach) and away from the phenomenological.

8. Schroeder contests the mutual exclusion in Sartre's account, namely, the idea that in the interaction one is either a subject seeing the other as an object, or an object seen by the other as subject, but not both. "One can experience the Other as looking while simultaneously experiencing his previous look as looked-at; one can even anticipate the new look" (*SHP*, 198). But Sartre is not speaking of the psychological, or of an empirical reality as it might appear to a third person, but to one's moments of ontological awareness. Schroeder posits two people looking into each other's eyes, which may look as if the mutual exclusion had been transcended. But this again is a third-person point of view. Yet to be engaged in such a closeness, for each participant, to see only one pair of eyes and speak to only one listener, engenders an exchange that obeys the Sartrean exclusion principle, insofar as the objectivations take hold ontologically even in intimacy. As I argue later, to listen is to be the look, and to speak is to be the one looked at and discovered. Ultimately, Schroeder's empiricism privileges the situational over the ontological, his own view over that of the first person in the account.

9. Interestingly enough, this has presented more of a political than a philosophical problem to some commentators. For both Flynn and Aronson, the absence of a possible synthesis for one's being-for-others is a problem. And both see the problem emerging from the very absoluteness of Sartrean ontological freedom and the endlessness of interpersonal conflict it entails. The problem is that Sartre seems to obviate any possibility of social solidarity or collective responsibility. For Aronson, this would then contradict Sartre's pretensions to revolutionism; it renders impossible a society in which free individuals treat all others as free. Thus, he is mystified, as is Wilfrid Desan, by the confusion Sartre creates in using the term *freedom* for both ontological being, as the foundation for both subjectivity and objectivation, and the situational freedom of the political or historical.

10. Sartre's notion of freedom is a similar conflation of disparate dimensions, which constitutes a sense of "ontological difference" for freedom in Sartre's discourse. As Thomas Flynn and David Detmer have argued, there is such a distinction to be made between ontological and situational freedom. Ontological freedom is the foundation of the for-itself, the ground of the subject and one's choice of being. Situational freedom refers to one's choices of strategies and tactics within one's choice of being, one's choice of fundamental project, but taken in terms of the constraints and unfreedoms given by one's situation. Cf. Flynn, *Sartre and Marxist Existentialism*; and Detmer, *Freedom as a Value*.

11. Schroeder argues that the situation of the look does not exclude positive or pleasurable feelings (*SHP*, 190) and attempts to broaden this generally by renaming the Sartrean notion of being-for-others as the "social self." For Schroeder, "the social self is like a blank slate that the Other-as-subject fills in, like a cage created and sustained by the Other-as-subject" (*SHP*, 184). That is, the "social self" is a kind of "border between Other and self" (*SHP*, 215). But the notion that this "social self" is a self sets it somewhat at odds with Sartre; it makes it difficult to find residence for it in Sartre's scheme of things, either as a self that comes and goes situationally or as an ontological moment of the for-itself, the subject. But I would argue that Schroeder's cases of positive feelings are proper examples of the look, and not at all outside Sartre's purview (that is, not requiring additional theoretical framework); they only appear to be if one neglects the difference between existential shame and moral shame. The central element of Sartre's narrative is the transformation from being

prereflectively and selflessly engrossed to being given an awareness of oneself as a "myself"—one's presence to oneself through one's presence to the other's eyes without distance. And this would not necessarily be obviated by a situation of face-to-face encounter, insofar as one "loses oneself" in what one is attempting to convey to the other, and insofar as the other has become embedded in one's act of discourse. Indeed, one's being-for-others, in its lived facticity, may be the situation in which one loses oneself. If Sartre abstracts the transformation to selfhood, it is in order to focus on it. Sartre often accentuates the negative to highlight his examples. One might add that if the longing look appeared to violate a taboo, it might produce repulsion rather than attraction, while the structure of the self-as-object would remain the same.

12. Cf. Chapter 4, note 29. It is interesting to note that Derrida takes issue with this. In an interview published in *Gendai Shiso*, in Japan ("Pourquoi pas Sartre?"), Derrida complains that Sartre writes his biographies under the continual aegis of a general philosophical notion that one arrives at identity through the other, in which case, there is a common core, a universality already built into Sartre's attempts to present the figures of his biographies in their individuality (Derrida mentions Genet, Baudelaire, and Mallarmé).

13. I use the male pronoun because Sartre does—and is, as first-person narrator. Sartre omits any mention of there being a gender orientation to the look. But given gender roles as they exist in this culture, can the look be gender neutral, even as Sartre is using it? If not, then the subject and Other-as-object that emerges from the self-as-object is gender-specific and gendered, a political operation of différance (not simply a difference) that must be understood. No critique of the gender specificity of Sartre's account has been done. Laura Mulvey has written on the male gaze with respect to cinema, and a number of authors have investigated the Lacanian gaze from the point of view of a gender critique, assuming that it is structurally the same as Sartre's, simply because Lacan invokes the Sartrean "look" in his use of it. But the Lacanian gaze is not the look. The "gaze" as deployed by Lacan is a third-person *regard*, experienced by a first-person subject, but then used to semiotize the world through that third-person presence rather than to apprehend the other (third person) as a subject. In Lacan's discourse, the gaze would be homologous to the self-as-other-as-object; that is, it pertains to the self but has the structure of Sartre's account of the other-as-object. For film theory, the gaze is often understood in the first person, the nature of the audience gaze at the cinematic image. All could be considered "ontic" variants of Sartre's ontological account. Hence they shift the look away from its ontologically interactive quality of subjectivizing the other to a means of studying moments of objectification. Some steps toward a gender critique of the look are attempted later in this work.

14. In his autobiographical work, *The Words*, a similar structure is engendered. Sartre writes his past self as one who can then look into the future in order to render the present writer the object "Sartre." That is, the former already-lived "Sartre" becomes the imagined other who sees the present Sartre (at the historical keyhole), and through whom the present Sartre tells of the present Sartre's meaning through that past Sartre in a metanarrative. Jean-Paul Sartre, *The Words*, trans. Bernard Frechtman (Greenwich, CT: Fawcett, 1964).

15. It is the existence of possible alternate systems of descriptions or morality of conduct, such as an absence of reprobation for voyeurism, that indicate the centrality of a narrative system as the only way of not generalizing one mode of ethical response. Indeed, the Other, upon discovery, might surprise the "I" by wanting to take a look through the keyhole himself. Or the "I" might interpret the discoverer's disapproving look as referring to the possibility of exclusion and invite him to take a look. The narrativity and the ethics of the situation are inseparable.

16. Sartre would not deny this. One lives the stories that provide meaning to comportment, feeling, etc. in passivity; one is beset by them, as indirect means of making oneself who one already is (*CDR*, 234). See also *CDR*, Book I, Chapter 3, Sections 3 and 4.

17. This gives added weight to Sartre's notion that anger does not simply sweep one away, but that one submits to it, accedes to it. Cf. Jean-Paul Sartre, *An Outline for a Theory of Emotions*, trans. B. Frechtman (New York: Philosophical Library, 1948), Chapter 3; hereafter cited in the text as *Emotions*. One chooses anger by choosing to interpret a situation, or the actions of an Other, as angering, as being in violation in a manner that deserves anger; that is, one narrativizes the other as one who has chosen to act in an angering manner. Though the notion of double recognition (and double narrativity itself) is an extrapolation from his account of the look, Sartre would later develop it into an important element of his critique of the social. In the *CDR*, it becomes what he calls "exigency," and in *L'idiot de la famille*, it becomes part of the entire process of acculturation (cf. Chapter 6).

18. Maurice Merleau-Ponty starts to make a similar point in *The Phenomenology of Perception* (trans. Colin Smith, New York: Routledge Kegan Paul, 1962) when he says that "feelings and passional conduct are invented like words" (p. 189) in the context of his assertion that "the most familiar thing appears indeterminate as long as we have not recalled its name" (p. 177) and "the act by which I lend myself to the spectacle must be recognized as irreducible to anything else" (p. 185). Where he stops short is in associating the sociality of recognition with the name rather than the narrative. We shall see below how that fits into the scheme being developed here.

19. This should not be confused with "training." When a child eats his mashed potatoes with his fingers and his mother smacks his hand and says, "You should be ashamed," a content is given to the term *shame*, or *ashamed*. But to interdict oneself as a result of such castigation and to understand Others' reprehension (what is narrated for their look as Other-as-subject), their feeling of disgust, for instance, at seeing mashed potatoes eaten with the fingers, are two different things. The latter requires a system of explanations (of reprehensibility) and analogy (about reactions of disgust), all of which narrativize the person (directly or indirectly) within and with respect to descriptions or presentations of disgusting things, or Others' actions toward the disgusting. One understands another's facial expressions that enact feelings of disgust because at one time someone explained disgust as "I don't like it; it makes me feel . . ." together with an enactment of those expressions (generally engendered between children most overtly). In principle, it could also stretch forward into the future as an endless chain of narrative signifiers.

20. A certain confirmation of this can be gleaned from its contrary. There are accounts of feelings that have not been narrativized, that remain forms of background malaise and are not seen as common experiences. An example is the dissatisfaction with the life of the middle-class housewife revealed by Betty Friedan in her book *The Feminine Mystique* (New York: Dell, 1970). It was not until Friedan herself brought women together to tell each other their similar stories that these feelings became articulated. At that moment of mutual recognition, these women realized that they were not alone, that the feelings were commonly experienced by others. Thus, the first step toward generating a community known as the women's movement was taken. But prior to that, the inchoate dissatisfaction with what had been presented as the epitome of success in life had no way of naming or recognizing itself.

21. *Gram*, 60. In this passage, Derrida is addressing "experience" as it appears to the history of metaphysics and argues that an understanding of "its ultimate foundation"

(avoiding "naïve" critiques) will involve a deconstruction having already "exhausted the resources of the concept of experience" (*Gram*, 60). But if experience is always recognized through prior social narratives (i.e., without origin, and in particular without origin in "experience"—though perhaps in the "history" of experience), then the concept of experience would in principle be inexhausible. To encounter that inexhausibility would be to escape the realm of familiarity, of recognizability, of repetition, of all that would name and reify experience as an object to be apprehended. With the particularity of narrative that engenders experience for the subject from an originless elsewhere, one is at its ultimate foundation.

22. The interplay of social discourse and individual experience has generally been understood as a dialectic. That is the way Gould (see note 4, chapter 4) treats it, for instance. But through the NMN-structure, a more complex structure of discursivity can be discerned, functioning underneath the appearance of dialectical articulations. In the look, it forms an interface between the individual and the social by deconstructing the spacing between the self-as-object and the Other-as-subject.

23. One could bring this meditation down to earth in terms of the various denigrations that people suffer as the objects of such socially instituted regimes of domination as class exploitation, racialization, gender hierarchy, etc. In a sense, they reflect and rely on a social refusal on the part of the dominant to be read by the other, a refusal to be the other to others. While the dominant attain their subjectivity because it is granted them by those they objectify, they withhold from those others, through that subject-object relation, the ability to be apprehended as subjects. To be read, to grant the other, the dominated, their subjectivity, their ability to speak for themselves, to present oneself as readable while reading the other, would break the relation of domination. It is that refusal on the part of the dominant that renders their relation non-reciprocal, non-dialectical, a one-sided structure of recognition and non-recognition.

24. In the "dialogue" Derrida enters into with Socrates (cf. "Plato's Pharmakon" in *Dissemination*), Socrates extols the virtue of speech because the listener confronts the speaker in dialogue and thus can question his/her assumptions. When reading a text, because the writer is not there, one must accept those assumptions in order to follow the text's argument; writing is if not fraudulent at least subjecting. Derrida rejoins that Socrates's argument is fraudulent because it is Plato's argument, and it is in writing. Indeed, it could be presented to us in no other way, because all meaning is constituted by some kind of inscription. And still, a reader can question a text's assumptions. One of the ways this is done is precisely by inventing an author (Plato) who lurks within the text and whom the reader can confront. This gives the reader distance from the text, from what that author says, across which to question it; and positions the text within a global discourse in which to judge it fraudulent or not.

25. One might merely mention the fact that many men feel isolated or alone in their relations to women; in part this is because the man generalizes the woman he is with as a woman and hence renders her unknowable to himself. In his joint activities with this woman, he participates as if with a stranger whom he apprehends as more than familiar and with a non-stranger he has already rendered nonexistent through having generalized her. To the extent that she lives the present with him, with neither past nor future that is her own, he is alone. In Sartre's terms, the project of intersubjectivity may be unrealizable, but the act of generalization of the other short-circuits the oscillation of objectivations in which the affections, intimacies, and desires of conjoint activity have a ground on which to overlay their meanings.

from its foundation" (p. 119). His charge is that Derrida is inventing a duplicity in order to reveal it.

But in Rousseau's obsessive concern with his detractors in the *Reveries*, the duplicity is there. Rousseau's writing undermines what he attempts to "say." First, Rousseau's speech against his detractors, if it were speech and were addressed to them, would put him in total choler, on his own "confession." It is writing that modifies this and indeed makes it possible for him to not address them while addressing them. Speech becomes possible because he writes. Second, Rousseau undergoes agonies, at his detractors' hands, at a considerable distance from any self-control or self-instigation, as presence. That he runs from them to be alone, and thus unaffected, both manifests his affect in writing and dispells their presence to the level of the inoperative in writing of them as if they were not there and thus do not have any effect upon him. The "delicate transposition from literary statement to its empirical referent" (p. 120) that de Man invokes does not occur. The referent is rewritten. Third, the detractors are a metaphor for Rousseau's aloneness, a state to which he fled not only at the moment of encountering them but all his life. His fear of encountering them is metaphoric for this aloneness, the meaning given by the form of distance he adopts in both *The Confessions* and *Reveries*. What de Man is blind to is the shift produced by a written narrative of the other; he centers his thinking in the critic (insight), from which the other is excluded (not in sight) through his (de Man's) abstraction of critical "sight."

By presenting Rousseau's notion of fear as a utility rather than a passion, de Man rewrites Rousseau. When Derrida quotes Rousseau's view of fear and its language (*Gram*, 276), fear is preserved as a passion, as relative to an Other. De Man criticizes Derrida for not seeing the figurative in Rousseau's passion and thus rewriting Rousseau. That is, Derrida has not taken Rousseau's psychology into account. But there is a psychology in Derrida that de Man is missing. If the passions can be known only through a figure, then the figure becomes the real referent for knowledge of the passion; though metaphoric of the passion, it then literalizes itself as that passion. Because fictions are literary and figural, de Man thinks they must operate as such; that is, as reference rather than referent. But the figure can operate only literally; otherwise "operation" itself makes no sense. In de Man's exposition, the figure flattens the passion against the figural. There is no metaphoric meaning if only the metaphor is possible. In Derrida, Rousseau's passion is sandwiched between two levels of discourse; in de Man, the two levels have been shifted; they no longer sandwich Rousseau, but vie for which will represent him. De Man may be correct when he says that there is a difference between Rousseau's story and Derrida's story of Rousseau's story, but what he points to is not the difference.

10. On this sense of the act of naming, cf. Merleau-Ponty; *The Phenomenology of Perception*, pp. 120, 176ff.

11. Irene Harvey is another who is fascinated by Derrida's terms and seeks to philosophize them. In her book, *Derrida and the Economy of Différance* (Bloomington: Indiana University Press, 1986), she regards these "terms" not as a system but as a critique of anteriority itself with respect to language. And she wonders if these terms or instrumentalities perhaps become a language themselves for textuality, one heretofore inaccessible to philosophical thought. And if so, then they present a theorization of that language. In approaching this, Harvey takes a Kantian path, focusing on the "necessary conditions of possibility" for textuality, such as its inevitable nontransparency. Where Kant offers a critique of reason, Derrida offers a critique of critique (p. 6). And to address this, Harvey focuses on Derrida's neologisms as the place where a form of Kantian transcendental would function. If différance, for instance, is the condition of possibility for difference, and thus of

signs, it is then the condition of possibility of any metaphysics, because it is the condition of possibility of textuality and hence of any text. It becomes part of the foundation of metaphysics as well. If différance is one of the points of deconstruction of metaphysics, that is, metaphysics as a condition of possibility for deconstruction, then metaphysics becomes what makes deconstruction possible. By operating in the interstices between the given (as assumption) and the non-given (as the conditions of possibility of assumption), Derrida's neologisms are themselves the necessary condition of possibility even for a deconstructive argument (p. 51).

But the notion of transcendental would be too conceptual for Derrida (and he has said so; States of Theory). To see the Derridean instrumentalities as transcendentals implies that the instrumentalities are also artifacts of language, as opposed to an infrastructure, precisely because of the priority of their form. If they are to reveal something fundamental about the structure of meaning, it must be beyond the interstice between the metaphysical and the anagogic or unspeakable (unspoken). Yet, the analogics between Derrida and Kant move to a space beyond language itself, a space of a uniqueness of idiom, imagination, death, and writing (p. 150). If language produces meaning as a structure (of differences), when metaphysics effaces those differences in order to claim to be that source itself (p. 190), for Harvey, this means that language begins with a certain negativity, a retreat out of earshot in order to become language. The double retreat of language from its anterior conditions that Harvey describes invokes a phenomenological descriptiveness that is not dissimilar in form to the Sartrean double flight of consciousness in fleeing toward the future and from self toward its project. Sartre is even more germaine to a sense of negativity that threads its way through her account of language—for instance, in understanding the Derridean notion of the trace as memory. It is as if she started in one language and ended in the other.

12. There are, however, fictional narratives that project idealizations of a post-patriarchal world. One might mention Monique Wittig, *Les guerrillieres*, trans. David LeVay (Boston: Beacon, 1969); or Marge Piercy, *Woman at the Edge of Time* (New York: Knopf, 1976).

13. Simone de Beauvoir, *The Second Sex*, trans. H. M. Parshley (New York: Knopf, 1953).

14. Helene Cixous, "The Laugh of Medusa," in *Signs*, I(4), (Summer, 1976), p. 892.

15. Sartre was oddly far from being a feminist theorist. While he attempted to understand and theorize the colonial relation and the racism it engendered to disguise itself and abrogate its responsibility for its oppressions, he did not extend this to gender domination and the sexism it established as its mask and cutting edge. And while he theorized anti-Semitism and sought to understand the situation that forced a no-win choice of authenticity upon the Jew, he did not extend this type of analysis to patriarchy, to the parallel way in which it was antiwoman and situationally forced no-win choices of authenticity upon women. In *The Second Sex*, Simone de Beauvoir addresses the latter question in terms of the situational necessities faced by women, that "one is not born a woman, but becomes one" through acquiescence or rejection of given avenues of authenticity. And in *The Ethics of Ambiguity* (trans. Bernard Frechtman, New York: Citadel Press, 1964), she addresses the chauvinist mind and its many forms of bad faith—in greater detail, and with more grounded thinking, than Sartre.

16. An interesting study on such cultural specificity, though written from a colonialist point of view, designed to outflank the politically obstructive effects of cultural differences, is Edward Hall, *The Silent Language* (Greenwich: Fawcett, 1959).

17. In terms of distant (metanarrated) representation, we might note the following. The ability to address the sociality of a "designated" non-social question such as emotion opens

another avenue of discourse on the "reality" of the subject, history, and how the empiricism of metaphysical presupposition manifests itself in human operations and structures. For instance, Foucault addressed the question of how to discover the foundations of human relations and power, and not fall prey to a determinism or an ineluctable self-referentiality. But to view such things as social power or sexuality through a historicity that is discernible in discursive transformation leaves a gap to be bridged between the structure of those discourses and the way in which people live them experientially. The NMN-structure suggests a bridging of that gap. What the NMN-structure provides is the separation and immediacy by which social discourses and human lived experience become instrumentalities for each other.

18. Silverman, *Inscriptions*, pp. 236ff.

19. Considering the leader of a movement or organization in this way is not to place that personage within any of the group dynamics that Sartre describes in the *Critique of Dialectical Reason*, namely group-in-fusion, pledged group, or institution. There he is concerned with the forms of group subjectivity as they oscillate between seriality and fusion. The focus of this discussion of the leader is the "look" at the level of the social, of appearing in the eyes of a group, at whatever level of cohesion it exists, and of its members apprehending themselves in the look of the leader. What is at stake here is not social dynamics or historical motility as in the *Critique*, but the significations that constitute the relation of members and leaders through the operation of their being-for-others.

20. Iteration, différance, and spacing are the operations rather than the characteristics or qualities of arche-writing, writing in general (*Gram*, 56, 70, 91). (This is also the central argument of "Signature Event Context" in *Margins of Philosophy*.) Writing in general subsumes the interstices of what becomes articulable, what becomes language; that is, writing in general is that for which language is a metaphor (*Gram*, 15). This suggests that one of the problems of language is the intelligibility of a metaphor whose metaphoric meaning remains unknowable or inarticulable. Such a metaphor must literalize itself, that is, substitute its literal meaning for its unknowable metaphoric meaning. "It is not, therefore, a matter of inverting the literal meaning and the figurative meaning but of determining the 'literal' meaning of writing as metaphoricity itself" (*Gram*, 15).

CHAPTER 7

1. These are not the same dimensions that Northrop Frye, for instance, gives to narrative. What I am looking at is the fundamental dimensions of narrative in general, which Frye was claiming only characterized plot. For him, plot consists of someone doing something. What then fills out narrative, which is roughly synonymous to fiction for him, consists of the modes of development (tragic, comic, and thematic), narrative modes such as mythic, romantic, etc., and the ethical moments of the narrative, consisting of the hero and his actions, the hero's social framework in the narrative, the writer of the narrative, and its readers. In other words, there is an empiricism in the way he approaches the question that is neither structurally abstract nor schematic.

2. It could be added here that the circle of narrativity provides a graphic indication of the insularity and incommensurability of narrative paradigms. If a system of narratives nestles at the core of a culture, as that culture's determination of common experience for itself, then the distinctions between cultures, their emotional and temperamental particularity, for which the absence of origin is general, would both refuse universalization and be the source of each one's self-universalization toward others. That is, as a culture, people live the content of the narratives that purvey them as people to others to be experienced as such

under the aegis of common exprience. Different systems of narrative would necessarily produce exclusive modes of familiarity and recognition, and hence incommensurabilities of feeling, emotion, and ways of apprehending experience, and thus ways of apprehending people. The metaphysics of universality, and the violation of others that is always attendant upon its imposition elsewhere, derives precisely from the desire to traverse those incommensurabilities, to articulate the inarticulability contained in the disparity of narrative systems.

3. The keyword here is "derangement," which Derrida uses often to describe the deconstruction of the metaphysical assumptions of a text under his own reading for form (cf. Derrida and McDonald, "Choreographies"; and *Positions*). The hermeneutic (dyadic) circle is not such a derangement because it only plays elements of form against each other and does not de-structure them into separate and interwoven form and content through the operation of form itself.

4. Intuitively, this can be expanded, in terms that Derrida has elucidated in many ways, in particular in *Limited, Inc.* Spacing individuates, and thus makes possible a repetition of what in the process obtains entityhood; repetition, or repeatability, is the possibility of discerning differences, of structuring differences, and is thus the possibility of the presence of the trace of what differs structurally; and the trace of what differs is what points to an elsewhere, an absence, and hence to a space between this and its elsewhere. In this "companion" circle, the hymen is the condition for dissemination; dissemination is the condition for the supplement; and the supplement is the condition for the hymen. And we can understand this intuitively by substituting the terms that Derrida uses to characterize these instrumentalities and that allow us to recapitulate and anticipate them in our own discussions of them. Separation and immediacy are the conditions for recapitulation and anticipation, which are the conditions for substitution and addition (adding on), which are the conditions for separation and immediacy. But this is a circle of inarticulables. Its interior relations are contingent upon the type of transformations at work in the mappings among these terms. It is given this form by the semiotic operations that Derrida's critique reveals for language as a structure.

5. The unitarity of the narrative circle is what transforms the sentences of a story into a narrative; it is the foundation upon which narrative codes dwell and effect themselves, which Barthes elucidates in *S/Z*. For Sartre, the meaning or theme of the narrative circle becomes a real transformation of the subject who reads, and who then sees, looks, apprehends, and incorporates the fact of the relation to the text's lurking subject into his/her projects (cf. the *esprit objectif*, in Flaubert; i.e., the formation of a common present through the notion that what is read forms a common past for the projected future of its readers). It is also in this sense that writing is engaged. For Derrida, the circle is the inarticulable itself, the anteriority to language (as writing in general) that can only be originless, the foundation for the absence of foundation.

6. Derrida also makes use of this figure (the circle and the center) in his critique of Heidegger's notion of time (*Marg*, 60).

7. Valéry's objection to psychoanalysis is its need to narrativize everything. It was on this basis that he rejected Freud (*Marg*, 300). For Valéry, narrative is a chain of ex post facto descriptions and transcriptions of experience whose being is essentially to be nameless (*Marg*, 299). And this suggests that Valéry is not as interested in contentless form as he is in formless content (like Heidegger). What he seeks is what can be left inarticulable behind articulations whose form is their content.

8. Both Fell and Flynn accept the notion that subject-object relations are primary to subject-subject relations in Sartre. Also Bell, *The Ethics of Authenticity*.

9. See Desan, *The Tragic Finale*, and Flynn, *Sartre and Marxist Existentialism*, for instance, on the assumption of the subject and the diffusion of the ontological difference.

10. It is also different from Heidegger's notion of being-with. Sartre establishes a language (of object and seeing) in which to articulate subject-subject relations; for Heidegger, these are precisely what must be left unarticulated in order for being-with to belong to Being.

11. A literalized metaphor is a metaphoric meaning that presents itself as denotational; it is a second-order meaning that presents itself as first-order. For example, an electron is a literalized metaphor. To understand it as a particle is a way of metaphorically expressing its mathematical description, its quantized energy, its orbital status around a nucleus. But to think in terms of the electron as a particle, like a grain of sand or a billiard ball, in spite of other mathematical dimensions for which the notion of particle is meaningless, is to literalize the metaphor. Though experiments can be designed to measure its "mass," the process of measurement deploys energy interactions that are already derived through an assumption of electrons and their mass. If they work, it is because they are consistent with the terms of literalization, rather than with the physical substrate metaphorized. Similarly, the concept of consciousness, or the positing of consciousness as a substance, are also literalized metaphors.

12. The triadic circle appears in Sartre's text in the same way that it appears in Heidegger's, that is, as a discursive form rather than as a geometry. The circle peppers Sartre's text more often than it does Heidegger's, but usually in dyadic form, as a version of the hermeneutic circle. Linda Bell points out the deployment of this circle in her commentary on Sartre (*Sartre's Ethics of Authenticity*, 81).

13. It is this that Heidegger is looking at, in "The Thing" (*Poetry Language Thought*, 163), when he speaks of its form, what the object "holds" and brings together. By breaking the circle, metaphysics renders human existence unintelligible, for which it must then provide substitute a priori intelligibilities, ideologies, and invented prior codings. The history of this process, as a rereading of the history of philosophy and Western culture, is what has been implicit in the post-structuralist critique. If metaphysics is the search for foundations, its postulation of a ground is that part of its project that derails the rest, producing interior aporias that render it coherent but unintelligible.

14. But it is unrepresentable as an NMN-structure. The homological relation that constitutes iteration for the other glyphs is replaced by allegory and metaphor and the iteration to which it gives rise by literalization. Allegory is not just a different form of homology; and it does not just function as a different form of narrativization of subject-subject encounter. Where homology maps the same form across differential textual content, allegory marks the same discursive content mapped across different rhetorical (or social) forms, as the many ways an object is come upon on its way to becoming a perceived object. Both function to mediate the inscription of the hidden, the subjective, as common experience.

CHAPTER 8

1. Sartre gives an extensive description of the modes of concrete relations with the other that emerge from the for-itself's choice of attitude toward the other in returning an objectivizing look, whether in dominance or subordination to the other. The attitudes that are paradigmatic of assimilation are love and masochism. Those that are paradigmatic of objectivization are indifference, desire, hate, and sadism. Neither paradigm constitutes being-for-others; being-for-others is a conflation of these, a synthesis that is not a dialectical synthesis. It is interesting to note that desire, as ontic desire, stands opposite love and forms

part of a spectrum that stretches from indifference to hate. Cf. Aronson, *Philosophy in the World*; Desan, *The Tragic Finale*; Iris Murdoch, *Sartre: Romantic Rationalist* (New Haven: Yale University Press, 1953).

2. Sartre uses the first person in order to locate all the effects, apprehensions, transformations, and modes of being of the encounter with the other as subject in the subject as a for-itself, in a phenomenological sense. I am recasting his first-person account in the third person, using the pronouns "one" and "the other" in order to maintain my being as a reader of Sartre, to not substitute myself for Sartre (although his text lends itself to such substitutions, and other commentators have deployed that well, such as Hazel Barnes in her most excellent commentaries), and to be able to focus, in the text, on the interface between ontology and narrative.

3. This being-as-a-look is outside the subject-object relation; it cannot be derived from either that relation or from the being of the for-itself. It opens on a different dimension of existence (*BN*, 272).

4. In a sense, this is a mode in which the Sartrean being-for approximates the Heideggerian "being-with." Sartre critiques the Heideggerian *mit-sein* on the grounds that a sense of being-with must be grounded in one's own being; and that mode of being that grounds being-with is what Sartre calls one's being-for-others. The other "knows" *what* I am (in an NMN mode of knowledge); but "the meaning of my being is outside me, imprisoned in an absence" (*BN*, 363). Rather than seek to retrieve or reappropriate one's being, to make it wholly one's own again, which would both objectivize the other and relinquish the narrative of the original discovery, one can seek to identify oneself with or assimilate the other's freedom.

5. In a hierarchical situation, the dominant will attribute a level of violence to a returned look, which serves to disguise the initial violence of domination, and to give the hierarch's response an aura of counterviolence or self-defense. The possibility of overt violence will always be immediate, to the extent that non-reciprocity is assumed by one and reciprocity enacted by the Other. In the situation of racialization, where white racial identity has to define a non-white "race" in order to define itself as white, and narrativize the non-white as given, this structure of definition in which the members of the defined group do not participate, yet against which they are unable to act, produces a situation of non-reciprocity. Indeed, in real hierachical domination, even the oscillation of alternating objectivations is not possible. Only the road of dispelling the structure of domination constituted through those definitions and their narratives will provide the space for reciprocity, or even mutual oscillating objectivations. The Hegelian master-slave relation assumes that mutual recognition is a possibility. Thus, ironically, slavery itself is not one of those situations; for white supremacy, there is no mutual recognition. Though an alternation of seeing "each other" as objects would seem to be the basic condition presumed by Sartre's account, such an oscillation could be seen as a somewhat special case.

6. A similar trace structure operates in the other moment of one's returned look, that pole at which it becomes objectivizing and makes the Other an object for oneself. One renders the Other an object in terms of grasping the negation for which one is not responsible (*BN*, 287), the original objectivation that put one out of play, stripped of transcendence. In negating this, in turn, to recapture one's own consciousness self-consciously, what becomes a possibility is grasping a sense of oneself again as a "myself" and operating within one's own "free spontaneity," at one's own limit, reasserted in "[wrenching] away from the Other" (*BN*, 287). It is not the same, because one negates that Other as an Other who had become the source of one's being an object. The Other becomes an object, a signifier whose trace is "the one I am not but for whom my for-itself is." Again, one makes the Other be.

7. This clarifies the problem that Sartre had noticed in Heidegger and gives an account of one becoming who one is in the "they" without depending on it, while founded on the ability of the for-itself, which already exists, to grant itself and the Other subjectivity.

8. When Sartre argues that "being-for-others is not an ontological structure of the for-itself" (*BN*, 376), being neither inherent nor derivable from the for-itself, he is claiming that it comes into existence as a fact of the for-itself's existence in the presence of Others. But the notion of its coming into existence in the context of his deconstruction of subject-object and subject-subject relations invokes an alternate meaning. It entails a domain of the in-articulable, of a socius of meta-NMN-structure whose only articulation can lie in its own unfolding, as a recursivity of the meta-NMN-structure. This unfolding becomes a second meaning adjoined to its being a proto-socius in relation to its Other.

9. This relationship is not a self-reflective self-consciousness, since the Other is a freedom, a subjectivity. And it is not a subject-object relation, for the same reason. As a subject-subject relation of facticity, it becomes a mode of being for oneself through a metaphorics and an incommensurability of images, in which the other becomes an organization of the world, as a subject-totality (*BN*, 293). It is this mode of being of the for-itself set up between oneself and the other that Sartre calls "I-and-the-Other" (*BN*, 299).

10. Jean-Paul Sartre, *Hope Now*, trans. Adrian Van Den Hoven (Chicago: University of Chicago Press, 1996), p. 73.

11. This is a dimension of sociality that Sartre leaves out of the *Critique of Dialectical Reason*. He posits the seriality of people engaged in common endeavor as individuals—for instance, people waiting for a bus are serialized in line, or people all watching the same movie are serialized inside the theater. And he proposes that people move to a group subjectivity through what he calls a group-in-fusion, whereby they become, as a group, a historical actor. But dialogue is already an escape from seriality, even while waiting for the bus—people talking to each other out of mutual recognition. They do not thereby become historical agents, but they have overcome the alienation of seriality in the formation of each microsocius, which is, prior to the kinds of crises that Sartre postulates must function for the construction of the group-in-fusion, an intermediary stage toward becoming a historical actor. Each person enters the dialogue as serial (participant), as being-for-others (listener), and as fused (mini) group in the dialogic substance or content, an affinity transcending seriality. In the sense of interaction engaged by Sartre in the *Critique*, this structure is homologous to the structure he gives the dialectic itself. It is far afield from the Hegelian or Marxian in the sense that he contextualizes it within his existentialist thought, and through the paradoxical logic of his thinking. If the dialectic has a structure in his *Critique* (and it does), it can be understood as three-layered. On the existential core of his understanding of being-for-itself, he laminates the traditional mode of dialectic, of interpenetration and contradiction of negation; but between those two there is a mediating layer of aporia, of the discursive, which Sartre submits to his own version of a post-structuralist critique. Cf. Steve Martinot, "The Site of Postmodernity in Sartre," *Sartre Studies International* 5, no. 2 (1999): 45–60.

12. For Sartre, speech and conversation would guarantee the freedom of the other, even in the event of using speech to command or manipulate, because both command and manipulation, dominance and nuanced control begin with the tacit affirmation that the other is not controlled, and proceed only by taking account of the other's possibility of saying "no." The enactment of mastery has always already assumed the social bedrock of non-mastery. For Derrida, the conversation is itself a double and continual act of mastery of the other, in the sense that each plays in the space of difference between what the other speaks,

and what the spoken words are made to say. That is, *vouloir-dire* always plays in the space between *savoir-dire* and *pouvoir-dire*. Knowledge is not power, but it is the difference that engenders each as the response (and adjunct) to the other. Derrida would not understand speech as "granting subjectivity" to the other. One cannot grant what escapes one's control the minute one enacts it, whether as speech or any other gesture. While for Sartre the anteriority of freedom opens the space of mastery and domination, for Derrida the anteriority of mastery opens the space for freedom.

13. Listening to a lecture, or a political or academic speech, does not constitute a dialogue in its immediacy. But it is predicated on prior dialogues in which the words and phrases used in the lecture have been given a familiarity and meaning. What does hold is that listening to a lecture is to be granted a subjectivity by the speaker and to encounter a lurking subjectivity in the speech, with which one engages in being interpretive or critical, as a listener.

14. This equivalence of writing and consciousness, to recapitulate, is to be understood as an equivalence of circularities that function as foundational. The Sartrean circle is constituted by the for-itself, the Other-as-subject, and being-for-others, as an endless progression of stages, each the anteriority of the next, each a form of proper name for that anteriority which constitutes its content. The circle is not simply a mode of ontological precedence. It is a way each moment exists as an interstice between moments that grant each other existence across that intermediation. The circle exists as a sign for itself. Similarly, a Derridean circle is constituted for writing by iteration, spacing, and the trace. But these elements reflect the circle of deconstructive glyphs, of the supplement, hymen, and dissemination, which are homologous to the elements of the Sartrean circle.

CHAPTER 9

1. As a "sidebar" on Chomskyan linguistics, we can consider the following extension of the theory of the glyph. The deep structure that Chomsky describes for the language function takes on whatever compelling aspect it does because it works off the structure of narrative. If narrative is the deep structure, it is because it represents the way in which individual experience of coming upon the world is first told, prior to generalization. As such, it forms part of the glyph of the terms and phrases that get put together as language. But the glyph, to the extent it amalgamates the interactive use of a term, and the term as the name for an enacted narrative in social encounter (this is other than the notion of pointing out by which objects are individuated), becomes simply an icon for the cumulative memory of all those instances of experience that relate through the same or similarly named narratives. In other words, there is no other "deep structure" than memory itself and the way in which narratives are built from encounter through the attribution of narratives in dialogic situations (whose atomic level is the look), which dialogues then become the second level of narrative for the term or phrase.

2. Cf. Michel Foucault, *Archeology of Knowledge*, trans. A. M. Sheridan Smith (New York: Pantheon, 1972) and Pierre Bourdieu, *Outline of a Theory of Practice*, trans. Richard Nice (Cambridge: Cambridge University Press, 1977). Foucault develops the more stringent theory of the subject's constraint by discursive formations, the forms of historical conditioning by discourses that become paradigmatic of thought as an episteme. Bourdieu presents a similar structure of organization of activity, of and by the subject, in his theory of the habitus.

3. Aaron David Gresson III, *The Dialectics of Betrayal.* (Norwood, NJ: Ablex Publishing, 1982). He begins with a long quote from Michael Hammond on Durkheim:

CHAPTER 6

1. W.E.B. DuBois, *The Souls of Black Folk* (Greenwich, CT: Fawcett, 1961), p. 16.

2. It is the chiasmus of this situation, the incommensurability of the space it defines for those seen across the color line itself that is maddening, and which has become historically inescapable. The "racializing look" has, in the United States in particular, functioned as a historical force conditioning an entire culture. One might add that in the case of women (in the West at least), the fact of being for show, to be seen, with entire industries dedicated to this simple command, functions as one of the bases upon which Western history has been made, though not with the overt historical force that race has been in the last 400 years. The racialization of social relations, as the very invention of race itself, occurs at the hands of a social situation in which such a look is unending, never blinking. White supremacy begins with never allowing the other to be other as a subject, but always foremost a socially constructed object for itself. And insofar as this is the operation by which white people defined themselves as white, it resides in every aspect of a white person's identification of him/herself as white.

3. Derrida discusses this most succinctly and fully in *Limited, Inc.*, in which he expands on more dispersed analysis given in "Signature Event Context" (*Marg*) and *Of Grammatology*.

4. Cf. John Searle, "Reiterating the Differences; A Reply to Derrida," *Glyph* no. 1 (1977). Also, Ellis, *Against Deconstruction* (see chapter 1, note 24). To interpret Derrida in such a hyperliteralizing manner insulates one from grasping the form of what Derrida is doing, in particular, his logic of the supplement.

5. Jacques Derrida, *Spectres of Marx*, trans. Peggy Kamuf (New York: Routledge, 1994), p. 51.

6. Ralph Ellison allegorizes this notion perfectly in *The Invisible Man* (New York: Vintage Books, 1972) in speaking about the Liberty Paint factory and the necessary addition of a bit of black pigment to make the white paint a paint that will "cover." It might be added here that race is not a biological entity; it exists, but only as a social relation. For instance, one black foreparent renders a person black, while one white foreparent does not render a person white. A white woman can give birth to a black child, but a black woman cannot give birth to a white child. "White" and "black" are social designations, not biologically descriptive terms. There are no natural dividing lines on the spectra of skin color or any other body trait. And no two traits necessarily occur together. Therefore, there is no basis on which to define racial division biologically.

7. Jean-Jacques Rousseau; *The Confessions*, trans. J. M. Cohen (Middlesex: Penguin, 1953; originally published as *Les confessions*), p. 108; translation modified. Hereafter abbreviated in the text as *Con*.

8. Jean-Jacques Rousseau; *The Reveries of the Solitary Walker*, trans. Peter France (New York: Penguin, 1979), p. 132; hereafter cited in text as *Reveries*.

9. Paul de Man, in *Blindness and Insight* (Minneapolis: University of Minnesota Press, 1983), claims Derrida presents Rousseau as revealing a "pattern of duplicity" in which Rousseau knew "that his doctrine (of unmediated presence) disguised his insight into something closely resembling its opposite, but chose to remain blind to this knowledge." Derrida then "bring[s] to light what had remained unperceived by the author and his followers" (p. 116). De Man further says, "The question remains why he (Derrida) postulates within Rousseau a metaphysics of presence which can then be shown not to operate, or to be dependent on the implicit power of a language which disrupts it and tears it away

> Durkheim presents two basic existential dilemmas in the construction of a human social world. First of all, there do not exist any significant instinctual, innate, or absolute guidelines with which to forge this world.... A human world needs to be "bounded" by "imaginary walls," "contrived boundaries," and "determinate rules." ... Secondly, without guidelines from an innate human nature, there is always an enormous variety of possible beliefs and practices for such a fabrication.... The key tools in a human construction are affective and these forces are limited. To make possible this reduction in behavioral alternatives, a sacred or moral quality must be "added" or "superimposed." This ultimately affective addition creates a degree of "distance" such that certain beliefs and practices become filled with meaning, and other alternatives become incompatible. (p. 26)

Then Gresson comments on this passage as follows: "With this view of the social construction of reality we get a sense of the tensions—deception, sacrifice, and sacredness—called into play by the "original" social act. Man is deceived into seeing life in a normative and deterministic manner; he is asked to sacrifice his primary impulse and to suppress his creator role; and, finally, he is taught to reify the resultant configuration, society" (p. 26).

First, Durkheim points out, through Hammond, that one constructs the possibilities of social interaction through structuring, as boundaries and rules. Second, the way in which people interact, which is affective, is given meaning through discourses of the sacred and of morality, which depend at a fundamental level on narrative. But then, the social person takes himself out of this picture and reifies the personal reality he lives not as coming from a social elsewhere.

4. Gresson exemplifies a problem with the sociological. It attempts to critique, and at times oppose, social determinism and social totalitarianism while deploying a language that does not escape that very totalitarianism, neither through critique nor discursive alternative. Social determination is a power-oriented or power-generated repression of the aporia between the individual and the social in the name of the social. While avenues of escape and resistance begin by recognizing and embracing that aporia, that is something sociological language, with its pretension to scientificity, cannot do. It would have to develop a language that respected incommensurability.

5. In Sartre's description of the "fundamental project," the primordial choice of who one is to be in the world, to which other projects are subordinate both in motivation and conceptualization, involves a moment of reading the world in which the content is nevertheless acted upon by the reader, critically, rebelliously, poetically, acquiescingly, imaginatively.

6. The layering of these spectra of acceptance/non-acceptance of socially given narratives of comportment that each person lives both strategically and intuitively is generally only describable in literature, in fiction, poetry, or drama. It is only literature that can make the attempt to fathom the depths of a specific angst, or the unfolding of a particular agonistics. Literature is thus different from the mythic structures that Eric Gould investigates, as the fundamental narratives of a socius, though it may contain or even analyze them. Literature provides the explicit discursive component of the glyphs in a multi-glyphic enactment within a particular situation of confrontation with others.

7. The other is rendered not only unknown, but in principle unknowable. The narratives substitute themselves for any real experience of those generalized and leave them hidden behind their systematicity. This is one of the reasons many men feel alone when with women they are intimate with; while the sense of togetherness should be the greatest, men's

masculinist generalization of the woman (of who women are and how they think, for instance) leaves the woman unknowable, regardless of how close, and out of relation.

8. Sartre, *Anti-Semite and Jew.* Continuing the dialogue between Sartre and Elizabeth Grosz, we can note that he attempts to explicate this structure with respect to anti-Semitism without elucidating the role of the anti-Semitic narratives in the look. His leaving out the question of narrative language and its role in the anti-Semitic "look" forms part of his omission of the disparity between the a priori anti-Semitic definition of the Jew and the Jewish project itself. While the former gets interiorized, whether in acquiescence or in rejection and rebellion, the latter, the meaning of being Jewish for Jews, their embrace of Jewish culture and thought in its own right, constitutes a prior narrativization, a prior language. Cf. E. Grosz (see chapter 4, note 25). For Sartre, "being a Jew" as an identity means "being made a Jew" as a location in a social hierarchy, which does not depend on a person's relation to Jewish thought and culture.

9. Two questions immediately arise, of course: Where does one get the generalization that is then imposed on the individual, and to whom is one relating when one generalizes another? These are photonegative questions. If the generalization is brought to the encounter, its source can only be others who have defined themselves through that act of generalization. The generalizations about women are created by men as the way they define themselves as a group for dominance over women; the racialization of African Americans is an act of generalization by whites, through which they define themselves as white and as dominant. Thus, chauvinism is a social structure that depends on one group's ability to define itself through another group that it subordinates in the process. That is, it reflects the social force (power) to define another group through which to define itself as "superior" by dint of that force.

10. Many homophobic men think a certain violence becomes justified, not to distance the gay man but to reduce him in status, to manifest the gay man's inferiority. This is part of the identity the homophobic man's homophobia gives him. Similarly, the white supremacist will think, and all too often enact, pure barbarism against an autonomous black or brown person, having renamed that autonomy as "arrogance," while at the same time renaming his violence as an expression of "civilized decency." Each of these modes of violence, though expressing hate in their enactment, are actually concrete moments of identity construction, the way a person in a dominant group speaks to himself about who he is through his victim. There is nothing the target of his violence can do to turn it aside. It is the target's existence he is establishing (as a target) to confirm his own dominance by reducing him in status.

11. In the United States, as a corollary, the racializing discourses for African Americans and "ethnic minorities" all contain a dimension that could be metaphorized as being "empty-handed." It is also found in various colonialist discourses. Cf. Albert Memmi, *Dominated Man* (Boston: Beacon Press, 1969). It implies having insufficient strength, culture, reasoning, creativity, or ingenuity for self-sufficiency; it is represented by the social enlistment of those so designated for the purposes of spectacle and, in that sense, disappeared. Native Americans have suffered this imposition continually, not only directly but indirectly through the iconicity of the white Nativist movements of the nineteenth century. African Americans, women, Latinos, and Asians, each in their own way, have been transformed into a mode of spectacle, as a form of overt and concealed colonialism. Sitting Bull was both legitimized and delegitimized as the icon of all Native Americans when he was placed in "Buffalo Bill" Cody's Wild West Show. O. J. Simpson was first the mythic (magic) black athlete, and then the mythic (magic) black male criminal threat, without ever having been given personhood. Cf. Earl Ofari Hutchenson, *Beyond O.J.* (New York: Black Rose Press, 1996).

12. Like Memmi, Derrida locates the source of racism in Western colonialism. But he then looks at the way in which the word represents a discourse, and that discourse presents itself as the origination, the moment of invention of racism itself, whose "last word" is apartheid, apartness, the artificial separation that Europe and the Western tradition, as Western universalism and humanism, have made in the world—in its most extreme form in South Africa.

"APARTHEID: by itself the word occupies the terrain like a concentration camp. System of partition, barbed wire, crowds of mapped out solitudes.... The word concentrates separation, raises it to another power and sets separation itself apart. ("Racism's Last Word," in *Critical Inquiry* vol. 12(1), Autumn 1985, p. 292). Derrida points out that it gets its apartness as a word from the world's refusal to translate it. "No tongue has translated this name—as if the languages of the world were defending themselves,... refusing to give an equivalent." But as being apart, separated, and the being of separation itself, "like all racisms, it tends to pass segregation off as natural" (p. 292). For Derrida, racism and apartheid indict "the whole of western history" (p. 294).

13. Edward Said, *Orientalism* (New York: Vintage Books, 1979). The notion of being "disappeared" has reached its most horrible materialization in Latin America under the operation of local and national police forces, as in Argentina, Guatemala, or El Salvador, in which opponents of the regime are simply killed and buried without judicial process by the army or the police forces.

14. Sartre would call this a situation in which one is rendered subhuman, rather than attributing hyper-subjectivity to the colonizer, but there are certain conceptual limitations to that kind of articulation.

15. One effect is to foster the notion among the hierarchs that they are the universal human because, within the paradigm of hierarchy, they grant each other subjectivity; they thus see themselves as such. In that sense, the discourse of domination (white supremacy or masculinism, for instance) is a discourse of what it means to be human, as against those inferiorized a priori by that discourse. Indeed, the equivalence of "white" and "man" and "human being" is one of the services provided white men by colonialism. At the same time, the institutedness of these discourses becomes a standard for individual comportment for the dominant group. Their subjectivity is always in question because it emerges from the dominated, an allegiance to domination, and a violence in the service of canceling the autonomy of the subordinated, all at once. One becomes dependent on the subordinated for one's own identity (i.e., it is not one's own), and one becomes dependent on the dominant group for one's own autonomy (i.e., one is not autonomous). In order to live the narrative of superiority over women that masculinist men have told themselves, they must place themselves in denial of their dependence on women as the obsessive center of their identity. And they live the masculinist identity given by other men as if it really was an autonomous attribute of themselves as individuals.

16. One sees this exemplified in the notion of a minority. A group does not exist as a minority because it has less voting strength; as such, it is just a small voting bloc. A group is created as a minority by having been separated from society through a definition that renders its members different, and thus minoritized, by which the separating or excluding group creates itself as a majority. That is, it is defined as "outvoted" before any vote is taken. Difference is seen as representing differential status, but the power to define represents a differential status of power that then sees its own effects as "objective" difference. An ethnic "minority" is thus a group that has been renarrativized as outside, inferiorized as a justification for exclusion, and invisibilized as a generalization that conceals the process of minoritization behind the imposition of being a minority. Minoritization, and the existence

of an ethnic minority, are thus instances of the operation of the colonial principle that "disappears" those whom it is about.

17. Should the dominant wish to rebel, against what would they rebel? They cannot rebel against the oppression of the other; they are not oppressed by it. They would have to rebel against themselves, though they are not oppressed by themselves. If they rebel against the socius that commands them and demands solidarity of them, they will betray the agreement they made when they accepted membership in the dominant group. And they had to accept such an agreement to have put themselves in a position to seek escape in the first place. They have no option to resign their membership in order not to betray it when they rebel. Between the inability to rebel, and the inability not to betray, they are stuck. Those of the dominant group, even if they abhor the oppression that makes them who they are, are unable to rise up against it and still be who they think they are.

18. This also implies that transforming the critique of domination into different philosophical terms is not just a word game. Changing the articulation of a situation, as the Derridean glyphs do, opens new possibilities of understanding its structure by articulating different relations in it, with different emphases. To point out that masculinism only brings itself into existence through an a priori definition and an enforced inferiorization of women implies not only that there are other ways of living, of being male, of relating to women, but that masculinism, along with its universalized, "humanist" discourse of "Man," is not the universal it pretends to be. One need not be trapped in its terms.

19. In Schroedinger's quantum theory, elementary particles could be described by wave equations, which are particular kinds of series functions. Because they worked, they became a way of naming a characteristic of the elementary particle. Particles were then understood to have a wave nature and were conceptualized as such for experimental purposes. Similarly, such recently described psychological phenomena as co-dependency take politico-social dependency as a metaphor and use it to name a psychological syndrome.

20. For example, the story of September 11, 2001. The facts, as presented by the government, were that four planes were hijacked by nineteen Arabs who flew two of them into the World Trade Center and a third into the Pentagon, with the fourth crashing in Pennsylvania because the passengers fought back. We consider these events as facts, look at their unfolding from a distance, ask ourselves why people would do that to us ("to us!"), and are properly terrorized. If I then consider Thierry Meyssan's argument that there is no evidence that an airliner crashed into the Pentagon (no wreckage, a hole too small for a 757, not deep enough into the building) L'Effroyable Imposture (Chatou: Editions Caret, 2002), and add that the single tunnel bored by the massive engine is actually evidence of a single-engine plane—meaning that the government faked a 757 crash—most people will accuse me of spreading a conspiracy theory. That is because they are thinking in terms of a knowledge of what happened, a factual story; and my disruption of that factuality simply means the story of who did it and how becomes difficult, implying a different agent and a different telos. But what my statement does is shift the center of the story from the government's account, in which a certain "knowledge" of the events resides, to "our" relation to the events. We are no longer at a distance but become participants in its meaning. We no longer know the story, and the one thing we then know is that we have been stripped of that former knowledge; we do not know what happened. What happened on 9/11 is not known. That is the difference between a conspiracy theory, which makes the same assumptions metaphysically as the account of events it contests (the government's), and a contestation of those assumptions.

21. In a conversation, after certain things have been generalized, to return to an earlier level of particularity, whether to critique the presuppositions or to counterimpose a differ-

ent axiomatics, becomes very difficult. It entails more than merely backtracking in the conversation. First, to look back, after having established certain presuppositions for the purposes of reasoning, means looking back through those presuppositions. In addressing them in order to move them aside, they are revalorized through recognition rather than being erased. Thus, one moves back through their reapplication, retroactively deploying them upon the previous realm of particularity to which one seeks to return. This is not to say it is impossible to return to that prior domain, but the difficulties are structural rather than conceptual. They cannot be resolved simply through a clarification of terms or a sharpening of theory.

Bibliography

Adorno, Theodor. *Negative Dialectics*. New York: Continuum, 1973.

Alcoff, Linda. "Cultural Feminism vs. Post-structuralism: The Identity Crisis in Feminist Theory." *Signs* 13, no. 3 (1988): 405–36.

Althusser, Louis. "Ideology and Ideological State Apparatuses." In *Lenin and Philosophy, and Other Essays*. Trans. Ben Brewster. New York: Monthly Review Press, 1972.

Arendt, Hannah. *The Origins of Totalitarianism*. New York: Meridian Books, 1958.

Aronson, Ronald. *Jean-Paul Sartre: Philosophy in the World*. London: NLB, 1980.

Barnes, Hazel. *An Existentialist Ethics*. Chicago: University of Chicago Press, 1967.

Barnes, Hazel. *Sartre and Flaubert*. Chicago: University of Chicago Press, 1981.

Barnes, Hazel. "Sartre and Sexism." *Philosophy and Literature* 14, no. 2 (1990).

Barthes, Roland. *La chambre claire: Note sur la photographie*. Paris: Cahiers du Cinema, 1980.

Barthes, Roland. *Elements of Semiology*. Trans. Annette Lavers and Colin Smith. New York: Hill and Wang, 1967.

Barthes, Roland. *The Fashion System*. Trans. Matthew Ward and Richard Howard. New York: Hill and Wang, 1983.

Barthes, Roland. *Image, Music, Text*. Trans. Stephen Heath. New York: Hill and Wang, 1977.

Barthes, Roland. *Mythologies*. Trans. Annette Lavers. New York: Hill and Wang, 1972.

Barthes, Roland. *S/Z*. Trans. Richard Miller. New York: Hill and Wang, 1974.

Barthes, Roland. "Writing: An Intransitive Verb?" In *The Structuralist Controversy*. Eds. Richard Macksey and Eugenio Donato. Baltimore: Johns Hopkins University Press, 1972.

Barthes, Roland. *Writing Degree Zero*, trans. Annette Lavers and Colin Smith. New York: Hill and Wang, 1967. Originally published as *Le degré zéro de l'écriture*. Paris: Éditions du Seuil, 1953.

Baudrillard, Jean. *Simulations*. New York: Semiotext(e), 1983.

Beckett, Samuel. *Molloy*. Trans. Patrick Bowles and Samuel Beckett. New York: Grove Press, 1955.

Bell, Linda. *Sartre's Ethics of Authenticity*. Tuscaloosa: University of Alabama Press, 1989.

Bennington, Geoffrey. *Jacques Derrida*. Chicago: University of Chicago Press, 1993.

Bergson, Henri. *Matter and Memory*. Trans. Nancy Margaret Paul and W. Scott Palmer. New York: Humanities Press, 1978.

Bergson, Henri. *Time and Free Will*. Trans. F. L. Pogson. New York: Harpers, 1960.

Bernasconi, Robert. *The Question of Language in Heidegger's History of Being*. Atlantic Heights, NJ: Humanities Press, 1985.

Boas, Franz. "The Origins of Totemism." *American Anthropologist* 18 (1916): 319–26.

Borges, Jorge Luis. *Labyrinths*. Eds. Donald A. Yates and James E. Irby. New York: New Directions, 1964.

Bourdieu, Pierre. *Outline of a Theory of Practice*. Trans. Richard Nice. Cambridge: Cambridge University Press, 1977.

Boyne, Roy. *Foucault and Derrida: The Other Side of Reason*. London: Unwin Hyman, 1990.

Bree, Germaine. *Camus and Sartre: Crisis and Commitment*. New York: Delacorte Press, 1972.

Brown, Marshall. "Unheard Melodies: The Force of Form." *PMLA* 107 (May 1992): 465–81.

Bruns, Gerald. *Heidegger's Estrangement: Language, Truth and Poetry in the Later Writings*. New Haven: Yale University Press, 1989.

Busch, Thomas. *The Power of Consciousness and the Force of Circumstances*. Bloomington: Indiana University Press, 1990.

Butler, Judith. *Gender Trouble: Feminism and the Subversion of Identity*. New York: Routledge, 1990.

Camus, Albert. *L'etranger*. Paris: Gallimard, 1949.

Cannon, Betty. *Sartre and Psychoanalysis*. Lawrence: University Press of Kansas, 1991.

Caputo, John D. "Meister Eckhart & The Later Heidegger: The Mystical Element in Heidegger's Thought" (2 part essay). *Journal of the History of Philosophy* 12(4) (October 1974): 479–494, and 13(1) (January 1975): 61–80.

Caputo, John D. *The Mystical Element in Heidegger's Thought*. Athens: Ohio University Press, 1978.

Caputo, John D. "The Poverty of Thought: Reflections on Heidegger and Eckhart." In *Heidegger: The Man and the Thinker*. Ed. Thomas Sheehan. Chicago: Precedent, 1981.

Caputo, John D. *Radical Hermeneutics: Repetition, Deconstruction, and the Hermeneutic Project*. Bloomington: Indiana University Press, 1987.

Carroll, David. *Paraesthetics: Foucault, Lyotard, Derrida*. New York: Methuen, 1987.

Catalano, Joseph. *A Commentary on Jean-Paul Sartre's "Being and Nothingness."* Chicago: University of Chicago Press, 1980.

Clark, Timothy. *Derrida, Heidegger, Blanchot: Sources of Derrida's Notion and Practice of Literature*. New York: Cambridge University Press, 1992.

Cohen-Solal, Annie. *Sartre: A Life*. Trans. Anna Cancogni. New York: Pantheon Books, 1987.

Collins, Margary, and Christine Pierce. "Holes and Slime: Sexism in Sartre's Psychoanalysis." *Philosophical Forum* 5 (1973), pp.112–127.

Cornell, Drucilla. *The Philosophy of the Limit*. New York: Routledge, 1992.

Culler, Jonathan. *On Deconstruction: Theory and Criticism after Structuralism*. Ithaca: Cornell University Press, 1982.

Danto, Arthur. *Jean-Paul Sartre*. New York: Viking Press, 1975.

De Beauvoir, Simone. *The Ethics of Ambiguity*. Trans. Bernard Frechtman. New York: Citadel Press, 1964.

De Beauvoir, Simone. *The Second Sex*. Trans. H. M. Parshley. New York: Knopf, 1953.

Deleuze, Gilles. *Nietzsche and Philosophy*. Trans. Hugh Tomlinson. New York: Columbia University Press, 1983.

Deleuze, Gilles, and Félix Guattari. *Anti-Oedipus*. Minneapolis: University of Minnesota Press, 1983.

Deleuze, Gilles, and Felix Guattari. *Nomadology: The War Machine*. Trans. Brian Massumi. New York: Semiotext(e), 1986.

Deleuze, Gilles, and Claire Parnet. *Dialogues*. Trans. Hugh Tomlinson and Barbara Habberjam. New York: Columbia University Press, 1987.

De Man, Paul. *Blindness and Insight*. Minneapolis: University of Minnesota Press, 1983.

Derrida, Jacques. *La carte postale: De Socrate à Freud et au-delà*. Paris: Flammarion, 1980.

Derrida, Jacques. "La différance." *Bulletin de la Société Française de Philosophie* 62, no. 3 (1968): 73–101.

Derrida, Jacques. *Dissemination*. Trans. Barbara Johnson. Chicago: University of Chicago Press, 1981. Originally published as *La dissémination*. Paris: Éditions du Seuil, 1972.

Derrida, Jacques. *Eperons: Les styles de Nietzsche/Spurs: Nietzsche's Styles* (bilingual edition). Trans. Barabara Harlow. Chicago: University of Chicago Press, 1979.

Derrida, Jacques. *Glas*. Trans. John P. Leavey Jr. and Richard Rand. Lincoln: University of Nebraska Press, 1986.

Derrida, Jacques. Interview with Catherine David. *Le Nouvel Observateur* 983 (September 9, 1983): 84–90. Trans. Contemporary Texts Seminar, State University of New York at Stony Brook.

Derrida, Jacques. "Limited, Inc." (trans. Samual Weber). *Glyph* 2 (1977), pp. 162–254.

Derrida, Jacques. *Limited, Inc*. Ed. Gerald Graff. Evanston: Northwestern University Press, 1988.

Derrida, Jacques. *Margins of Philosophy*. Trans. Alan Bass. Chicago: University of Chicago Press, 1982. Originally published as *Marges de la philosophie*. Paris: Éditions de Minuit, 1972.

Derrida, Jacques. *Of Grammatology*. Trans. Gayatri Spivak. Baltimore: Johns Hopkins University Press, 1974. Originally published as *De la grammatologie*. Paris: Éditions de Minuit, 1967.

Derrida, Jacques. "Pourquoi pas Sartre?" (trans. David Yum). *Gendai Shiso* 15 (1987): 58–80.

Derrida, Jacques. *Positions*. Trans. Alan Bass. Chicago: University of Chicago Press, 1981. Originally published as *Positions*. Paris: Éditions de Minuit, 1972.

Derrida, Jacques. *Signéponge/Signsponge*. Trans. Richard Rand (bilingual edition). New York: Columbia University Press, 1984.

Derrida, Jacques. *Speech and Phenomena*. Trans. David Allison. Evanston: Northwestern University Press, 1973. Originally published as *La voix et le phénomène*. Paris: Presses Universitaires, 1967.

Derrida, Jacques. *The Truth in Painting*. Trans. Geoff Bennington and Ian McLeod. Chicago: University of Chicago Press, 1987.

Derrida, Jacques. *Writing and Difference*. Trans. Alan Bass. Chicago: University of Chicago Press, 1978. Originally published as *L'écriture et la différence*. Paris: Éditions du Seuil, 1967.

Derrida, Jacques, and Christie McDonald. "Choreographies." *Diacritics* 12 (1982): 66–76.

Desan, Wilfrid. *The Tragic Finale*. New York: Harper, 1960.

Descartes, Rene. *Discourse on Method*. Trans. Laurence J. Lefleur. Indianapolis: Bobbs-Merrill, 1956.

Detmer, David. *Freedom as a Value*. LaSalle: Open Court Press, 1986.

DuBois, W.E.B. *The Souls of Black Folk*. Greenwich: Fawcett, 1961.

Ellis, John M. *Against Deconstruction*. Princeton: Princeton University Press, 1989.

Ellison, Ralph. *The Invisible Man*. New York: Vintage Books, 1972.

Evans, Joseph Claude. *Strategies of Deconstruction: Derrida and the Myth of the Universe*. Minneapolis: University of Minnesota Press, 1991.

Fanon, Frantz. *Wretched of the Earth*. Trans. Constance Farrington. New York: Grove Press, 1968.

Fell, Joseph. *Heidegger and Sartre*. New York: Columbia University Press, 1979.

Flaubert, Gustave. *Madame Bovary*. Trans. Eleanor Marx Aveling. New York: Modern Library, 1950.

Flynn, Thomas. *Sartre and Marxist Existentialism*. Chicago: University of Chicago Press, 1984.

Foucault, Michel. *Archeology of Knowledge*. Trans. A. M. Sheridan Smith. New York: Pantheon, 1972.

Foucault, Michel. *Language, Counter-Memory, Practice*. Ithaca: Cornell University Press, 1977.

Foucault, Michel. *Power/Knowledge*. Ed. Colin Gordon. Trans. Colin Gordon, Leo Marshall, John Mepham, Kate Soper. New York: Pantheon Books, 1980.

Foucault, Michel. *The Order of Things*. New York: Random House, 1970.

Friedan, Betty. *The Feminine Mystique*. New York: Dell, 1970.

Gadamer, Hans-Georg. *Philosophical Hermeneutics*. Trans. David E. Linge. Berkeley: University of California Press, 1976.

Gardner, Sebastian. "Splitting the Subject." *Auslegung* 13, no. 2 (1983): 186–92.

Gasché, Rodolphe. *The Tain of the Mirror*. Cambridge, MA: Harvard University Press, 1986.

Gelley, Alexander. "Form as Force." *Diacritics* 2, no. 1 (1972): 9–13.

Genet, Jean. *The Maids and Deathwatch*. Trans. Bernard Frechtman. New York: Grove Press, 1962.

Gerassi, John. *Jean-Paul Sartre: Hated Conscience of His Century*. Chicago: University of Chicago Press, 1989.

Goldberg, Jonathan. *Writing Matter*. Stanford: Stanford University Press, 1990.

Goldmann, Lucien. *Toward a Sociology of the Novel*. Trans. Alan Sheridan. London: Tavistock, 1975.

Gould, Eric. *Mythical Intentions in Modern Literature*. Princeton: Princeton University Press, 1981.

Grene, Marjorie. *Sartre*. Washington, DC: University Press of America, 1983.

Grusson, Aaron David III. *The Dialectics of Betrayal: Sacrifice, Violation, and the Oppressed*. Norwood, NJ: Ablex Publishing, 1982.

Grosz, Elizabeth. "Judaism and Exile: The Ethics of Otherness." *New Formations* 12 (winter), pp. 77–88.

Guerlac, Suzanne. "Sartre and the Powers of Literature: The Myth of Prose and the Practice of Reading." *MLN* 108 (1993): 805–24.

Hall, Edward T. *The Silent Language*. Greenwich: Fawcett, 1959.

Hall, Stuart. *The Hard Road to Renewal*. London: Verso, 1988.

Harari, Josu V., ed. *Textual Strategies: Perspectives in Post-Structuralist Criticism*. Ithaca: Cornell University Press, 1979.

Haraway, Donna. "A Manifesto for Cyborgs: Science, Technology, and Socialist Feminism in the 1980s." In *Feminism/Postmodernism*. Ed. Linda Nicholson. New York: Routledge, 1990.

Hartsock, Nancy. "Rethinking Modernism: Minority vs. Majority Theories." *Cultural Critique* vol. 7, (Fall 1987), pp. 187–206.

Hegel, G.W.F. *Phenomenology of Mind*. Trans. J. B. Baillie. New York: Harper and Row, 1967.

Heidegger, Martin. *Basic Writings*. Ed. David Krell. New York: Harper and Row, 1977.

Heidegger, Martin. *Being and Time*. Trans. John Macquarrie and Edward Robinson. New York: Harper and Row, 1962.

Heidegger, Martin. *Identity and Difference*. Trans. Joan Stambaugh. New York: Harper and Row, 1969.

Heidegger, Martin. "Letter on Humanism," In *Basic Writings*. Ed. David Krell (New York: Harper and Row, 1977).

Heidegger, Martin. *The Metaphysical Foundations of Logic*. Trans. Michael Heim. Bloomington: Indiana University Press, 1984.

Heidegger, Martin. *On the Way to Language*. Trans. Peter D. Hertz. New York: Harper, 1971.

Heidegger, Martin. *Poetry, Language, Thought*. Trans. Albert Hofstadter. New York: Harper, 1971.

Heidegger, Martin. *Vorträge und Aufsätze*. Tübingen: Gunther Neske Pfullingen, 1954.

Heidegger, Martin. *Wegmarken*. Frankfurt am Main: Vittorio Klostermann, 1967.

Hendley, Steve. *Reason and Relativism: A Sartrean Investigation*. Albany: SUNY Press, 1991.

Hindess, Barry, and Paul Hirst. *Mode of Production and Social Formation*. London: Macmillan, 1977.

Hollier, Denis. *The Politics of Prose*. Trans. Jeffrey Mehlman. Minneapolis: University of Minnesota Press, 1986. Originally published as *Politique de la prose: Jean-Paul Sartre et l'an quarante*. Paris: Gallimard, 1982.

Howells, Christina. "Sartre and Derrida: Qui Perde Gagne." *Journal of the British Society of Phenomenology* 13, no. 1 (1982): 26–34.

Howells, Christina. *Sartre: The Necessity of Freedom*. New York: Cambridge University Press, 1988.

Hoy, David. *The Critical Circle*. Berkeley: University of California Press, 1978.

Husserl, Edmund. *Ideas: General Introduction to Pure Phenomenology*. Trans. W. R. Boyce Gibson. New York: Collier Books, 1962.

Husserl, Edmund. *Phenomenology of Internal Time Consciousness*. Trans. James S. Churchill. Bloomington: Indiana University Press, 1964.

Hutcheons, Linda. *The Politics of Postmodernism*. London: Routledge, 1989.

Jameson, Fredric. *Marxism and Form: Twentieth-century Dialectical Theories of Literature*. Princeton: Princeton University Press, 1972.

Jameson, Fredric. *The Prison-House of Languages*. Princeton: Princeton University Press, 1972.

Jameson, Fredric. *Sartre: The Origin of a Style*. New Haven: Yale University Press, 1961.

Jeanson, Francis. *Sartre and the Problem of Morality*. Trans. Robert Stone. Bloomington: Indiana University Press, 1980.

Joyce, James. *Ulysses*. New York: Vintage Books, 1961.

Kant, Immanuel. *Critique of Judgment*. Trans. J. H. Bernard. New York: Hafner Press, 1951.

Kant, Immanuel. *Critique of Practical Reason*. Trans. Lewis White Beck. Indianapolis: Bobbs-Merrill, 1956.

Kant, Immanuel. *Critique of Pure Reason*. Trans. Norman Kemp Smith. New York: St. Martin's Press, 1965.

Kellner, Douglas. *Critical Theory, Marxism, and Modernity*. Baltimore: Johns Hopkins University Press, 1989.

Keohane-O'Connor, Noreen. "Intentionality, Analysis, and the Self and Others." *Journal of British Society of Phenomenology* 13, no. 2 (1982): 186–92.

Lacan, Jacques. *Ecrits*. Trans. Alan Sheridan. New York: W.W. Norton, 1977.

Lacan, Jacques. *The Four Fundamental Concepts of Psycho-Analysis*. Trans. Alan Sheridan. New York: W.W. Norton, 1981.

LaCapra, Dominick. *A Preface to Sartre*. Ithaca: Cornell University Press, 1978.

Laclau, Ernesto, and Chantal Mouffe. *Hegemony and Socialist Strategy*. London: Verso, 1985.

Lautréamont, Comte de [Isador Ducasse]. *Maldoror*. Trans. Guy Wernham. New York: New Directions, 1965.

Lavers, Annette. *Roland Barthes: Structuralism and After*. Cambridge: Harvard University Press, 1982.

Lawler, Leonard. "A Little Daylight: A Reading of Derrida's 'White Mythology.'" *Man and World* 24 (1991): 285–300.

Leitch, Vincent B. *Deconstructive Criticism*. New York: Columbia University Press, 1983.

Levi, Primo. *The Drowned and the Saved*. Trans. Raymond Rosenthal. New York: Summit Books, 1988.

Levinas, Emmanuel. *The Theory of Intuition in Husserl's Phenomenology*. Trans. Audre Orianne. Evanston: Northwestern University Press, 1978.

Levi-Strauss, Claude. *Structural Anthropology*. Trans. Claire Jacobson and Brooke Grundfest Schoepf. Garden City: Basic Books, 1963.

Levi-Strauss, Claude. *Totemism*. Trans. Rodney Needham. Boston: Beacon Press, 1963.

Llewelyn, John. *Derrida on the Threshold of Sense*. New York: St. Martin's Press, 1986.

Lorde, Audre. *Zami: A New Spelling of My Name*. Watertown: Persephone Press, 1982.

Lyotard, Jean-Francois. *The Differend: Phrases in Dispute*. Trans. Georges Van den Abbeele. Minneapolis: University of Minnesota Press, 1988.

Mallarmé, Stephane. *Un coup de des*. Paris: Baudouin, 1979.

Martinot, Steve. "The Languages of Racial Loyalty." *APA Newsletter* 92, no. 2 (1993): 8–12.

Martinot, Steve. "Sartre's Being-for-Heidegger: Heidegger's Being-for-Sartre." *Man and World* 24 (1991): 63–74.

Marx, Karl. *Capital*, Vol. I. Trans. Samuel Moore and Edward Aveling. Moscow: Foreign Languages Publishing House, 1962.

Marx, Karl. *The 18th Brumaire of Louis Napoleon*. Trans. Eden Paul and Cedar Paul. New York: International Publishers, 1967.

McBride, William. *Sartre's Political Theory*. Bloomington: Indiana University Press, 1991.

Megill, Allan. *Prophets of Extremity*. Berkeley: University of California Press, 1985.

Merleau-Ponty, Maurice. *Adventures in the Dialectic*. Trans. Joseph Bien. Evanston: Northwestern University Press, 1973.

Merleau-Ponty, Maurice. *The Phenomenology of Perception*. Trans. Colin Smith. New York: Routledge Kegan Paul, 1962.

Merleau-Ponty, Maurice. *The Visible and the Invisible*. Trans. Alphonso Lingus. Evanston: Northwestern University Press, 1968.

Michelfelder, Diane, and Richard E. Palmer, eds. *Dialogue and Deconstruction: The Gadamer-Derrida Debate*. Albany: SUNY Press, 1989.

Mohanty, Satya. "Us and Them: On the Philosophical Bases of Political Criticism." *Yale Journal of Criticism* 2, no. 2 (1989): 1–31.

Mui, Constance. "Sartre's Sexism Reconsidered." *Auslegung* 16, no. 1 (1990), pp. 31–41.

Mulvey, Laura. "Visual Pleasure and Narrative Cinema." *Screen* 16, no. 3 (1975): 6–14.

Murdoch, Iris. Sartre: *Romantic Rationalist*. New Haven: Yale University Press, 1953.

Nietzsche, Friedrich. *The Birth of Tragedy and the Genealogy of Morals*. Trans. Francis Golffing. Garden City: Doubleday, 1956.

Nietzsche, Friedrich. *The Twilight of the Idols*. Trans. R. J. Hollingdale. Middlesex: Penguin, 1968.

Norris, Christopher. *Deconstruction: Theory and Practice*. London: Methuen, 1982.

Peirce, Charles S. *Collected Papers of Charles Sanders Peirce*. Eds. Charles Hartshorne and Paul Weiss. Cambridge: Harvard University Press, 1953.

Peirce, Charles S. *The Philosophy of Peirce: Selected Writings*. Ed. Justus Buehler. New York: Harcourt Brace, 1940.

Plato. *Phaedrus*. Trans. W. C. Helmbold and W. G. Rabinowitz. Indianapolis: Bobbs-Merrill, 1956.

Poster, Mark. *Critical Theory and Poststructuralism: In Search of a Context*. Ithaca: Cornell University Press, 1989.

Poster, Mark. *Marxist Existentialism in Post-War France: From Sartre to Althusser*. Princeton: Princeton University Press, 1975.

Poster, Mark. *Sartre's Marxism*. London: Pluto Press, 1977.

Proust, Marcel. *Remembrance of Things Past*. Trans. C. K. Scott Moncrieff. New York: Vintage Books, 1970.

Rappaport, Herman. *Heidegger and Derrida: Reflections on Time and Language*. Lincoln: University of Nebraska Press, 1989.

Robbe-Grillet, Alain. *The Erasers*. Trans. Richard Howard. New York: Grove Press, 1964.

Rorty, Richard. "Is Derrida a Transcendental Philosopher?" *Yale Journal of Criticism* 2, no. 2 (1989), pp. 107–117.

Rorty, Richard. *Philosophy and the Mirror of Nature*. Princeton: Princeton University Press, 1979.

Rosenstein, Leon. "Mysticism as Preontology: A Note on the Heideggerian Connection." *Philosophy and Phenomenological Research* 39, no. 1 (1978): 57–73.

Rousseau, Jean-Jacques. *The Confessions*. Trans. J. M. Cohen. Middlesex: Penguin, 1953. Originally published as *Les confessions*. Paris: Garnier Freres, 1891.

Rousseau, Jean-Jacques. *Essai sur l'origine des langues*. Paris: Le Graphe, 1967.

Rousseau, Jean-Jacques. *The Reveries of the Solitary Walker*. Trans. Peter France. New York: Penguin, 1979.

Ryan, Michael. *Marxism and Deconstruction*. Baltimore: Johns Hopkins University Press, 1982.

Said, Edward. *Orientalism*. New York: Vintage Books, 1979.

Said, Edward. "The Problem of Textuality: Two Exemplary Positions." *Critical Inquiry* 4, no. 4 (1978): 673–714.

Sallis, John. *Delimitations: Phenomenology and the End of Metaphysics*. Bloomington: Indiana University Press, 1986.

Sartre, Jean-Paul. *Anti-Semite and Jew*. Trans. George Becker. New York: Grove Press, 1948.

Sartre, Jean-Paul. *Being and Nothingness*. Trans. Hazel Barnes. New York: Philosophical Library, 1956. Originally published as *L'etre et le néant*. Paris: Gallimard, 1957.

Sartre, Jean-Paul. *Between Existentialism and Marxism*. New York: Morrow, 1974.

Sartre, Jean-Paul. *Critique of Dialectical Reason*, Vol. 1 and 2. Trans. Alan Sheridan. London: Verso, 1982, 1991. Originally published as *Critique de la raison dialectique*, Vol. 1 and 2. Paris: Gallimard, 1960, 1985.

Sartre, Jean-Paul. [debate with Foucault] L'Arc, no. 30, October 1966, pp. 87–96. *La Quinzaine Litteraire* 14 (October 15, 1966), pp. 5.

Sartre, Jean-Paul. *The Devil and the Good Lord*. Trans. Kitty Black. New York: Vintage Books, 1960.

Sartre, Jean-Paul. "Existentialism is a Humanism." *Existentialism and Human Emotions*. Trans. Bernard Fruchtman. New York: Philosophical Library, 1957.

Sartre, Jean-Paul. *The Freud Scenario*. Trans. Quintin Hoare. Chicago: University of Chicago Press, 1985.

Sartre, Jean-Paul. *L'idiot de la famille*, 3 volumes. Paris: Gallimard, 1971.

Sartre, Jean-Paul. Interview with Alain Koehler. *Perspectives du Theatre* 3 (March 1960): 18–23; 4 (April 1960): 5–9.

Sartre, Jean-Paul. "Jean-Paul Sartre." *Que peut le litterature?* Series L'inedit. 10/18. Buin, Yves, ed., 1966. pp. 107–127.

Sartre, Jean-Paul. *Les jeux sont faits*. London: Methuen, 1961.

Sartre, Jean-Paul. *Literary and Philosophical Essays*. Trans. Annette Michelson. New York: Collier Books, 1962.

Sartre, Jean-Paul. *Mallarmé: The Poet of Nothingness*. Trans. Ernest Sturm. University Park: Pennsylvania State University Press, 1988.

Sartre, Jean-Paul. *Nausea*. Trans. Lloyd Alexander. New York: New Directions, 1964.

Sartre, Jean-Paul. *No Exit, and Three Other Plays*. Trans. Stuart Gilbert and Lionel Abel. New York: Vintage Books, 1956.

Sartre, Jean-Paul. *An Outline for a Theory of Emotions*. Trans. B. Frechtman. New York: Philosophical Library, 1948.

Sartre, Jean-Paul. *Saint Genet: Actor and Martyr*. New York: Braziller, 1963.

Sartre, Jean-Paul. *Search for a Method*. Trans. Hazel Barnes. New York: Vintage Books, 1963.

Sartre, Jean-Paul. *Situations*. Trans. Benita Eisler. Greenwich: Fawcett, 1964.

Sartre, Jean-Paul. *The Transcendence of the Ego*. Trans. Forrest Williams. New York: Noonday Press, 1957.

Sartre, Jean-Paul. *The Wall*. Trans. Lloyd Alexander. New York: New Directions, 1948.

Sartre, Jean-Paul. *What Is Literature?* Trans. Bernard Frechtman. New York: Washington Square Press, 1966.

Sartre, Jean-Paul. *The Words*. Trans. Bernard Frechtman. Greenwich: Fawcett, 1964.

Saussure, Ferdinand de. *Course in General Linguistics*. Trans. Wade Baskin. New York: McGraw-Hill, 1966.

Scarry, Elaine. *The Body in Pain*. New York: Oxford University Press, 1985.

Schroeder, William R. *Sartre and His Predecessors*. Boston: Routledge, 1984.

Schurmann, Reiner. "Trois Penseurs du délaissement: Maitra Eckhart, Heidegger, Suzuki" (2 part essay). *Journal of the History of Philosophy* 12(4) (October 1974): 455–78.

Schurmann, Reiner. *Journal of the History of Philosophy* 13(1) (January 1975): 43–60.

Sheehan, Thomas, ed. *Heidegger: The Man and the Thinker*. Chicago: Precedent, 1981.

Silverman, Hugh. *Inscriptions: Between Phenomenology and Structuralism*. New York: Routledge & Kegan Paul, 1987.

Silverman, Kaja. *The Subject of Semiotics*. New York: Oxford University Press, 1983.

Smith, Paul. *Discerning the Subject*. Minneapolis: University of Minnesota Press, 1988.

Spivak, Gayatri. *In Other Worlds*. New York: Routledge, 1988.

Spivak, Gayatri, and Ranajit Guha, eds. *Subaltern Studies*. New York: Oxford University Press, 1988.

Staten, Henry. *Derrida and Wittgenstein*. Lincoln: University of Nebraska Press, 1984.

Tynan, Stephen. "Mysticism and Gnosticism in Heidegger." *Philosophy Today* 28, no. 4 (1984): 358–77.

Vycinas, Vincent. *Earth and Gods*. The Hague: M. Nijhoff, 1961.

Welte, Bernhard. "God in Heidegger's Thought." *Philosophy Today* 26, no. 1 (1982): 85–100.

White, Hayden. *The Content of the Form: Narrative Discourse and Historical Representation*. Baltimore: Johns Hopkins University Press, 1987.

White, Hayden. *Metahistory: The Historical Imagination in Nineteenth Century Europe*. Baltimore: Johns Hopkins University Press, 1973.

Wittgenstein, Ludwig. *Philosophical Investigations*. Trans. G.E.M. Anscombe. Oxford: Blackwell, 1989.

Wood, David. *Philosophy at the Limit*. Boston: Unwin Hyman, 1990.

Wood, David, and Robert Bernasconi. *Derrida and Différance*. Evanston: Northwestern University Press, 1988.

Wood, Philip R. "Derrida Engagé and Post-structuralist Sartre: A Redefinition of Shifts in Recent French Philosophy." *MLN* 104, no. 4 (1989): 861–79.

Wood, Philip R. *Understanding Jean-Paul Sartre*. Columbia: University of South Carolina Press, 1990.

Wright, Richard. *Black Boy*. New York: Harper and Row, 1966.

Young, Iris. "The Idea of Community and the Politics of Difference." In *Feminism/Postmodernism*. Ed. Linda Nicholson. New York: Routledge, 1990.

Young, Iris M. *Justice and the Politics of Difference*. Princeton: Princeton University Press, 1990.

Index

About the Author

Steve Martinot is Instructor at the Center for Interdisciplinary Programs at San Francisco State University. He is the author of *The Rule of Racialization: Class, Identity, Governance* (Temple), editor of two previous books, and translator of *Racism* by Albert Memmi. He has written extensively on Sartre and his relation to other continental philosophers.